RETURN OF MARXIAN MACRO-DYNAMICS IN EAST ASIA

RESEARCH IN POLITICAL ECONOMY

Series Editor: Paul Zarembka
State University of New York at Buffalo, USA

Recent Volumes:

Volume 21:	Neoliberalism in Crisis, Accumulation, and Rosa Luxemburg's Legacy – Edited by P. Zarembka & S. Soederberg
Volume 22:	The Capitalist State and Its Economy: Democracy in Socialism – Edited by P. Zarembka
Volume 23:	The Hidden History of 9-11-2001 – Edited by P. Zarembka
Volume 24:	Transitions in Latin America and in Poland and Syria – Edited by P. Zarembka
Volume 25:	Why Capitalism Survives Crises: The Shock Absorbers – Edited by P. Zarembka
Volume 26:	The National Question and the Question of Crisis – Edited by P. Zarembka
Volume 27:	Revitalizing Marxist Theory for Today's Capitalism – Edited by P. Zarembka and R. Desai
Volume 28:	Contradictions: Finance, Greed, and Labor Unequally Paid – Edited by P. Zarembka
Volume 29:	Sraffa and Althusser Reconsidered; Neoliberalism Advancing in South Africa, England, and Greece – Edited by P. Zarembka
Volume 30A:	Theoretical Engagements In Geopolitical Economy – Edited by Radhika Desai
Volume 30B:	Analytical Gains of Geopolitical Economy – Edited by Radhika Desai
Volume 31:	Risking Capitalism – Edited by Susanne Soederberg

RESEARCH IN POLITICAL ECONOMY VOLUME 32

RETURN OF MARXIAN MACRO-DYNAMICS IN EAST ASIA

EDITED BY

MASAO ISHIKURA
Hitotsubashi University, Japan

SEONGJIN JEONG
Gyeongsang National University, South Korea

MINQI LI
University of Utah, USA

emerald PUBLISHING

United Kingdom – North America – Japan
India – Malaysia – China

Emerald Publishing Limited
Howard House, Wagon Lane, Bingley BD16 1WA, UK

First edition 2017

British Library Cataloguing in Publication Data
A catalogue record for this book is available from the British Library

ISBN: 978-1-78714-478-1 (Print)
ISBN: 978-1-78714-477-4 (Online)
ISBN: 978-1-78714-941-0 (ePub)

ISSN: 0161-7230 (Series)

Printed and bound by CPI Group (UK) Ltd, Croydon, CR0 4YY

ISOQAR certified Management System, awarded to Emerald for adherence to Environmental standard ISO 14001:2004.

ISOQAR REGISTERED
Certificate Number 1985
ISO 14001

INVESTOR IN PEOPLE

CONTENTS

PART II
STATE AND HEGEMONY IN EAST ASIA IN THE CONTEXT OF TRANSNATIONAL CAPITALISM

PART III
CONSIDERATION OF ASPECTS FOR A MARXIAN ALTERNATIVE FOR EAST ASIA

PART IV
COMMUNICATIONS ON CHAPTERS ON SRAFFA IN *RPE*

LIST OF CONTRIBUTORS

Taro Abe	Nagoya Gakuin University, Japan
Scott Carter	University of Tulsa, USA
Dae-oup Chang	Sogang University, South Korea
Lorenzo Fusaro	Universidad Autónoma Metropolitana, Mexico
Taiji Hagiwara	Kobe University, Japan
Masao Ishikura	Hitotsubashi University, Japan
Sangjun Jeong	Mokpo National University, South Korea
Seongjin Jeong	Gyeongsang National University, South Korea
Gyu Cheol Lee	Kyungpook National University, South Korea
Minqi Li	University of Utah, USA
Takeshi Nakatani	Onomichi City University, Japan
Kenshiro Ninomiya	Shiga University, Japan
Hao Qi	Renmin University of China, China
Robert M. Solow	Massachusetts Institute of Technology, USA
Jeb Sprague-Silgado	University of California Santa Barbara, USA
Masaaki Tokuda	Shiga University, Japan
Yoann Verger	National Institute for Agronomic Research (INRA), France
Anna Zakharzhevskaya	State Academic University for the Humanities, Russia

EDITORIAL ADVISORY BOARD

INTRODUCTION: RETURN OF MARXIAN MACRO-DYNAMICS IN EAST ASIA

Masao Ishikura, Seongjin Jeong and Minqi Li

For many economists, regardless of their political positions, the economic growth in East Asia has been believed to be the model case of the triumph of capitalism. Indeed, conservative mainstream economists still quote "miracle" stories of the Japanese, South Korean, and Chinese economy as the best examples of economic catch-up based on market economy. On the other hand, some progressive economists (like the developmental state theorists) also viewed the East Asian model (including Japanese, South Korean, and Chinese variants) as the progressive alternatives to neoliberal market fundamentalism, despite their substantial shortcomings.

However, with the sudden advent of "Lost Decade of Japan" in the 1990s, and the ensuing "IMF Crisis" of South Korea in 1997, and now the slowing down of the Chinese economy, the East Asian "miracle" story seems to be a thing of the past. On the contrary, East Asia has become an epicenter of the contradictions and crisis of global capitalism. Today, deepening economic crisis, exacerbation of social polarization, rising popular discontents, and escalating geopolitical tensions are common to China, Japan, and the Korean peninsula. East Asia (especially China) has also been at the center of global ecological contradictions. Indeed, East Asia has become the typical place of Marxian macro-dynamics. Although "miracle" stories of East Asia are still on

Return of Marxian Macro-dynamics in East Asia
Research in Political Economy, Volume 32, 1–12

ISSN: 0161-7230/doi:10.1108/S0161-723020170000032001

sale by the developmental state theorists as well as mainstream ideologues, it is obvious that their audience substantially shrank. Instead, critiques of and resistances to capitalism rapidly proliferate in East Asia. Several million peoples' candlelight in Korea against President Park Geun-hye's abuse of power and corruption, culminated in her impeachment, was just a recent example.

With the deepening contradictions of capitalism, interests in anti-capitalism and Marxism began to revive in East Asia after a long period of marginalization under "miracle" regimes.[1] Also, as it became clear that the export-led or investment-led growth model, which has sustained the "miracles" in East Asia, is petering out, some progressive economists are now trying to find new alternative in the Keynesian wage-led growth model or the universal basic income program, triggering the new interesting debates with Marxists.

In this spirit, current volume features 10 papers, which discusses the issues of macro-dynamics, state and hegemony in the context of globalization, and socialist alternatives in East Asia, mostly concentrated on three countries: China, Japan, and South Korea.

MACRO-DYNAMICS IN EAST ASIA

A review of economic growth and fluctuations in East Asian countries since the 1980s shows how Marxian-dynamics regarding overaccumulation, devalorization, and the subsequent restructuring of capital have evolved in various historical and institutional contexts. The evolution is exemplified by the Japanese experience from the late 1980s to the mid-2010s.

Following the Louvre Accord signed by the G7 countries in February 1987, in order to halt the dollar's sharp depreciation caused by the Plaza Accord in September 1985, the Bank of Japan cut the official discount rate to 2.5 percent and maintained the same rate from February 1987 to May 1989. This led to a surge in both stock and land prices and a concomitant credit expansion in the banking sector. This situation supported an accelerated pace of capital accumulation and a higher production capacity. However, following the subsequent monetary tightening from May 1989 to July 1991, both stocks and land prices started declining, and the assets offered as collateral for loans also depreciated, being directly triggered by the administrative guidance of the Ministry of Finance from March 1990 through December 1991, which requested financial institutions to restrict the lending growth to real estate firms below total lending growth. The result was an increased concern over repaying existing loans and the overaccumulation of capital that manifested as a high amount of uncollected loans.

In the post-war Japanese economy, the financial sector was protected by the "convoy system" of financial regulations, where the Ministry of Finance arranged an insolvent bank to be merged with another bank to protect the interests of depositors and borrowers. Since the middle of 1997, when the financial administration of this system was abandoned, even large and influential banks were forced to leave the market in case of financial difficulties.[2] In parallel with the financial administration reform, the ban on financial holding companies (defined as holding companies, the subsidiaries of which were financial institutions such as banks, insurers, brokerages) was lifted in 1998, which facilitated the restructuring of the financial sector.

Regarding the three large banks that failed between 1997 and 1998,[3] the financial authorities did not allow them to survive, and their nonperforming loans were settled through injections of taxpayer money. The nonperforming loans held by the other ailing financial institutions were disposed of during the period of quantitative monetary easing by the Bank of Japan from March 2001 to March 2006. Following the intensive disposal of nonperforming loans, firms in financial distress were forced to bankruptcy, leading to accelerated devalorization of capital in both real and financial sectors. Concomitantly, there was a series of alliances and mergers between financial institutions under financial holding companies, leading to capital restructuring in the financial sector.[4]

Since the mid-1990s, when the financial crisis started, deregulation regarding non-regular employment – namely a series of amendments to the Worker Dispatching Law – allowed companies to utilize dispatched workers more flexibly in response to an increasing pressure for cost reduction in the global market. In the post-war Japan, the worker dispatching businesses had been prohibited by the Employment Security Law enforced in 1947. Following the enforcement of the Worker Dispatching Law in 1986, the ban on worker dispatching was lifted for 13 specialized jobs (software developers, operators of office equipment, translators, etc.). The amendment of the law in 1987 also removed the ban on worker dispatching in another three jobs (designers of machinery, operators of broadcast equipment, etc.). Afterward, the 1996 further amendment of the law permitted companies to utilize dispatched workers in the 26 specialized jobs, including the 16 jobs mentioned above, specified by the government ordinance. Then, the amendment of the law in 1999 opened the way for worker dispatching in all jobs except construction, port and harbor transportation, security, manufacturing, and medical-related businesses.

Subsequently, with the amendment of the Worker Dispatching Law in 2004, the ban on worker dispatching in manufacturing jobs was further lifted. Under the amended law, for 26 specialized types of jobs specified by the government ordinance, the client companies could use workers dispatched from temporary staff agencies with no restriction on duration. On the other hand, for other types of jobs, including manufacturing jobs, companies could use dispatched workers for one year, which could be extended to three by consulting a majority representative of the employees in each company. Following yet another 2015 amendment of the law, for all types of jobs, companies could use dispatched workers in the same department for more than three years by replacing a currently dispatched worker with a new one and after consulting a majority representative of the company's employees.[5] The deregulation on worker dispatching implies that the capital and wage-labor relationship was restructured as follows: the worker dispatching agencies could have more opportunities for earning profits and the client companies could use the labor force of dispatched workers in more flexible ways, although some dispatched workers would find their income insufficient to make a living.

The Japanese economy experienced a relatively long expansion that began in the second quarter of 2002, amid monetary easing, and ended in the first quarter of 2008, two years after the end of monetary easing.[6] Afterward, the economy entered contraction, adversely affected by the collapse of Lehman Brothers through the fourth quarter of 2009. Subsequently, the economy returned to expansion, which lasted through the first quarter of 2012, supported by the supplementary fiscal measures on the negative impact of the global financial crisis. However, during the same period, on March 11, 2011 the Great East Japan Earthquake and Fukushima nuclear plant disaster occurred, having disastrous effects on the regional economies. Since then, following a mild recession, the Japanese economy has been in expansion from the fourth quarter of 2012 to the present (early 2017).

The current cabinet of Shinzo Abe, leader of the Liberal Democratic Party who took office as prime minister in December 2012, advocated an economic policy package, the so-called "Abenomics," that comprised bold monetary easing, flexible fiscal policy, and growth strategies for promoting private investment. Monetary easing in tandem with fiscal policy implies the coordination of both government and the central bank. Indeed, in January 2013, the Japanese government and the Bank of Japan announced a strengthening of their policy coordination in order to overcome deflation and achieve sustainable economic growth with price stability.[7] As shown below, monetary easing was implemented mainly through the Bank of Japan's purchase of long-term government bonds.

In April 2013, the Bank of Japan announced the introduction of quantitative and qualitative monetary easing (QQE) to achieve more quickly the price stability target of 2 percent annual inflation in terms of consumer price index. Its main measures were the money market operations that would cause the monetary base to increase at an annual pace of around JPY 60–70 trillion through purchases of long-term Japanese government bonds and extending their maturity.[8] In the balance sheet of the Bank of Japan at the end of March 2013, just before the introduction of the QQE, the total assets amounted to JPY 164.8 trillion, including long-term government bonds of JPY 91.3 trillion, and the liabilities included JPY 83.4 trillion of banknotes, and JPY 58.1 trillion of current deposits.[9] At the end of March 2015, two years after the introduction of the QQE, the total assets doubled to JPY 323.6 trillion, including JPY 220.1 trillion of long-term government bonds, which significantly exceeded the banknotes issued, and the total liabilities included JPY 89.7 trillion of banknotes, and JPY 201.6 trillion of current deposits held by financial institutions. During the two years after the introduction of the QQE, the long-term government bonds held by the Bank of Japan increased 2.4 times and, correspondingly, the current deposits of the bank increased 3.5 times.

As the target of 2 percent annual inflation in terms of consumer price index was not achieved, the Bank of Japan maintained the QQE with a series of modifications. In January 2016, the Bank of Japan announced the introduction of the "QQE with a negative interest rate" for the purpose of achieving as early as possible the price stability target of 2 percent annual inflation in terms of consumer price index. Its main measures were to apply negative interest rates to current deposits and cause the monetary base to increase at an annual pace of about JPY 80 trillion through purchases of long-term Japanese government bonds and extending their maturity.[10] Following these measures, since mid-February 2016, the unsecured overnight call rate fell into the range of 0 and −0.1 percent and the Japanese 10-year government bond yield became negative and lower than the unsecured overnight call rate. This behavior of long- and short-term interest rates implied the decline and flattening of the yield curve, leading to increased concerns about its negative impacts on the bottom lines of financial institutions.

In light of this situation, in September 2016, the Bank of Japan announced the introduction of "QQE with yield curve control" to achieve as early as possible the price stability target of 2 percent annual inflation in terms of consumer price index. The main measures to control the long- and short-term interest rates were as follows. First, a negative interest rate of −0.1 percent should be applied to the component called "policy-rate balance" in the current deposits held by financial institutions. Second, the bank should purchase long-term government bonds so that the Japanese 10-year government bond yield would remain around 0 percent. Further, the Bank of Japan committed to continuing the "QQE with yield curve control" until an observed annual rate of increase in the consumer price index exceeded the price stability target of 2 percent.[11] Following the introduction of yield curve control, in the middle of November 2016, the Japanese 10-year government bond yield returned to positive values.

Even after the introduction of the "QQE with a negative interest rate," both the Japanese long-term government bonds held by the Bank of Japan and the current deposits held by financial institutions at the bank increased. In the balance sheet of the Bank of Japan at the end of December 2016, the total assets amounted to JPY 476.5 trillion, including JPY 360.7 trillion of the long-term government bonds, and the total liabilities included JPY 102.5 trillion of banknotes, and JPY 330.2 trillion of current deposits held by financial institutions. From the end of March 2013 to the end of December 2016, the long-term government bonds held by the Bank of Japan increased 4 times and, correspondingly, the current deposits of the bank increased 5.7 times. Moreover, there has been a rise in the proportion of government bonds held by the central bank. According to the flow of funds statistics,[12] at the end of September 2016, the Bank of Japan held 37.9 percent of the outstanding long- and short-term bonds issued by the central government and the Fiscal Loan Fund, while it held 13.2 percent at the end of March 2013, just before the introduction of the QQE. While the Bank of Japan noted that "The aforementioned Japanese government bond purchases are executed for the purpose of conducting monetary policy and not for the purpose of financing fiscal deficits,"[13] there are increasing concerns that further increases in the central bank's holding of government bonds could eventually lead to the monetization of fiscal deficits. The Bank of Japan has yet to suggest the withdrawal from monetary easing.

One of the key issues in contemporary political economy is the valorization and accumulation of capital in the global economy. In the paper titled "Labor Value and Exploitation in the Global Economy," Taiji Hagiwara constructs a theoretical model to measure the labor value of commodities in the context of international division of labor. To measure the total labor time embodied in goods that domestic workers produce using both domestic and foreign products as materials, we need to consider the labor time embodied in imported materials, and the direct labor time of domestic workers and the labor time embodied in domestic materials. Using data from the World Input Output Database, the author measured the labor value of the wage goods basket consumed by workers in four Asian countries: namely, China, Japan, Korea, and Taiwan, and two groups: namely, advanced countries and developing countries. Then, the author investigated the exploitation of labor in the global economy through the composition of domestic and foreign labor embodied in the wage goods basket.

In the late 1990s, the Japanese economy experienced increasing financial anxieties with banks holding a huge amount of nonperforming loans and financial institutions experiencing a series of failures. One of the critical issues regarding contemporary financial crisis is the effect financial anxieties have on the macroeconomy. In the paper titled "Financial Instability in Japan: Debt, Confidence, and Financial Structure," Kenshiro Ninomiya and Masaaki Tokuda measure financial anxieties using a proxy variable called "the instability of confidence," which was econometrically estimated using the diffusion indexes of changes in interest rates on borrowings and corporate financial positions declared by the Bank of Japan. The instability of confidence rose from the early 1990s, peaked at the end of 1998 amid the financial crisis, and then started to decline. Using a recursive vector autoregressive model with interest rates, income, debt burden, and the instability of confidence as the variables, the authors demonstrated the presence of a negative response of the instability of confidence to an increase in the debt burden in the period from the first quarter of 1980 to the fourth quarter of 1996 and a positive response of the instability of confidence to an increase in the debt burden in the period from the first quarter of 1997 to the fourth quarter of 2014. This result implies that the macroeconomic structure has become unstable following the financial crisis in the late 1990s.

With the restructuring of capital in both the real and financial sectors, as well as the deregulation of the labor market, the Japanese economy has yet to find a path to sustainable growth. To address this problem, we need to examine the economic policies implemented since the 2000s and their consequences. In the paper titled "A Historical Perspective and Evaluation of Abenomics," Takeshi Nakatani and Taro Abe critically examine the effectiveness of the economic policy package implemented by the current cabinet of Shinzo Abe, also known as "Abenomics," which is marked by bold monetary easing, flexible fiscal policy, and growth strategies for promoting private investment. Based on the following facts, the authors investigated the reason behind the failure of the QQE that started in April 2013 in increasing production and employment. From 2012, just before the introduction of monetary easing, till 2015, the money stock held by the nonfinancial private sector increased at a slower rate than the monetary base. In the same period, GDP growth stagnated. Although the unemployment rate declined, the average disposable income per workers' household hardly improved. Following the labor-related deregulation that led to an increase in non-regular workers, the growth of workers' income was curbed and employment became increasingly precarious. The authors pointed out that higher wages and job security are essential for achieving a sustainable economic recovery in Japan.

Mainstream neo-classical economics tend to regard the "miracle" of the South Korean economy as a vindication of the efficiency of the market. On the contrary, for most heterodox economics, especially developmental statists, it was the result of "getting the price wrong." What is missing in this age-old debate between free marketeers and statists is the recognition of the central role of Marxian macro-dynamics, or "Marx-biased technical change," in the capitalist development in Korea. Indeed, without it, neither the previous success nor the current difficulties of the Korean economy can be properly understood. Sangjun Jeong tries to tackle this issue in his paper, "Biased Technical Change and Economic Growth: The Case of Korea, 1970–2013." Jeong establishes that "Marx-biased technical change" has predominated in Korea for the period of 1970–2013 by econometrically evidencing the unidirectional causality from real wages to labor productivity and labor-saving *cum* capital-using technical change against the increase of workers' power. Admitting that the capital productivity appreciation after the 1997 crisis is a deviation from the long-run trend of "Marx-biased technical change," Jeong does not attribute it to the vitality of new technological innovations but to the class dynamics over extracting productivity under weaker capital deepening. For Jeong, the recent deterioration of labor share due to weakened labor unions is the main culprits of the low incentive for technological progress in Korea, which contributes to prolonged stagnation.

China has been the leading engine of global capital accumulation. In "Dynamics of the Rate of Surplus Value and the "New Normal" of the Chinese Economy," Hao Qi studies the long-term dynamics of capital accumulation by measuring key Marxian variables such as the rate of surplus value, value composition of capital, and the profit rate in the context of the Chinese economy.

Qi's data series cover the extended period from 1956 to 2014, illustrating the changing dynamics of the Chinese economy from the state socialist period to the market transition. The author finds that China's rate of surplus value followed a U-shape from 1978 to 2008. It rose strongly from 1997 to 2008 and reached its historical peak when the global economic crisis broke out. The rate of surplus value then fell slightly after 2008. The financial and economic crisis led to persistent stagnation in leading capitalist economies, depressing demand for China's exports. On the other hand, the reduction in the reserve army of labor has enhanced the bargaining power of the Chinese workers. And the massive investment in fixed assets has led to rapid increase in value composition of capital. The combination of rising value composition of capital and stagnating rate of surplus value implies a falling profit rate, jeopardizing the sustainability of China's economic growth. Qi contends that major institutional changes promoting pro-labor redistribution and a wage-led economic growth may be necessary for China to sustain economic development in the future.

STATE AND HEGEMONY IN EAST ASIA IN THE CONTEXT OF TRANSNATIONAL CAPITALISM

As components of society, social classes contain individuals who are carriers of productive relationships. In the era of global capitalism, as chains of accumulation functionally integrate across national borders and regions, the formation of productive relationships has been deeply transformed. In "The Transnational Capitalist Class and Relations of Production in Asia and Oceania," Jeb Sprague-Silgado raises several important questions in the time of transnational global capitalism. How can we understand the changing class relations in the global era, and in the context of regions and countries of Oceania and East and South Asia? How can the political economy of Asia and Oceania be seen in light of the novel dynamics of the globalist era, with the rise of transnational social, economic, and political processes? How are one-time nationally or internationally oriented state apparatuses, institutions, and corporations converging with new transnational processes? How do social classes and various social groups in Asia and Oceania connect objectively and subjectively to transnational and global processes? How do shifting social and material relations play out regionally or within particular frontiers or built environments?

To address these questions, Sprague-Silgado reviews the existing studies on transnational class relations and the associated political and economic changes and analyzes contradictions connected to the transnational capitalist processes. In particular, Sprague-Silgado evaluates the crisis of legitimacy that occurs through the abandonment by state managers of national development as they seek transnational capitalist integration with consequences in social polarization and the deepening of the global environmental crisis.

An important aspect of Marxist political economy has to do with analyzing the interaction between capital accumulation, class struggle, and the role of the state. In "A Critical Review of China's Reform," Gyu Cheol Lee reviews the socioeconomic reform policies employed by China's party-state system from the early 1980s to the mid-2000s. Unlike conventional frameworks seeing the reform process as an economic development project designed for "national interests," Lee interprets China's reform as a political attempt of the party-state in response to the late-Maoist political and economic crisis as slow growth of labor productivity made it difficult for the party-state to reproduce dominance over the working class.

The state managers of the post-Mao era embarked on the reform as a way to restore the state's ability to impose work discipline upon the workers. By depoliticizing exploitative social relations of production, the market-oriented reform helped the party-state effectively repress workers without the risk of serious damage to political legitimacy. However, Lee does not think that China's reform as a depoliticizing strategy of class dominance was completely successful and non-problematic. Beneath the apparent success of the reform, a growing tendency toward crisis has emerged. Faced with the burgeoning workers' struggles, growing problems of overproduction and overaccumulation, and the looming banking system crisis, the party-state has been under growing pressure to bring economic management back into the sphere of politics, as the underlying political risks continues to grow.

One of the central questions regarding the future direction of global capitalist economy has to do with China's position in the capitalist world system in the 21st century. In "Why China is Different: Hegemony, Revolutions and the Rise of Contender States," Lorenzo Fusaro assesses the question from the perspective of international political economy. Unlike some theorization that sees China as being integrated within US hegemony or other accounts that claim we are witnessing the "terminal crisis" of US hegemony accompanied by a hegemonic transition toward China, Fusaro argues that China has been able to gain "relative geopolitical autonomy" as a result of the revolutionary processes it went through and will eventually assert itself as a contender state.

Dissatisfied with the existing theorization on hegemonies, Fusaro draws on the critical edition of Gramsci's *Quaderni* and attempts to offer a new perspective. Applying the elaborated framework of analysis to the current situation, Fusaro argues that while the United States successfully managed challenges from its traditional imperial rivals such as Germany and Japan, the United States is facing difficulties in countering China's ascent. However, the idea of a "crisis of US hegemony" is premature and China remains distant from fully realizing hegemonic relations, even at the regional level of East Asia.

CONSIDERATION OF ASPECTS FOR A MARXIAN ALTERNATIVE FOR EAST ASIA

What is needed first for the progressives who try to design a Marxian alternative for East Asia is to accept that none of the East Asia models is one of them. Even China is far from suggesting some sort of progressive "non-capitalist market economy" alternative, as Giovanni Arrighi has argued.[14] Indeed, China is only a variant of state capitalist exploitative and repressive regime. It is also required for the left to break with any variant of nationalistic "socialism in one country" model, and pursue a Marxian internationalist alternative in East Asia, as was historically exemplified in the slogan for "United States of Socialist Europe" before the World War I. Struggles for Marxian internationalist alternative is not only realistic and desirable, considering the close economic nexus between the East Asian economies – highlighted by the "flying-geese model" or "East Asian production networks" etc., and their historically shared cultural commonalities – but also urgently needed to resist the escalation of the recent inter (sub-)imperialist geopolitical competitions in East Asia or the second coming of "Greater East Asia Co-Prosperity Sphere."

In this respect, the recent attempt for socialist renewal in Chongqing is remarkable. From 2007 to 2012, China's Chongqing Municipality undertook a number of bold policy experiments, including a successful campaign against organized crimes, promotion of "red songs" and red culture, and a more egalitarian oriented economic development model under the leadership of Bo Xilai. In 2012, Bo Xilai was suddenly dismissed because of corruption charges. The Chongqing incident attracted widespread attention throughout the world. In "The Chongqing Model – Socialist Alternative or Propaganda Cliché?," Anna Zakharzhevskaya examines diverging views on the Chongqing model.

The model has impressed both supporters of socialist identity of China and supporters of liberal identity. Some leftists perceived the Chongqing model as a return to the genuinely socialist way of development. Other leftists criticized the Chongqing model for being no more than another liberal variant. In the meantime, the liberals tried to present the Chongqing model as a return to Mao's Cultural Revolution and denied Chongqing's economic success as a debt dependent investment bubble. Zakharzhevskaya discusses and helps to clarify to what extent the Chongqing model represented a genuine socialist experiment and the implications of the model for China's future.

In order to build a progressive alternative socioeconomic system in East Asia, breaking with statism and forging peoples' solidarity from below are essential. Dae-oup Chang's paper, "Subversive Migration, Citizenship from Below and Democracy against Bordered Capitalism," is written in this spirit. Chang defines contemporary capitalism as bordered capitalism, which functions to dilute tensions among "us" and strengthens the fetishistic state function by compartmentalizing the global working class within their nation states. From this understanding, Chang questions the prevalent form of internationalism as cooperation between parallel attempts of national working classes to change their own worlds within national borders. Chang argues that challenging capitalism requires us to subvert borders as a central class and racial institution to the reproduction of global capitalism while trying to overcome the injustice of capitalist social relations. Therefore, migrant workers emerge as crucial agency of subverting bordered capitalism. Chang's case study on the struggle of migrant labor in Hong Kong and South Korea shows that migrant labor ruptures the migrant control regimes and struggles to form citizenship from below by exercising "social movement citizenship," that is, social movement toward universal citizenship that goes beyond borders. Indeed, abolishing bordered capitalism is unthinkable without the struggles of migrant workers for universal citizenship.

Communications on chapters on Sraffa in *RPE* Volume 29 (2014) of the *Research in Political Economy* began by "Reconsidering Sraffa," including a long chapter by Scott Carter, comments thereafter by Robert M. Solow, a response to him by Carter, and ending with a chapter by Bangxi Li related to the Chinese experience. In this issue, Yoann Verger offers an addendum to Carter's response to Solow, to which Carter and Solow offer their reactions. We are thankful to Paul Zarembka for organizing this exciting debate on Sraffa.

NOTES

1. For example, refer to Hart-Landsberg, M., Jeong, S., & Westra, R. (Eds.). (2007). *Marxist perspectives on South Korea in the global economy*. Aldershot: Ashgate; Li, M. (2015). *China and the 21st century crisis*. Chicago: The University of Chicago Press.
2. Ministry of Finance, *Financial system reform: Toward the early achievement of reform*, released on June 13, 1997 (http://www.fsa.go.jp/p_mof/english/big-bang/ebb32.htm).
3. The three failed large banks are as follows: Hokkaido Takushoku Bank, the tenth largest bank, which failed in 1997, and the Long-Term Credit Bank of Japan and the Nippon Credit Bank, both of which failed and were placed under temporary nationalization in 1998.
4. For the transformation of the Japanese financial system following the financial deregulation from the late 1970s through the early 2000s, see Ishikura, M. (2007). Reassessing the Japanese response to globalization: Causes and consequences of Japanese financial crisis. In J.-S. Shin (Ed.), *Global challenges and local responses: The East Asian experience* (pp. 116–139). London: Routledge.
5. For further details on the regulation of worker dispatching in Japan, see *Labor Situation in Japan and Its Analysis: General Overview 2015/2016*, edited by the Japan Institute for Labour Policy and Training, released in March 2016 (http://www.jil.go.jp/english/lsj/general/2015-2016.html), p. 162.
6. For dating the business cycles in Japan, see the Economic and Social Research Institute, the Cabinet Office, *The determination of business-cycle peak and trough*, released on July 24, 2015 (http://www.esri.cao.go.jp/en/stat/di/150724rdates.html).

7. Cabinet Office, Ministry of Finance, Bank of Japan, *Joint statement of the Government and the Bank of Japan on overcoming deflation and achieving sustainable economic growth*, released on January 22, 2013 (http://www5.cao.go.jp/keizai1/2013/130122_joint_statement_of_the_government_and_the_bank_of_japan.pdf).

8. For further details on the quantitative and qualitative monetary easing, see the Bank of Japan, *Introduction of the 'quantitative and qualitative monetary easing'*, released on April 4, 2013 (http://www.boj.or.jp/en/announcements/release_2013/k130404a.pdf).

9. Data on the balance sheet of the Bank of Japan are available from the site of the bank (http://www.boj.or.jp/en/statistics/boj/other/ac/index.htm/).

10. For more detail on the QQE with a negative interest rate, see the Bank of Japan, *Introduction of 'quantitative and qualitative monetary easing with a negative interest rate'*, released on January 29, 2016 (http://www.boj.or.jp/en/announcements/release_2016/k160129a.pdf).

11. For further details on QQE with yield curve control, see the Bank of Japan, *New framework for strengthening monetary easing: 'Quantitative and qualitative monetary easing with yield curve control,'* released on September 21, 2016 (http://www.boj.or.jp/en/announcements/release_2016/k160921a.pdf).

12. Data from the flow of fund accounts are available on the site of the Bank of Japan (http://www.boj.or.jp/en/statistics/sj/index.htm/).

13. Bank of Japan, *Introduction of the 'Quantitative and qualitative monetary easing'*, released on April 4, 2013, p. 2.

14. For more critique of Giovanni Arrighi's thesis of "non-capitalist market economy," refer to Seongjin Jeong, "Karl Marx in Beijing," *International Socialism*, No. 123, 2009.

PART I
MACRO-DYNAMICS IN EAST ASIA

LABOR VALUE AND EXPLOITATION IN THE GLOBAL ECONOMY

Taiji Hagiwara

ABSTRACT

This paper discusses labor value and the rate of exploitation in the global economy using international input–output tables. Labor value is defined as the multiplication of the labor coefficient and Leontief inverse. Exploitation means that the amount of labor embodied in the received wage commodity is less than the amount of the labor actually sold. Therefore, the Fundamental Marxian Theorem, which states that the conditions for the existence of profit and those for the existence of exploitation are the same, should be modified to stipulate that the existence of profit requires exploitation in at least one country. In other words, exploitation may not exist in some countries (non-exploitation). In the context of international input–output tables, we introduce the concept of global labor value, which is the vector of embodied labor in various countries. In the empirical study using an international input–output table, we find that (1) there are non-exploitation cases in several countries. (2) During the time period 1995–2009, the rate of exploitation increased in Asian countries, namely China, Japan, Korea, and Taiwan, whereas the advanced countries other than Asia faced a decreased rate of exploitation.

Keywords: Exploitation; global economy; input–output tables; Fundamental Marxian Theorem; labor value

Return of Marxian Macro-dynamics in East Asia
Research in Political Economy, Volume 32, 15–37

ISSN: 0161-7230/doi:10.1108/S0161-723020170000032003

INTRODUCTION

In classical economics, including Marx, labor *value* was considered as a good proxy for price. Since the marginal revolution, economists have explained prices as being determined by demand and supply, and the concept of labor value was thought to be obsolete. But Marx found a more important role for labor value as a good tool to explain the existence of exploitation. He insisted that the existence of profit is conditioned by the existence of exploitation.

According to Marx, labor value is the sum of *living labor* and *dead labor*. While the notion of *living labor* is obvious, that of *dead labor* is arguable. *Dead labor* is the value of *constant capital* which is *circulation capital* (intermediate input) and *fixed capital*. However, measuring the value of a commodity requires a value for *constant capital*. Okishio (1955) formulated this as labor value in his system of equations, using the input–output framework developed by Leontief (1941) which he then proved mathematically. Later, Morishima (1973) named this the *Fundamental Marxian Theorem*.

Among numerous discussions on the Theorem, two points receive the maximum attention. The first point is joint production which means that multiple outputs are produced in single production activity. However, many cases of joint production except fixed capital seem to have less importance in the real economy. Fixed capital, in turn, can be treated in a more simplified way.

The second point is heterogeneity of labor. There are various kinds of jobs, whose skill levels vary. However, if not unified as simple labor, the Theorem may not hold. Okishio (1965) showed how various labor types can be unified by incorporating training labor. Bowles and Gintis (1977) took another approach and proved that although some types of labor may not be exploited, at least one kind of labor must be exploited in order for profit to exist under a heterogeneous labor situation. This paper aims to expand on this approach by using international input–output (IO) tables to determine the existence of non-exploited labor in several Asian countries.

Various empirical studies have used input–output tables, for example, Okishio (1958), Gupta and Steedman (1971), Nakatani (1976), Ochoa (1989), Nakajima and Izumi(1995), Fröhlich (2012), and so on. Some compromises are required when using these tables in an empirical study. One important compromise is international trade. Until the 1980s, only single-country IO tables existed. In a single-country IO table, economic transactions are not closed within the country. The labor value of import commodities must be defined. Okishio (1958) assumed that this equals the labor value of export commodities, for which the monetary value is the same as that of imports.

When international input–output tables were first planned, Katano (1984) tried to formulate labor value in the international IO framework but this attempt was incomplete. Nakatani and Hagiwara (in Nakatani, 1994) defined global labor value and expanded the Fundamental Marxian Theorem as heterogeneous labor value (Bowles & Gintis, 1977). Hagiwara (2004) examined global labor using Japan-USA-Asia-Europe international IO tables 1985–1990 and found that the labor value of Japan's laborers' wage commodity basket is larger than their working hours. Following this approach of using international IO tables to measure labor value across countries, this paper uses IO tables to investigate the presence of non-exploited labor in several Asian countries.

LABOR VALUE AND EXPLOITATION IN A SINGLE ECONOMY

Labor value is defined as the labor embodied in one commodity. In the commodity's production process, labor is incorporated as direct labor. In addition, the commodity is used as intermediate input or fixed capital. Intermediate input and fixed capital are also, in turn, products of labor, intermediate input and fixed capital, and so on. Although such calculations may seem to go back indefinitely, labor value is solved in a system of equations.

Labor Value in a Single Economy

Suppose there are N commodities. Each commodity needs some commodity and labor inputs. That is, a_{ij} units of commodity[1] i and τ_j units of labor are required to produce one unit commodity j

$$1 \leftarrow (a_{1j}, a_{2j}, \ldots, a_{Nj}, \tau_j), \quad 0 \leq a_{ij}, \ 0 < \tau_j$$

Labor value, t, is defined as

$$t_j = \sum_i t_i a_{ij} + \tau_j$$

Labor value t_j represents the total labor inputs needed to produce commodity j and may therefore be considered the labor embodied in commodity j. In the matrix form,

$$\mathbf{t} = \mathbf{tA} + \boldsymbol{\tau} \tag{1}$$

where

$$\mathbf{A} \equiv \begin{pmatrix} a_{11} & \cdots & a_{1N} \\ \vdots & \ddots & \vdots \\ a_{N1} & \cdots & a_{NN} \end{pmatrix}, \quad \boldsymbol{\tau} \equiv (\tau_1, \ldots, \tau_N), \quad \mathbf{t} \equiv (t_1, \ldots, t_N)$$

Its solution is

$$\mathbf{t} = \boldsymbol{\tau}(\mathbf{I_N} - \mathbf{A})^{-1} \tag{2}$$

where $\mathbf{I_N}$ represents an $N \times N$ identity matrix. Since the reciprocal of labor value shows the amount of product produced by a unit of labor either directly or indirectly, $1/t_j$ can be called labor productivity. In the context of input–output analysis, labor value can be called an employment multiplier. Labor value t is positive if the matrix $(\mathbf{I_N} - \mathbf{A})$ satisfies the Hawkins–Simon condition.[2]

Conditions for Profit's Existence in a Single Economy

Profit in each sector should be positive.

$$0 < \pi_j = p_j - \sum_i p_i a_{ij} - w\tau_j$$

where p_j is the output price of sector j, and w is the nominal wage rate. In matrix form,

$$0 < \boldsymbol{\pi} = \mathbf{p} - \mathbf{pA} - w\boldsymbol{\tau} \tag{3}$$

where $\mathbf{p} \equiv (p_1, \ldots, p_N)$.

Wage laborers purchase certain amounts of consumption commodities (wage basket)

$$\mathbf{b} \equiv (b_1, \ldots, b_N)'$$

$$w = \mathbf{pb} \tag{4}$$

Substituting Eq. (4) for Eq. (3), we get

$$0 < \mathbf{p}(\mathbf{I_N} - \mathbf{A} - \mathbf{b}\boldsymbol{\tau}) \tag{5}$$

Prices must satisfy inequality (5). Therefore, the matrix $(\mathbf{I_N} - \mathbf{A} - \mathbf{b\tau})$ must satisfy the Hawkins–Simon condition.

Exploitation in a Single Economy

From the viewpoint of demand and supply, it is possible to choose some positive output vector $(\mathbf{x})$ such that surplus product $(\mathbf{z})$ is positive in all sectors.

$$0 < \mathbf{z} = \mathbf{x} - \mathbf{Ax} - \mathbf{b\tau x} = (\mathbf{I_N} - \mathbf{A} - \mathbf{b\tau})\mathbf{x} \tag{6}$$

The condition for a positive output $(\mathbf{x})$ in all sectors to produce surplus product $(\mathbf{z})$ is that the matrix $(\mathbf{I_N} - \mathbf{A} - \mathbf{b\tau})$ satisfies the Hawkins–Simon condition, which is equivalent to the condition for positive prices to exist as positive profit in all sectors.

Multiplying Eq. (6) with labor value $(\mathbf{t})$ from the left, we get

$$0 < \mathbf{tz} = \mathbf{t}(\mathbf{I_N} - \mathbf{A} - \mathbf{b\tau})x = \mathbf{t}(\mathbf{I_N} - \mathbf{A})x - \mathbf{tb\tau}x = \boldsymbol{\tau}x - \mathbf{tb\tau}x = (1 - \mathbf{tb})\boldsymbol{\tau}x \tag{7}$$

Since total employment $(\boldsymbol{\tau}\mathbf{x})$ is positive, $\mathbf{tb}$ must be less than unity:

$$0 < 1 - \mathbf{tb} \tag{8}$$

Here, $\mathbf{tb} = \sum_i t_i b_i$ is the sum of labor value embodied in wage basket $(\mathbf{b})$. Unity means one unit of labor is sold. Since $\mathbf{b}$ is the wage basket a laborer received by selling one unit of his/her own labor and $\mathbf{t}$ is amount of labor embodied in each commodity, $\mathbf{tb}$ means the amount of labor embodied in the wage basket. Therefore, Eq. (8) means the amount of the worker's labor embodied in the wage basket by selling his/her labor is smaller than amount of labor that he/she sold. That is, exploitation, that is, the worker not receiving the full value created by his or her labor, exists. The rate of exploitation is defined as a fraction of surplus value $(1 - \mathbf{tb})$ and variable capital $(\mathbf{tb})$

$$e = (1 - \mathbf{tb})/\mathbf{tb} \tag{9}$$

The so-called *Fundamental Marxian Theorem* states the condition of profit's existence is equivalent with the condition of exploitation's existence.

Measuring Labor Value in Single Economy

Several researches have addressed the estimation of labor value in the context described above. First was Okishio (1958), followed by Okishio and Nakatani (1985), and Nakajima and Izumi (1995). Another stream is Gupta and

Steedman (1971), Ochoa (1989), Fröhlich (2012), and so on. When applying input–output tables to labor value measurement, Okishio (1958) noted three points.

First, he noted that the difference between the physical term and monetary term. Input–output tables are measured in terms of money, whereas labor value is measured in physical terms, because labor value should be independent from price. Monetary input–output tables from the cost side are

$$p_j x_j = \sum_i p_i a_{ij} x_j + w\tau_j x_j$$

Dividing by the monetary amount of output, $p_j x_j$, we get

$$1 = \sum_i \frac{p_i a_{ij}}{p_j} + \frac{w\tau_j}{p_j}$$

The input coefficient used in input–output analysis is the product of a physical input coefficient (a_{ij}) and relative price (p_i/p_j), and the labor coefficient is the quotient of the physical labor coefficient (τ_j) divided by price (p_j)

$$a^*_{ij} = p_i a_{ij}/p_j \tau^*_j = \tau_j/p_j \quad A^* = \hat{p}A\hat{p}^{-1}, \quad \tau^* = \tau\hat{p}^{-1}$$

where the symbol ˆ indicates a diagonal matrix. The solution of Eq. (1) with monetary coefficient **A*** and **τ*** is

$$\mathbf{t}^* = \mathbf{t}^*\mathbf{A}^* + \boldsymbol{\tau}^* \tag{10}$$

$$\mathbf{t}^* = \mathbf{t}^*\hat{\mathbf{p}}\mathbf{A}\hat{\mathbf{p}}^{-}1 + \boldsymbol{\tau}\hat{\mathbf{p}}^{-}1$$

Multiplying with diagonal p from the right yields

$$\mathbf{t}^*\hat{\mathbf{p}} = \mathbf{A}\mathbf{t}^*\hat{\mathbf{p}} + \boldsymbol{\tau} \tag{11}$$

Comparing Eq. (11) with Eq. (1), we get

$$\mathbf{t}^*\hat{\mathbf{p}} = \mathbf{t}$$

This means that the solution to Eq. (10) is t_j/p_j, that is, the rate of unequal exchange. In the following analysis, the symbols **A**, **τ**, and t are used as monetary terms, instead of **A***, **τ***, and **t***.

The second point addresses the treatment of fixed capital. Input coefficients a_{ij} include only intermediate inputs. Using depreciation per output (d_j) as an approximation of the unit cost of fixed capital and sectoral share of investment

(s_i^I) as the composition of capital, the cost of fixed capital is endogenized as follows:

$$t_j = \sum_i (a_{ij} + d_j s_i^I) t_i + \tau_j \tag{12}$$

The third point is the treatment of imports.[3] The labor value of domestic commodities is endogenously determined by Eq. (1), whereas the value of imported commodities is not. Okishio (1958) used the labor value of an exported commodity as the labor value of an imported commodity, that is, one monetary unit of imports is earned by one monetary unit of exports. Let m_j be the import coefficient of sector j and s_i^E be the share of exports. The labor value of the imported commodity is

$$t_m = \sum_i s_i^E t_i \quad t_m = \mathbf{s^E t}$$

The labor value equation is modified as

$$\begin{aligned} t_j &= \sum_i a_{ij} t_i + a_{mj} t_m + \tau_j \\ &= \sum_i a_{ij} t_i + a_{mj} \sum_i s_i^E t_i + \tau_j \end{aligned}$$

In the matrix form, it reads

$$\begin{aligned} \mathbf{t} &= \mathbf{tA} + \mathbf{a_m} t_m + \boldsymbol{\tau} = \mathbf{tA} + \mathbf{a_m s^E t} + \boldsymbol{\tau} \\ &= \mathbf{t}(\mathbf{A} + \mathbf{a_m s^E}) + \boldsymbol{\tau} \end{aligned} \tag{13}$$

Since export share, $\mathbf{s^E}$, and import inputs, $\mathbf{a_m}$, are measured in monetary terms, they reflect both export and import prices. That is, terms of trade will influence the value of imports. This treatment of imports was unavoidable when only single-country input–output tables were available.

Recently, in a reflection of the globalized economy, several international input–output tables have been compiled.[4] Labor value can be applied to the new situation described in the next section.

GLOBAL ECONOMY

In this section, we discuss how the *Fundamental Marxian Theorem* should be modified in the international input–output framework. In short, we will treat labor as heterogeneous among countries due to substantial wage differences among countries.

Labor Value in a Global Economy

We extend the concept of labor value in a global economy. There are R countries with N sectors in each country. Therefore, there are RN sectors in the world. Complete specialization is assumed. For example, the agricultural product produced in country r is different from that produced in country s.

One unit of production in sector j of country s requires a_{ij}^{rs} units of the commodity from sector i in country r and l_j^s units of labor from country s. In the matrix form, the input coefficient matrix is

$$\mathbf{A}^{rs} \equiv \begin{pmatrix} a_{11}^{rs} & \cdots & a_{1N}^{rs} \\ \vdots & \ddots & \vdots \\ a_{N1}^{rs} & \cdots & a_{NN}^{rs} \end{pmatrix}, \quad \mathbf{A} \equiv \begin{pmatrix} \mathbf{A}^{11} & \cdots & \mathbf{A}^{1R} \\ \vdots & \ddots & \vdots \\ \mathbf{A}^{R1} & \cdots & \mathbf{A}^{RR} \end{pmatrix}$$

The direct labor coefficient vector of country s is

$$\boldsymbol{\tau}^s \equiv (\tau_1^s, \ldots, \tau_N^s)$$

Although it is possible to combine each country's labor coefficient in the same row, we locate each country's labor in a different row in order to treat them as different kind of labor, namely, heterogeneous labor.[5] Because each economy's wage level differs,[6]

$$\boldsymbol{\tau} \equiv \begin{pmatrix} \boldsymbol{\tau}^1 & \cdots & \mathbf{0} \\ \vdots & \ddots & \vdots \\ \mathbf{0} & \cdots & \boldsymbol{\tau}^R \end{pmatrix}$$

Labor value is defined in the same way as Eq. (1).

$$\mathbf{T} \equiv \mathbf{T}\mathbf{A} + \boldsymbol{\tau} \tag{14}$$

where

$$\mathbf{t}^{rs} \equiv (t_1^{rs}, \ldots, t_N^{rs}) \quad \mathbf{t}^r \equiv (\mathbf{t}^{r1}, \ldots, \mathbf{t}^{rR}) \quad \mathbf{T} \equiv \begin{pmatrix} \mathbf{t}^1 \\ \vdots \\ \mathbf{t}^R \end{pmatrix} = \begin{pmatrix} \mathbf{t}^{11} & \cdots & \mathbf{t}^{1R} \\ \vdots & \ddots & \vdots \\ \mathbf{t}^{R1} & \cdots & \mathbf{t}^{RR} \end{pmatrix}$$

Labor value is an R × RN matrix. t_j^{rs} represents one unit of the commodity of sector j in country s which embodies labor from country r. A commodity is a bundle of labor from various countries (t_j^{rs}, $r = 1, \ldots, R$). We call the matrix $\mathbf{T}$ as global labor matrix.

Condition for Profit's Existence in Global Economy

The profit of industry j in country s (π_j^s) is determined by own output price (p_j^s), input prices (p_i^r, $i = 1, \ldots, N$, $r = 1, \ldots, R$) and wages (w^s) in addition to input coefficient (a_{ij}^{rs}) and labor coefficient (τ_j^s). The condition for positive profit to exist is

$$0 < \pi_j^s = p_j^s - \sum_r \sum_i p_i^r a_{ij}^{rs} - w^s \tau_j^s \tag{15}$$

Using matrix notation, it is expressed as

$$0 < \mathbf{p} - \mathbf{pA} - \mathbf{w}\boldsymbol{\tau}$$

$$\mathbf{p}^s \equiv (p_1^s, \ldots, p_N^s), \quad \mathbf{p} \equiv (\mathbf{p}^1, \ldots, \mathbf{p}^R), \quad \mathbf{w} \equiv (w^1, \ldots, w^R)$$

Laborers in country s purchase various countries' consumption commodities (b_i^{rs}, $i = 1, \ldots, N$, $r = 1, \ldots, R$) and the total cost for purchasing wage commodities equals the wage in country s:

$$w^s = \sum_r \sum_i p_i^r b_{ij}^{rs}$$

In matrix notation, the wage basket is expressed as

$$\mathbf{b}^{rs} \equiv \begin{pmatrix} b_1^{rs} \\ \vdots \\ b_N^{rs} \end{pmatrix} \quad \mathbf{b}^s \equiv \begin{pmatrix} \mathbf{b}^{1s} \\ \vdots \\ \mathbf{b}^{Rs} \end{pmatrix}$$

$$\mathbf{B} \equiv \begin{pmatrix} \mathbf{b}^1 & \cdots & \mathbf{b}^R \end{pmatrix} = \begin{pmatrix} \mathbf{b}^{1s} & \cdots & \mathbf{b}^{1R} \\ \vdots & \ddots & \vdots \\ \mathbf{b}^{R1} & \cdots & \mathbf{b}^{RR} \end{pmatrix} \tag{16}$$

$$\mathbf{w} = \mathbf{pB} \tag{17}$$

The condition for profit's existence can be rewritten as

$$\mathbf{p}(\mathbf{I}_{RN} - \mathbf{A} - \mathbf{B}\boldsymbol{\tau}) > \mathbf{0} \tag{18}$$

The condition for the existence of a positive price assuring a positive profit in all sectors is that the matrix $(\mathbf{I}_{RN} - \mathbf{A} - \mathbf{B}\boldsymbol{\tau})$ satisfies the Hawkins–Simon condition.

Exploitation in the Global Economy

Since matrix (18) satisfies the Hawkins–Simon condition, there exists a positive column vector of output ($\mathbf{x}$) for any positive vector of surplus product ($\mathbf{z}$):

$$\mathbf{0} < \mathbf{z} = (\mathbf{I}_{RN} - \mathbf{A} - \mathbf{B}\boldsymbol{\tau})\mathbf{x}$$

Multiplying the global labor value matrix ($\mathbf{T}$) from the left, we get

$$\begin{aligned} \mathbf{0} < \mathbf{Tz} &= \mathbf{T}(\mathbf{I}_{RN} - \mathbf{A} - \mathbf{B}\boldsymbol{\tau})x \\ &= \mathbf{T}(\mathbf{I}_{RN} - \mathbf{A})x - \mathbf{TB}\boldsymbol{\tau}x \\ &= \boldsymbol{\tau}x - \mathbf{TB}\boldsymbol{\tau}x \\ &= (\mathbf{I}_R - \mathbf{TB})\boldsymbol{\tau}x \end{aligned} \tag{19}$$

Although Eq. (19) looks similar to Eq. (8) in the previous section, $\mathbf{TB}$ is an $\mathrm{R} \times \mathrm{R}$ matrix and $\boldsymbol{\tau}\mathbf{x}$ is an R-dimensional column vector of each country's employment:

$$\mathbf{TB} = [\mathbf{t}^r\mathbf{b}^s] = \begin{pmatrix} \mathbf{t}^{11} & \cdots & \mathbf{t}^{1R} \\ \vdots & \ddots & \vdots \\ \mathbf{t}^{R1} & \cdots & \mathbf{t}^{RR} \end{pmatrix} \begin{pmatrix} \mathbf{b}^{11} & \cdots & \mathbf{b}^{1R} \\ \vdots & \ddots & \vdots \\ \mathbf{b}^{R1} & \cdots & \mathbf{b}^{RR} \end{pmatrix} \tag{20}$$

where the (r,s) factor of TB is $\boldsymbol{t}^r\boldsymbol{b}^s$. Since the vector of employment ($\boldsymbol{\tau}\mathbf{x}$) is positive, the matrix

$$(\mathbf{I}_R - \mathbf{TB}) \tag{21}$$

satisfies the Hawkins–Simon condition.

What is the implication of Eq. (21) satisfying Hawkins-Simon condition? Consider its dual problem. Multiplying the positive row vector $\boldsymbol{\mu}$ from the left, we get

$$\boldsymbol{\omega} \equiv \boldsymbol{\mu}(\mathbf{I}_R - \mathbf{TB}) \text{ in scalar terms, } \omega^s \equiv \mu^s - \sum\nolimits_r \mu^s \mathbf{t}^r \mathbf{b}^s \tag{22}$$

where ω^s reflects the surplus value in country s evaluated by the conversion rate of labor ($\boldsymbol{\mu}$). If Eq. (21) satisfies the Hawkins–Simon condition, some conversion rate of labor ($\boldsymbol{\mu}$) exists, which generates a positive surplus value in all countries ($\omega^s > 0$ for all s). That is,

$$0 < \boldsymbol{\omega} = \boldsymbol{\mu}(\mathbf{I}_R - \mathbf{TB})$$

In scalar terms,

$$0 < \omega^s = \mu^s - \sum\nolimits_r \mu^s \mathbf{t}^r \mathbf{b}^s$$

It can be rewritten as

$$1 > \sum_r \frac{\mu^r}{\mu^s} \mathbf{t}^r \mathbf{b}^s \quad \text{for all } s \tag{23}$$

> **Proposition:** The condition for the existence of positive profit in global economy (18) is equivalent to the condition that there exists some conversion rate of labor ($\boldsymbol{\mu}$) in Eq. (23) such that labor is exploited in all countries.

To illustrate the proposition, we consider a two-country case:

$$\begin{cases} \omega^1 = \mu^1 - (\mu^1 \mathbf{t}^1 \mathbf{b}^1 + \mu^2 \mathbf{t}^2 \mathbf{b}^1) \\ \omega^2 = \mu^2 - (\mu^1 \mathbf{t}^1 \mathbf{b}^2 + \mu^2 \mathbf{t}^2 \mathbf{b}^2) \end{cases}$$

For a positive surplus of labor to exist in both the countries ($0 < \omega^1$ and $0 < \omega^2$), the conversion rate of labor (μ^1, μ^2) must satisfy

$$\frac{\mathbf{t}^1 \mathbf{b}^2}{1 - \mathbf{t}^2 \mathbf{b}^2} < \frac{\mu^2}{\mu^1} < \frac{1 - \mathbf{t}^1 \mathbf{b}^1}{\mathbf{t}^2 \mathbf{b}^1} \tag{24}$$

If the conversion rate of labor (μ^2/μ^1) is lower than the lower bound $\mathbf{t}^1\mathbf{b}^2/1 - \mathbf{t}^2\mathbf{b}^2$, surplus labor in country 2 is negative, whereas that in country 1 is positive ($\omega^2 < 0 < \omega^1$). If the conversion rate (μ^2/μ^1) is higher than the upper bound $1 - \mathbf{t}^1\mathbf{b}^1/\mathbf{t}^2\mathbf{b}^1$, surplus labor in country 1 is negative, whereas that in country 2 is positive ($\omega^1 < 0 < \omega^2$). If the conversion rate of labor (μ^2/μ^1) is between the lower and upper bounds, surplus labor is positive in both countries ($0 < \omega^1$ and $0 < \omega^2$) (Fig. 1).

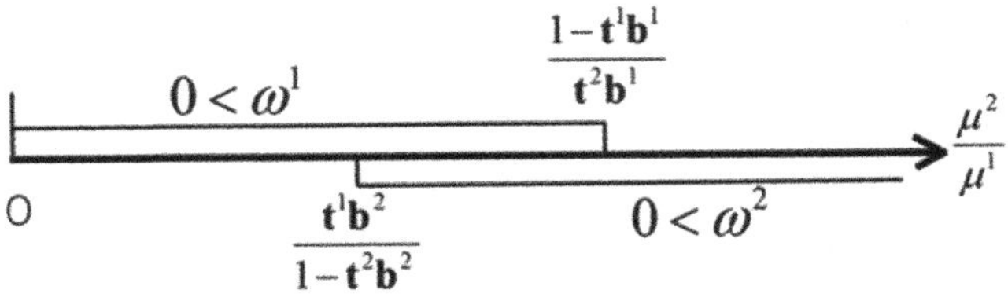

Fig. 1. Conversion Rate of Labor and Surplus Value.

The existence condition of the conversion rate of labor (μ^2/μ^1) needed to assure Eq. (23) is

$$\frac{\mathbf{t}^1\mathbf{b}^2}{1-\mathbf{t}^2\mathbf{b}^2} < \frac{1-\mathbf{t}^1\mathbf{b}^1}{\mathbf{t}^2\mathbf{b}^1}$$

That is,

$$0<(1-\mathbf{t}^1\mathbf{b}^1)(1-\mathbf{t}^2\mathbf{b}^2)-(\mathbf{t}^1\mathbf{b}^2)(\mathbf{t}^2\mathbf{b}^1)$$

The right-hand side of inequality is a second-order principle minor of Eq. (21). Since the Hawkins–Simon condition requires any principal minor of Eq. (21) is positive, there exists some range of the conversion rate of labor (μ^2/μ^1) to assure the existence of Eq. (23).

The lower bound of the conversion rate of labor (μ^2/μ^1) in Eq. (24) increases as the wage basket in country 2 ($\mathbf{b}^2$) increases, and the upper bound decreases as the wage basket of country 1 ($\mathbf{b}^1$) increases. If the wage basket ($\mathbf{b}^1$ and/or $\mathbf{b}^2$) increases enough, the Hawkins–Simon condition is violated and the range of the conversion rate of labor (μ^2/μ^1) satisfying the positive surplus labor conditions ($0<\omega^1$ and $0<\omega^2$) will diminish. Positive surplus labor exists exclusively in two countries. If the surplus value in country 1 is positive, that in country 2 is negative, and *vice versa*.

The important point is that the conversion rate of labor satisfying Eq. (23) is not always plausible. The possibility exists that some country's laborers enjoy a rich wage basket which embodies more labor than those laborers sold:

$$1<\sum_r \frac{\mu^r}{\mu^s}\mathbf{t}^r\mathbf{b}^s$$

for some s

Even in this case, there exists at least one country in which labor is exploited:

$$1 > \sum_r \frac{\mu^r}{\mu^s} \mathbf{t}^r \mathbf{b}^s$$

If laborer is not exploited in all countries, the inequality $0 > \boldsymbol{\omega} = \boldsymbol{\mu}(\mathbf{I} - \mathbf{TB})$ holds, which contradicts Eq. (23)

> **Corollary 1:** There exists some conversion rate of labor (μ) such that labor is not exploited in some countries. Nonetheless, there exists at least one country in which labor is exploited.

The rate of exploitation in country s (e^s) is

$$e^s \equiv \frac{\left(1 - \sum_r \sum_i (\mu^r/\mu^s) \mathbf{t}^r \mathbf{b}^s\right)}{\sum_r \sum_i (\mu^r/\mu^s) \mathbf{t}^r \mathbf{b}^s} = \frac{\left(\mu^s - \sum_r \sum_i \mu^r \, \mathbf{t}^r \mathbf{b}^s\right)}{\sum_r \sum_i \mu^r \mathbf{t}^r \mathbf{b}^s} = \frac{\omega^s}{1 - \omega^s} \tag{25}$$

If the conversion rate of labor ($\boldsymbol{\mu}$) satisfies Eq. (23), the exploitation rate in all countries is positive. Conversely, there is a possibility that a plausible conversion rate of labor ($\boldsymbol{\mu}$) may not satisfy Eq. (23) and rate of exploitation is negative in some countries.

Another point is that the own-country's labor embodied in a worker's labor basket is less than unity independent from the choice of conversion rate of labor ($\boldsymbol{\mu}$):

$$0 < 1 - \mathbf{t}^s \mathbf{b}^s$$

The right-hand side of inequality is a first-order principle minor of Eq. (21). The Hawkins–Simon condition requires any principal minor of Eq. (21) to be positive. Therefore, the inequality holds.

> **Corollary 2:** Whatever the conversion rate of labor ($\boldsymbol{\mu}$) is chosen, the own-country labor embodied in wage basket $\mathbf{t^s b^s}$ is less than unity.

Since the total labor embodied in a wage basket is a country's own labor plus foreign labor, the own-country labor is its lower bound. The case of non-exploitation occurs when foreign labor is large due to the conversion rate of labor.

EMPIRICAL STUDY

In this section, we examine exploitation in the context of global labor using international input-output tables.

First, we need to specify the conversion rate of labor (μ). It is natural to assume that labor is the same across countries even if serious wage gaps exist; that is, the essential nature and value of labor in a rich country and that in poor country are the same. We employ a simple weight wherein the conversion rate for any country's labor equals unity.[7]

$$\boldsymbol{\mu} = \boldsymbol{\iota}_{\mathbf{R}} \equiv (1, 1, ..., 1) \tag{26}$$

Then surplus value (22) is specified as

$$\boldsymbol{\omega} = \iota_R(\mathbf{I}_R - \mathbf{TB}) \text{ in scalar term } \omega^s = 1 - \sum\nolimits_r \mathbf{t}^r \mathbf{b}^s \tag{27}$$

It should be noted that Eq. (27) does not guarantee a positive surplus value in all countries ($\omega^s > 0$ for all s). As shown later, there are countries where the surplus value is negative.

Exploitation is the gap between the labor sold and the amount of labor purchased as wage commodity by selling his/her own labor. The amount of labor purchased by selling unit labor is expressed as the sum of the value of labor in the wage basket $\left(\sum_r \mathbf{t}^r \mathbf{b}^s\right)$ in Eq. (27). If it is less than unity, exploitation prevails; otherwise laborers in the country enjoy being paid for more labor than he/she provides (non-exploitation).

Data

We use the World Input Output Database (WIOD)[8] which covers 40 countries and the rest of the world (RoW). It includes 27 EU countries (except Croatia), three NAFTA countries, four East Asian countries, and six resource-rich countries. The 40 WIOD countries cover nearly 90% of global GDP and include major rich and large countries.

We aggregate countries into four separate countries and two regions: China, Japan, Korea, Taiwan, Advanced Countries (ADCs hereafter) and Developing Countries (DVCs hereafter). The list of regions is given in Table 1. A total of

Table 1. Definitions of Countries and Regions.

Country and Region	Description
China	People's Republic of China
Japan	Japan
Korea	Republic of Korea
Taiwan	Republic of China
*Ad*vanced Countrie*s* (ADCs)	USA, Australia, Canada, EU15 (Austria, Belgium, Denmark, Finland, France, Germany, Greece, Ireland, Italy, Luxembourg, Netherlands, Portugal, Spain, Sweden, UK)
*De*veloping Countrie*s* (DVCs)	Brazil, India, Indonesia, Mexico, Russia, Turkey, EU12 (Bulgaria, Cyprus, Czech, Estonia, Hungary, Latvia, Lithuania, Malta, Poland, Romania, Slovakia, Slovenia)

Table 2. Wages and Labor Hours.

		China	Japan	Korea	Taiwan	ADCs	DVCs
Nominal wage	1995	0.33	24.71	8.10	8.21	19.59	0.89
	2009	1.35	26.12	10.98	9.64	32.75	2.03
	Change rate	310%	6%	36%	17%	67%	129%
Real wage	Change rate	137%	11%	42%	40%	26%	47%
Labor hour engaged	1995	1,215	128	51	22	541	1,512
	2009	1,556	106	54	22	592	1,821
	Change rate	28%	−17%	5%	0%	9%	20%

Source: Author's calculation using WIOD database.
Unit: Nominal wage: US$ per hour. Labor hours engaged: trillion hours.

35 industry sectors are aggregated into nine sectors, namely, (1) agriculture, hunting, forestry, and fishing; (2) mining and quarrying; (3) manufacturing; (4) electricity, gas, and water Supply; (5) construction; (6) commerce; (7) transport and communication; (8) financial intermediation, real estate, renting, and other business services; and (9) other service. Using the previous year's price table, we constructed an input–output table with fixed prices (1995 prices).

WIOD does not serve consumption of fixed capital (CFC) by industry. We used statistics of United Nations and World Development Indicators (WDI) of the World Bank. UN statistics were used first; then, a cross-country average ratio of CFC to value added and the WDI macro ratio are used to fill in the missing data. Since those statistics are not disaggregated as in the WIOD, we assume that the WIOD ratio of depreciation to value added is common to UN statistics. WIOD has no data on labor and value added for Rest of the World. We therefore ignored labor of the Rest of the World. Therefore, the result shown below underestimates the real labor value.

Table 2 shows wage and labor hour differences among countries in 1995 and 2009. The top wage group was Japan and ADCs. Korea and Taiwan were the second group. The third group was China and DVCs. The wage level in the second group was around 40% of that of top group, whereas that in the third group was around 5% of that in the first group. Wages in China increased rapidly, whereas those in Japan stagnated in both nominal and real terms.

As for labor hour engaged, China and DVCs were the largest, followed by ADCs. Korea and Taiwan are the smallest group. While labor hour of China and DVCs increased more than 20%, that of Japan decreased.

Composition of Wage Basket in Terms of Global Labor Value

The labor embodied in the wage basket ($\mathbf{t}^{r}\mathbf{b}^{s}$) in 1995 and 2009 is shown in Table 3. The sum of labor embodied ($\Sigma_{r}\mathbf{t}^{r}\mathbf{b}^{s}$) is less than unity in China,

Table 3. Composition of Labor Embodied in Countries' Wage Baskets.

	Country r	Year	China	Japan	Korea	Taiwan	ADCs	DVCs
			Wage Basket of Country s					
Labor r embodied in wage basket of s ($\mathbf{t^r b^s}$)	China	1995	0.565	0.287	0.180	0.116	0.184	0.006
		2009	0.489	0.268	0.235	0.148	0.302	0.021
	Japan	1995	0.000	0.679	0.010	0.020	0.008	0.000
		2009	0.001	0.618	0.011	0.018	0.009	0.001
	Korea	1995	0.000	0.014	0.796	0.010	0.007	0.000
		2009	0.001	0.008	0.691	0.007	0.009	0.001
	Taiwan	1995	0.000	0.008	0.002	0.543	0.005	0.000
		2009	0.001	0.006	0.004	0.470	0.005	0.000
	ADCs	1995	0.001	0.039	0.031	0.049	0.656	0.003
		2009	0.003	0.032	0.030	0.030	0.724	0.006
	DVCs	1995	0.002	0.133	0.085	0.080	0.237	0.542
		2009	0.009	0.106	0.097	0.077	0.365	0.551
	Sum of Labor $\mathbf{\Sigma_r t^r b^s}$	1995	0.569	1.160	1.105	0.818	1.098	0.552
		2009	0.504	1.038	1.067	0.751	1.415	0.579
Surplus Value:		1995	0.431	−0.160	−0.105	0.182	−0.098	0.448
$\omega^s=1-\Sigma_r t^r b^s$		2009	0.496	−0.038	−0.067	0.249	−0.415	0.421
Rate of exploitation:		1995	0.757	−0.138	−0.095	0.223	−0.089	0.810
$e^s=\omega^s/(1-\omega^s)$		2009	0.986	−0.037	−0.063	0.332	−0.293	0.727

Source: Author's calculation using WIOD database.

Taiwan, and DVCs, whereas Japan, Korea, and ADCs exceed unity (non-exploitation case). Laborers in the latter countries purchase wage commodities which embody more labor than they sold their labor. The rate of exploitation is negative. Labor embodied in the wage basket of Asian countries decreased during the period 1995–2009, whereas that of ADCs and DVCs increased. In other words, the rate of exploitation increased in the four Asian countries, whereas it decreased in ADCs and DVCs.

Own-country labor embodied in the wage basket ($\mathbf{t^s b^s}$) diagonal factor in Table 3 is the largest among column countries. It is less than unity, between 0.47 and 0.80, which is consistent with the *Fundamental Marxian Theorem* in a global economy. Own-country labor increased in ADCs and DVCs but decreased in Asian countries during the period 1995–2009.

Regarding the foreign labor in a country's wage basket, the sum of the off-diagonal factors ($\mathbf{\Sigma_{r \neq s} t^r b^s}$) for labor in China and the DVCs are largely embodied in these countries' wage baskets. Since China (top row) and DVCs (bottom row) have large labor forces and low wages, more advanced countries take advantage. The share of Chinese labor embodied in the Japanese wage basket ($t^{China}b^{Japan}$) is around 0.287 and 0.268. In Korea and ADCs, the share of Chinese labor was 0.18 in 1995, increasing to 0.235 and 0.302, respectively. In DVCs, the share of Chinese labor is small. The amount of DVCs labor embodied in ADCs, 0.237 and 0.365, is larger than that in Japan, Taiwan and Korea, between 0.077 and 0.133. In China, the share of DVCs labor is quite low.

The time series of labor embodied in wage baskets are shown in Figs. 2(a)–(f). Labor embodied in the wage basket of China (Fig. 2(a)) decreased during the period 1998–2007, then slightly recovered. Own-country labor is almost all labor embodied the wage basket, with negligible labor coming from other countries. In Japan (Fig. 2(b)), the sum of embodied labor was 1.2 then moved between 1.08 and 0.97. The embodied Japanese own-country labor decreased

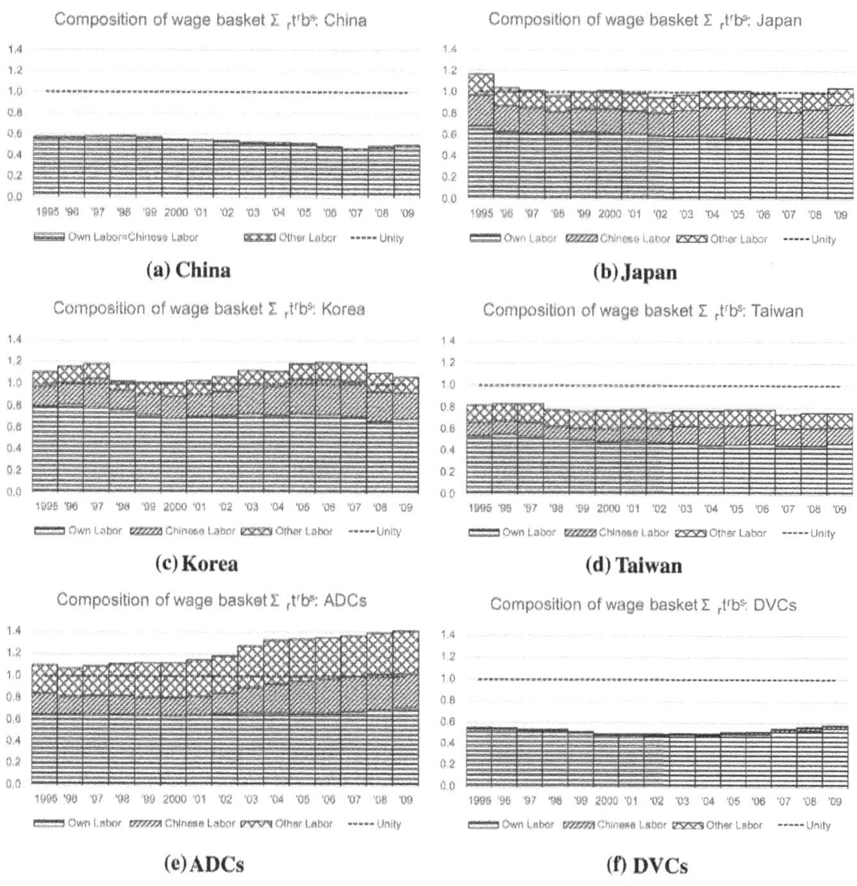

Fig. 2. (a) China, (b) Japan, (c) Korea, (d) Taiwan, (e) ADCs, (f) DVCs.

until 2007 and then slightly increased. Embodied Chinese labor decreased until 2002 and then increased. Other 7 decreased. In Korea (Fig. 2(c)), there are two sudden decreases, in 1998 and 2008, respectively. In Taiwan (Fig. 2(d)), a decreasing trend can be seen in the sum of embodied labor, whereas Chinese embodied labor increased. ADCs (Fig. 2(e)) show an increasing trend, especially for embodied Chinese labor. DVCs (Fig. 2(f)) share decreased until 2000 and then gradually increased.

Contribution Analysis

From Figs. 2(a)–(f), we see that labor embodied in the wage baskets ($\boldsymbol{t}^r\boldsymbol{b}^s$) of the four examined Asian countries decreased, whereas that in ADCs increased. We explore the factors that contributed to these changes in labor embodied in wage baskets. The studied factors are wage basket b, input coefficient A, and labor coefficient τ. The sum of the effects of A and τ is the effects of labor value. Taking the time difference of Eq. (22), we get the following formula for contribution analysis:[9]

$$\begin{aligned}\Delta(\iota\mathbf{TB}) &= \iota\mathbf{T}\Delta\mathbf{B} + \iota\Delta\mathbf{TB} = \iota\mathbf{T}\Delta\mathbf{B} + \iota(\mathbf{T}\Delta\mathbf{A} + \Delta\boldsymbol{\tau})(\mathbf{I}_{RN} - \mathbf{A})^{-1}\mathbf{B} \\ &= \iota\mathbf{T}\Delta\mathbf{B} + \iota\mathbf{T}\Delta\mathbf{A}(\mathbf{I}_{RN} - \mathbf{A})^{-1}\mathbf{B} + \iota\Delta\boldsymbol{\tau}(\mathbf{I}_{RN} - \mathbf{A})^{-1}\mathbf{B}\end{aligned}$$

$$\begin{aligned}\Delta\left(\sum_r \mathbf{t}^r\mathbf{b}^s\right) &= \left(\sum_r \mathbf{t}^r\Delta\mathbf{b}^s\right) + \left(\sum_r \mathbf{t}^r\Delta\mathbf{A}(\mathbf{I}_{RN} - \mathbf{A})^{-1}\mathbf{b}^s\right) \\ &\quad + \left(\sum_r \Delta\boldsymbol{\tau}^r(\mathbf{I}_{RN} - \mathbf{A})^{-1}\mathbf{b}^s\right)\end{aligned}$$

The first term on the right-hand side is the effect of a wage basket change ($\boldsymbol{\Delta b}^s$). The second term is the effect of an input coefficient change (ΔA). The third term is the effect of a labor coefficient change ($\boldsymbol{\Delta\tau}$).

We compare ADCs and four Asian countries during the period 1995–2009. The sum of labor embodied in the wage baskets (line 1) of ADCs increased, whereas that in the four Asian countries decreased. From Table 4, it can be seen that the contribution of wage basket changes (line 2) is positive and high except in Japan. The contribution of labor value (line 3) is negative and large in China, Korea, and Taiwan, but negative and small in ADCs. The contribution of direct labor coefficient (line 4) is large negative for every country. The difference between ADCs and the four Asian countries lies in the input coefficient (line 5). In ADCs, the effects of wage basket, b, and input coefficient, A, overcome the negative effect of the direct labor coefficient. In contrast, the effect of the input coefficient is not so large and the sum of tb decreases in the four studied Asian countries.

Table 4. Contribution to Change in the Sum of Labor Embodied in Wage Basket: $\mathbf{\Delta(\Sigma_r t^r b^s)}$.

		Wage basket of Country *s*					
		China	Japan	Korea	Taiwan	ADCs	DVCs
(1) $\mathbf{\Delta(\Sigma_r t^r b^s)}$	=(2)+(3)	−0.066	−0.121	−0.038	−0.067	0.316	0.027
(2) $\mathbf{\Sigma_r t^r \Delta b^s}$		0.450	0.173	0.431	0.346	0.427	0.184
(3) $\mathbf{\Sigma_r \Delta t^r b^s}$	=(4)+(5)	−0.515	−0.294	−0.469	−0.413	−0.111	−0.158
(4) $\mathbf{\Sigma_r \Delta \tau^r (I\text{-}A)^{-1} b^s}$		−0.595	−0.547	−0.700	−0.521	−0.625	−0.178
(5) $\mathbf{\Sigma_r \tau^r \Delta A (I\text{-}A)^{-1} b^s}$		0.080	0.253	0.231	0.108	0.514	0.021

Source: Author's calculation from WIOD database.

Table 5. Contribution to Change in Own-Country Labor Embodied in Wage Basket: $\mathbf{\Delta(t^s b^s)}$.

		Wage Basket of Country *s*					
		China	Japan	Korea	Taiwan	ADCs	DVCs
(1) $\mathbf{\Delta(t^s b^s)}$	=(2)+(3)	−0.076	−0.061	−0.106	−0.073	0.068	0.009
(2) $\mathbf{t^s \Delta b^s}$		0.442	0.055	0.228	0.205	0.155	0.166
(3) $\mathbf{\Delta t^s b^s}$	=(4)+(5)	−0.518	−0.116	−0.334	−0.278	−0.087	−0.157
(4) $\mathbf{\Delta \tau^s (I\text{-}A)^{-1} b^s}$		−0.592	−0.123	−0.382	−0.282	−0.167	−0.155
(5) $\mathbf{\tau^s \Delta A (I\text{-}A)^{-1} b^s}$		0.073	0.006	0.048	0.004	0.080	−0.002

Source: Author's calculation from WIOD database.

Table 6. Contribution to Change in Foreign Labor Embodied in Wage Basket: $\mathbf{\Delta(\Sigma_{r\neq s} t^r b^s)}$.

		Wage Basket of Country *s*					
		China	Japan	Korea	Taiwan	ADCs	DVCs
(1) $\mathbf{\Delta(\Sigma_{r\neq s} t^r b^s)}$	=(2)+(3)	0.011	−0.060	0.068	0.006	0.248	0.018
(2) $\mathbf{\Sigma_{r\neq s} t^r \Delta b^s}$		0.008	0.118	0.203	0.141	0.272	0.018
(3) $\mathbf{\Sigma_{r\neq s} \Delta t^r b^s}$	=(4)+(5)	0.003	−0.178	−0.135	−0.135	−0.024	0.000
(4) $\mathbf{\Sigma_{r\neq s} \Delta \tau^r (I\text{-}A)^{-1} b^s}$		−0.004	−0.424	−0.318	−0.239	−0.458	−0.023
(5) $\mathbf{\Sigma_{r\neq s} \tau^r \Delta A (I\text{-}A)^{-1} b^s}$		0.006	0.246	0.183	0.104	0.434	0.023

Source: Author's calculation from WIOD database.

The sum of labor embodied in the wage basket ($\mathbf{\Sigma_r t^r b^s}$) is divided into the own-country's labor (Table 5) and foreign labor (Table 6).

$$\Delta(\mathbf{t}^s\mathbf{b}^s) = (\mathbf{t}^s\Delta\mathbf{b}^s) + (\mathbf{t}^s\Delta\mathbf{A}(\mathbf{I}_{RN} - \mathbf{A})^{-1}\mathbf{b}^s) + (\Delta\boldsymbol{\tau}^s(\mathbf{I}_{RN} - \mathbf{A})^{-1}\mathbf{b}^s)$$

$$\Delta\left(\sum\nolimits_{r\neq s}\mathbf{t}^r\mathbf{b}^s\right) = \left(\sum\nolimits_{r\neq s}\mathbf{t}^r\Delta\mathbf{b}^s\right) + \left(\sum\nolimits_{r\neq s}\mathbf{t}^r\Delta\mathbf{A}(\mathbf{I}_{RN} - \mathbf{A})^{-1}\mathbf{b}^s\right) + \left(\sum\nolimits_{r\neq s}\Delta\boldsymbol{\tau}(\mathbf{I}_{RN} - \mathbf{A})^{-1}\mathbf{b}^s\right)$$

In ADCs, the large contribution of *b* and *A* comes from foreign labor. In the four Asian countries, it is not so large. Therefore, differences between ADCs and the four Asian countries arise from the extent of the shift from domestic purchases to international purchases, especially in low-wage countries. The contribution of this factor to changes in Chinese labor (Table 7) does not show a significant difference between ADCs and the three Asian countries of Japan, Korea, and Taiwan. Tables 6 and 7 are similar in terms of these three Asian countries, which means that the shift to global purchases is limited to China. In ADCs, the share of labor from China is large but other foreign labor is also significant, which is obvious from Figure 2(a).

In case of China and DVCs, the effect of foreign labor is negligible; own-country labor dominates (Tables 5 and 6), as can be seen in these countries' own labor value far exceeding other countries' labor values.

China in Table 7 is omitted because it is the same as Chinese own-country labor in Table 5.

Table 7. Contribution to Change in Chinese Labor Embodied in Wage Basket: $\mathbf{\Delta(t^{China}b^s)}$.

		Wage Basket of Country *s*					
		China	Japan	Korea	Taiwan	ADCs	DVCs
(1) $\mathbf{\Delta(t^{China}b^s)}$	=(2)+(3)		−0.018	0.055	0.032	0.118	0.015
(2) $\mathbf{t^{China}\Delta b^s}$			0.120	0.163	0.113	0.172	0.015
(3) $\mathbf{\Delta t^{China}b^s}$	=(4)+(5)		−0.138	−0.109	−0.080	−0.054	0.000
(4) $\mathbf{\Delta\tau^{China}(I\text{-}A)^{-1}b^s}$			−0.363	−0.276	−0.190	−0.348	−0.021
(5) $\mathbf{\tau^{China}\Delta A(I\text{-}A)^{-1}b^s}$			0.225	0.167	0.109	0.294	0.020

Source: Author's calculation from WIOD database.

CONCLUSION

In this paper, we discussed labor value and exploitation in the context of international input–output analysis. Each country's labor is treated as heterogeneous. Evaluation of exploitation needs a conversion rate for labor. There exists a conversion rate for labor such that each country's laborers are exploited, whereas the non-exploitation case may happen in some countries.

From international input–output analysis, we found (1) non-exploitation in Japan, Korea, and advanced countries (ADCs); (2) during 1995 and 2009, the rate of exploitation declined in Asian countries, whereas it increased in ADCs. There is a tendency that increases in the effect of wage baskets and decreases in the effect of labor value coexist; and (3) the labor embodied in ADCs' wage basket increased, whereas that in the four Asian countries decreased. This difference can be traced back to the spread of globalization.

NOTES

1. The input coefficient generally used in input–output analysis is an intermediate input coefficient. In this paper, the input coefficient is defined as intermediate input coefficient plus fixed capital consumption per output. Consumption of fixed capital of the *i*th commodity in the *j*th sector is defined as the *i*th share of capital formation multiplied by the rate of depreciation.

2. Assuming a square matrix **H** with a positive diagonal and non-positive off-diagonal and vector **b**, the Hawkins-Simon theorem states following four conditions are equivalent:

(1) $\mathbf{Hx} = \mathbf{b}$ has a non-negative solution $\mathbf{x} \geq \mathbf{0}$ for some $\mathbf{b} > \mathbf{0}$,
(2) $\mathbf{Hx} = \mathbf{b}$ has a non-negative solution $\mathbf{x} \geq \mathbf{0}$ for any $\mathbf{b} \geq \mathbf{0}$,
(3) Any principal minor of **H** is positive (Hawkins-Simon Condition), and
(4) The inverse of **H** is non-negative.

3. Researches in line with Sraffa (1960), like Gupta and Steedman (1971), Ochoa (1989) and Fröhlich (2012), neglected the labor value of imports. Steedman (2008) commented that the labor value of imports can be incorporated by using exports, an idea similar to that of Okishio (1958).

4. For example, the Institute of Development Economics (Japan) complied an Asia table covering China, Indonesia, Japan, Korea, Malaysia, Taiwan, the Philippines, Singapore, Thailand, and the United States for 1985, 1990, 1995, 2000, and 2005 (Asian International Input-Output Project (2013). Groningen University compiled tables covering 40 countries during 1995 and 2009, WIOD, which we use in this research. Other data are GTAP (Hertel, 1997) and EORA (Lenzen, 2013).

5. Bowles and Gintis (1979).

6. Wage differences exist among laborers in a single economy, which are justified as the reflection of differences in labor quality. Although labor quality differences, like skill level, between economies exist, it is not a major reason of international wage difference.

7. An alternative conversion rate of labor is a weight-reflecting skill level. The database explained later supplies hours worked by high-skilled, medium skilled and low-skilled persons, as classified by attained education. To apply this alternative, we need to determine the weight among these three skill levels.

8. Timmer, Dietzenbacher, Los, Stehrer, and de Vries (2015). Calculation based on WIOD release 2013.

9. Applying a time difference on the product, there are several alternatives for timing: $\Delta(xy) = x_1y_1 - x_0y_0 = \Delta xy_0 + x_1\Delta y = \Delta xy_1 + x_0\Delta y = \Delta x(y_0 + y_1)/2 + (x_0 + x_1)\Delta y/2$ we adopt the third formulation.

REFERENCES

Asian International Input-Output Project. (Ed.). (2013). *Asian International Input-Output Table* 2005, IDE-JETRO.

Bowles, S., & Gintis, H. (1977). The Marxian theory of value and heterogeneous labor: A critique and reformulation. *Cambridge Journal of Economics*, *1*(2), 173–192.

Fröhlich, N. (2012). Labour values, prices of production and the missing equalisation tendency of profit rates: Evidence from the German economy. *Cambridge Journal of Economics*, *37*(5), 1107–1126.

Gupta, S., & Steedman, I. (1971). An input-output study of labor productivity in the British economy. *Bulletin of the Institute of Economics and Statistics*, *33*(1), 21–34.

Hagiwara, T. (2004). Measurement of global labor value. *Kokumin Keizai Zasshi*, *189*(2), 17–31 (in Japanese).

Hertel, T. (1997). *Global trade analysis: Modeling and applications*. Cambridge: Cambridge University Press.

Katano, H. (1984). Basics of international input-output relations. *Kokumin Keizai Zasshi*, *151*(4), 1–14 (in Japanese).

Lenzen, M., Moran, D., Kanemoto, K., & Geschke, A. (2013). Building Eora: A global multi-regional input-output database at high country and sector resolution. *Economic Systems Research*, *25*(1), 20–49.

Leontief, W. (1941). *The structure of American economy, 1919–1929*. Cambridge, MA: Harvard University Press.

Morishima, M. (1973). *Marx's Economics*. Cambridge: Cambridge University Press.

Nakajima, A., & Izumi, H. (1995). Economic development and unequal exchange among nations: Analysis of the U.S., Japan and South Korea. *Review of Radical Political Economics*, *27*(3), 86–94.

Nakatani, T. (1994). *Economics of Value, Price and Value*. Tokyo: Keiso Shobo (in Japanese).

Ochoa, E. M. (1989). Values, prices, and wage-profit curves in the US economy. *Cambridge Journal of Economics*, *13*, 413–429.

Okishio, N. (1955). Value and price – Labor value theory and equilibrium price theory. *Annals of Economics Research (Kobe University)*, *1*, 211–296, (Okishio (**1977**), in Japanese).

Okishio, N. (1958). Empirical study of unequal exchange. *Shogaku ronshu (Fukushima University)*, *27*(3), 156–175, (Okishio (1977), in Japanese).

Okishio, N. (1965). *Fundamental theory of capitalist economy*. Tokyo: Sobunsha (in Japanese).

Okishio, N. (1977). *Marxian economics*. Tokyo: Chikuma Publishers (in Japanese).

Okishio, N., & Nakatani, T. (1985). A measurement of the rate of surplus value in Japan: The 1980 case. *Kobe University Economic Review*, *31*, 1–13.

Sraffa, P. (1960). *Production of commodities by means of commodities – Prelude to a critique of economic theory*. Cambridge: Cambridge University Press.

Steedman, I. (2008). Marx after Sraffa and the open economy. *Bulletin of Political Economy*, *2*(2), 165–174.

Timmer, M. P., Dietzenbacher, E., Los, B., Stehrer, R., & de Vries, G. J. (2015). An illustrated user guide to the world input–output database: The case of global automotive production. *Review of International Economics*, *23*, 575–605.

FINANCIAL INSTABILITY IN JAPAN: DEBT, CONFIDENCE, AND FINANCIAL STRUCTURE

Kenshiro Ninomiya and Masaaki Tokuda

ABSTRACT

The Japanese economy experienced prosperity during the bubble economy and has suffered from a prolonged recession since the bubble economy collapsed. This paper examines how the interest-bearing debt burden, structural change, and instability of confidence affect dynamic systems. Moreover, it examines these factors in the Japanese economy by applying a recursive vector autoregression analysis. This paper emphasizes the interest-bearing debt burden, the economic structure resulting from the instability of confidence, and the instability of confidence resulting from debt burden play important roles in the instability of the economy. As a result, Japan's economy was determined to be relatively stable from 1980 to 1996, but was unstable, thereafter.

Keywords: Interest-bearing debt burden; structural change; instability of confidence; recursive VAR; Japanese economy

INTRODUCTION

The Japanese economy experienced prosperity during the "bubble economy," but after its collapse, it suffered from a prolonged recession, referred to as "the

Return of Marxian Macro-dynamics in East Asia
Research in Political Economy, Volume 32, 39–61

ISSN: 0161-7230/doi:10.1108/S0161-723020170000032004

lost two decades." Several economists have keenly studied these two phases in the Japanese economy.

Nakatani and Skott (2007) combined demand- and supply-side aspects in a Harrodian model to analyze Japanese growth and stagnation.[1] They assumed an S-shaped "output expansion function" and discussed the high economic growth in the 1960s and the prolonged recession post-1990. They emphasized labor constraints as a factor of the economic stagnation. However, they largely ignored financial matters.[2]

Ninomiya and Tokuda (2011) introduced the concept of the "instability of confidence" and showed that it increased in Japan in the mid-1990s. By applying vector autoregression (VAR) analysis, they indicated the fragility in the Japanese economy's financial structure.[3] Asada (2006b) presented a high-dimensional, dynamic Keynesian model with debt accumulation, and showed that the monetary authority can stabilize an unstable economy by conducting sufficiently credible inflation-targeting policy, even in the case of a liquidity trap. Asada (2006b) implied that the inadequate monetary policy of the Bank of Japan was a reason for the prolonged recession.

The financial instability hypothesis, which was proposed by heterodox economist Hyman P. Minsky, and the related mathematical models stressed the debt burden as a factor of financial instability.[4] By applying a VAR model, Nishi (2012a) investigated the dynamic relationships among income distribution, the debt ratio, and capital accumulation in the Japanese economy after the 1990s.[5]

On the other hand, the Japanese economy suffered from a cumulative interest-bearing debt burden after the bubble economy collapsed. Nonperforming loans were regarded as one of the main reasons for the prolonged recession in Japan. Ninomiya (2006) noted the cumulative interest-bearing debt burden as an aspect of financial instability. Although his research yielded interesting results, he did not consider structural change or the instability of confidence; therefore, his paper lacked a comprehensive empirical analysis.[6]

The present paper begins by presenting a Keynesian macro-dynamic model, which considers the interest-bearing debt burden. It examines how the interest-bearing debt burden, structural change, and the instability of confidence affect dynamic systems in the model. Moreover, it examines these factors in the Japanese economy by applying a recursive VAR analysis.

The present paper argues both theoretically and empirically about the relationship among these factors in the dynamic economic systems. We believe that our discussion provides some insight into the global recession after the US subprime loan crisis, even though we focus on the Japanese bubble economy and its subsequent prolonged economic stagnation.

THE THEORETICAL MODEL

This section presents a Keynesian macro-dynamic model that considers the interest-bearing debt burden by further developing Ninomiya (2006). This paper proposes an oligopolistic economy, and assumes that the price level, p, is decided by the mark-up principle as follows:

$$p = \frac{(1+\tau)WN}{Y} \tag{1}$$

where τ is the mark-up rate, W is the nominal wage, N is the employment, and Y is the net income.

Real profit, Π, which constitutes the internal reserve, is defined as follows:

$$\Pi = Y - \frac{W}{p}N = \frac{\tau}{1+\tau}Y = \theta Y \tag{2}$$

where θ is the rate of profit share. The real wage income, H_W, is obtained from Eq. (1) as follows:

$$H_W = \frac{W}{p}N = \frac{1}{1+\tau}Y = (1-\theta)Y, \quad 0<\theta<1 \tag{3}$$

The investment function, I, is defined as follows:

$$\begin{aligned} I &= I(Y, B, i, \sigma^2) + I_0 \\ I_Y \equiv \frac{\partial I}{\partial Y} > 0, \quad I_B &\equiv \frac{\partial I}{\partial B} < 0, \quad I_i \equiv \frac{\partial I}{\partial i} < 0, \quad I_\sigma \equiv \frac{\partial I}{\partial \sigma^2} < 0 \end{aligned} \tag{4}$$

where B is the debt burden, i is the interest rate, and I_0 is the independent investment. $I_B(<0)$ shows that firms reduce their investment demand on the basis of an increase in their debt burden. This is one type of borrower risk.

σ^2 is the instability of confidence. $I_\sigma(<0)$ shows that firms reduce their investment demand on the basis of an increase in the instability of their confidence level. The instability of confidence declines when the economy is in a state of "euphoria." Investment demand increases considerably when the absolute value of I_σ is large. On the contrary, investment demand decreases considerably in case of a decrease in the instability of confidence. I_σ is often referred to as the "animal spirits" that co-exist with many investment opportunities. For example, the investment demand does not increase considerably, in spite of a decrease in the instability of confidence, if the absolute value of I_σ is small.[7]

The money demand function, M^{d}, and the money supply function, M^{s}, are defined as follows:

$$M^{\mathrm{d}} = L(Y, i), \quad L_Y \equiv \frac{\partial L}{\partial Y} > 0, \quad L_i \equiv \frac{\partial L}{\partial i} < 0 \tag{5}$$

$$M^{\mathrm{s}} = \mu(B, i, \sigma^2)H, \quad \mu_B \equiv \frac{\partial \mu}{\partial B} < 0, \quad \mu_i \equiv \frac{\partial \mu}{\partial i} > 0, \quad \mu_\sigma \equiv \frac{\partial \mu}{\partial \sigma^2} < 0 \tag{6}$$

where μ is a monetary multiplier and H is high-powered money. We assume that H is constant ($H = \overline{H}$). $\mu_B(<0)$ and $\mu_\sigma(<0)$ indicate lender risks. μ_B, for example, shows that commercial bank loans decrease with an increase in debt burden, B. On the other hand, the instability of confidence considerably declines when the economy is euphoric. $\mu_\sigma(<0)$ shows that the money supply increases considerably with an increase in bank loans. We assume that there is no asymmetry between the instability of confidence of borrowers and lenders.

The consumption function is assumed to be a linear function of the real wage income, H_W:

$$C = cH_W + C_0 = c(1-\theta)Y + C_0, \quad 0 < c < 1, \quad C_0 > 0 \tag{7}$$

where c is the marginal propensity to consume and C_0 is basic consumption.

Following Okishio (1986), Ninomiya (2007), and Ninomiya and Tokuda (2012), we suppose that the following equation determines the interest rate, i:

$$EB = -[EX + EM] = -[(C + I - Y) + (M^{\mathrm{d}} - M^{\mathrm{s}})] = 0 \tag{8}$$

where EX, EB, and EM are the excess demand for goods, bonds, and money, respectively. Equation (8) indicates that the interest rate is determined by the relationship between lenders and borrowers.

By ordering Eqs. (4)–(8), and solving them with respect to the interest rate, we obtain the following equation:

$$\begin{aligned} &i = i(Y, B, \sigma^2), \quad i_Y \equiv \frac{\partial i}{\partial Y} = -\frac{I_Y - \{1 - c(1-\theta)\} + L_Y}{I_i + L_i - \mu_i H} > 0 \\ &i_B \equiv \frac{\partial i}{\partial B} = -\frac{I_B - \mu_B H}{I_i + L_i - \mu_i H} \gtrless 0, \quad i_\sigma \equiv \frac{\partial i}{\partial \sigma^2} = -\frac{I_\sigma - \mu_\sigma H}{I_i + L_i - \mu_i H} \gtrless 0 \end{aligned} \tag{9}$$

The sign of i_Y depends on I_Y and L_Y. However, the following empirical study supports $i_Y > 0$. Therefore, we assume $i_Y > 0$ in this paper.[8] The sign of i_B depends on I_B and $\mu_B H$ as follows:

$$I_B - \mu_B H \gtreqless 0 \Leftrightarrow i_B \gtreqless 0 \tag{10}$$

For example, we obtain $i_B < 0$ when the absolute value of μ_B is small. As mentioned above, this implies that bank loans do not decrease, in spite of an increase in the debt burden of firms. We also obtain $i_B < 0$ when the absolute value of I_B is large. On the other hand, $i_B > 0$ shows that the interest rate rises in spite of a recession, if the lenders' risk is enhanced by factors such as an increase in the debt burden. The following empirical analysis supports $i_B < 0$ in Japan, after the 1980s. Therefore, we assume $i_B < 0$ in this paper.[9]

The sign of i_σ depends on I_σ and $\mu_\sigma H$ as follows:

$$I_\sigma - \mu_\sigma H \gtreqless 0 \Leftrightarrow i_\sigma \gtreqless 0 \tag{11}$$

For example, we obtain $i_\sigma > 0$ when the absolute value of μ_σ is relatively large. As mentioned above, this means that commercial banks refrain from granting loans when there is an increase in the instability of confidence. On the contrary, we obtain $i_\sigma < 0$ when the absolute value of μ_σ is relatively small. This means that commercial banks do not refrain from granting loans, despite an increase in the instability of confidence. This situation is termed as a state of euphoria. We also obtain $i_\sigma < 0$ when the absolute value of I_σ is relatively large. Kregel (1997) emphasizes that the margins of safety proposed by Minsky are significant for financial instability. When an economic boom reduces lenders' risks, lenders, including commercial banks, promote lending despite erosion in margins of safety. This situation leads to increased financial fragility. Instability of confidence is different from margins of safety. However, erosion in margins of safety also increases when instability of confidence increases. Therefore, we believe that the sign of i_σ also indicates the economic structure, which is fragile when $i_\sigma > 0$.[10]

Firms first utilize their internal reserves, Π, on investment and then make-up for the deficit with loans. Therefore, the dynamic equation of debt burden, B, is formulated as follows:

$$\dot{B} = I - \Pi + iB = I(Y, B, i, \sigma^2) + I_0 - \theta Y + iB \tag{12}$$

For example, the rise in the interest rate increases the interest-payment burden. As a result, there is a possibility that firms cannot help but issue new debt to facilitate interest payments. In other words, the cumulative interest-bearing debt burden affects the economy.

The dynamic equation for the net income, Y, is formulated as follows:

$$\dot{Y} = \alpha(C + I - Y), \quad \alpha > 0 \tag{13}$$

Equation (13) describes the quantity adjustment process of the goods market, where α is the parameter.

First, we examine a basic model in which the instability of confidence does not depend on income and the debt burden ($\sigma^2 = \overline{\sigma}^2$). By sequencing Eqs. (4)–(7), (9), and (12)–(13), we obtain the basic dynamic system (S_a) as follows:

$$\dot{Y} = \alpha[c(1-\theta)Y + C_0 + I(Y, B, \overline{\sigma}^2, i(Y, B, \overline{\sigma}^2)) + I_0 - Y], \quad \alpha > 0 \qquad (S_a.1)$$

$$\dot{B} = I(Y, B, i(Y, B, \overline{\sigma}^2)) + I_0 - \theta Y + i(Y, B, \overline{\sigma}^2)B \qquad (S_a.2)$$

The Jacobian matrix of the system (S_a) at the equilibrium point can be expressed as follows:

$$J_a = \begin{pmatrix} \alpha(I_Y + I_i i_Y - s) & \alpha(I_B + I_i i_B) \\ I_Y + I_i i_Y - \theta + i_Y B & I_B + I_i i_B + i_B B + i \end{pmatrix} \qquad (14)$$

where $s = 1 - c(1-\theta)$.

The characteristic equation of the dynamic system (S_a) is as follows:

$$\lambda^2 + a_1\lambda + a_2 = 0 \qquad (15)$$

where

$$a_1 = -\alpha(I_Y + I_i i_Y - s) - [I_B + (I_i + B)i_B + i] \qquad (16)$$

$$a_2 = \alpha(\theta - 1)(1 - c)(I_B + I_i i_B) + \alpha(I_Y + I_i i_Y - s)i + \alpha[(I_Y - s)i_B - I_B i_Y]B \qquad (17)$$

We adopt the following assumption:

$$-\alpha(I_Y + I_i i_Y - s) - (I_B + i) > 0 \qquad (A.1)$$

In the case, where the cumulative interest-bearing debt burden is not significant ($i_B = 0$), we obtain $a_1 > 0$ under Assumption 1 (A.1). We obtain $a_2 > 0$, if $\alpha(I_Y + I_i i_Y - s)i$ is sufficiently small. Therefore, the dynamic system (S_a) becomes locally stable in this case. This means that the economy is stable if the cumulative interest-bearing debt burden is not significant.

We obtain the following propositions when $i_B < 0$.

> **Proposition 1:** We suppose that $i_B < 0$ and the absolute value of i_B is sufficiently large. The dynamic system (S_a) becomes locally stable when $I_Y - s < 0$ and the absolute value of I_i is small. The dynamic system (S_a) is locally unstable when the absolute value of I_i is sufficiently large.

Proof. We obtain $a_1>0$ when $I_i+B>0$. We obtain $a_2>0$ when $I_Y-s<0$ and the absolute value of I_i is small. Therefore, the Routh–Hurwitz conditions are satisfied in this case. On the contrary, we obtain $a_1<0$ when $I_i+B<0$. Therefore, the Routh–Hurwitz conditions are not satisfied when $I_i+B<0$. ■

Proposition 1 indicates that the economic stability mainly depends on the sign of I_i+B when $i_B<0$ and the absolute value of i_B is sufficiently large. The instability mechanism, for example, is as follows. We assume that the economy is booming and the investment demand is increasing. The debt burden increases with an increase in the investment demand. However, the interest rate decreases in spite of the increase in the debt burden and the investment demand continues to increase. This situation is consistent with the Japanese economy before the collapse of the bubble economy in 1990.

$$Y\uparrow \Rightarrow I\uparrow \Rightarrow B\uparrow \Rightarrow i\downarrow \Rightarrow I\uparrow \Rightarrow Y\uparrow$$

Proposition 1 indicates that the dynamic system is stable when the absolute value of I_i is small. However, the Japanese economy has suffered from a prolonged recession and the absolute value of I_i has been marginal since the 1990s. Therefore, it is likely that other factors have destabilized the Japanese economy.

Next, we consider the case where the instability of confidence depends on income and the debt burden as follows:

$$\sigma^2=\sigma^2(Y,B)=\sigma_Y^2 Y+\sigma_B^2 B, \quad \sigma_Y^2<0, \quad \sigma_B^2 \gtreqless 0 \tag{18}$$

$\sigma_Y^2<0$ means, for example, that the instability of confidence increases when the economy is in recession. $\sigma_B^2>0$ indicates that the instability of confidence increases with an increase in the debt burden. $\sigma_B^2<0$ indicates that the instability of confidence decreases in spite of an increase in the debt burden. The following empirical analysis suggests that $\sigma_B^2<0$ before the 1990s and that $\sigma_B^2>0$ after the 1990s.[11]

Considering Eq. (18), we now examine the following simplified dynamic system to focus on the instability of confidence and the interest-bearing debt burden:

$$\dot{Y}=\alpha[c(1-\theta)Y+C_0+I(Y,B)+I_0-Y], \quad \alpha>0 \tag{S$_b$.1}$$

$$\dot{B}=I(Y,B)+I_0-\theta Y+i(Y,B,\sigma_Y^2 Y+\sigma_B^2 B)B, \quad \sigma_Y^2<0, \ \sigma_B^2 \gtreqless 0 \tag{S$_b$.2}$$

The Jacobian matrix of the system (S_b) at the equilibrium point can be expressed as follows:

$$J_b = \begin{pmatrix} \alpha(I_Y - s) & \alpha I_B \\ I_Y - \theta + (i_Y + i_\sigma \sigma_Y^2)B & I_B + (i_B + i_\sigma \sigma_B^2)B + i \end{pmatrix} \tag{19}$$

The characteristic equation of the dynamic system (S_b) is as follows:

$$\lambda^2 + b_1\lambda + b_2 = 0 \tag{20}$$

where

$$b_1 = -i_\sigma B\sigma_B^2 - \alpha(I_Y - s) - (I_B + i_B B + i) \tag{21}$$

$$\begin{aligned} b_2 = {} & \alpha(I_Y - s)i_\sigma B\sigma_B^2 - \alpha I_B i_\sigma B\sigma_Y^2 \\ & - \alpha(s - \theta)I_B + \alpha(I_Y - s)(i_B B + i) - \alpha I_B i_Y B \end{aligned} \tag{22}$$

If $\sigma_Y^2 = 0$ and $\sigma_B^2 = 0$, we obtain similar results for the dynamic system (S_a). The following empirical analysis suggests that the sign of i_σ changed from $i_\sigma > 0$ to $i_\sigma < 0$ between 1980 and 1996. As mentioned above, the empirical analysis suggests that $\sigma_B^2 < 0$ before 1996 and that $\sigma_B^2 > 0$ after 1997. Considering these facts, we present the following proposition:

> **Proposition 2:** We suppose $\sigma_B^2 < 0$. The dynamic system (S_b) is locally stable if $i_\sigma > 0$ and $I_Y - s < 0$. On the contrary, the system (S_b) is unstable if $i_\sigma < 0$. We suppose $\sigma_B^2 > 0$. The dynamic system (S_b) is locally unstable, even though $i_\sigma > 0$.

> **Proof.** We obtain $b_1 > 0$ when $\sigma_B^2 < 0$ and $i_\sigma > 0$. We obtain $b_2 > 0$ when $I_Y - s < 0$, $\sigma_B^2 < 0$, and $\sigma_Y^2 < 0$. Therefore, the Routh–Hurwitz conditions are satisfied in this case. On the contrary, we obtain $b_1 < 0$ when $\sigma_B^2 < 0$ and $i_\sigma < 0$. We also obtain $b_1 < 0$ when $\sigma_B^2 > 0$ and $i_\sigma > 0$. Therefore, the Routh–Hurwitz conditions are not satisfied in these cases. ■

We examine Proposition 2 in an economic sense. Proposition 2 indicates that the economic stability mainly depends on the signs of i_σ and σ_B^2. As mentioned above, the sign of i_σ indicates the economic structure. Therefore, Proposition 2 suggests that the instability of confidence has an important role in terms of the stability and the economic structure. The following empirical analysis indicates that the sign of i_σ changed from $i_\sigma > 0$ to $i_\sigma < 0$ between 1980 and 1996. The bubble economy in Japan occurred after the Plaza Accord in 1985 and collapsed in 1990. We believe that the economic structure changed during this period, and that the fragile economic structure made the Japanese economy unstable.

On the other hand, the following empirical analysis suggests that $\sigma_B^2 < 0$ before 1996 and that $\sigma_B^2 > 0$ after 1997. The increase in the instability of confidence due to the debt burden ($\sigma_B^2 > 0$) played a crucial role in the instability of the Japanese economy after 1997 because we believe that the absolute value of I_i was not large enough and that $i_B < 0$ after 1997. The next section examines these theoretical results in more detail using a recursive VAR analysis.

EMPIRICAL ANALYSIS

As mentioned above, there is almost no empirical analysis that includes both debt and instability, although a few include either debt or instability. Therefore, this paper includes both debt and instability in the analysis of the Japanese economy.

In previous dynamic systems (S_b), we emphasized that the signs of the condition, i_σ, and the instability of confidence, σ^2, play important roles in the stability of a dynamic system. Here, we examine the changes in the economic structure using data on the Japanese economy. One characteristic of this analysis is that it is a subsample comparative analysis that focuses on the creation of a proxy variable, which indicates the instability of confidence, and a recursive VAR model, which introduces this proxy variable.

Straightforward Observation of the Survey of Business Sentiments

We observe the business survey, which is deeply concerned with the instability of confidence level, σ^2. We examine Fig. 1, which shows the association of the periods in which $i_\sigma < 0$ in the diffusion index (DI) of financial position, and the DI of the level of interest rates on loans. The solid line represents the DI of the estimated general cash position of the responding enterprises on the basis of the level of cash and cash equivalents, the lending attitude of financial institutions, and the payment and repayment terms. These estimates were only requested at the time of the survey. A high value suggests an easy financial position. The dotted line represents the accumulated value of the DI of the estimated changes in the interest rate on the borrowings of the responding enterprises. A high DI suggests that the enterprises consider a higher borrowing interest rate.

Generally, in a situation where the financing of an enterprise is considered to be "easy," the enterprise believes that a commercial bank's borrowing

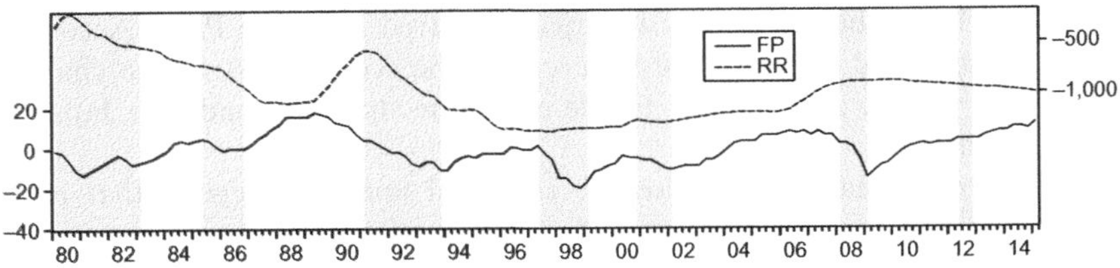

❖ Gray zone shows a phase of recession.
❖ FP: Diffusion index of financial Position/All/All industries/Actual result
❖ RR: Diffusion index of change in Interest Rate on Loans (Accumulation value) /All/All industries/Actual result

Fig. 1. Transition of DIs. *Source*: Bank of Japan, TANKAN Business Survey.

interest rate will decline. For this, we observe both indices 1980 onward. In addition, in terms of the borrowing interest rate, we show the accumulation level to focus on the actual interest rate rather than on the direction of change in the interest rate.

According to Fig. 1, we observe a clearly negative correlation for both indices until at least the beginning of the 1990s. This suggests that the lender's risk was stable during this time. On the other hand, it is difficult to observe the correlation after the 1990s. Such a situation will occur until the following company sentiment changes: Financing is difficult because of loan tightening by the financial institutions, even though the borrowing interest rates are low enough. If this inference is correct, it suggests that the risk to the lender (who is the counterpart to any borrowing) is unstable. The correlation coefficient will enable one to account for this situation. Just prior to the collapse of the bubble economy (1991Q1), the correlation coefficient of both variables was significantly negative (−0.87). That is, there was a relationship between the estimation of the borrowing interest rate, which the business evaluates, and financing of the business at this time. However, the absolute value of the correlation coefficient later fell to 0.40 and the correlation was low. We then shifted our time period and divided it by the 1996Q4 data, which was just before the breakup of the large financial institutions. We found a negative correlation of −0.65 before this time period, but we were able to verify that the absolute value of correlation declined to 0.50 thereafter.

This time period corresponds to the time when the large credit cooperatives (e.g., COSMO and KIDU) and HYOGO Bank, one of the regional banks continued to fail. Furthermore, it constituted a time of many negative incidents affecting Japanese society, such as the Great Hanshin Earthquake, the chemical terrorism in the Tokyo subway system, and the appreciation of the yen. Reflecting these situations, we can conclude that the reliance on the financial system collapsed in the second half of the 1990s because the bank myth – a bank never goes bankrupt – also collapsed. We surmise that a change in the financial structure arose when the lender's risk became unstable compared with the earlier period. Assuming that this interpretation is correct, a model that excludes the change in economic structure cannot account for this change. Therefore, we assume that the Japanese economy changed structurally in the 1990s. Moreover, we are able to verify the change in economic structure in our comparison before and after the incidences that affected Japanese society.

In the theoretical model presented below, we quantify the instability of the confidence levels that play a crucial role in our theoretical model, and use this information as the basis for identifying different periods. We also construct a recursive VAR model and examine the spillover effects of shocks to the economic system. Finally, we implement simulations based on the resulting VAR parameters.

Quantification of the Instability of Confidence σ^2

The variable defined by the theoretical model, called the "instability of confidence," does not exist in the observational data. Therefore, to directly evaluate this variable, it is necessary to define or create a certain proxy. We use a volatility model widely used in the field of finance and quantify the instability of confidence equivalent to the concept of variance. More precisely, we incorporate a method using the Generalized Autoregressive Conditional Heteroscedasticity (GARCH) model to quantify the variable, using the short-term economic survey of enterprises in Japan (Tankan). Having used this method for a time-series analysis to identify the discrepancy of the change in interest rates on loans and financial positions, we now define σ_t^2 as the instability of confidence.

Initially, Fig. 1 shows that, at least until the beginning of 1990, the view of the current loan rate had a strong correlation with the view of financial position. That is, business administrators believed that there was a strong correlation between difficult (easy) financing and high (low) borrowing interest rates. For simplification, we assume that the DI of the financial position and the accumulation value of the DI of the borrowing interest rate at a given time is a linear relationship. This is shown as follows:

$$\mathrm{RR}_t = \alpha_0 + \alpha_1 \mathrm{FP}_t + \mu_t \tag{23}$$

where RR_t is the accumulated value of DI of the borrowing interest-rate level, FP_t is the DI of the financial position, μ_t is the error term, and α_0 and α_1 are parameters.

Equation (23) shows the relevance of the expectation of financing an enterprise and an evaluation of the borrowing interest rate according to a linear relation. The error term, μ_t, represents disturbing and/or irregular factors, and the variance in these factors represents the uncertainty about the economic environment. In other words, increases in the variance of the error term imply that certain factors, which cannot be explained by the assessment of economic conditions, greatly influence the economic environment expectations. The increases also indicate that the instability of confidence in the economy is increasing.

This error-term variance is not stable across the period, but it has a tendency to continually increase whenever a large shock occurs. To model the heterogeneity of the error-term variance, we use the GARCH model, as shown below:

$$\sigma_t^2 = \gamma_0 + \gamma_1 \mu_{t-1}^2 + \gamma_2 \sigma_{t-1}^2 \quad \mu_t | \text{Info}_{t-1} \sim N(0, \sigma_t^2) \tag{24}$$

Here, $\gamma_0 > 1, \gamma_1 > 1$ where γ_2 is a parameter that shows how many influences (shocks) in the previous period continue, and is taken as $|\gamma_2| < 1$. μ_t indicates the prediction error during the previous period. $\text{Info}_{t\text{-}1}$ denotes information that is set at time $t-1$, and it represents a usable information set. We assume that the conditional distribution of μ_t is normal and the conditional variance σ_t^2 is heterogeneous, depending on past shocks, as well as on μ_{t-1} and σ_{t-1}^2. The economic instability factors estimated by this GARCH model are as follows:

$$\text{RR}_t = \underset{(-33.9)}{-832.8} - \underset{(-9.73)}{18.43}\,\text{FP}_t + \mu_t \tag{25}$$

$$\sigma_t^2 = \underset{(4.24)}{66887} + \underset{(2.69)}{1.738\mu_{t-1}^2} - \underset{(-26.72)}{0.879\sigma_{t-1}^2} \tag{26}$$

The sample period is from 1974Q2 to 2015Q1 and the numbers in parentheses represent z-statistics.

The estimation results show that each parameter satisfies the 5% significance level, as well as the sign condition. Fig. 2 shows the estimated conditional variance distribution, σ_t^2, which is synonymous with the instability of confidence. The instability of confidence rapidly increased after the mid-1990s, and experienced a declining trend after peaking in 1998. More recently, it increased again in 2009 due to the economic recession that resulted from the US subprime loan

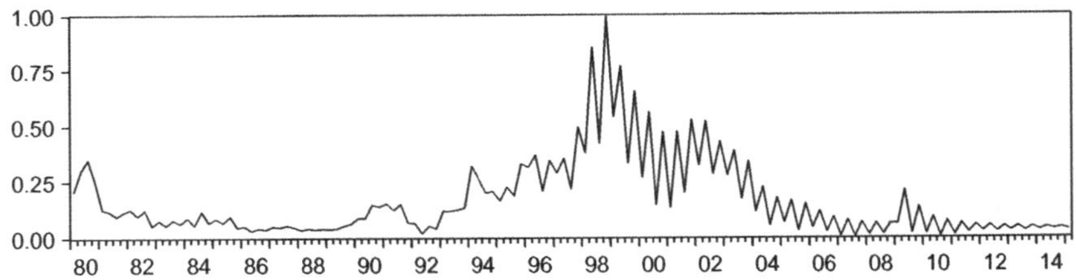

❖ Large numerical values mean an increase in the instability of confidence.

Fig. 2. Conditional Variance σ_t^2.

crisis. However, the increase in the variance is marginal compared with the latter half of the 1990s.

Borrowers and lenders receive the instability of confidence recognized and shared as expanded from the middle of the 1990s. However, the appropriate long-term time-series data, which accounted for the lender's sentiment, does not exist. Therefore, we suppose that there is no or very little asymmetry of information. Moreover, we assume that the borrower's financial risk and the lender's risk (that the borrower will default on its obligation to the lender) are identical. From such a perspective, we can consider that σ_t^2, which is related to a company's DI and used in this paper's empirical analysis, represents the whole chain of the lender's risk in our theoretical analysis.

In this way, the large fluctuations in financial sentiment result in significant changes in funding positions when an enterprise's liquidity preference arises. Such fluctuations beyond a certain fixed threshold value result in structural changes in connection with the financial transmissions to the real economy. The VAR analysis in the next section uses the quantified σ^2 to represent the instability of confidence and incorporates it into a recursive VAR model, dividing the estimation period into two for the 1996 period. We determined the boundary of this division based on the following three points:

1. the relative change in the levels of RR_t and FP_t;
2. the time period that the stability of conditional variance, σ^2, is maintained at a low level;[12] and
3. ensuring the degree of freedom to estimate.

After dividing the estimation period into two parts, we compare the differences in the results for each subsample estimation.

Analysis Using a Recursive VAR Model

According to the previous theoretical model, the macroeconomic variables that form the core of a VAR model include the following: interest rate, i_t, income, y_t, debt burden, b_t, and the quantified instability of confidence, σ^2. These variables take the form of series transition of the data. We use quarterly data and derive our estimates from the logarithmic values. The data sources are shown in Table 1, while Fig. 3 shows the time-1980Q1 to the 2014Q4 period, which is the timeframe where we have continuous data. The data for 1996Q4 are divided into subsamples.

From the above process, we specify the following recursive VAR model, where $\mathbf{x_t}$ is an endogenous variable vector, $\mathbf{A_0}$ is a simultaneous coefficient matrix, $\mathbf{A_i}$ is a coefficient matrix, $\mathbf{c}$ is a constant vector, $\boldsymbol{\varepsilon}_t$ is an innovation vector, and $\mathbf{L}$ represents a lag operator. The innovation vector, $\boldsymbol{\varepsilon}_t$, is mutually independent and not correlated. Therefore, $\mathbf{D}$ is a diagonal matrix.

Table 1. Dataset.

Variables	Data	Unit	Source
i: interest rate	Outstanding Loans and Bills Discounted/Long-term Loans/City Banks	%	Bank of Japan
y: income	Real GDP of chained (2005) yen, s.a.	Billion yen	Cabinet Office
b: debt burden	Leverage ratio	%	Financial Statements Statistics of Corporations by Industry
σ^2: instability of confidence	FP: Diffusion index of financial Position/All/All industries/Actual result	Index	Bank of Japan, TANKAN Judgment Survey
	RR: Diffusion index of change in Interest Rate on Loans (Accumulation value)/All/All industries/Actual result		

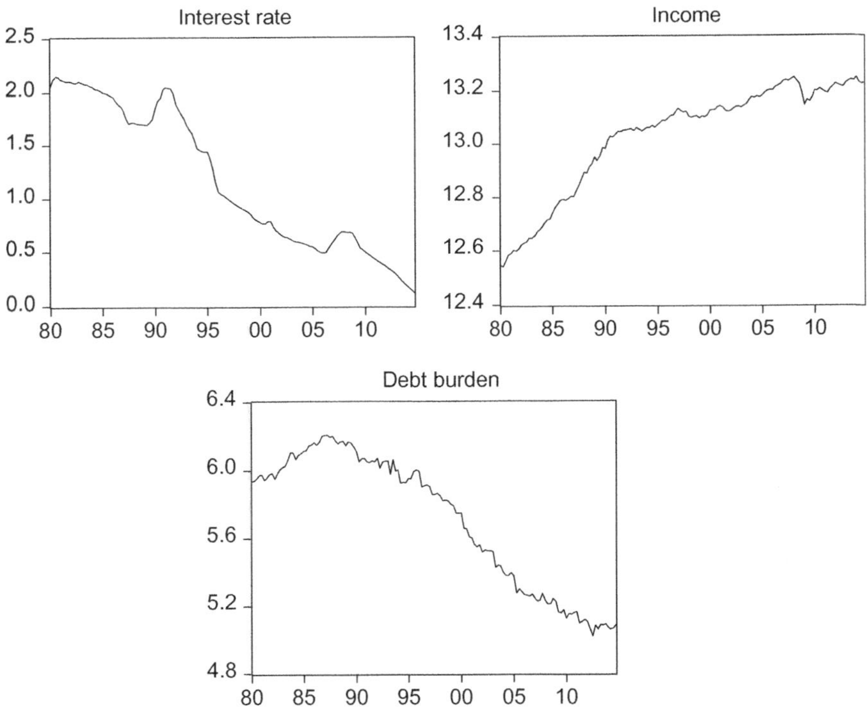

❖ All data are represented by their logarithms.

❖ Refer to Fig. 2 on the data of instability of confidence $(= \sigma^2)$.

Fig. 3. Transition of Data.

$$\mathbf{A_0x_t} = \mathbf{c}+\mathbf{A(L)x_t}+\boldsymbol{\varepsilon}_t, \quad \boldsymbol{\varepsilon}_t \sim \text{i.i.d.}(0,\mathbf{D})$$

$$\mathbf{X_t} = \begin{bmatrix} \Delta i_t \\ \Delta y_t \\ \Delta b_t \\ \Delta \sigma_t \end{bmatrix}, \quad \boldsymbol{\varepsilon}_t = \begin{bmatrix} \varepsilon_{it} \\ \varepsilon_{yt} \\ \varepsilon_{bt} \\ \varepsilon_{\sigma t} \end{bmatrix} \quad \mathbf{D} = E(\boldsymbol{\varepsilon}_t \ \boldsymbol{\varepsilon}'_t) = \begin{bmatrix} v_i^2 & 0 & 0 & 0 \\ 0 & v_y^2 & 0 & 0 \\ 0 & 0 & v_b^2 & 0 \\ 0 & 0 & 0 & v_\sigma^2 \end{bmatrix}$$

$$\mathbf{A_0} = \begin{bmatrix} 1 & 0 & 0 & 0 \\ a_{yi} & 1 & 0 & 0 \\ a_{bi} & a_{by} & 1 & 0 \\ a_{\sigma i} & a_{\sigma y} & a_{\sigma b} & 1 \end{bmatrix} \quad \mathbf{A_i} = \begin{bmatrix} a_{ii.i} & a_{iy.i} & a_{ib.i} & a_{i\sigma.i} \\ a_{yi.i} & a_{yy.i} & a_{yb.i} & a_{y\sigma i.i} \\ a_{bi.i} & a_{by.i} & a_{bb.i} & a_{b\sigma.i} \\ a_{\sigma i.i} & a_{\sigma y.i} & a_{\sigma b.i} & a_{\sigma\sigma.i} \end{bmatrix} \quad (i = 1, \ldots, n) \tag{27}$$

To avoid simultaneity bias, Eq. (27) is changed into its following reduced form:

$$\begin{aligned} &\mathbf{x_t} = \mathbf{k}+\mathbf{B(L)x_t}+\mathbf{u_t}, \quad \mathbf{u_t} \sim \text{i.i.d.}\left(0,\textstyle\sum_{\mathbf{u}}\right) \\ &\mathbf{k} = \mathbf{A_0^{-1}c}, \quad \mathbf{B_i} = \mathbf{A_0^{-1}A_i} \quad (i = 1, \ldots, n) \\ &\mathbf{u_t} = \mathbf{A_0^{-1}}\boldsymbol{\varepsilon}_t \Rightarrow E(\mathbf{u_t} \ \mathbf{u'_t}) = \textstyle\sum_{\mathbf{u}} = \mathbf{A_0^{-1}}E(\boldsymbol{\varepsilon}_t \ \boldsymbol{\varepsilon}'_t)(\mathbf{A_0^{-1}})' \end{aligned} \tag{28}$$

Since these reduced innovations, $\mathbf{u_t} = [u_{it} \ u_{yt} \ u_{bt} \ u_{\sigma t}]$, are usually correlated, $\sum_{\mathbf{u}}$ has non-zero values in the non-diagonal elements. In this case, $\mathbf{A_0}$ has six zero restrictions, since the identification for conversion requires six restrictions. By conducting OLS estimations of Eq. (28) drawn in this way, we avoid simultaneous bias.

Prior to performing the recursive VAR analysis, we conducted a unit root test for the stationarity of each variable in each subsample, using the augmented Dicker–Fuller (ADF) test. Then, using our model, which basically includes trends and constants, we confirmed that the variables are in a differential stationary process; that is, $I(1)$. Next, we applied Johansen's cointegration test (maximum eigenvalue test) to various models, but the results did not strongly support cointegration. As such, we used log differential variables in the analysis below. To ensure the degree of freedom in our VAR model, we chose a two-term lag model.[13] We set the order of the variable group to i_t, y_t, b_t, σ_t^2.

Next, we examined Eq. (28) in terms of the impulse response function and used the orthogonal transformation estimated from the structural factorization matrices for the generation of the impulses. Figs. 4 and 5 show the impulse response functions for the earlier subsample (1980Q1–1996Q4) and the later subsample (1997Q1–2014Q4), respectively. Structural one s.d. shock (innovation) to the endogenous variable affects not only this variable but also other endogenous variables through the dynamic lag structure of the recursive VAR model. Using the impulse response function, we quantify the effects of the shock in the current period and the movements in the endogenous variables over the preceding 10 periods (2½ years). The solid lines show the value of each impulse, while the dotted lines show the ± 2 standard-error bands.

As space limitations prohibit a complete review of the effects on the endogenous variables, we examine the shocks and subsequent responses, focusing on the empirical results relating to the instability of confidence, σ^2. Fig. 4 shows the responses for the earlier subsample. With regard to the instability of confidence, it shows that for the increase in the instability, albeit not significant, the interest rate rose for the first four periods and then declined (first row, fourth column). On the other hand, although it was only at the beginning of the time period, the influence of the debt burden was significantly negative (third row,

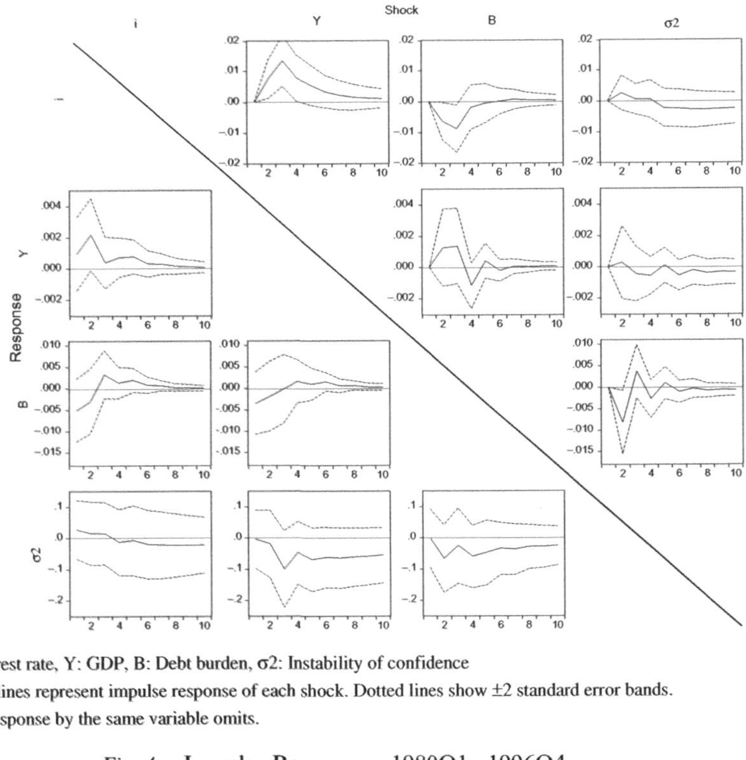

❖ i: interest rate, Y: GDP, B: Debt burden, σ2: Instability of confidence

❖ Solid lines represent impulse response of each shock. Dotted lines show ±2 standard error bands.

❖ The response by the same variable omits.

Fig. 4. Impulse Responses: 1980Q1–1996Q4.

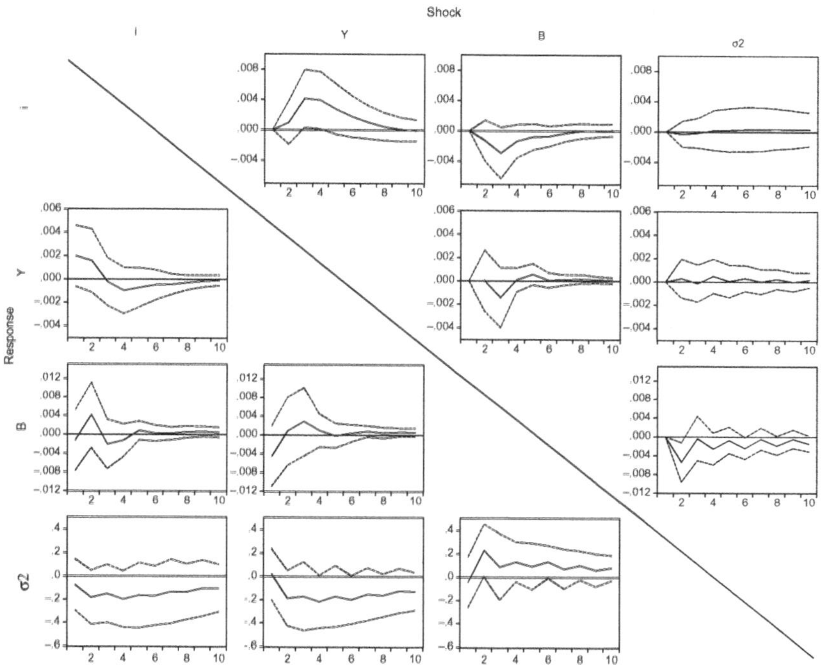

❖ i: interest rate, Y: GDP, B: Debt burden, σ2 : Ins tability of confidence

❖ Solid lines represent impulse response of each shock. Dotted lines show ±2 standard error bands.

❖ The response by the same variable is omitted.

Fig. 5. Impulse Responses: 1997Q1–2014Q4.

fourth column). The response of GDP was indefinite (second row, fourth column).

The instability of confidence showed that it had a tendency to decline when there was an increase in the debt burden. This response suggests that both enterprises and banks evaluated the rise of the enterprises' debt ratio as positive. The response of the instability of confidence to the interest rate and GDP was negative, in general. However, neither of these responses was significant.

Fig. 5 shows the responses of the later subsample. The response of the interest rate to the shock brought about by increased instability is not clear (first row, fourth column). On the other hand, the influence of the debt burden was negative (third row, fourth column). The response of GDP was indefinite, similar to the earlier subsample (second row, fourth column).

The response of the instability of confidence to the debt burden was interesting, since the variable showed an upward tendency due to the shock of the debt burden. This response suggests that enterprises and banks evaluated the increase in the enterprises' debt ratio as negative. On the other hand, the response of the interest rate and GDP to the instability was negative, similar to the reaction in the earlier subsample.

In contrast with the earlier subsample, the instability of confidence showed an upward trend. As is clear from Fig. 3, the debt burden in Japan shows a continuous decline from the latter half of the 1980s. Until the second half of the 1990s, the mitigation shock of the debt burden made instability expand on the contrary. The economic structural change may have arisen by having exceeded the threshold value in this situation. Such a situation after a structural change leads to a reverse reaction. The decline of the debt burden suppressed the instability of confidence level.

Even if this response is accompanied by a rise in the debt ratio, a $\sigma_B^2 < 0$ situation occurred because the enterprises and banks believed that greater investment resulted in larger profits. According to Proposition 2, under the $i_\sigma > 0$ condition, the economy was stable to these dynamics. However, if based on Minsky's (1986) financial instability hypothesis, the form of financing will soon shift to Ponzi, according to the complicated financial architecture inherent in capitalism. In the final stage, the shock affecting the enterprises and banks became a serious dilemma that transformed the economic structure and resulted in the avoidance of investment activities that caused the debt ratio to rise. This suggests that the investment activities that were funded by retained profits or equity capital were adopted more than those relying on debt financing. In the economy, the credit-creating functions of institutions fell and the individual businesses and banks became more sensitive to risk. Such dynamics signal an unstable economy. That is, Japan's situation in the second sub-period aligns with the cases where $\sigma_B^2 > 0$ and $i_\sigma > 0$ in Proposition 2. The economic structure was locally unstable. It could be considered that these macro variables were the end result that reflected the change in sentiment of the business enterprises and banks in Japan.

In addition, the case where $i_B < 0$ was checked, irrespective of the second portion in the first half (first row, third column). This suggests not suppressing bank loans irrespective of the rise in the debt ratio. Either of the subsamples increases for the first three periods, and the reaction decreases after that. Therefore, the $i_B > 0$ assumed by the previous works of Ninomiya (2006) or Asada (2006a, 2006b) may be able to conclude that the situation of $i_B > 0$ is not so large concerning Japan, at least.

Finally, we simulate the stochastic dynamics using the parameters obtained from our VAR model. This technique uses the value of each equation's error term to solve the model. It is a random number in the VAR model based on a standard error that is not equal to zero. The number of simulation iterations is set at 1,000. After extracting the debt burden, B, and the instability of confidence, σ^2, from the results of the simulation, and taking note of their percentage changes, we plotted the values shown in the scatter diagrams in Fig. 6. The

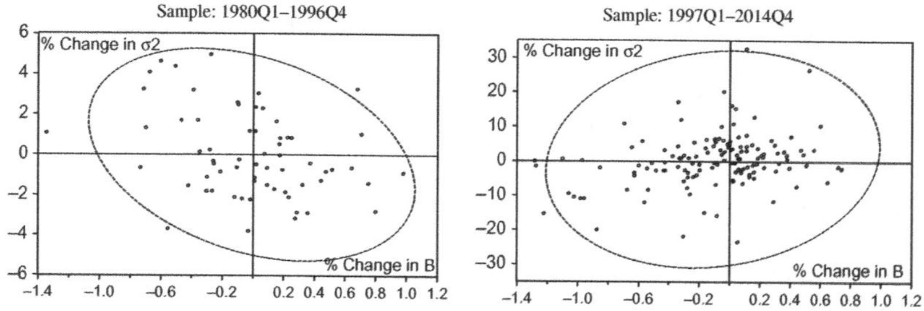

❖ The vertical and horizontal axes represent the percentage change in the forecasted instability of confidence and the percentage change in the forecasted debt burden, respectively.

Fig. 6. Stochastic Simulations.

plotted points indicate the average values of the trials obtained from the simulations, and the values inside the ellipse have a confidence interval of 95%. When the distribution of the change of both variables is checked, the second and fourth quadrants in the earlier subsample have relatively more plots. This suggests that the state of $\sigma_B^2<0$ is dynamic and similar to the results of the previous impulse response function. Therefore, this time period was somewhat stable, according to the dynamics of Proposition 2. On the other hand, in terms of the latter half of the subsample, the upward-slanting distribution to the right indicates that the situation where $\sigma_B^2>0$ is apparent. According to Proposition 2, the dynamics of this situation can be interpreted as unstable.

Accordingly, the results of these simulations suggest that the economic structure was unstable after a structural change.

CONCLUSION

This paper examined how the cumulative interest-bearing debt burden, structural change, and the instability of confidence affected a dynamic economic system. Next, it examined these factors in the Japanese economy by applying a recursive VAR analysis. The main conclusions drawn from this paper are as follows. First, in the theoretical analysis,

1. we suppose that $i_B<0$ and the absolute value of i_B is sufficiently large. The dynamic system (S_a) is locally stable when the absolute value of I_i is small, under some conditions, and locally unstable when the absolute value is large.
2. we assume that $\sigma_B^2<0$. The dynamic system (S_b) is locally stable if $i_\sigma>0$, under some conditions, and unstable if $i_\sigma<0$. We suppose $\sigma_B^2>0$. The dynamic system (S_b) is locally unstable, even though $i_\sigma>0$.

These results indicate that the interest-bearing debt burden, the economic structure resulting from the instability of confidence, and the instability of confidence resulting from the debt burden play important roles in the instability of the economy.

In addition, in the empirical analysis,

3. The possibility that Japan's economic structure changed late in the 1990s is high, according to a GARCH analysis using sentiment indexes.
4. The recursive VAR model was built and the data was used to divide the sample period into two sub-periods. From the responses of variables to our impulse response analysis, although we did not find an instability factor in the Japanese economy from 1980 to 1996,[14] we did find it after this period.
5. Using the parameters obtained by our VAR model, the results of our stochastic simulations support the findings in (4).

We emphasize that financial factors were the reason for the prolonged recession in Japan, although we do not deny that labor constraints[15] and the decline of productivity were among the other reasons for the recession. Several countries have suffered from financial crises since the US subprime loan crisis. We believe that our method of theoretical and empirical analysis contributes toward the understanding of these crises.

Furthermore, our analysis did not consider monetary policy. The Bank of Japan adopted its zero-interest-rate policy and its quantitative-easing policy after the collapse of the bubble economy. Asada (2006b) criticized this monetary policy. Our analysis did not evaluate whether these policies, along with inflation-targeting policy, helped to stabilize the Japanese economy. These policy developments need to be examined in future studies.

NOTES

1. Hayashi and Prescott (2002) pointed out the decline in the productivity of Japanese economy from the viewpoint of mainstream economics.

2. Ninomiya and Sanyal (2009) presented a macro-dynamic model with debt accumulation that is based on a stylized view of the Japanese situation during the bubble period.

3. The structural change in Ninomiya and Tokuda (2011) is different from the hedge, speculative, and Ponzi finance indicated by Minsky (1986). Ninomiya and Tokuda (2012) extended their model to include an open economy and examined the structural change in the Korean economy. By applying a reduced VAR analysis, they showed that the Korean economic structure became more robust after the Asian monetary crisis. The structural change in this chapter follows Ninomiya and Tokuda (2011, 2012).

Ninomiya and Tokuda (2011, 2012) also presented a financial cycle and showed by numerical simulation that the interest rate rises despite the decline in income immediately after the business cycle peaks. Uno (1953), one of Japan's foremost Marxian economists, pointed out that the interest rate rises at the peak of the business cycle, after which the economy plunges into an economic crisis. Uno (1953) emphasized the importance of credit in business cycles and crises. Okishio (1992) formulated a mathematical model that considers Uno's discussion. He captured Uno's crisis theory as a "Rising Real Wage Rate Leads to a Falling Rate of Profit" model and indicated that the model is the same as Goodwin's (1967). Therefore, it also ignored financial factors.

4. Recent Kaleckian models introduced the accumulation of firm debt. See, for example, Hein (2007) and Sasaki and Fujita (2012). Nishi (2012b) and Sasaki and Fujita (2014) introduced the relationship between a financial growth regime and Minskyan taxonomy in a dynamic model.

5. Few empirical studies on financial instability were presented. For example, Isenberg (1988) examined the validity of the Minskyan financial instability hypothesis using US macroeconomic data in the 1920s. Dafermos (2012) quantified the influences of instability on business using a calibration with an appropriate parameter. Thus, although there are few empirical analyses that include debt or instability, almost none include both factors.

6. Many economists considered the interest-bearing debt burden and discussed financial instability and financial growth. See, for example, Jarsulic (1990), Keen (1995), Asada (2006a, 2006b), Charles (2008a, 2008b), Ryoo (2010), and Sasaki and Fujita (2012). However, these studies did not consider the structural change and the instability of confidence, and they lacked a comprehensive empirical analysis.

7. See Keynes (1937), p. 161.

8. The sign of $i_Y$depends on $I_Y$and $L_Y$as follows:

$$I_Y - \{1 - c(1 - \theta)\} + L_Y \gtreqless 0 \Leftrightarrow i_Y \gtreqless 0$$

We obtain $i_Y < 0$ when $I_Y$and $L_Y$are small. Ninomiya (2007) examined the case of $i_Y < 0$, and discussed financial instability in an open economy. Ninomiya (2016) also examined the case of $i_Y < 0$, and discussed financial instability and the effect of inflation targeting in a mixed competitive-oligopolistic system.

9. Ninomiya (2006) examined both the cases of $i_B > 0$ and $i_B < 0$. As we mentioned above, many studies took the interest-bearing debt into account and discussed the financial instability and financial growth. However, Asada (2006a, 2006b), for example, also assumed that the interest rate is an increasing function of the debt-capital ratio. Sasaki and Fujita (2012) assumed that the interest rate is constant by following the Post Keynesian "horizontalist" view.

10. Taylor and O'Connell (1985) present a simple macroeconomic model of financial instability and prove that an economy would fall into a "true Minsky crisis" if the decline in expected profit rates ρ worsened firms' financial condition and increased household preference for liquidity. The interest rate i increases in this situation ($i_\rho < 0$). For more on this subject, see Ninomiya and Tokuda (2011, 2012). Adachi (1994) provides the micro-foundation of Taylor and O'Connell (1985) on the basis of Okishio (1986).

11. As we mentioned, the following empirical analysis supports $i_B < 0$ in Japan after the 1980s. The sign of i_B presents a financial structure. However, this means that structural change has not occurred since the 1980s. Therefore, we consider the effect of σ_B^2. This suggests that debt burden B affects interest rates by influencing the instability of confidence σ^2 in the following theoretical and empirical analysis.

12. Although σ^2itself is the endogenous variable in the next VAR model, we consider the possibility that the large shock (i.e., the crises in the financial system) triggered the change in the economic structure.

13. We set the maximum lag degree as 2 and measured Akaike's Information Criteria (AIC) and Schwarz Bayesian Information Criteria (SBIC). According to AIC, two lags were supported in each subsample. In contrast, one lag was supported according to

SBIC. In addition, although an estimation using the same model with one lag was performed as an additional verification, the result did not change significantly with two lags.

14. The Japanese economy might have been unstable during the bubble economy. We do not consider the accumulation of financial asset in this chapter. However, we did construct macro-dynamic models, which consider the accumulation of financial assets, as noted in Ninomiya and Tokuda (2016). Applying a VAR analysis, we also found an instability factor from the accumulation of financial assets.

15. In the 1990s, the unemployment rate actually rose and the labor market was slack. We believe that the increase in unemployment was triggered by the collapse of the bubble economy. In fact, the Japanese economy faced a shortage of young and skilled laborers during these lost decades, and a declining birth rate is now evident in Japan. However, we do not consider the labor market in this chapter; examination of the labor market is a topic for future research.

ACKNOWLEDGMENTS

The authors are grateful to anonymous referees, Professor Yasuhiro Sakai (Shiga University/University of Tsukuba) and Professor Masao Ishikura (Hitotsubashi University) for their many valuable comments. This paper has been financially supported by the Grant-in-Aid for Scientific Research (16K03633) (23530325) from the Japan Society for the Promotion of Science and the academic support fund from the Department of Economics, Shiga University. Any errors remaining in this paper are the authors' sole responsibility.

REFERENCES

Adachi, H. (1994). The theory of macrodynamics. Tokyo: Yuhikaku Publishing Co., Ltd. (in Japanese).

Asada, T. (2006a). Stabilization policy in a Keynes-Goodwin Model with debt accumulation. *Structural Change and Economic Dynamics*, *17*, 466–485.

Asada, T. (2006b). Inflation targeting policy in a dynamic Keynesian Model with debt accumulation: A Japanese perspective. In C. Chiarella, P. Flaschel, R. Franke, & W. Semmler (Eds.), *Quantitative and empirical analysis of nonlinear dynamic economic dynamics* (pp. 206–235). Amsterdam; Tokyo: Elsevier.

Charles, S. (2008a). Corporate debt, variable retention rate and the appearance of financial fragility. *Cambridge Journal of Economics*, *32*, 781–795.

Charles, S. (2008b). Teaching Minsky's financial instability hypothesis: A manageable suggestion. *Journal of Post Keynesian Economics*, *31*(1), 125–138.

Dafermos, Y. (2012). Liquidity preference, uncertainty, and recession in a stock-flow consistent model. *Journal of Post Keynesian Economics*, *34*(4), 749–776.

Goodwin, R. M. (1967). A growth cycle. In C. H. Feinstein (Ed.), *Socialism, capitalism, and economic growth: Essays presented to Maurice Dubb* (pp. 54–58). Cambridge: Cambridge University Press.

Hayashi, F., & Prescott, E. C. (2002). The 1990s in Japan: A lost decade. *Review of Economic Dynamics*, *5*, 206–235.

Hein, E. (2007). Interest rate, debt, distribution and capital accumulation in a post Kaleckian Model. *Metroeconomica*, *56*(2), 337–352.
Isenberg, D. L. (1988). Is there a case for Minsky's financial fragility hypothesis in the 1920s? *Journal of Economic Issues*, *22*(4), 1045–1069.
Jarsulic, M. (1990). Debt and macro stability. *Eastern Economic Journal*, *16*, 91–100.
Keen, S. (1995). Financial and economic breakdown: Modeling Minsky's financial instability hypothesis. *Journal of Post Keynesian Economics*, *17*(4), 607–635.
Keynes, J. M. (1936). *The general theory of employment, interest, and money*. London: Macmillan.
Kregel, J. A. (1997). Margin of safety and weight of argument in generating financial fragility. *Journal of Economic Issues*, *31*(2), 543–548.
Minsky, H. (1986). *Stabilizing an unstable economy*. New Haven, CT: Yale University Press.
Nakatani, T., & Skott, P. (2007). Japanese growth and stagnation: A Keynesian perspective. *Structural Change and Economic Dynamics*, *18*, 306–332.
Ninomiya, K. (2006). *Macroeconomics of Financial Crises*. Tokyo: Chuo-Keizai-sha, Inc. (in Japanese).
Ninomiya, K. (2007). Open economy financial instability. *Journal of the Korean Economy*, *8*(2), 329–355.
Ninomiya, K. (2016). Financial structure, financial instability, and inflation targeting. *Evolutional Institutional Economics Review*, *13*(1), 23–36.
Ninomiya, K., & Sanyal, A. (2009). Bubble without inflation. *Journal of the Korean Economy*, *10*(1), 55–79.
Ninomiya, K., & Tokuda, M. (2011). Structural change and financial instability. *Political Economy Quarterly*, *48*(2), 81–95 (in Japanese).
Ninomiya, K., & Tokuda, M. (2012). Structural change and financial instability in an open economy. *Korea and the World Economy*, *13*(1), 1–37.
Ninomiya, K., & Tokuda, M. (2016). *Accumulation of financial asset and economic structural change*. CRR Discussion Paper, J-48. Faculty of Economics, Shiga University (in Japanese).
Nishi, H. (2012a). Structural VAR analysis of debt, capital accumulation, and income distribution in the Japanese economy: A Post Keynesian perspective. *Journal of Post Keynesian Economics*, *34*(4), 685–712.
Nishi, H. (2012b). A dynamic analysis of debt-led and debt-burdened growth regimes with Minskian financial structure. *Metroeconomica*, *63*(4), 634–660.
Okishio, N. (1986). The movement of interest rate and exchange rate. *The Kokumin Keizai Zasshi*, *154*(6), 46–69. (in Japanese).
Okishio, N. (Ed.) (1992). *Business cycle: Theories and numerical simulation*. Frankfurt am Main; New York: Peter Lang.
Ryoo, S. (2010). Long waves and short cycles in a model of endogenous financial fragility. *Journal of Economic Behavior and Organization*, *74*(3), 163–186.
Sasaki, H., & Fujita, S. (2012). The importance of the retention ratio in a Kaleckian model with debt accumulation. *Metroeconomica*, *63*(3), 417–428.
Sasaki, H., & Fujita, S. (2014). Pro-shareholder income distribution, debt accumulation, and cyclical fluctuations in a post-Keynesian model with labor supply constraints. *European Journal of Economics and Economic Policies: Intervention*, *11*(1), 10–30.
Taylor, L., & O'Connell, S. A. (1985). A Minsky crisis. *Quarterly Journal of Economics*, *100*, 871–886.
Uno, K. (1953). Theory of crises *(*Kyokoron*)*. Tokyo: Iwanami-Shoten, Inc. (in Japanese).

A HISTORICAL PERSPECTIVE AND EVALUATION OF ABENOMICS☆

Takeshi Nakatani and Taro Abe

ABSTRACT

This paper examines policies of Abenomics and explains their ineffectiveness through historical comparisons. In conclusion, Abenomics raises serious concerns about Japanese economy. It offsets the effects of its aggressive monetary expansion by increasing consumption taxes. It has tilted the distribution of income in favor of financial speculation, but the returns have not benefitted the nonfinancial economy. It has enriched investors, corporate profits, and exporters but not Japan's workers, households, and general economy. It ignores the structural problems. Specifically, its deregulation of labor markets reduced household income by raising the number of nonregular workers. Higher wages in general and providing more workers with stable, well-paid employment are among necessary reforms. It will be difficult to achieve a sustainable economic recovery in Japan without proceeding with these types of policy changes.

Keywords: Abenomics; Japanese economy; neoliberal policies; deregulation of labor markets

☆This paper is based on a report published at the interdisciplinary Life Research Institute meeting in April 2016. This is supported by scientific research expenses 16K03555 and part of the 2016 research scholarship of the Nagoya Gakuin University School of Economics. This paper will be translated into Spanish and published as chapter of *Análisis teóricos y aplicados de la política monetaria actual.*

Return of Marxian Macro-dynamics in East Asia
Research in Political Economy, Volume 32, 63–79

ISSN: 0161-7230/doi:10.1108/S0161-723020170000032005

INTRODUCTION

Regarded as a shining example of economic performance during the 1980s, Japan's economy entered a long period of stagnation after the bubble burst in the early 1990s. The Bank of Japan (BOJ) became the world's first central bank to implement numerous and well-known nontraditional monetary policies to revive the economy. After the Abe administration's re-election in December 2012, it embarked upon a set of monetary, fiscal, and growth policies collectively called "Abenomics." Nonetheless, Japan still suffers continuing deflation and economic stagnation. Considering that an adequate period of time has elapsed since the beginning of Abenomics, this study examines these policies and explains their ineffectiveness through historical comparisons. Section 1 explains the concept of Abenomics. Section 2 sets the historical context for its emergence. Section 3 discusses the goals of Japanese monetary policy. Section 4 examines the joint effectiveness of Abenomics and monetary policy. Section 5 concludes the study.

WHAT IS ABENOMICS?

Abenomics is a policy of "three arrows" of bold monetary easing, flexible fiscal policy, and growth strategies for promoting private investments. The three arrows refer to an apocryphal story concerning Samurai Motonari Mouri of the 16th century. He exhorted his sons on his deathbed to cooperate in preserving the Mouri family because it is more difficult to snap three arrows bundled than a single arrow. How does Abenomics adopt this philosophy?[1]

The first arrow – bold monetary easing – reflects the notion that the BOJ was primarily responsible for reversing Japan's economic stagnation. To meet a monetary target of 2% inflation and doubling of the monetary base, the BOJ bought five-year and 10-year government bonds, investment trusts, and real-estate investment trusts, although it previously had bought only short-term government bonds for monetary easing. It removed the upper limit for the regulation of fund purchases[2] and extended the period in which the policy was to be conducted to when those targets were achieved. In January 2016, the BOJ adopted a negative interest rate policy.

The second arrow – flexible fiscal policy – addresses Japan's already substantial financial deficit. In February 2013, the House of Councilors enacted a supplementary budget of 13.1 trillion yen by one vote. The government issued 53 trillion yen in new debt as a result.

The first and second arrows were intended to stimulate demand, but the third was intended to stimulate long-run economic growth. It included opening Japanese markets as a signatory to the Trans-Pacific Partnership, de-regulating labor markets, and raising the consumption tax to refill the nation's coffers. These growth strategies were intended to strengthen international competitiveness.

HISTORICAL BACKGROUND LEADING TO ABENOMICS

To understand Abenomics and its implications, we must review Japan's post-war economic performance (Fig. 1).

Fig. 1 illustrates Japan's inflation-adjusted economic growth for 60 years after World War II. The average annual growth from the late 1950s to the 1970s was 9.1%. During that period, private investment drove Japan's economy, with the government playing a passive role of creating the infrastructure to promote private industry. Faced with soaring crude oil prices and increasingly serious environmental problems during the 1970s, however, the average annual growth declined to 4.2% by the 1990s. The decline was accompanied by falling corporate profits and revenues and stagnating production and employment.

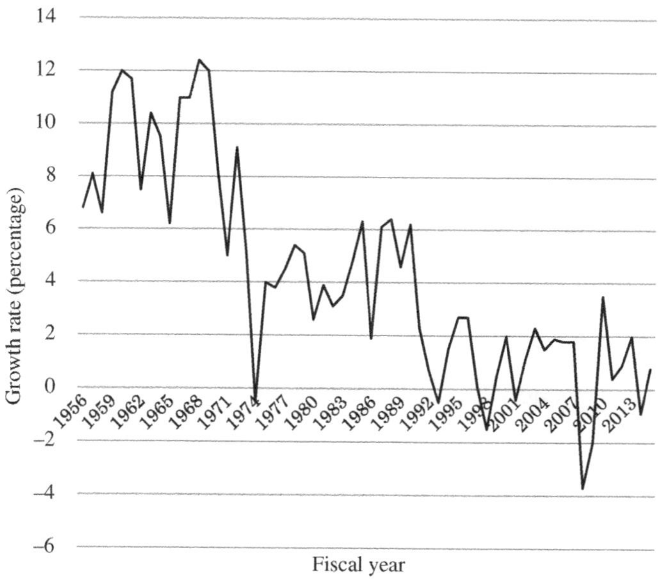

Fig. 1. Rate of Real Economic Growth. *Source*: Data preceding 1980 are from the Annual Report on National Accounts 2000. Data spanning 1981–1994 are from the Annual Report on National Accounts 2009. Remaining data are from a preliminary release (June 8, 2016). *Notes*: 1956–1973 average was 9.1%, 1974–1990 average was 4.2%, and 1991–2015 average was 0.9%. Data are from Japan Cabinet Office, 93SNA estimates. Averages are simple averages for each year.

As more assertive fiscal policies became necessary in response to oil shocks, Japan's government initiated deficit spending for the first time in 1975 by issuing government bonds. The deficit began to accumulate in 1985, when a substantial appreciation of the yen following the Plaza Accords provoked an economic downturn. Deficit spending stimulated Japan's economy to some extent, but after that, national debt continued to accumulate. Fig. 2 depicts how the trend continued after the 1990s.

Another issue is exports. Japan's trade surplus occasioned trade deficits among its trading partners, and their criticism of Japan's torrent-like exports emerged during the late 1980s. In essence, Japan's high growth before the 1970s and moderate growth thereafter originated in policies to stimulate the economy. This was done by supporting private investment and creating demand from the government and foreign countries. In this sense, these policies were principally Keynesian.

Japan has endured large economic fluctuations. The transition of economic growth rate from a high of 9.1% to a low of 0.9% during the 70 years after the war is notable compared with that of other advanced countries, which exhibited milder fluctuations albeit with declining trends.

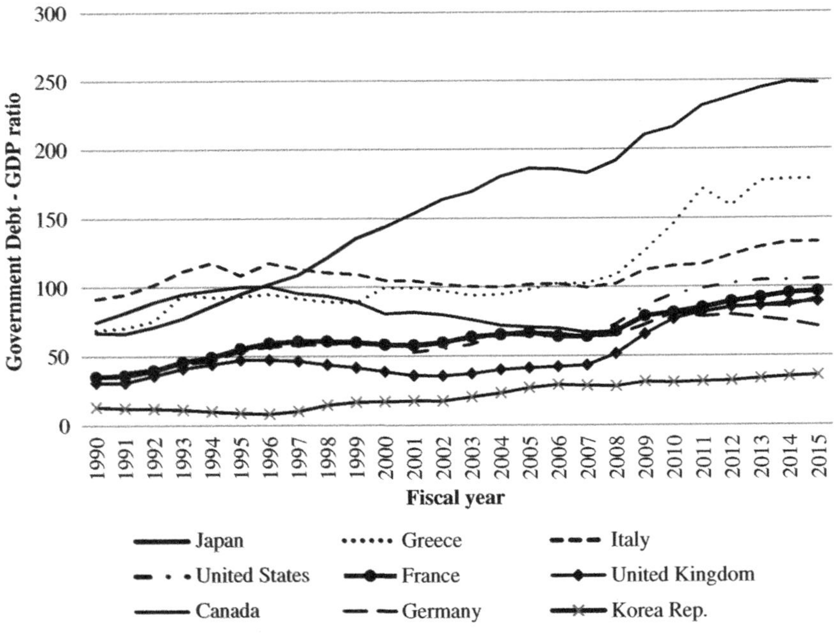

Fig. 2. Government Debt to GDP. *Source*: Data are from the International Monetary Fund. *Notes*: Government includes the central and local governments, municipalities, and the social security fund.

Weak domestic demand underlies the volatility in Japan's economic growth. Domestic consumption constitutes 60% of Japan's GDP; the remainder is composed of private investment, government spending, and exports. If investment demand is positive, the economy grows, but when it stagnates during downturns, weakened governmental spending and exports exacerbate the slump. As consumption centers upon domestic demand, weak consumption causes volatile economic fluctuations. Consumption constitutes 68% of GDP in the United States and 64% in the United Kingdom; the share of consumption in both countries is slightly higher than that in Japan. The consumption ratio of Japan is similar to those of other European countries; however, consumption spending could not compensate for the large change in investment.[3]

When the economic bubble burst in 1991, Japan's economy entered a 20-year recession. This era renders Japan's economic policies highly instructive. Japan's economic policies after 1992 can be divided into two periods. The first is an era of affirmative fiscal policy (1993–2001) during the administrations of Hosokawa, Murayama, Hashimoto, Obuchi, and Mori. The second is an era of structural reform (2001–2012) under the administrations of Koizumi, the first Abe term, Fukuda, Asou, and the Democratic Party administration that started in 2009.[4]

The first period exhibits many similarities with Abenomics. For example, Obuchi positioned former Prime Minister Miyazawa as the Minister of Finance, following five quarters of declining economic growth. The Mori administration after the Obuchi administration also inherited policies with similar stances. Consequently, the issuance of new government bonds reached 34.0 trillion yen in FY1998 and 37.5 trillion yen in FY1999, the highest ever. This elevated the stock market – the Nikkei Stock Average hit a high of 20,000 yen. However, the economic growth rate decreased to −1.5% in 1998 and 0.5% in 1999. Thus, despite an aggressive policy, the road to economic recovery was steep, and the fiscal deficit also expanded. Abenomics presents a similar situation.[5] The Abe cabinet positioned the former Prime Minister Asou as the Minister of Finance and implemented an aggressive fiscal and monetary policy. Consequently, a rise in stock prices and devaluation of the exchange rate occurred, which occurred in the era of the Obuchi cabinet.

In the second phase since 2000, the LDP's economic policy began shifting from an aggressive fiscal and monetary policy to a policy focusing on structural reform. Let's consider deregulation of the labor market and an increase in irregular employment, for example. Deregulation of the labor market began in 1986. During that time, the Nakasone administration approved the prohibited worker dispatch in 16 industries, the Hashimoto administration expanded it to 26 industries in 1996, and the Obuchi government, in principle, released the regulation in 1999. Consequently, the number of irregular workers (such as temporary and temporary staffing workers) significantly increased during this period. However, as indicated in Fig. 3, the increase in irregular labor has been rapidly developing since 2000.

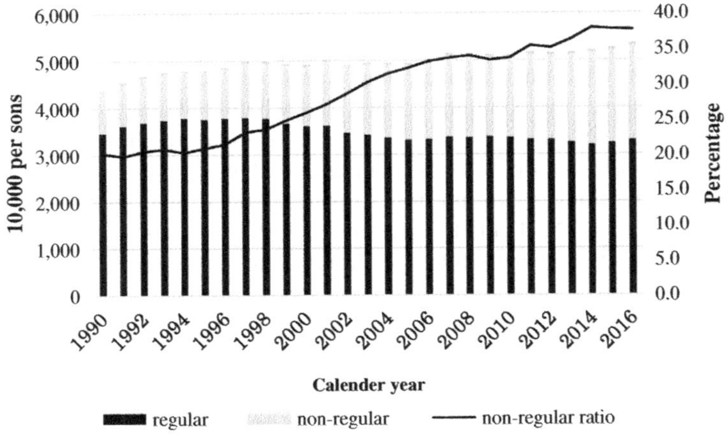

Fig. 3. Regular and Nonregular Employees. *Source*: Data are from the Labor Force Survey, Statistics Bureau. *Notes*: Averages span January to March each year. Nonregular employees include part-time and temporary workers, workers dispatched from temporary labor agencies, contract employees, and entrusted employees. Figures exclude company or corporate executives.

As illustrated in Fig. 3, the number of regular workers decreased by 2.96 million between 2000 and 2012, during which the number of irregular workers increased by 5.32 million. The proportion of irregular employment to regular employment has been large in the past for people aged above 60; recently, it has spread to young workers aged between 15 years and 24 years.

Entering the 2000s, Japan's economic policy shifted from Keynesian to Neoclassical, emphasizing free market mechanisms. In a nutshell, Keynesian policy emphasizes profit by selling goods, and neoclassical policy emphasizes cutting costs. Cutting costs requires introducing technical innovations (e.g., new IT technologies) and/or restraining labor costs, a major element of total cost. Suppressing labor costs reduces household income and consumption. Therefore, it produces two consequences for firms – reduction of production costs (positive) and erosion of demand for their products (negative). If an economy is largely export-oriented with a weak domestic demand, firms advocate wage cuts to attract foreign demand. In this sense, the global economy pits businesses against households.

During the low-growth economy following the late 2000s, Koizumi's structural reforms have proceeded and labor costs have declined. Neoclassical structural reform had apparently failed as Japan's recession deepened.

Neoliberal structural reforms ideally would have restored growth without raising prices by lowering production costs. Aggregate supply in Fig. 4 would shift from S to S′, and equilibrium supply and demand would expand from A

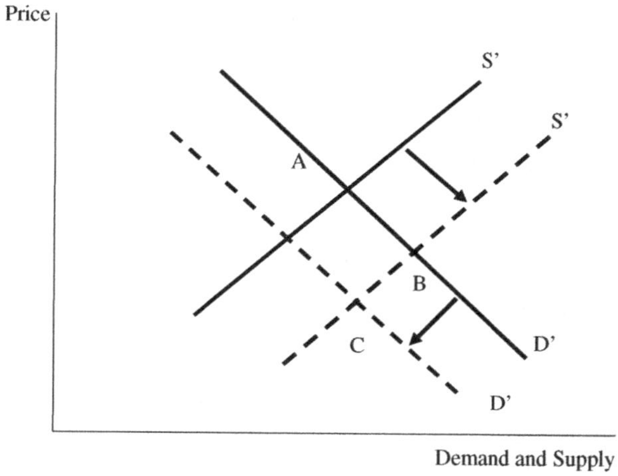

Fig. 4. Neoclassical Policy and the Economy's Response.

to B, a point of greater output. The result should be lower prices with increased production and employment.

However, regular employment was replaced by nonregular employment, which now exceeds 35% of Japan's workforce. Although wages have declined since the mid-1990s, employment has been undependable. Workers who have less income and more fear for their livelihoods consume less, as indicated by the contraction in demand to D′. Thus, the policies that reduced production costs in the hope of stimulating demand also reduced household income and curtailed domestic demand. The economy that was supposed to accelerate from A to B actually decelerated to C. As an economy recedes, lower prices engender a deflationary recession.

THE INTENT OF MONETARY POLICY UNDER ABENOMICS

Abenomics arrived in the midst of this economic situation. It included an ultra-expansionary monetary policy during the early stages of stagnation and more extensive structural reforms later. In sum, Abenomics is a more intense version of Obuchi's economic policy.

Abe's ultra-expansionary policy centered upon monetary policy, not fiscal policy, to achieve the inflation target. However, raising the consumption tax was a fiscal maneuver that contravened the expansionary monetary policy.

Structural reforms included in the Abe administration's yearly plans for Japan's revival sought to strengthen returns on capital, enable cooperation in the Trans-Pacific Partnership, and induce flexibility in the labor market.

The aims of its monetary policy are as follows:

(a) Increase the monetary base
(b) Raise the money stock
(c) Stimulate demand for goods and exports
(d) Increase production and employment

Monetary policy is effective if an economy smoothly transitions from (a) to (d). The elements are well known: an increase in the monetary base raises the money stock through the lending behavior of financial institutions; this increases the demand for goods and exports via inflation expectations, decreases real interest rate and depreciates exchange rate and ultimately increases production and income.

Through long-recognized transmission mechanisms, the BOJ could increase the monetary base; however, it failed to raise the money stock sufficiently because the money stock is endogenously determined. The increase in the money stock depends on whether financial institutions can lend to the private nonbank sector when the monetary base swells. In short, money does not flow from the BOJ to the nonbank economy when the private sector is reluctant to invest, even if the BOJ buys national bonds and deposits its proceeds in banks. The route from (a) to (b) has been blocked as Japan has been in a liquidity trap since the 1990s.

In addition, an increase in the money stock does not ensure increased demand for goods. If money is directed to the purchase of stock and foreign exchange, boosting stock prices and foreign exchange rates, domestic production and employment are not affected directly. Even if consumers become richer via increases in stock prices, they might spend their money on imported luxuries. The routes from (b) to (c) and (d) are also not always guaranteed.

EFFECTIVENESS OF ABE'S MONETARY POLICY

This section examines the effectiveness of Abe's monetary policy.

The Nikkei Stock Average increased from 9,000 yen during the Noda years to more than 15,000 yen in 2016 (Fig. 5).

The yen has depreciated versus the dollar since the late 1970s (Fig. 6).

According to Figs. 7 and 8, the CPI and Japan's expected inflation rate have risen since 2013, although the CPI has not reached 2%. Shioji (2015) argued that rising prices of imported goods have elevated the inflation rate and decreased the real interest rates. However, Japan's real economy has continued to stagnate.

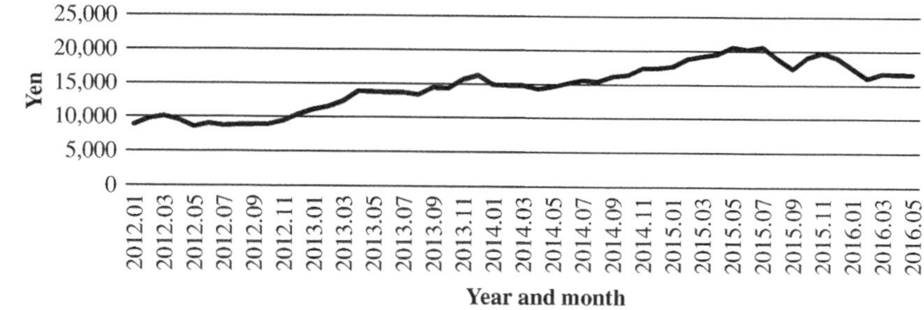

Fig. 5. Nikkei Stock Average. *Note*: Closing price.

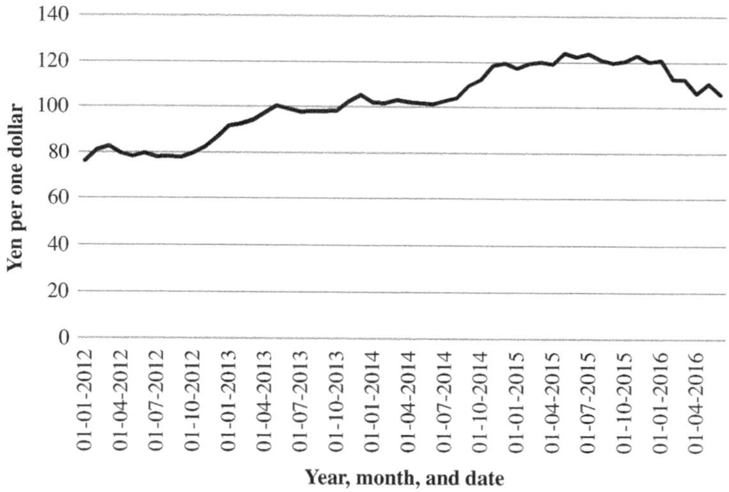

Fig. 6. Exchange Rate.

According to Figs. 9–12, the GDP, private consumption, private investment, and exports have seesawed between 2011 and 2016. Raising the consumption tax in April 2014 affected domestic demand. According to Fig. 13 and Table 1, the declines in real wages and real disposal income have reduced private consumption. Real disposable income fell as prices rose, although nominal disposable income was almost unchanged. On the other hand, retained earnings rose from 69 trillion yen in December 2012 to 343 trillion yen in September 2015 according to the Ministry of Finance's Financial Statement Statistics of Corporations by Industry. According to Oshio (2016), the increase in the number of nonregular workers and the diversion of benefits resulting from high stock prices have polarized income and assets. These factors have decreased consumption.

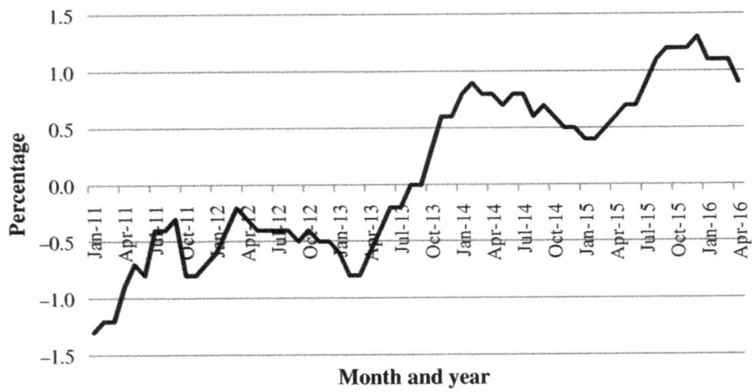

Fig. 7. Core-Core CPI. *Source*: Data from the Bank of Japan. *Notes*: Excludes the effect of the increase in consumption tax. Relative change from previous year.

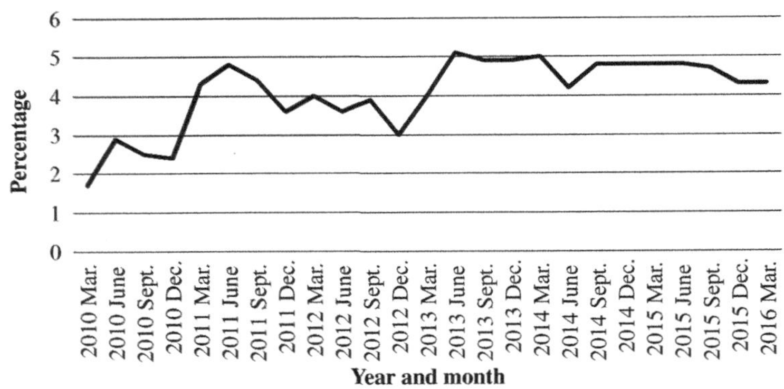

Fig. 8. Expected Inflation Rate. *Source*: Data from the Bank of Japan. *Notes*: Relative change from previous year.

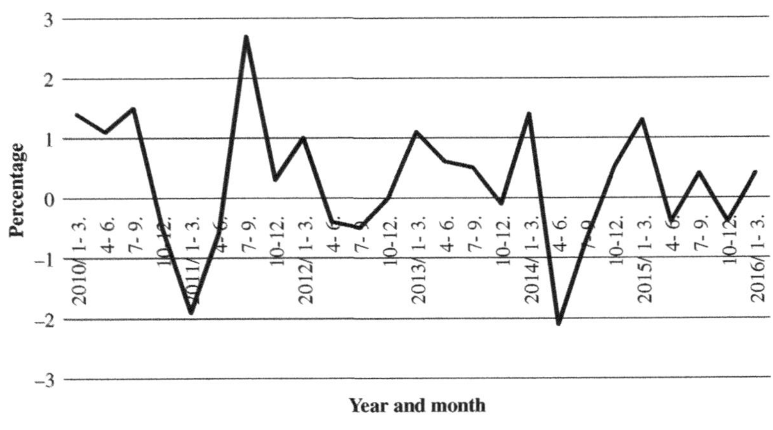

Fig. 9. Growth Rate of Real GDP. *Source*: Data from Cabinet Office.

Exports are not robust despite a weaker yen. As explained by Shimizu and Sato (2014), Japanese firms proceeded with systems of international division of labor in response to a strong yen after the 2008 financial crisis. Their action raised the imports of intermediate goods (e.g., components). A weak yen made it difficult to profit from expanding exports. Moreover, Japanese firms did not change their dollar-denominated prices in dollars to expand margins from the weaker yen.

However, over this time period, the unemployment rate declined (Fig. 14), one of the real economy's few achievements. Tsuri (2016) attributed the increased demand for labor to the consumption of medical and social services by Japan's aging populations, an outcome unrelated to Abenomics. However, the increased demand for workers did not see an increase in real wages in Japan because many workers are nonregular and low-paid (Fig. 13).

In short, the effects of (a) and (b) in Section 2 do not lead to outcomes (c) and (d).

Fiscal policy changes have direct effects because they generate direct purchases. However, the effects of monetary policy are indirect because they must be translated into action by the private sector.

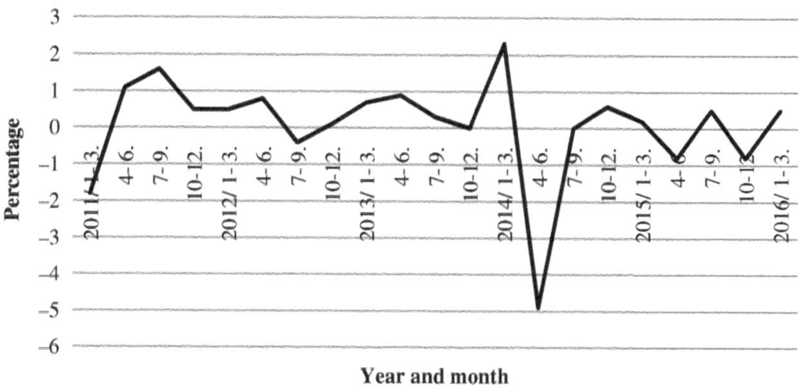

Fig. 10. Growth Rate of Real Private Consumption.
Source: Data from Cabinet Office.

The effects of the monetary base on Japan's economy are as follows.

	1980	2007	Magnification
Monetary base	18	90	5.00
Money stock	198	723	3.65
Real GDP	245	507	2.06

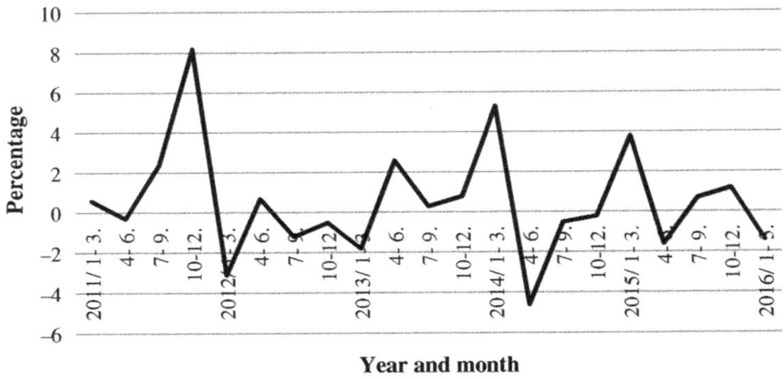

Fig. 11. Growth Rate of Real Private Investment. *Source*: Data from Cabinet Office.

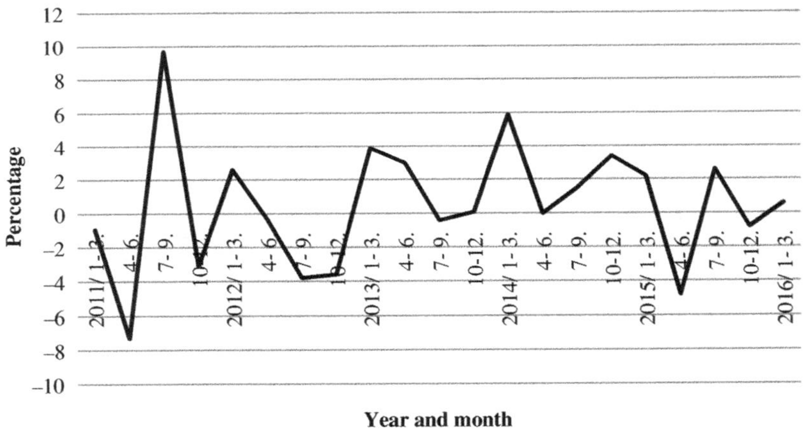

Fig. 12. Growth Rate of Real Exports. *Source*: Data from Cabinet Office.

Japan's monetary base increased five-fold from 1980 to 2007. However, money stock and GDP increased by factors of 3.65 and 2.06, respectively.

Changes from 2006 to 2011 are as follows.

	2006	2011	Magnification
Monetary base	94	125	1.32
Money stock	708	796	1.12
Real GDP	512	509	0.99

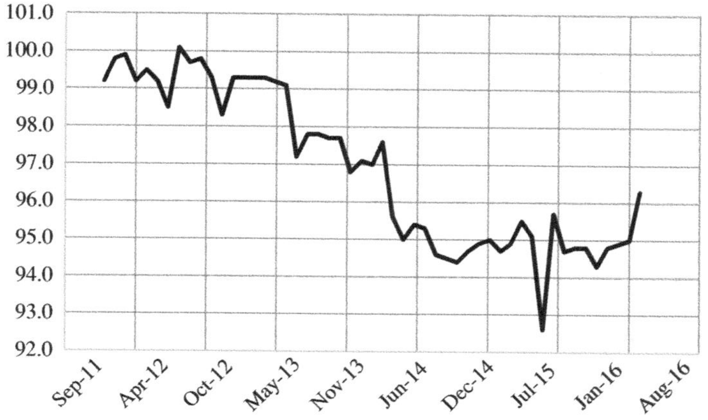

Fig. 13. Real Wages. *Source*: Data from Ministry of Health, Labor and Welfare. Seasonally Adjusted. 2010 Average = 100.

Table 1. Nominal Disposal Income.

2012	2013	2014	2015
383,851	380,966	381,929	381,193

Source: Data from household means test by Ministry of Internal Affairs and Communications
Notes: The unit is yen. The total households of workers (per household and during a month).

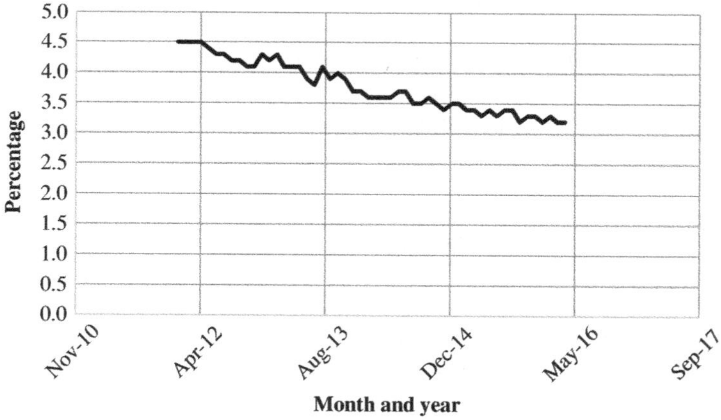

Fig. 14. Unemployment Rate. *Source*: Data from Statistics Japan.

From 2006 through 2011, the monetary base increased by a factor of 1.32, money stock increased by a factor of 1.12, and real GDP declined. Firms and households did not borrow, although the BOJ supplied an abundance of base money. Output did not increase, and GDP stagnated.

The endogeneity of money remained a factor after Abenomics.

	2012	2015	Magnification
Monetary Base	121	313	2.58
Money Stock	1122	1223	1.09
Real GDP	519	528	1.00

CONCLUSION

Our results reveal that monetary policy under Abenomics has not affected Japan's real economy, although it has stimulated stock prices and lowered the yen's exchange rate. It has been ineffective for several reasons. First, Abenomics holds that deflation has caused Japan's economy to stagnate. Unfortunately, that reasoning includes a tautology. Second, Abenomics seized upon monetary easing without considering the structural causes of Japan's stagnation. Specifically, its deregulation of labor markets reduced household income by raising the number of nonregular workers. Third, the third arrow of Abenomics missed its mark. The real economy will remain stagnant, and liquidity from an aggressively expansionary monetary policy will flow into financial speculation.

Further, there is a question whether a 2% inflation target is achievable. Japan's CPI has not exceeded 2%, and some economists and policymakers now doubt if the BOJ can achieve that goal. Indeed, there is a question whether 2% inflation is desirable. Inflation creates economic winners and losers. Pensioners and smaller enterprises cannot always increase their incomes or raise products prices correspondingly. Inflation also expands the inequality of income and assets.

A weaker yen creates similar effects: it benefits exporters but increases the prices of imported goods and intermediate inputs. Inflation expands inequality among producers and sellers.

Wage increases are more effective when prices increase.[6]

Figs. 15 and 16 indicate that nominal wages and the CPI operate in tandem. Wage increases increase business costs as well as workers' income and household consumption.

Moreover, Keynesian demand policies and Abe's tax and growth policies contradict. Monetary easing and a higher consumption tax operate at opposite ends, as the Hashimoto and Obuchi administrations demonstrated years ago.[7]

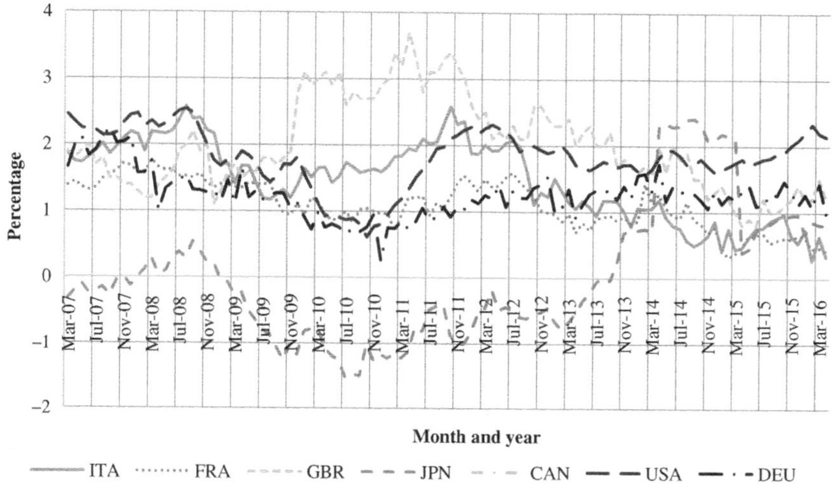

Fig. 15. Core CPI. *Source*: Data from OECD.

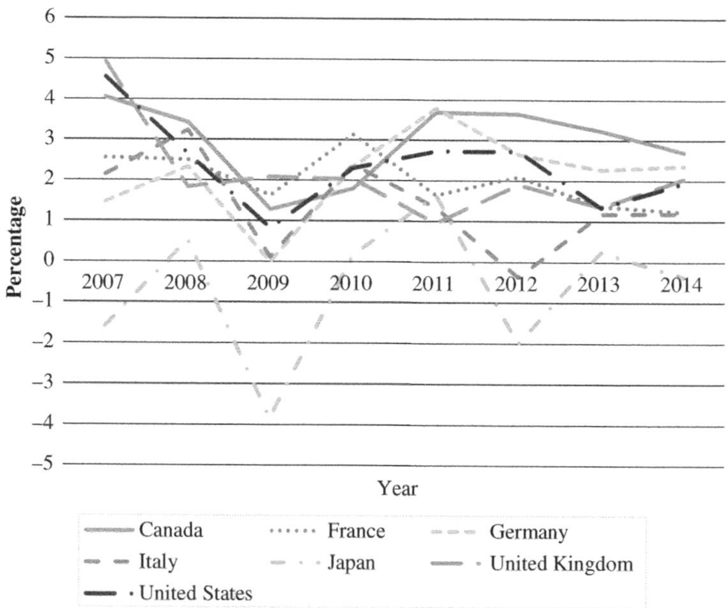

Fig. 16. Rate of Change of Nominal Wages. *Source*: Data from OECD. Total. Current price in National Currency Unit.

In sum, Abenomics raises many concerns. It offsets the effects of its aggressive monetary expansion by increasing consumption taxes. It has tilted the distribution of income in favor of financial speculation, but the returns have not benefitted the nonfinancial economy. It has enriched investors, corporate profits, and exporters but not Japan's workers, households, and general economy. Abenomics ignores the structural problems underlying Japan's economic dilemma. Higher wages in general and providing more workers with stable, well-paid employment are among necessary reforms. It will be difficult to achieve a sustainable economic recovery in Japan without proceeding with these types of policy changes.[8,9]

NOTES

1. This story is not based on historical fact. However, Motonari wrote nearly the same episode in his book (1557). The three sons were Takamoto, Harumoto, and Takakage. It is said that Takamoto did not have what it took to be a Samurai because he was inactive and unassertive. The brothers did not help each other. The younger brothers ignored the eldest son. Harumoto and Takakage became well-known Samurai of the Mouri family, even if the story is untrue.
2. The regulation kept the holdings of long-term government bonds not exceeding the amount of banknotes issued.
3. It is under 40% in China, which is extremely low although common among developing countries like Japan in the 1950s and 1960s.
4. Only the Koizumi administration implemented austerity policy in this era. However, the administration introduced structural reforms in full swing. Neoliberal policies dominated after the administration, although there had been some such policies in place prior to then.
5. According to Daiwa Institute of Research (2013), the effects of fiscal policies have been weaker since the early 1990s.
6. Yoshikawa (2013) and Porcellacchia (2016) also shared the same opinion.
7. The consumer tax increase was determined by the preceding administration of the Democratic Party of Japan. However, the Abe administration did not postpone it, although it had two chances to do so.
8. "Reflationist" has supported Abenomics based on Krugman's (1998) model. They insist that Abenomics was effective to stop deflation and revive the Japanese economy as Wakatabe (2015, chap. 5), although they were concerned with the negative effects of the consumption tax hike. However, in 2013, when Abe administration claimed to have achieved a great success, the growth rate of real GDP was about 2.0%, which is not as high compared with the rates since 1990 except for the period of the world economic shocks: Asian monetary shock of 1997–1998, Lehman shock of 2007–2008, and United States credit-rating shock of 2011.The points where our arguments differ from that of the Reflationist are as follows: price is not only a monetary phenomenon but reflects real economic conditions, so a monetary easing policy will not be guaranteed successful when the real economic structures like the labor market, welfare system, and innovation promoting mechanism remain invariant. A monetary easing policy itself has effects only in the short run while its effects on expectations remain. Therefore, it is natural that Abenomics has failed because of its major emphasis on expectation formation. More

emphasis should be placed on real structural changes in the production, distribution and innovation, the effects of which last longer.

9. The monetary policy of Abenomics has sometimes been compared with the monetary easing, which began in March 2001 and ended in March 2006. From 2001 to 2006, the growth rate of real GDP recovered to 1–2%, the unemployment rate decreased, and stock prices increased. On the other hand, core-core CPI remained negative and the yen did not depreciate dramatically. We should focus on the similarity, although there are such differences. During the time, the monetary base did not correlate money stock and core-core CPI, and the nominal wage level continued to decrease. In short, the Japanese economy is vulnerable to economic shocks such as the Lehman Shock and the consumption tax hike as long as there is a weak economic structure.

REFERENCES

Daiwa Institute of Research. (2013). *Japan's Economy: Monthly Review 2013.* (in Japanese). Retrieved from http://www.dir.co.jp/research/report/japan/outlook/monthly/20130220_006827.pdf. Accessed on October 2.

Krugman, P. R. (1998). It's Baaack: Japan's slump and the return of the liquidity trap. *Brookings Papers on Economic Activity, 1998*(2), 137–205.

Oshio, T. (2016). Abenomic expands inequalities of income and asset. Monetary-Fiscal Business. January 14, 2016 (in Japanese).

Porcellacchia, D. (2016). *Wage-Price Dynamics and Structural Reforms in Japan.* IMF Working Paper No. WP/16/20.

Shimizu, J., & Sato, K. (2014). *Abenomics, yen depreciation, trade deficit and export competitiveness.* Research Institute of Economy, Trade and Industry Discussion Papers No. 14-J-022 (in Japanese).

Shioji, E. (2015). Time varying pass-through: Will the yen depreciation help Japan hit the inflation target? *Journal of the Japanese and International Economies, 37*, 43–58.

Tsuri, M. (2016). Does employment really improve? *THE PAGE*, April 16, 2016 (in Japanese). Retrieved from https://thepage.jp/detail/20160405-00000018-wordleaf?pattern=6&utm_expid=90592221-74.LdrGpjcWS4Czgnu3l9N7Eg.3&utm_referrer=https%3A%2F%2Fwww.google.co.jp%2F

Wakatabe, M. (2015). *Japan's great stagnation and abenomics: Lessons for the world.* New York, NY: Palgrave Macmillan.

Yoshikawa, H. (2013). *Deflation. Nihon Keizai Shinbun sya.* (In Japanese).

BIASED TECHNICAL CHANGE AND ECONOMIC GROWTH: THE CASE OF KOREA, 1970–2013

Sangjun Jeong

ABSTRACT

This paper explores the pattern of technical change in the Korean economy from 1970 to 2013 and investigates its determinants. We use the Classical growth-distribution schedule to show that the labor-saving and capital-using pattern has predominated. For the rationale behind this Marx-biased technical change, we focus on the relationship between technical change and real wage growth via the evolution of labor and capital productivity, and verify the historical direction of technical change against the rise and fall of the working class. Furthermore, we find that the deviation during the post-crisis period from the long-run trend of Marx-biased technical change is not attributable to the vitality of new technological innovations, but rather the reflection of class dynamics over extracting productivity under weaker capital deepening. The results suggest that the recent deterioration of labor share and labor unions in Korea is closely associated with low incentive for technological progress, which contributes to prolonged stagnation.

Keywords: Growth-distribution schedule; Marx-biased technical change; labor productivity; capital productivity

Return of Marxian Macro-dynamics in East Asia
Research in Political Economy, Volume 32, 81–103

ISSN: 0161-7230/doi:10.1108/S0161-723020170000032006

INTRODUCTION

Korea had been one of the fastest-growing countries in the post-war period. It recorded a real growth rate of 8.5%, 9.3%, and 8.4% during the 1970s, 1980s, and mid-1990s, respectively, which earned Korea the title of the "East Asian miracle economy". Although its dazzling state-led development model declined sharply with the 1997–1998 Asian crisis and the subsequent sweeping neoliberal reforms led to the secular bear phase during the 21st century with a 3.6% growth rate, Korea remains a role model for catching up and even of quickly recovering from the crisis. Given that technical progress is an inherent feature of economic growth, unsurprisingly, Korea's remarkable technical innovation as a driver of its rapid growth has been in the spotlight for decades.

However, while Korea's technical progress is allegedly attributed to human capital accumulation fostered by education and trade openness (Lucas, 1993) or the strong industrial policies that allocate rents to private entities, which have enabled *chaebols* to defy comparative advantage (Lee, Lin, & Chang, 2005), the dynamics of technical change associated with the contradictions of capital accumulation have attracted little interest. That is, by belittling the bloody Taylorism, harsh labor repression, the *chaebol*'s overgrown social power, and U.S.-Japan auspices, all of which structured the institutional architecture supporting the capitalist operation in Korea (Hart-Landsberg, Jeong, & Westra, 2007), the above conventional interpretations have treated technical progress as practically neutral with respect to income distribution and as exogenous to class conflict.

The mainstream economic growth literature freely relied on the elusive concept of total factor productivity (hereafter "TFP") for understanding technical change (Easterly & Levine, 2001). Even when addressing theoretically relatively uncontentious labor productivity growth, the literature generally and unavoidably invoked TFP change as its contributing factor. However, despite much effort to estimate the size of TFP in growth accounting, its unreliable assumptions of production functions have baffled the proper investigation of technical changes (Felipe & McCombie, 2013). In Korea's case, we still run up against mixed TFP calculations which even contradict one another.[1] Moreover, within the common framework of calculating TFP, which is nothing more than the residual of growth accounting formulas, we are given few explanations as to where technical progress has originated from and why it has favored capitalists rather than the working class or both.

Instead, we considered how technical progress emerges from within the economic system following in the steps of Classical economists such as Ricardo and Marx, who emphasized the struggle between classes as a motive for technical change (Kurz, 2010). In that vein, we explored endogenous patterns of technical change in the Korean economy for the period 1970–2013, the most recent time span of data available. We aimed to find whether technical change has a biased direction and investigated the specific bias determinants, both of which have seldom been discussed in textbook economics.

The induced innovation literature includes Neoclassical research such as Kennedy (1964) and Drandrakis and Phelps (1966), who modeled the theoretical logic according to which capitalist firms adopt technologies using a specific production factor more intensively in response to a decrease in its relative cost.[2] Meanwhile, without depending on production function or its unrealistic and tautological assumptions, Duménil and Lévy (1995) and Foley and Michl (1999) stressed the inevitability of the biased technical change, which promises to increase the profit rate at the existing wage so that only "viable techniques" are embraced.[3] Accordingly, a growing body of analysis, like that of Foley and Marquetti (1999), Marquetti (2003), Ferretti (2008), Felipe, Laviña, and Fan (2008), and Vaona (2011), has attempted to empirically demonstrate the bias in the real economy. They show, albeit with some variations in the individual countries and time spans, that the predominant form of technical change in recent decades has been labor-saving and capital using. Additionally, in explaining why the Industrial Revolution was British in origin, Allen (2011) proves that the very high wages in 18th-century Britain not only induced British firms to invent technologies that substituted capital for labor but also generated the firms' demand for literacy, numeracy, and trade skills that were necessary for the technological revolution to unfold.

We followed the above studies and employed Foley and Michl's (1999) growth-distribution schedule (hereafter "GDS"). By adding econometrical analyses within a historical context, we revealed the endogenous feature of the bias in technical change. In particular, we cautioned that the above-referenced empirical literature measures and discusses technical progress in terms of labor productivity growth and thus explicitly omits capital productivity or implicitly assumes constant capital productivity. This practically fails to distinguish a form of Marx-biased capital-using technical change and labor-augmenting or neutral technical change. As Groll and Orzech (1990, p. 99) properly points out: "whereas the former imposes changes that are advantageous to the owners of the means of production, the latter, by definition, preserves the distribution of the total product between labor and capital unchanged." Hence, we drew a distinct line between biased and neutral technical change by looking at separate trends in labor and capital productivity and identified the factors driving the biases in both productivities, which will help evaluate the relevance of Marx dynamics in technical change in Korea and clarify its implications for the current lengthy recession.

The rest of the paper is structured as follows. The next section presents a brief framework of the GDS and characterizes the different patterns of technical change. The following section provides the schedule in Korea and its interpretations. Then, bias-inducing factors are explored and the deviation of capital productivity from the long-run trend during the post-crisis period is specifically discussed. Finally, the findings are summarized and concluded with a policy implications discussion.

ANALYTICAL FRAMEWORK: GDS

Following the pioneering work of Foley and Michl (1999), we consider a simple capitalist economy using only capital and labor. The production technique and its direction of change are represented in the GDS. For a given year, X is the real gross output, K is the net stock of non-residential fixed assets, C is the aggregate consumption, I is the gross investment, D is the depreciation, N is the number of workers employed, W is the total worker compensation, and R is the net profit. Using both national income accounting identity, $X \equiv W + R + D$, and expenditure identity, $X \equiv C + I$, the following GDS is easily derived:

$$c = x - (g + d)k \tag{1}$$

where $x = X/N$ is the labor productivity, $w = W/N$ is the wage rate, $c = C/N$ is the social consumption per worker, $k = K/N$ is the capital per worker, $d = D/K$ is the depreciation rate, and $g + d = I/K$ is the rate of capital accumulation. Considering the identity, $x \equiv w + vk$, where v is the gross rate of profit, we can rearrange Eq. (1) into Eq. (2), where $\rho = x/k$ is the output per unit of capital or capital productivity.

$$w = x(1 - (v/\rho)) \tag{2}$$

In the $(c, g + d)$ space, the schedule of Eq. (1) is a straight line with the vertical and horizontal intercepts of (x, ρ), respectively. Additionally, in the (w, v) space, the schedule of Eq. (2) is the same straight line with the same intercepts. The schedules imply an inverse relationship between the real wages and the profit rate as well as the consumption and capital accumulation. As both schedules are mathematically identical and have an equal $-k$ slope, we can depict them graphically in the same quadrant as in Fig. 1.

The GDS movements reflect the bias in the adoption of technical change, which a combination of changes in labor and capital productivity presents. When labor productivity(x) increases, the vertical intercept shifts outward, and when capital productivity(ρ) increases, the horizontal intercept shifts outward. Accordingly, we are able to identify some common technical change patterns in the relevant literature as follows, and any pattern below can be depicted in the GDS.

For example, a pure labor-saving (Harrod-neutral) technical change that increases x while keeping ρ constant corresponds to a clockwise rotation of the GDS around its horizontal axis. Inversely, a pure capital-saving

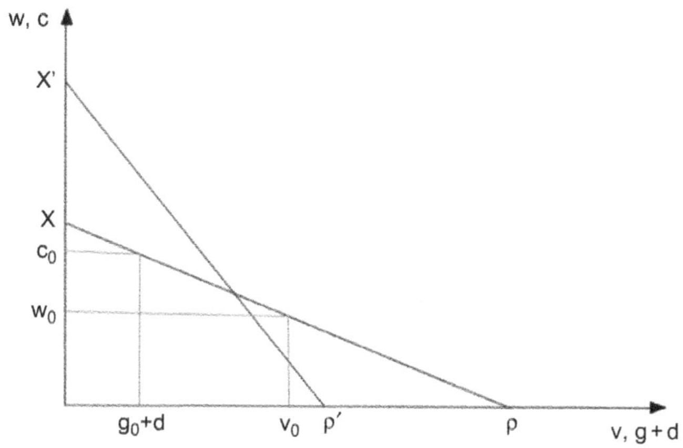

Fig. 1. GDS, Marx-Biased Technical Change.

(Solow-neutral) technical change that increases ρ while keeping x constant corresponds to a counter-clockwise rotation of the GDS around its vertical axis. The other GDS shifts are relevant; a nearly equal labor- and capital-saving (Hicks-neutral) technical change that increases ρ and x alike corresponds to a near-parallel outward shift of the GDS, while a labor-saving and capital-using (Marx-biased) technical change that increases ρ and decreases x corresponds to a clockwise pivot around the switching point in the positive GDS orthant. This final movement is illustrated from (x, ρ) to (x', ρ') in Fig. 1.

As the GDS assumes a one-commodity production economy and is not free from the issues the Cambridge controversy raised, the GDS has a chance to be non-linear in the actual economies. Marquetti (2003) and Basu (2010) observe that this point poses a potential caveat to the GDS framework. We have yet to devise an alternative model that can address, for example, the problems due to capital aggregation in a non-linear GDS. However, from a pragmatic perspective, as Ochoa (1989) showed for the United States, da Silva (1991) for Brazil, and Tsoulfidis and Rieu (2006) for Korea, all estimated GDSs are quasi-linear and display few curvatures, which justifies our simple analytic framework.

HISTORICAL DIRECTIONS IN TECHNICAL CHANGE

In this section, we investigate the direction of bias in technical change for the Korean economy. We used the National Income at factor cost as a measure of output (X). For the real net capital stock (K), we employed the national balance sheet accounts the Bank of Korea construct using the perpetual inventory method. The capital stock excludes both inventories and non-produced assets such as land, mineral, and energy reserves. Based on the data Statistics Korea and the Ministry of Employment and Labor collected, we calculated the total number of hours worked for labor productivity denominator (L).

The analysis is divided into three phases: 1970–1987, 1988–1997, and 1998–2013. Both the first and second phases were periods of rapid export-led industrialization and successful catching up, while the second period was marked by the explosive growth of labor movements as well as large conglomerates that compete in global high-technology industries. The third phase is a post-Asian crisis period characterized by the thoroughgoing liberalization of financial markets and labor market deregulation. Fig. 2 presents the movement of the GDS over all three phases and the above principal moments.

The clockwise pivot of GDS in Fig. 2 shows that the Marx-biased pattern of technical change has been dominant for the entire period in Korea. Labor productivity has risen steadily with only a few exceptions when the economic crises occurred. The average labor productivity growth for all industries reached 4.85%. Conversely, capital productivity declined over all periods with an average growth rate of −2.79%. This long-run Marx-biased technical change (MBTC) trend also occurred with manufacturing.

This pictured MBTC touches upon an important issue on the ascending evolution of labor productivity, which is at odds with the overall decrease of capital productivity. As Duménil and Lévy (1995) who explain technical change in probabilistic terms noted, Korea's case again confirms that technical innovation which increases both labor and capital productivity, contrary to Neoclassical claims, is intrinsically difficult to achieve. Thus, economic growth under capitalism likely strays from a balanced growth path. Besides, when constant labor share accompanies this "trajectory *à la* Marx" (Duménil & Lévy, 2003), the profit rate falls. That is to say, the trajectory of the Korean economy with technical progress has been endogenously crisis-prone and inevitably has entailed class conflict to offset the tendency toward a crisis. This Marxian point is a sine qua non, which mainstream textbooks praising Korea's growth performance scarcely address.

As Marquetti (2003) found, a strong MBTC tendency characterizes the evolution of less-developed economies that adopted capital-intensive technology from highly developed economies. In other words, capital-intensive investments usually accompany developing countries' catching-up process. With an average capital accumulation rate of over 12% during the high-growth regime in the first and second phases, the case of Korea with MBTC is the byword for dynamic but contradictory capitalist development.

As a side note, during the post-1998 period when the financial crisis severely hit Korea and forced it to implement IMF-imposed structural adjustment programs, the increasing speed of labor productivity began to decelerate, while the decreasing trend of capital productivity slackened or grew positively over intermittent years, as shown in Table 1. That is, although the pervasive long-term pattern of technical change has been labor-saving and capital using, its

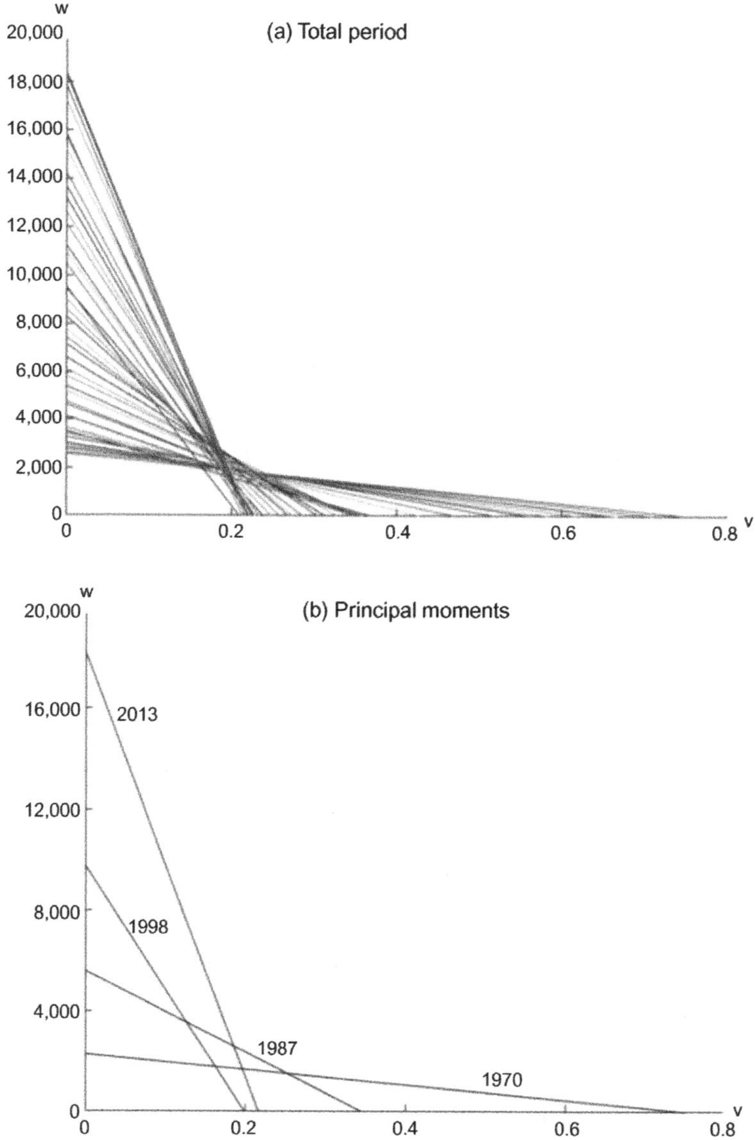

Fig. 2. GDS of Korea: All Industries. (a) Total Period. (b) Principal Moments.
Source: Author's Calculation from data available in Bank of Korea (2015a, 2015b).

Table 1. Average Growth Rates (%) of Labor and Capital Productivity.

Phases	All-Industry		Manufacturing	
	x	ρ	x	ρ
1970–1987	5.16	−4.21	5.75	−2.70
1988–1997	5.93	−3.68	9.47	−3.34
1998–2013	3.85	−0.58	7.39	1.79
Total (1970–2013)	4.85	−2.79	7.18	−1.24

evolutionary path was uneven, depending on the short phases of capitalist development. Overall, Korea in the 21st century, with lower economic growth and overly stagnant accumulation rates, has more frequently witnessed aspects of technical progress differing from the existing trend. This new phenomenon is more pronounced in the manufacturing sector, where productivity measurement is less controversial than compared with the entire economy, including the service sector.

Will this new path in the 21st century, with increased Harrod- and Hicks-neutral technical change characteristics, be only a temporary deviation or a complete disengagement from the long-run trend of the Marx-biased pattern? To answer this puzzling phenomenon, we attempted to identify the factors that underpinned and determined the GDS pivot movement.

RELATIONSHIP BETWEEN TECHNICAL CHANGE AND REAL WAGE

Conventional wisdom has it that the combination of low wages and cheap exports drove the Korean economy's high growth during the pre-1998 period. Taking into account a cruel military dictatorship with repressive labor laws and flagrant interventions into labor disputes, such opinions carried weight. However, the invincible developmental state was involved in the labor market not only as a conflict suppressor but also as a promoter of skill formation and learning (Ra & Shim, 2009; You & Chang, 1993). For the *chaebols* who started consolidating their power in the world market, cooperation with the interventionist state was vital for gaining de facto state-underwritten credit and tax incentives, and for expanding their business to more capital-intensive industries. Hence, keeping the wage increase in check was neither a priority nor advantageous for upgrading technologies (Seguino, 2000). In that vein, to maintain high accumulation levels, sustained and "guided" wage increases rather than low wages were more important.

Indeed, as the time series of real wages and labor productivity in Fig. 3 describes, both trends displayed almost consistent positive growth. For the real

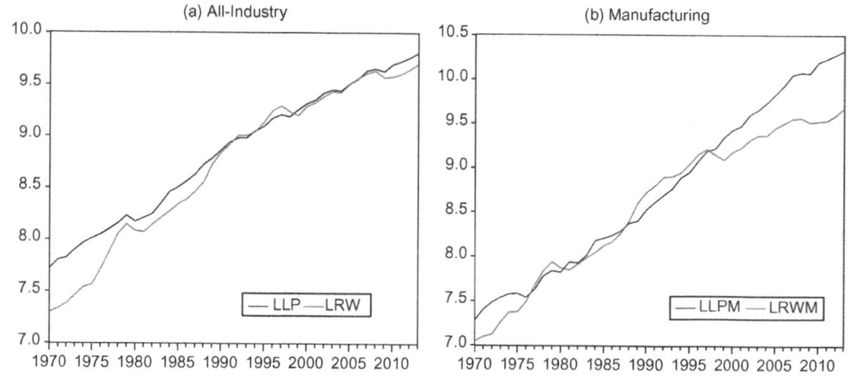

Fig. 3. Time Series of Labor Productivity and Real Wages. (a) All-Industry. (b) Manufacturing. *Source:* Statistics Korea (www.kosis.kr), Ministry of Employment and Labor (laborstat.molab.go.kr). *Note:* LRW, log-transformed real wage rate; LLP, log-transformed labor productivity.

wage, the total compensation per hour worked by an employee deflated by the consumer price index was used to provide a measure of the workers' real purchasing power. Although initially very low, real wages often grew more rapidly than labor productivity for the first two phases. In particular, when democratization movements finally ended the oppressive military regime, real wage growth was spurred and peaked in the early 1990s; hence, the labor share of the value added also surged, although for a relatively short period.

Instead, labor productivity reactively increased enough to offset the shrinking profit from the wage increase. It is noteworthy that the rise in labor productivity was accompanied by the acceleration of fixed capital formation until the advent of the crisis in 1997–1998. Against the rapid rise of working class power, big conglomerates began to enlarge their vertical subcontracting and supplier networks with small- and medium-sized firms, hence solidifying their monopoly power in technical innovation investment. Under the gradual change of the state-chaebol power dynamic toward the latter and freer overseas financing due to deregulation, these measures generated a mirage with another labor productivity boom that lasted until the mid-1990s, also acting as a carrot to appease the working class. After all, the case of Korea before the Asian crisis was an unusual example among developing countries, which successfully intensified both the absolute and relative surplus value extraction in Marxian parlance.

However, with the late-1990s currency crisis, labor market liberalization began to be forced, which included the labor protection law relaxation, mass dismissal law introduction, and employment flexibility enhancement. Due to these neoliberal measures, real wage growth decelerated considerably while the productivity series showed a slightly smoother growth, which implies the

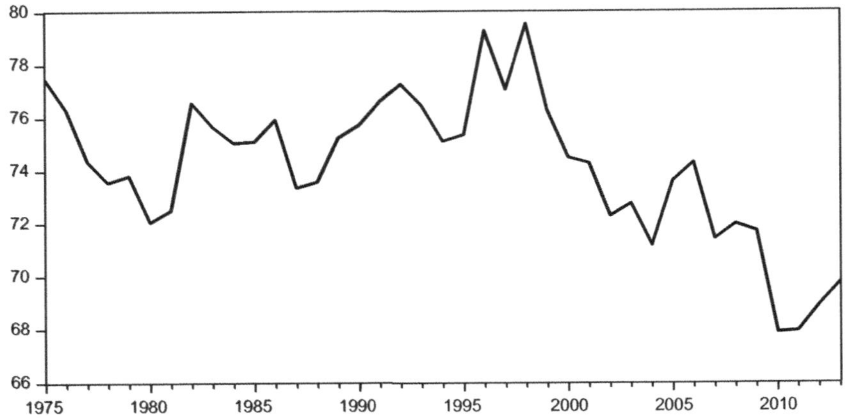

Fig. 4. Labor Income Share (Self-Employment Income Adjusted); All Industries, %. *Source:* Author's calculation from data in Bank of Korea (2015b). *Note:* Income data for adjustment are available only from 1975.

deterioration of labor income shares in the functional income distribution. Actually, the labor share dropped by almost 10 percentage points during the post-crisis period (see Fig. 4).[4] This reversal was more pronounced in manufacturing, which suffered from a mass employment reduction and became more vulnerable to price competition from rivals abroad compared to the non-tradeable service sector.

Based on the brief historical observations above, we econometrically examined the long-run relationship between real wages and labor productivity. As a relevant strategy, we applied cointegration and the Granger-causality test based on the vector error-correction model (VECM) for Korea, like Marquetti (2004) did for the United States and de Souza (2014) did for a panel of countries. Because unit root tests clearly show that both series are nonstationary and integrated of order one (see Appendix), we first ascertained the presence of a long-run equilibrium between the two time series by using the methodology Johansen (1991) developed. The results clearly indicated a single cointegrating vector, which implies some comovement between the two series in the long run (see Appendix). Then, we estimated the VECM as given in Eqs. (3) and (4),

$$\Delta \mathrm{LP}_t = \alpha_1 + \sum_{i=1}^{p} \beta_{1i} \Delta \mathrm{LP}_{t-i} + \sum_{i=1}^{p} \beta_{2i} \Delta \mathrm{RW}_{t-i} + \gamma_1 \hat{\epsilon}_{t-1} + u_{1t} \tag{3}$$

$$\Delta \mathrm{RW}_t = \alpha_2 + \sum_{i=1}^{p} \theta_{1i} \Delta \mathrm{RW}_{t-i} + \sum_{i=1}^{p} \theta_{2i} \Delta \mathrm{LP}_{t-i} + \gamma_2 \hat{\epsilon}_{t-1} + u_{2t} \tag{4}$$

where LP and RW denote labor productivity and real wages, ϵ is an error-correction term in a normalized form, and u is a random error term. Given that we have only 44 annual observations, a maximum lag length of 4 is imposed on the equations and the lag length is chosen based on the Akaike and Schwartz criterion. The optimal lags were mostly one or two, hence we reported both cases for a robustness check. Inasmuch as the existence of cointegration implies the Granger causality but does not indicate the direction of causality, we further examined both the short-run and long-run Granger causality within the VECM. The causality was obtained by testing the long-run (error-correction term) and short-run (differenced explanatory variables) effects together with the joint F-statistic (Gujarati, 2011, pp. 272–274; Lütkepohl, 2005, p. 262).[5] That is, for Eq. (3), if the null hypothesis $H_0 : \beta_{21} = \beta_{22} = \cdots = \beta_{2j} = 0$ and $\gamma_1 = 0$ is rejected, the real wages do Granger-cause labor productivity. The symmetrical hypothesis, whether labor productivity Granger-causes real wages, is also tested in the same manner. The results are reported in Table 2.

Table 2 reports the existence of unidirectional causality from real wages to labor productivity, and the causality is stronger for manufacturing than other industries overall. The empirical verification that real wages precede labor productivity, a more precise interpretation of Granger causality, implies that real wage increases entice capitalists, under competitive pressure from other capitalists, into implementing technological progress to secure their own profitability. The magnitude of such "wage-cost induced" labor productivity growth seems to be substantial given that Vergeer and Kleinknecht (2011) reported 0.31–0.39 percentage points for a panel data of OECD countries (1960–2004) and Naastepad (2006) attributed 90% of the Dutch productivity growth slowdown after 1982 to the decline in real wage growth. Meanwhile, the causal direction

Table 2. Granger-Causality Test Between the Real Wage Rate and Labor Productivity.

Direction of Causality		Lag 1	Lag 2
		Joint F-Statistic	
All-Industry	RW ⇏ LP	4.757**	4.359**
	LRW ⇏ LLP	2.290*	2.601*
	LP ⇏ RW	1.173	1.011
	LLP ⇏ LRW	2.701*	2.188
Manufacturing	RW ⇏ LP	16.773***	11.933***
	LRW ⇏ LLP	3.415**	4.280**
	LP ⇏ RW	0.267	0.873
	LLP ⇏ LRW	1.093	2.723*

Note: ⇏ means the null hypothesis of non-causality.
*Significant at 10%, **significant at 5%, ***significant at 1%.

from real wages to labor productivity runs counter to the Neoclassical marginal productivity theory, which states that wages are determined with respect to productivity. Except for variants of the efficiency wage theory, the Neoclassical proposition that higher productivity will cause higher real wages lacks empirical support, at least for Korea.[6]

CAPITAL PRODUCTIVITY PUZZLE

It is worth noting why we should proceed to the separate discussion of capital productivity changes. The direction of causality from real wages to labor productivity cannot be ascribed only to the MBTC. The causality can also be explained in the context of the Kaldor–Verdoorn effect, which suggests that aggregate demand spurred by wage share increases, more obviously in a wage-led economy, affects the learning-by-doing and division of labor leading to higher labor productivity. Similarly, the Neoclassical efficiency wage theory also suggests that higher wages attract more productive workers who rationally avoid being dismissed. That is, the econometric finding of causation from real wages to labor productivity is simply a confirmation of MBTC's necessary (but not sufficient) condition.[7] For this reason, the factors that underpin MBTC in terms of capital productivity change merit a detailed examination; hence, we first investigated the relationship between real wages and capital productivity.

Fig. 5, the scatter plot with regression line between the two variables, shows it is evident that capital productivity growth depends negatively on real wage growth.[8] This result implies that capital-using technological progress has been

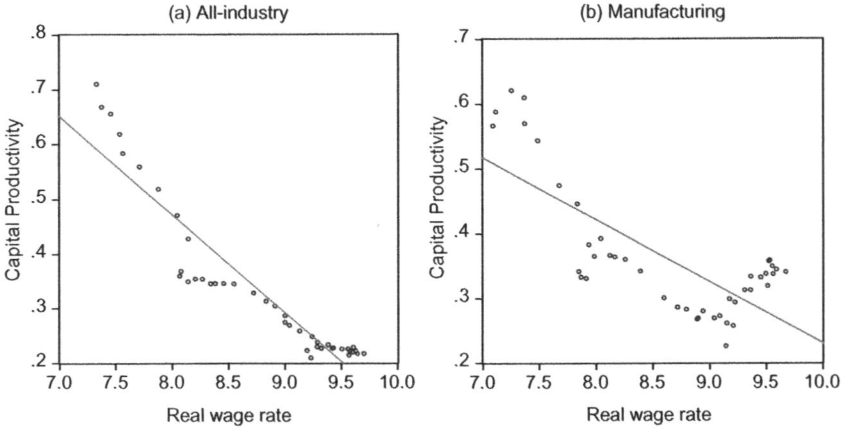

Fig. 5. Capital Productivity and (Log) Real Wage Rate, 1970–2013. (a) All-industry. (b) Manufacturing. *Source:* Author's Calculation from data available in Bank of Korea (2015a, 2015b) and Ministry of Employment and Labor (laborstat.molab.go.kr).

adopted more frequently against the increase of workers' power, which again confirms the predominance of MBTC in the long run.

However, as mentioned, the post-crisis period saw an impressive and positive capital productivity growth, particularly in manufacturing. Capital productivity increase per se can be interpreted as an enhanced efficiency of capital in terms of an output increase realized on the basis of a given stock of capital. If such dynamism was caused, as generally conceived, by virtue of the adoption of new innovative technologies, the hypothesis of MBTC's dominance is debatable, if not untenable. Michl (1992) stresses that endogenous capital-saving technical change may emerge as the effect of learning-by-doing driven by cumulative output while the exogenous natural direction of technology is capital using, and the opposite combination of exogenous capital-saving and endogenous capital-using technical change is also plausible. In other words, which aspect of capital productivity change will prevail depends not on a priori theorems but on empirical grounds. Hence, we explored several figures and statistics of potential factors that may have enhanced capital productivity, each of which would entail contrasting tenets from Neoclassical, Keynesian, or Marxian economics.

First, from the viewpoint of Neoclassical endogenous growth theory, R&D investment is critical for enhancing capital efficiency. The diffusion of innovative technologies can help an economy build new types of dynamic efficiency. Aside from methodological flaws like "setting up capital-like sectors for the production of human capital and R&D, bundling up and representing technical change through the device of treating it like a new factor of production" (Fine & Dimakou, 2016, p. 58), it is undeniable that technological advances related with so-called knowledge creation might have operated to some extent. However, examining the figures compiled in the OECD Structural Analysis database (2016), R&D intensity of high and medium-high technology manufacturers, which is calculated as R&D expenditures as a percentage of value added, rose from 10.1% in 1995 to 13.7% in 2009. Similar increments are neither uncommon among OECD economies nor comparable to those of advanced economies such as the United States (from 16.5% to 21.8%), the United Kingdom (from 11.0% to 15.2%), and Japan (from 14.2% to 22.7%), who are said to be in a Solovian steady state. Besides, the national balance sheet accounts (Bank of Korea, 2015a) show that, while the share of intellectual property products in total fixed assets of all corporations rose from 1.8% in 1970 to 9.9% in 2013, the share's annual growth rate has dropped from 4.8% in the pre-crisis to 2.6% in the post-crisis period. In summary, the Neoclassical orthodoxy which accentuates technology diffusion, knowledge accumulation, and the like, does not persuasively explain why capital productivity appreciates during economic downturns.

Second, we traced the cyclical demand-side factor's effect on capital productivity because Fig. 5 may have disclosed only the long-run trend aspect of capital productivity. It is motivated by the Kaleckian reasoning, which states that capital investment is a function of the changes in the expected profit rate and capacity utilization (hereafter, "CU", Bhaduri & Marglin, 1990; Hein, 2008).

The increase of CU, which commonly serves as a proxy for cyclical demand,[9] stimulates further investment, and the effect may well be reflected in capital productivity.

Hence, we plot the CU rate and the cyclical element of the HP-filtered ($\lambda = 100$) capital productivity in Fig. 6. Although a robust relationship between the level variables in different time periods has not been found, the cyclical series of capital productivity shows a very similar evolution to the CU rate, which means capital productivity moves procyclically.[10] In other words, the role of demand-side shocks in technical change is sufficiently relevant, aside from the traditional concern of the short-run versus the long-run breadth of analysis. Consequently, temporary aggregate demand rebounds including a short boom in the mid-2000s, contributed to the rise of capital productivity, if not a complete reversal of the long-run trend.

Last, but most importantly, turning to a Marxian perspective, exploitation and class conflict dynamics are another key to puzzle out capital productivity appreciation. As inferred from the simple identity $Y/K = (L/K) \times (Y/L)$, the movement of capital productivity is the combination of capital intensity and labor productivity.

Regarding the first term (L/K) of the identity, it is bound to decrease with higher capital deepening which substitutes capital for labor. But, the annual capital deepening growth rate has almost halved from 9.33% (1987–1997) to 5.11% (1998–2013) for all industries and from 11.83% to 6.70% for manufacturing. The primary culprit that put a damper on capital deepening is the rising price of capital goods. As Fig. 7 shows, although the cheap and stable price of capital goods, partly credited to the previous developmental state's resource allocation, fueled massive capital-intensive investment, the relative price to the price of output since the Asian crisis has steeply risen.

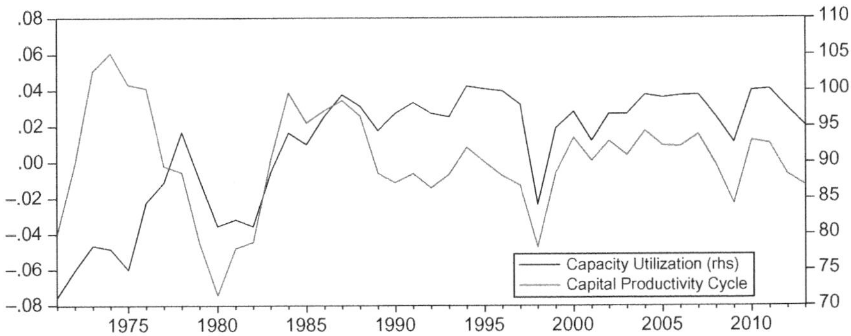

Fig. 6. Capacity Utilization and Cyclical Component of Capital Productivity; Manufacturing. *Source:* Bank of Korea, Author's calculation. *Note:* Capacity utilization rate's benchmark year is 2010.

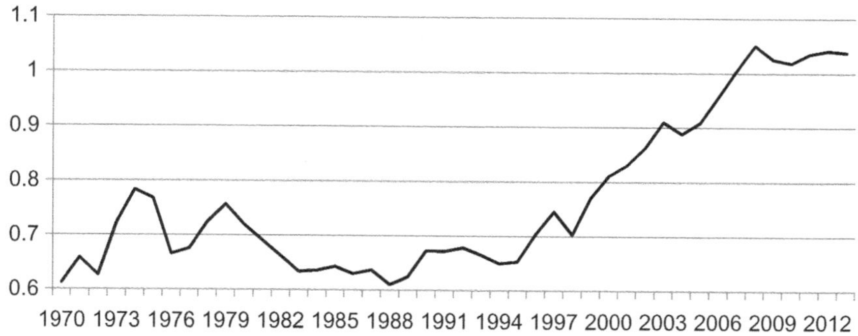

Fig. 7. Relative Price of Capital Goods to the GDP Deflator, Manufacturing. *Source:* Bank of Korea, Author's calculation.

The capital goods price hike clearly facilitates investment with capital-saving rather than capital-using technologies. But more expensive capital goods do not fully explain the decline in capital deepening. As implied by the data shown in Fig. 4, profit income share soared beginning with the crisis. The ratio of corporate saving to disposable income also increased drastically from 2.9% (1997) to 11.0% (2010). The corporate saving glut stemmed from surging operating surplus as well as benefits from radical tax breaks by the neoliberal state, and reduction of financial costs in a long, low-interest environment, etc. That is, it's unclear whether capitalists could ill afford to increase capital-intensive investment only owing to cost burden of capital goods. Rather, the slowdown in capital deepening also reflects worker's non-threatening bargaining power and moderated wage increase which contributed to the reduction of firms' incentives for capital-using technologies.[11]

As for the second term (Y/L) of the identity, the issues are more delicate. Labor productivity growth sizably contributed to sustaining and raising capital productivity for this period. Interestingly, for the period 1998–2013, though not appreciable as a pre-crisis period, average labor productivity growth per annum in manufacturing was over 7.4%. The record is noteworthy because it was achieved without vigorous capital deepening as explained above.

Given that the labor productivity series described in this paper was constructed as output per total hours worked, the labor productivity increase was primarily due to the working hours reduction demanded by Korean workers' strenuous struggle and international pressure, which crucially resulted in the 40-hour workweek system adoption in 2004. Fig. 8 shows there has been a gradual decline in average hours worked per worker since the mid-1980s, although Korea is still not free from the infamy of recording the first or second longest working hours among OECD economies.

On the other hand, the relatively high labor productivity growth reflects intensified worker exploitation. It became easier for firms to extract labor

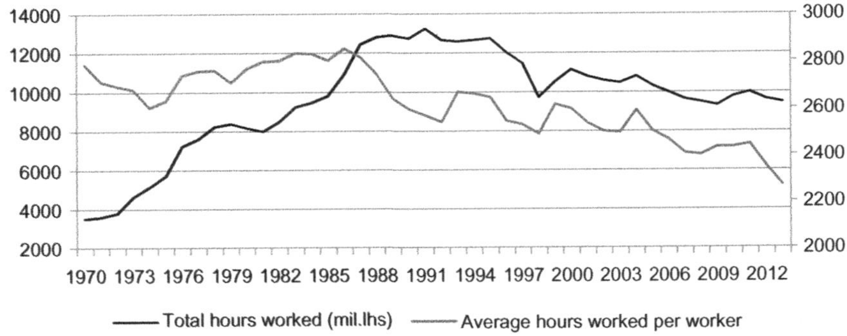

Fig. 8. Annual Working Hours; Manufacturing. *Source:* laborstat.molab.go.kr (Ministry of Employment and Labor).

productivity increases by further expanding the use of temporary workers and low-wage subcontractors. Labor market flexibility reforms for over a decade have not only greatly reduced workers' ability to negotiate higher wages and obtain employment stability but also frustrated worker solidarity. As a result, Korea has the highest incidence of low-paid work among full-time workers and the third-highest level of earnings dispersion, just below the United States and Israel as of 2011 (OECD, 2013; Figure 3.4). Moreover, temporary employment accounts for 22.4% of total dependent employment in Korea – the fourth largest among OECD members. Such workers are least likely to move into permanent employment among their counterparts in 15 other OECD members, which is true over both 1-year (11.1%) and 3-year (22.4%) horizon (OECD, 2013; Table 3.7).

It is doubtful whether such cost-cutting strategies as nonregular employment and external labor flexibility are sustainable for long-run economic growth (Lucidi & Kleinknecht, 2010).[12] But these organizational changes deserve to be called "effort-biased technical change" using Green's (2004) terminology, as they demand more highly committed and more productive "human capital" by using temporary workers and contractors in the absence of substantial capital deepening. After all, it was the highly strengthened power of capitalists vis-à-vis workers under the prolonged stagnation that enabled the contradictory capital productivity appreciation. In theory, the bias of technical change does not presuppose a high or low growth rate of capital intensity. However, as in our case, the United States (1982–1997), Argentina (1982–1994), and Chile (1964–1989) together show that Hicks-neutral technical change, where both labor productivity and capital productivity rise, occurred when capital deepening was lethargic (Mendoza, 2007; Mohun, 2009). And they have in common that those eras are marked by the relative weakening or defeat of the working class. It suggests that although the physical outcome of technical change may be neutral in the strict sense of the word, the driver of direction in technical change is far from being "neutral" as the class conflicts center on the adoption of specific technologies.

CONCLUDING REMARKS

This paper empirically examined the bias of technical change and investigated its determinants in Korea. The endogenous direction of technical change has been a rather neglected topic in Neoclassical growth literature, which is especially true for Korea who achieved extremely rapid growth. Instead, we used the GDS to show that the labor-saving and capital-using pattern have been the dominant type of technical progress. The relationship between technical change and real wage growth via the evolution of labor and capital productivity verified the historical direction of technical change against the rise and fall of the working class, which is the rationale behind the MBTC. Furthermore, the direction in technical change during the post-crisis period suggests that sluggish wage growth with undermined workers' power ironically contributes to attenuating the incentives for technological progress. Likewise, the contemporary deviation of capital productivity from the long-run trend of MBTC is not attributable to the vitality of new technological innovations, but rather is the reflection of class dynamics over extracting productivity under weaker capital deepening.

Our study's policy implications are straightforward. The alternative growth strategy against the contemporary secular recession should embrace policies that favor increases in real wages and wage shares. Taking MBTC into consideration, the recent deterioration of labor unions and their bargaining power prolongs the recession by deterring technical progress as well as by only stifling effective demand. In this regard, our findings suggest that higher wage-induced technical innovation under stable employment conditions will offer the tipping point for economic recovery with decent work.

However, two points are worth mentioning regarding growth dynamics. First, the dominance of the endogenous MBTC pattern may forecast a gloomy picture for workers because higher real wage growth may generate a lower employment by accelerating the worker-replacing technology. MBTC's job-loss potential can primarily reduce the wage-fueled growth effects that are strongly underlined by the recent Post-Keynesian literature. Although the question of whether such trade-offs will be substantively significant in Korea and other specific economies should be explored in future research, the effect of wage increase on aggregate demand may be overestimated if we pay scant attention to the aspects of technical change that appear in employment.[13] Second, as long as the trend of MBTC with a constant or rising labor share logically incurs the tendency for the rate of profit to fall, an intense class struggle from a capitalist counter-attack is inevitable, for which the Korean economy has been no exception as we have shown. In other words, the dominance of MBTC allows little room for class compromise or cooperative capitalist growth that is suggested by naive Keynesian wishes. These will be knotty points for the pro-labor economics camps to settle, when designing alternative growth policies.

NOTES

1. Recent empirical results such as OECD (2015) and Chun, Miyagawa, Pyo, and Tonogi (2015) find that Korea's TFP growth rate and its contribution to economic growth have long been fairly high even before the Asian crisis, while the more widespread recognition is that that the quantitative increase of factor inputs, rather than qualitative TFP, drove Korea's rapid growth (Krugman, 1994; Young, 1995).

2. More recently, Acemoglu (2010) emphasizes the way in which the relative abundance of the production factor, including different types of labor, determines the direction of technical change.

3. Basu (2010) and Hölzl (2010) address the subtle but significant differences between the Neoclassical- and Classical-induced innovation approaches.

4. It is well known that labor income share more commonly used in official statistics underestimates the share of employee compensation in value added, because it calculates all income of the self-employed as capital share. However, income of the self-employed comprises both labor and capital income, and there is a significant difference between the usual labor share and self-employment-income-adjusted labor share (Gollin, 2002). In particular, Korea has a 28.2% proportion of self-employed to fully employed, which is far higher than the United States (6.8%), Japan (11.8%), and the average of OECD members (15.8%) as of 2012 (OECD, 2014). Therefore, we recalculated the labor share by omitting the operating surplus of private unincorporated enterprises (OSPUE) from the denominator (Y), which is algebraically the same as assuming the proportion of labor and capital income of OSPUE is equal to that of the rest of the economy.

5. This methodology is challengeable as it not only requires unit root and cointegrating rank pretests but also might be biased toward rejecting the non-causality null since cointegration implies existence of long-run causality for at least one direction. Therefore, Toda and Yamamoto's (1995) methodology which estimates augmented VAR with level variables may be a better strategy which reduces the risks of wrongly identifying the order of integration. However, as Toda and Yamamoto (1995, p. 246) explicitly explains, when the VAR's lag length is just one as in our paper, the inefficiency caused by adding even one extra lag might be relatively large.

6. Although not based on the same framework as ours, previous research for other countries such as Australia (Kumar, Webber, & Perry, 2012) and Turkey (Bildirici & Alp, 2008) also confirm the causal direction from real wages to labor productivity.

7. The Kaleckian models, such as You (1994) and Cassetti (2003) described, successfully highlight the endogenous demand-side conditions of facilitating technological innovations, but the innovations' capital-using aspect is not addressed. Likewise, although Hein and Tarassow (2010) and Storm and Naastepad (2013) attempted to differentiate the mixed effects of technical change attributed to both the Kaleckian demand effect and the Marxian effect, their empirical estimations are limited to the change in labor productivity only.

8. We refrain from repeating the econometric inferences for capital productivity. The capital productivity series for all-industry does not have a unit root (see Appendix), as in both series of labor productivity and real wages, and the ECM specifications are not applicable due to the lack of evidence of cointegration. Hence, a more robust econometric specification against spurious regressions should employ a lengthy model, for example, the autoregressive distributed lag model with other control variables; however, we only present several graphs for the sake of brevity and intuitive obviousness.

9. The choice of the demand-side variable is an open issue, but we chose the CU rate as the best proxy. The comparison with other conventional options, such as the GDP's cycle component or output gap, runs the risk of tautology because the capital productivity variable already has the output term in the numerator. Moreover, output gap estimates based on potential output are neither theoretically flawless nor officially reported in Korea.

10. Schoder (2012) provides theoretical arguments as to capital productivity procyclicality for the reason that firms seek to adjust capital productivity to narrow the gap between realized and desired CU.

11. Other reasons for the remarkable discrepancy between corporate saving and investment can be deduced from various factors; for example, financialization (Stockhammer, 2004) and monopoly (Foster & McChesney, 2012). To verify these hypotheses in detail is beyond the scope of this paper.

12. Recently, even IMF researchers (Aoyagi & Ganelli, 2013) propose reducing the labor market duality and increasing wages to move toward higher growth.

13. Storm and Naastepad (2013, p. 109) correctly notes, "the higher is the sensitivity of productivity growth to real wage growth, the more limited will be the strength of the wage-led nature of aggregate demand."

ACKNOWLEDGMENTS

This Research was supported by Research Funds of Mokpo National University in 2015. I am grateful to the editor and the two anonymous referees for insightful critiques and helpful suggestions. Any and all errors that remain are my own.

REFERENCES

Acemoglu, D. (2010). When does labor scarcity encourage innovation? *Journal of Political Economy, 118*(6), 1037–1078.

Allen, R. (2011). Why the industrial revolution was British: Commerce, induced invention, and the scientific revolution. *The Economic History Review, 64*(2), 357–384.

Aoyagi, C., & Ganelli, G. (2013). *The path to higher growth: Does revamping Japan's dual labor market matter?* Working Paper 13/202. International Monetary Fund.

Bank of Korea. (2015a). *National balance sheet accounts* (ecos.bok.or.kr).

Bank of Korea. (2015b). *National income and product accounts* (ecos.bok.or.kr).

Basu, D. (2010). Marx-biased technical change and the neoclassical view of income distribution. *Metroeconomica, 61*(4), 593–620.

Bhaduri, A., & Marglin, S. (1990). Unemployment and the real wage: The economic basis for contesting political ideologies. *Cambridge Journal of Economics, 14*(4), 375–393.

Bildirici, M., & Alp, E. A. (2008). The relationship between wages and productivity: TAR unit root and TAR cointegration approach. *International Journal of Applied Econometrics and Quantitative Studies*, *5*(1), 93–110.

Cassetti, M. (2003). Bargaining power, effective demand and technical progress: A Kaleckian model of growth. *Cambridge Journal of Economics*, *27*(3), 449–464.

Chun, H., Miyagawa, T., Pyo H. K., & Tonogi, K. (2015). *Do intangibles contribute to productivity growth in East Asian countries? Evidence from Japan and Korea*. RIETI Discussion Paper Series, 15-E-055.

da Silva, E. A. (1991). The wage-profit curve in Brazil: An input-output model with fixed capital, 1975. *Review of Radical Political Economics*, *23*(1–2), 104–110.

de Souza, J. P. A. (2014). *Real wages and labor-saving technical change: Evidence from a panel of manufacturing industries in mature and labor-surplus economics*. Working Paper-03. University of Massachusetts at Amherst.

Drandrakis, E., & Phelps, E. (1966). A model of induced invention, growth, and distribution. *Economic Journal*, *76*, 823–840.

Duménil, G., & Lévy. D. (1995). A stochastic model of technical change: An application to the US Economy. *Metroeconomica*, *46*(3), 213–245.

Duménil, G., & Lévy. D. (2003). Technology and distribution: Historical trajectories *à la* Marx. *Journal of Economic Behavior and Organization*, *52*(2), 201–233.

Easterly, W., & Levine, R. (2001). What have we learned from a decade of empirical research on growth? It's not factor accumulation: Stylized facts and growth models. *World Bank Economic Review*, *15*(2), 177–219.

Felipe, J., Laviña, E., & Fan, E. X. (2008). The diverging patterns of profitability, investment and growth of China and India during 1980-2003. *World Development*, *36*(5), 741–774.

Felipe, J., & McCombie, J. S. L. (2013). *The aggregate production function and the measurement of technical change: 'Not even wrong'*. Cheltenham: Edward Elgar.

Ferretti, F. (2008). Patterns of technical change: A geometrical analysis using the wage-profit rate schedule. *International Review of Applied Economics*, *22*(5), 565–583.

Fine, B., & Dimakou, O. (2016). *Macroeconomics: A critical companion*. London: Pluto Press.

Foley, D. K., & Marquetti, A. (1999). Productivity, employment and growth in European integration. *Metroeconomica*, *50*(3), 277–300.

Foley, D. K., & Michl, T. R. (1999). *Growth and distribution*. Cambridge, MA: Harvard University Press.

Foster, J. B., & McChesney, R. W. (2012). *The endless crisis: How monopoly-finance capital produces stagnation and upheaval from the U.S.A. to China*. New York, NY: Monthly Review Press.

Gollin, D. (2002). Getting income shares right. *Journal of Political Economy*, *110*(2), 458–474.

Green, F. (2004). Why has work effort become more Intense? *Industrial Relations: A Journal of Economy and Society*, *43*(4), 709–741.

Groll, S., & Orzech, Z. B. (1990). Marx's social dynamics and neutral technical progress: a contradiction? *Australian Economic Papers*, *29*(54), 85–100.

Gujarati, D. (2011). *Econometrics by example*. Basingstoke: Palgrave Macmillan.

Hart-Landsberg, M., Jeong, S.-J., & Westra, R. (Eds.). (2007). *Marxist perspectives on South Korea in the global econo*. Aldershot: Ashgate.

Hein, E. (2008). *Money, distribution conflict and capital accumulation: Contributions to 'monetary analysis'*. Basingstoke: Palgrave Macmillan.

Hein, E., & Tarassow, A. (2010). Distribution, aggregate demand and productivity growth: Theory and empirical results for six OECD countries based on a post-Kaleckian model. *Cambridge Journal of Economics*, *34*(4), 727–754.

Hölzl, W. (2010). Was there a Marxian bias in Austrian manufacturing? Evidence on the direction of technical change, 1978-1994. *International Review of Applied Economics*, *24*(1), 35–56.

Johansen, S. (1991). Estimation and hypothesis testing of cointegration vectors in Gaussian vector autoregressive models. *Econometrica*, *59*(6), 1551–1580.

Kennedy, C. (1964). Induced bias in innovation and the theory of distribution. *The Economic Journal, 74*(295), 541–547.

Krugman, P. (1994). The myth of Asia's miracle. *Foreign Affairs, 73*(6), 62–78.

Kumar, S., Webber, D. J., & Perry, G. (2012). Real wages, inflation and labour productivity in Australia. *Applied Economics, 44*(23), 2945–2954.

Kurz, H. (2010). Technical progress, capital accumulation and income distribution in Classical economics: Adam Smith, David Ricardo and Karl Marx. *European Journal of the History of Economic Thought, 17*(5), 1183–1222.

Lee, K., Lin, J. Y., & Chang, H.-J. (2005). Late marketisation versus late industrialisation in east Asia. *Asian-Pacific Economic Literature, 19*(1), 42–59.

Lucas, R. E. Jr. (1993). Making a miracle. *Econometrica, 61*(2), 251–272.

Lucidi, F., & Kleinknecht, A. (2010). Little innovation, many jobs: An econometric analysis of the Italian labour productivity crisis. *Cambridge Journal of Economics, 34*(3), 525–546.

Lütkepohl, H. (2005). *New introduction to multiple time series analysis*. Berlin: Springer.

Marquetti, A. (2003). Analyzing historical and regional patterns of technical change from a Classical-Marxian perspective. *Journal of Economic Behavior and Organization, 52*, 191–200.

Marquetti, A. (2004). Do rising real wages increase the rate of labor-saving technical change? Some econometric evidence. *Metroeconomica, 55*(4), 432–441.

Mendoza, G. (2007). Economic growth models and growth tendencies in major Latin American countries and in the United States, 1963-2003. *Investigación Económica, 66*(262), 59–87.

Michl, T. (1992). Capital and labor productivity. *Review of Radical Political Economics, 24*(2), 45–50.

Mohun, S. (2009). Aggregate capital productivity in the US economy, 1964-2001. *Cambridge Journal of Economics, 33*(5), 1023–1046.

Naastepad, C. W. M. (2006). Technology, demand, and distribution: A cumulative growth model with an application to the Dutch productivity slowdown. *Cambridge Journal of Economics, 30*(3), 403–434.

Ochoa, E. (1989). Value, prices and wage-profit curves in the U.S. economy. *Cambridge Journal of Economics, 13*(3), 413–429.

OECD. (2013). *Strengthening social cohesion in Korea*. Paris: OECD Publishing.

OECD. (2014). *OECD Factbook 2014*. Retrieved from http://dx.doi.org/10.1787/factbook-2014-en

OECD. (2015). *OECD compendium of productivity indicators*. Paris: OECD Publishing.

OECD. (2016). *Structural analysis database*. Retrieved from http://www.oecd.org/sti/ind/stanstructuralanalysisdatabase.htm

Ra, Y.-S., & Shim, K.-W. (2009). *The Korean case study: Past experience and new trends in training policies*. World Bank SP Discussion Paper, no.0931.

Schoder, C. (2012). *Endogenous capital productivity in the Kaleckian growth model. theory and evidence*. Working Paper 102, Macroeconomic Policy Institute.

Seguino, S. (2000). The investment function revisited: Disciplining capital in South Korea. *Journal of Post Keynesian Economics, 22*(2), 313–338.

Stockhammer, E. (2004). Financialisation and the slowdown of accumulation. *Cambridge Journal of Economics, 28*(5), 719–741.

Storm, S., & Naastepad, C. W. M. (2013). Wage-led or profit-led supply: Wages, productivity and investment. In M. Lavoie & E. Stockhammer (Eds.), *Wage-led growth-an equitable strategy for economic recovery*. London: Palgrave Macmillan.

Toda, H. Y., & Yamamoto, T. (1995). Statistical inference in vector autoregressions with possibly integrated processes. *Journal of Econometrics, 66*(1), 225–250.

Tsoulfidis, L., & Rieu, D.-M. (2006). Labor values, prices of production, and wage-profit rate frontiers of the Korean economy. *Seoul Journal of Economics, 19*, 275–295.

Vaona, A. (2011). Profit rate dynamics, income distribution, structural and technical change in Denmark, Finland and Italy. *Structural Change and Economic Dynamics, 22*(3), 247–268.

Vergeer, R., & Kleinknecht, A. (2010-11). The impact of labor market deregulation on productivity: A panel data analysis of 19 OECD countries (1960-2004). *Journal of Post Keynesian Economics*, *33*(2), 371–408.

You, J.-I. (1994). Macroeconomic structure, endogenous technical change and growth. *Cambridge Journal of Economics*, *18*(2), 213–233.

You, J.-I., & Chang H.-J. (1993). The myth of free labour market in Korea. *Contributions to Political Economy*, *12*(1), 29–46.

Young, A. (1995). The tyranny of numbers: Confronting the statistical realities of the east Asian growth. *Quarterly Journal of Economics*, *110*(3), 641–680.

APPENDIX

Table A1. Unit Root Tests.

Variables		LP	LLP	RW	LRW	CP
All-Industry	*ADF* Levels	−1.152	−2.131	−2.395	−2.378	−6.895***
	First difference	−9.427***	−6.725***	−2.568*	−3.953***	−4.241***
	PP Levels	−1.804	−2.146	−2.372	−2.433	−5.409***
	First difference	−8.705***	−6.729***	−4.447***	−3.765***	−4.343***
Manufacturing	*ADF* Levels	2.368	−2.429	−2.660	−2.370	−2.263
	First difference	−7.437***	−6.961***	−2.706*	−3.971***	−4.498***
	PP Levels	−0.061	−2.429	−2.055	−2.089	−2.139
	First difference	−6.637***	−6.966***	−3.459*	−3.912**	−4.622***

Note: L, logarithm; RW, real wage rate; LP, labor productivity; CP, capital productivity; ADF, Augmented Dickey–Fuller test; PP, Phillips–Perron test.
*Significant at 10%; **significant at 5%; ***significant at 1%.

Table A2. Johansen Bivariate Cointegration.

Hypothesized Number of Cointegrating Equations			λ-Trace Statistic	λ-Max Statistic
All-Industry	LP-RW	None	22.018**	19.898**
		At most 1	2.120	2.120
	LLP-LRW	None	13.675*	12.526*
		At most 1	1.149	1.149
Manufacturing	LP-RW	None	23.611**	22.063**
		At most 1	1.547	1.547
	LLP-LRW	None	17.431**	15.766**
		At most 1	1.665	1.665

*Significant at 10%; **significant at 5%.

DYNAMICS OF THE RATE OF SURPLUS VALUE AND THE "NEW NORMAL" OF THE CHINESE ECONOMY

Hao Qi

ABSTRACT

This paper builds homogenous series of the rate of surplus value (RSV) for the Chinese economy over the extended period 1956–2014 with a Marxian approach. It finds that the high profitability that stimulated capital accumulation in the decade before the 2008 crisis had relied on the continuous growth in the RSV. Given that the global crisis and changes in the domestic economy undermine all the conditions maintaining the accumulation model (an expanding external market, a relatively large reserve army of labor, and a low debt-income ratio), the RSV has failed to increase and profitability declined since 2008. Thus, this paper interprets the so-called new normal of the Chinese economy as a stage of declining profitability that results mainly from the stagnant RSV and the rising value composition of capital.

Keywords: Rate of surplus value; profitability; new normal; Chinese economy

Return of Marxian Macro-dynamics in East Asia
Research in Political Economy, Volume 32, 105–129

ISSN: 0161-7230/doi:10.1108/S0161-723020170000032007

INTRODUCTION

This paper builds homogeneous series of the rate of surplus value (RSV, hereafter) for the Chinese economy using a Marxian approach. This method highlights the division between productive labor and unproductive labor and argues that the value that unproductive labor obtains is a transfer of surplus value. The origin of the approach dates back to classical economists including Adam Smith, David Ricardo, and Karl Marx; in recent decades, Moseley (1985) and Shaikh and Tonak (1994) developed the approach and made it empirically applicable with statistical data. Some country-specific studies have applied the approach and obtained interesting findings (Cronin, 2001; Maniatis, 2005; Mohun, 2005a, 2005b, 2013; Paitaridis & Tsoulfidis, 2011); nevertheless, no study following this method has been focused on the Chinese economy. The main barrier for applying the approach to the Chinese economy might be data availability; another might be theoretical issues of implementing the approach to an economy that experienced a transition from a state-socialist system to a capitalist system.

This paper has two objectives. First, it provides data series for the RSV and relevant Marxian variables (value composition of capital, the share of surplus value extracted by unproductive sectors, and gross and net rate of profit) by using recently published China's official statistical data. Although the calculation has to impose assumptions to the estimation procedures due to the lack of data, it makes those assumptions and procedures as transparent as possible. The data series cover an extended period of contemporary China from 1956 to 2014 – from the establishment of the state-socialist system to the seventh year since the global crisis broke out. This paper might be the first attempt to build series of Marxian variables for China over such an extended period.[1]

The second objective of this paper is to understand China's so-called new normal from the dynamics of the RSV and its crucial role in affecting profitability during the reform era.[2] The analysis finds that the RSV followed a U-shape from 1978 to 2008, reached the trough in 1997, stagnated, and slightly fell after 2008. While the RSV in China was not as high as that in the United States,[3] it reached its historical peak when the global crisis broke out. This paper uses a decomposition method to show that profitability had relied on the growth of the RSV underpinned by a series of economic and institutional conditions.[4] The global crisis and changes in the domestic economy, however, undermined all the conditions maintaining the accumulation model; therefore, this paper suggests the "new normal" be a stage of declining profitability caused by the failure of keeping the increase of the RSV. As the growth of the RSV cannot offset the increase in the value composition of capital, a falling tendency of profitability is threatening the Chinese economy.

In what follows, this paper is organized into four sections. Initially, theoretical issues on measuring Marxian variables for a transitioning economy are discussed. The following section constructs the RSV, discusses data issues, assumptions and estimation procedures, describes the trends of the RSV, and examines the relationship between the RSV and profitability. Then the conditions that had supported the growth of the RSV and why the RSV stagnated after the 2008 crisis are discussed. Finally, concludes the paper.

THEORETICAL ISSUES: MARXIAN VARIABLES IN A TRANSITIONING ECONOMY

The division between productive and unproductive labor is a perspective to see how the new value of an economy is circulated and distributed, which enables us to trace the flow of new value and measure critical Marxian variables (e.g. Marxian value added, variable capital, and surplus value). Some heterodox studies (e.g., Weisskopf, 1979) use distributive shares in GDP to measure the bargaining power of labor vis-à-vis capital; however, given that GDP accounting does not consider the transfer of surplus value, distributive shares in GDP do not necessarily reflect the distribution between labor and capital or the RSV. Another problem with GDP accounting is that it does not distinguish coexisting modes of production, which can also affect distributive shares.[5]

Current studies that take the transfer of surplus value into account start with restructuring the economy by the division of productive and unproductive labor (sectors) and then measure Marxian variables using data from input-output tables and GDP accounting. Empirical studies with this approach have achieved many interesting findings. Moseley (1985), Shaikh and Tonak (1994), and Paitaridis and Tsoulfidis (2011) find that the rise of unproductive activities in the United States after World War II has extracted an increasingly large share of surplus value, which repressed the net rate of profit of the economy. Mohun (2005a, 2005b, 2013) integrates the approach with a class analysis and finds that distributive shares of the working class (consisted of productive workers and unproductive workers) decreased in recent decades. However, most of the studies are focused on the US economy, whereas no study has applied to the Chinese economy.

China established a state-socialist economic system in 1956 when it accomplished the Socialist Transformation, and experienced the transition to a capitalism-dominated economic system that started in 1978 and accelerated after 1992. There was no capitalist component in the economy from 1956 to 1978, and the capitalist component did not play a major role until 1992. Given China's economic transition, can one apply the Marxian conceptions designed for a capitalist economy to the Chinese economy, in particular for the period before 1992?

We address this question in two steps. The first step is about the division between variable capital and surplus value. In a capitalist economy, it is the contested terrain in the workplace where exploitation occurs that generates the division between variable capital and surplus value. The micro-foundation of China's state-socialist economy was much different: all means of production were publicly owned assets; workers enjoyed job security and various benefits; before 1978, especially during the Cultural Revolution, workers had some rights to criticize cadres in factories; the economic inequality between workers and cadres was small. Although no capitalist-worker conflict existed in the socialist economy, there was a contradiction between workers and the state, between the national products distributed to workers as wages and that submitted to the state as surplus. Raising wages could enhance the living standards of workers; nevertheless, the state was aimed at not only enhancing the living conditions but also accomplishing industrialization, for which accumulation of surplus was obviously a prerequisite. Giving this contradiction, the distribution between workers and the state could reflect the realistic contradiction between workers' living standards and the aim of industrialization. For the sake of simplicity, admitting the difference between wages and variable capital and that between surplus and surplus value, the rest of the paper uses variable capital and surplus value for the entire period 1956–2014.

The second step is the division of productive and unproductive labor in a state-socialist economy. This division is not a new topic for Chinese economists. From the late 1970s to the early 1990s, intensive discussions on what is productive labor and unproductive labor in the socialist economy took place among Chinese economists. Meanwhile, China's official statistical system transited from the Material Product System (hereafter, MPS) to the U.N. System of National Accounts (hereafter, SNA). These discussions played a role in promoting the transition because reforming the official statistical system had to answer what is productive labor and unproductive labor in the first place. The main deficiency of the MPS is that it only treats "material production" (agriculture, mining, manufacturing, utilities, and construction) as productive activities and excludes all services from its scope, while the SNA treats the activities of all sectors as "productive" in the sense of creating GDP. As the state pursued the comparability with the national income of capitalist economies, it finally replaced the MPS with the SNA.[6] Among the Chinese economists who contributed to the discussions on productive labor and unproductive labor, Yu (1981) asserts that all services are productive and endorses the adoption of the SNA, while Sun (1981) and Wei (1981) insists that only "material production" is productive. Luo (1990) compares the differences between the MPS and SNA and argues that "material production" and some services are productive, whereas commerce, finance, and the state non-enterprise sector is unproductive, which shares many similarities with Shaikh and Tonak (1994). Both Luo (1990) and Shaikh and Tonak (1994) point out that there are a general distinction and a particular distinction (i.e., the difference in a specific relation of production) between productive and unproductive labor. Shaikh and Tonak (1994) suggest that household industry in a capitalist economy is productive because it

Table 1. The Chinese Economy from a Marxian Perspective.

The Whole Economy		
Enterprise Sector		Rest of the Economy
Productive sector	Unproductive sector	
Mining, manufacturing, utilities, construction, transportation, post and telecommunications, food and hotel services, social services	Commerce Finance Real estate	Agriculture Self-employment units Non-profit institutions for scientific research, education, culture, and medical services The state non-enterprise sector

produces certain use value according to the general distinction; however, it is unproductive of capital because it does not produce surplus value for capital according to the particular distinction. Similarly, Luo (1990) argues that agriculture in a socialist economy be unproductive according to the particular distinction.

Table 1 divides the Chinese economy into productive sectors and unproductive sectors with the Marxian approach based on Luo (1990) and Shaikh and Tonak (1994). "Productive sectors" means that there are some productive activities in these sectors, while "unproductive sectors" means that there is no productive activity in these sectors. A kind of labor is productive if it creates objects of use values, while labor is unproductive if it only distributes existing objects of use values or maintains social order (Shaikh & Tonak, 1994). Under this criterion, restaurant services are productive labor, while commercial and financial activities are unproductive labor. This paper focuses on the enterprise sector because first of all it was the dominant part of the economy over the entire period and secondly it was a relatively homogenous sector where the relation of production transited from the worker-socialist state relation to the worker-capital relation as the economic transition proceeded. Specifically, the enterprise sector consists of state-owned enterprises, state-holding enterprises, collective enterprises, and private enterprises.[7]

The enterprise sector does not include agriculture, self-employment units, non-profit institutions for scientific research, education, culture, and medical services (hereafter, non-profit institutions), and the state non-enterprise sector (governments, the legal system, and the military). People's communes were the main organization for agricultural production during the period before 1978, and rural households became the dominant production units after the de-collectivization reform in the early 1980s. Over the entire period 1956–2014, agriculture was different from the enterprise sector in distribution and employment. Luo (1990) suggests that agriculture does not belong to the dominant part of China's socialist economy. The self-employed sector expanded only after 1992, mainly based on household labor and a small fraction of wage labor.[8] Non-profit institutions were mostly public-funded over the entire period. Although Shaikh and Tonak (1994) treat public-funded institutions of education and medical services in the United States as government enterprises, the non-profit institutions in China are not any enterprises because they aimed at fulfilling certain needs of the state, rather than economic objectives such as output and profits.[9] The state non-enterprise sector obtains a transfer of surplus value from the enterprise sector in the form of taxes.

Within the enterprise sector, commerce, finance, and real estate are unproductive sectors in the sense that no productive activity exists in these sectors. In China's state-socialist economy, a part of the surplus value is transferred from productive sectors to unproductive sectors, similar to the transfer of surplus value in a capitalist economy. Supervisory labor in China's state-socialist economy was partially unproductive because it played a productive role in organizing production and meanwhile it aimed at promoting the absorption of surplus, similar to the supervisory labor in a capitalist economy.

DYNAMICS OF THE RSV AND RELEVANT MARXIAN VARIABLES IN THE ENTERPRISE SECTOR

This section introduces the procedures for calculating the RSV and related Marxian variables and discusses the assumptions for the estimation procedures and the potential biases that those assumptions may lead to; then this section discusses the trends of the RSV and relevant Marxian variables, and discusses the relationship between the RSV and the net rate of profit.

Methodology and Data

The RSV is the ratio of surplus value (SV) to variable capital (VC). The RSV, SV, and VC are given by Eqs. (1)–(3):

$$\mathrm{RSV} = \mathrm{SV}/\mathrm{VC} \tag{1}$$

$$\mathrm{VC} = (1-\alpha)\mathrm{EC_p} \tag{2}$$

$$\mathrm{SV} = \left(\mathrm{NV_p} - \mathrm{VC}\right) + \mathrm{TO_t} + \mathrm{RY_p} + \mathrm{RY_t} \tag{3}$$

In Eq. (2), $\mathrm{EC_p}$ is the employees' compensation of productive sectors, consisted of all the wages, salaries, and benefits of workers and managers; α is the share of supervisory labor's compensation in EC_p. In Eq. (3), NV_p is the net value added of the productive sector, which equals to the sum of EC_p, operating surplus and net taxes on production; TO_t is the total output of the commerce sector, which equals to the sum of intermediate inputs, depreciation of fixed capital, employees' compensation, operating surplus and net taxes of the commerce sector; RY_p and RY_t are royalty payments paid by productive sectors and the commerce sector to the finance sector as intermediate inputs, respectively.[10]

Regarding data sources, a rigorous calculation of the Marxian variables requires input-output tables. Although China began to compile input-output tables as early as 1973, the first input-output table that covers all sectors was compiled in 1992, whereas the previous tables only cover "material production" sectors of the MPS. Also, China's basic input-output table is updated every 5 years, so it is not continuous.[11] Thus, the paper uses the data of the income-approach national accounts instead, which covers almost all the years from 1978 to 2014. For the period 1956–1977, variables are estimated based on the data of national accounts and labor statistics.

The appendix introduces data sources, assumptions, and estimation procedures in detail. Here we discuss two of these assumptions. Due to the lack of data, we cannot measure supervisory labor's compensation. Thus, the first assumption is that $\alpha = 0$. This obviously unrealistic assumption will underestimate the RSV and is likely to cause more underestimation for the post-2000 period because there is evidence to show that since the late 1990s the management-worker inequality has increased for China's listed companies (Qi, 2014). On the other hand, some data show that the employment share of supervisory labor was stable. The supervisory share in mining, manufacturing, utilities, and construction employment varied within a narrow range from 9.8% to 11% over the period 1980-1997;[12] micro-level data also suggest that supervisory employees accounted for around 10% of total employment prior to 1990.[13]

The second assumption is that the redistribution of surplus value only takes place within the country. In reality, surplus value produced by China's productive sector can be distributed to a foreign trade sector, and vice versa. For instance, Wal-Mart who sells products imported from China in the United States may acquire surplus value created by the manufacturing exporter located in China. It is impossible to estimate this transfer of surplus value without detailed export and import input-output data. Given that current account surplus became increasingly large after 2001 when China joined the WTO, this kind of transfer might be considerable. Thus, this assumption is likely to underestimate the RSV after 2001.[14]

Long-term Trends of the RSV and Relevant Marxian Variables

Fig. 1 shows the long-term trend of the RSV. In the Maoist era (1956–1978), the RSV fluctuated severely in the 1950s and 1960s and became relatively

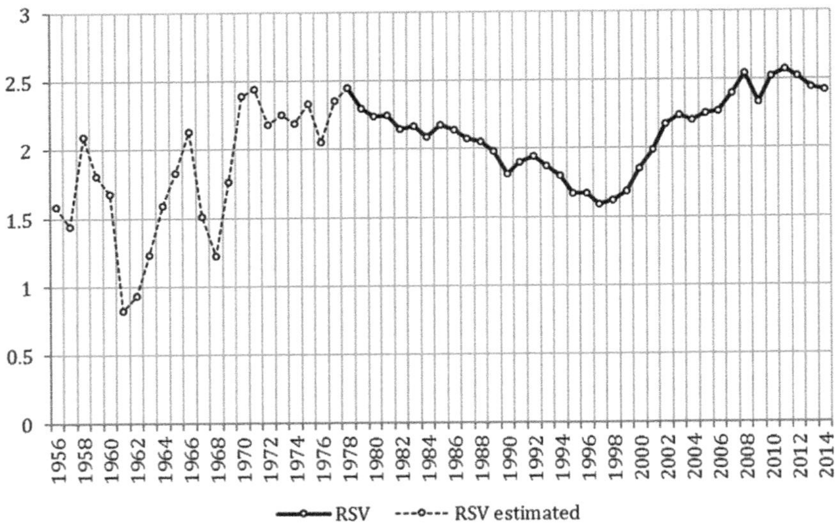

Fig. 1. Rate of Surplus Value, 1956–2014. *Data Sources*: See Data Appendix.

stable after 1970. Those severe fluctuations resulted from the massive accumulation during the Great Leap Forward movement (1958–1960) and the economic contractions in the early 1960s and the early period of the Cultural Revolution (1966–1976). In the reform era (1978 to present), the RSV shows a U-shape before 2009: it had a declining trend from 1978 to 1997 and then entered a rising trend until 2008. This U-shape of labor's share took place along with fast economic growth and development over the reform era. If we consider the RSV as a proxy for distribution inequality, this U-shape of the RSV contradicts the Kuznets curve that depicts the relationship between inequality and economic development (Kuznets, 1955). Using top income ratios and distributive shares in the national income, Piketty (2014) shows that the experiences of leading capitalist economies do not support the Kuznets curve. Here the Chinese facts do not support the Kuznets curve either.

Why did the RSV change in such a U manner? In the early stage of the reform era, the reformers undermined the incentive system within the factories of the Maoist era featured by nonmaterial incentives and encouraged the adoption of material incentives such as bonuses and piece wages. Workers lost some critical political rights but still enjoyed job security and various benefits. The economic inequality between workers and cadres in factories was small, and cadres tended to pursue higher wages and more benefits for both workers and themselves. In this situation, without the stick of unemployment, material incentives were increasingly ineffective in disciplining workers and absorbing surplus labor, which is why the RSV decreased from 1978 to the 1990s (Qi, 2015).

After 1997, despite lower than the RSV of the US economy, China's RSV grew much faster than the latter. The RSV fell from 2.45 in 1978 to 1.59 in 1997 and then increased to 2.55 in 2008. The RSV estimated with similar methods for the US economy was generally in a rising trend in the post-World War II period except the period 1964–1974 (Paitaridis & Tsoulfidis, 2011; Shaikh & Tonak, 1994); it increased from 2.2 in 1978 to 3.1 in 1997 and 3.5 in 2008 (Paitaridis & Tsoulfidis, 2011). The growth rate of China's RSV is comparable to that of the RSV in the Greek economy. Tsoulfidis and Tsaliki (2014) shows that the RSV in the Greek economy increased from 1.4 in 1990 to 2.3 in 2004 and after that slightly declined. Marina and Moseley (2000) find that the RSV in the Mexican economy grew rapidly from 1982 to 1993 at an average annual rate of 1.6%, which, however, is much slower than the growth of China's RSV from 1997 to 2008.

The fast growth of the RSV was possible, thanks to the expansion of the private sector and the reserve army of labor. Private enterprises use harsh management practices and disobey the Labor Law on signing labor contracts and restricting working hours. Thus, the RSV of the private sector is higher than that of the state-owned sector. The increase of the RSV echoes the falling share of the state-owned sector in the economy. In 1997, when the RSV reached its trough of the reform era, the Fifteenth National Congress of the Communist Party of China accelerated the reform on the state-owned sector, consisted of laying off workers, privatizing small- and medium-scale enterprises, and transforming large-scale enterprises into shareholding companies. Meanwhile, due to market competition and profit motivation, state-owned enterprises tended to adopt management and employment practices similar to those of private enterprises.

The reserve army of labor emerged as migrant workers from rural areas seek jobs in cities and the state-owned enterprises laid off massively. Despite a large rural underemployed population, the formation of a reserve army of labor requires institutional changes in both the rural and urban sectors. The de-collectivization of the rural economy, the stagnation of rural household income, the expansion of the urban private sector, and the tendency of the state-owned sector to replace urban workers with migrant workers prepared the necessary conditions for the influx of migrant workers. Meanwhile, laid-off workers of the state-owned sector also expanded the reserve army of labor. One of the objectives of the drastic reform of the state-owned sector was "increasing efficiency by reducing employment." In fact, workers had begun to be laid off even earlier; from the mid-1990s to the early 2000s, more than 30 million workers lost jobs from state-owned enterprises. Employment of state-owned and state-holding industrial enterprises dropped by 6% in 1997, by 7% in 1998, and by about 10% each year from 1999 to 2003.[15]

The loss of wage and job securities is evident from the comparison of the cyclicality of the RSV in different periods. The RSV was pro-cyclical throughout the entire period; however, it was more pro-cyclical in the Maoist era than in the reform era. Both the correlation between real GDP growth and the RSV and that between real GDP growth and the growth of RSV are higher in the Maoist era than in the reform era. Economic contractions in the Maoist era led to a fall in the new value, but also a drop in the RSV due to the relatively stable wages and job security. As the transition proceeded, economic fluctuations were increasingly relevant to wages and employment because workers increasingly lost their wage and job securities after the expansion of the private sector, the influx of migrant workers, and the drastic reform of the state-owned sector.

It is noteworthy that the RSV reached its historical peak in 2008,[16] which was even higher than that in 1978. At the beginning of the reform era, the reformers gained support from workers by raising wages, reducing the RSV, and criticizing that the distribution policies of the Maoist era failed to improve the living conditions of workers.[17] In 2008, when the RSV was higher than the 1978 level, it lost its momentum. One may expect that today a redistribution of income will also gain support from workers, which is likely to produce major institutional changes.

Fig. 2 shows the share of surplus value extracted by unproductive sectors, *u*:

$$u = \mathrm{UP}/\mathrm{SV} \tag{4}$$

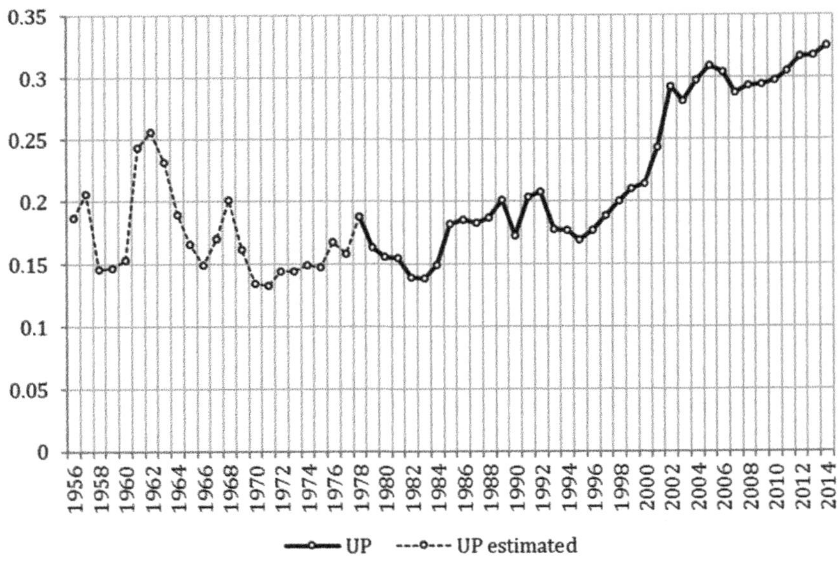

Fig. 2. Share of Surplus Value Extracted by Unproductive Sectors, 1956–2014. *Data Sources*: See Data Appendix.

In Eq. (4), UP is the surplus value extracted by unproductive sectors. Given that commerce and finance under the planning economy were small, they did not play a major role in the Maoist era. In the early stage of the reform era, the share of surplus value extracted by unproductive sectors rose slightly but was still relatively small before 2000. This proportion had increased substantially from about 20% to about 30% after 2000. A fast-growing RSV implies that the economy is likely to encounter the underconsumption crisis tendency. The economy had to rely more on not only investment and export but also unproductive activities such as commercial and financial activities to absorb surplus value and avoid an underconsumption crisis.

Fig. 3 shows the value composition of capital, σ:

$$\sigma = K/\text{VC} \tag{5}$$

In Eq. (5), K is the non-residential capital stock of the enterprise sector, measured by replacement costs. Although the measure is different from Marx's definition of value composition of capital (the ratio of constant capital to variable capital), it is likely to reveal the trend of Marx's measure. It is noteworthy that the value composition of capital shows a slightly downward trend during the reform era before 2008. One reason for this trend is the changes in the investment priorities of the state from heavy industries to light industries; another is the expansion of the private sector, which concentrate in more

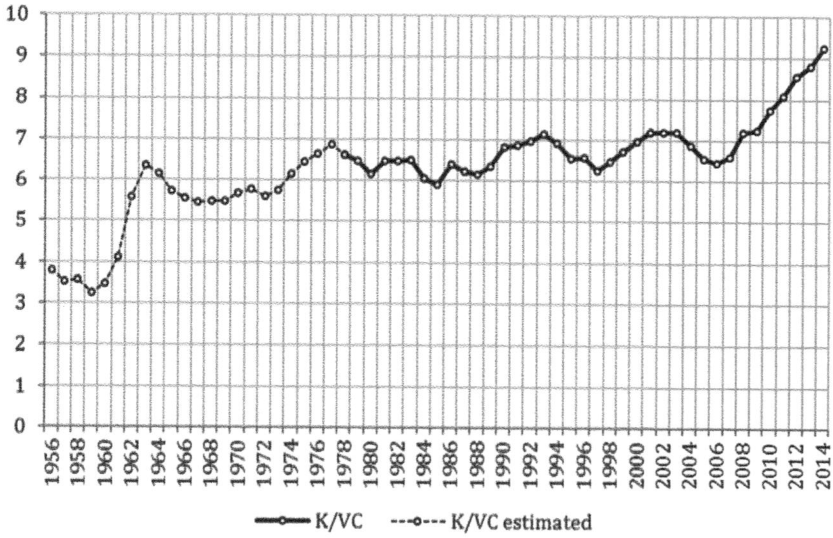

Fig. 3. Composition of Capital, 1956–2014. *Data Sources*: See Data Appendix.

labor-intensive industries. After 2008, as the global market stagnated and the Chinese economy relied more on massive investment to sustain economic growth, the value composition of capital increased substantially, which is likely to depress the rate of profit in the overall economy.[18]

Fig. 4 shows the gross rate of profit GRP and net rate of profit NRP:

$$\text{GRP} = \text{SV}/K \tag{6}$$

$$\text{NRP} = (\text{SV} - \text{UP})/K \tag{7}$$

As shown in Fig. 4, both the gross and net rates of profit in the 1950s were extremely high, partly because 1952 is the first year in the calculation of capital stock using the perpetual inventory method. From 1960 to 1978, the gross and net rate of profit was on average 33% and 27%, respectively. In the reform era, both rates of profit were stable from 1978 to 1985, quickly declined from 1985 to 1990, continued to decline slowly from 1990 to 1999, increased substantially from 1999 to 2007, and declined again after 2007. In 2014, the gross rate of profit was as low as the level in 2000, and the net rate of profit was the lowest of the reform era.

Decomposition of the Net Rate of Profit

To what extent did the net rate of profit rely on the growth of RSV? A decomposition of the net rate of profit is helpful to answer this question, although

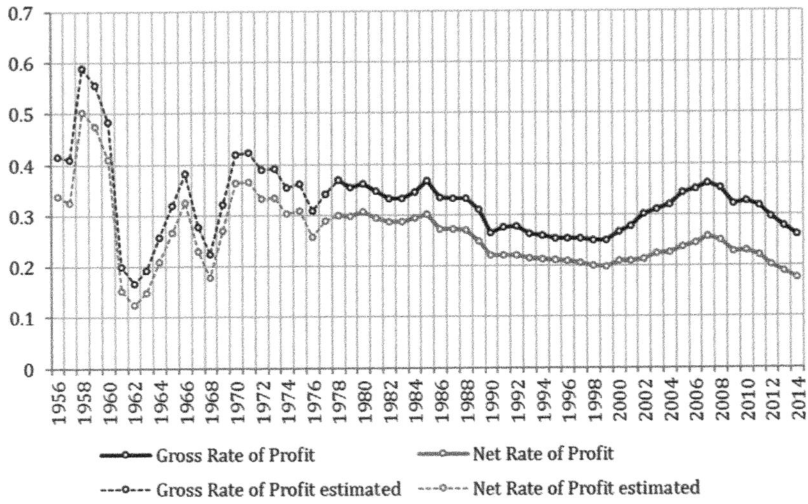

Fig. 4. Gross versus Net Rate of Profit, 1956–2014. *Data Sources*: See Data Appendix.

decomposition does not directly explore the causality between the two variables. Let $\tau = 1 - u$, that is, the share of surplus value retained by productive sectors. Rewrite the net rate of profit,

$$\text{NRP} = \text{RSV}\sigma^{-1}\tau \tag{8}$$

From Eq. (8), one can obtain the relationship between the growth rates of the variables. Let $\widehat{X}$ be the annual growth rate of X,

$$\widehat{\text{NRP}} \doteq \widehat{\text{RSV}} + \widehat{\sigma^{-1}} + \widehat{\tau} \tag{9}$$

Using Eq. (9), one can compare the growth rate of the net rate of profit and that of the RSV to measure the "contribution" of the RSV to the net rate of profit. We carry out the decomposition for the four phases of the net rate of profit: 1978–1990, 1990–1999, 1999–2007, and 2007–2014. Table 2 gives the decomposition results.

In the first phase (1978–1990), the RSV declined whereas the value composition of capital turned to increase. In this phase, the RSV was the dominant driving force for the growth of the net rate of profit. In the second phase (1990–1999), the pattern of the first phase persisted, and the RSV continued to be the dominant driving force. Although the value composition of capital slightly declined, its positive effect on the net rate of profit was offset by the increase in the surplus value absorbed by unproductive sectors. In the third phase (1999–2007), the substantial increase in the RSV reversed the declining trend of the net rate of profit, helping the economy achieve the fastest growth of the net rate of profit over the reform era. In this phase, value composition of capital and unproductive sectors played minor roles. In the fourth phase (2007–2014), due to the fast-rising value composition of capital, the net rate of

Table 2. Decomposition of the Net Rate of Profit.

%	$\widehat{\text{NRP}}$	$\widehat{\text{ROS}}$	$\widehat{\sigma^{-1}}$	$\widehat{\tau}$
1978–1990	−2.58	−2.49	−0.24	0.15
		(96.35)	(9.46)	(−5.73)
1990–1999	−1.13	−0.82	0.19	−0.51
		(71.91)	(−17.04)	(45.28)
1999–2007	3.36	4.50	0.20	−1.29
		(133.98)	(5.83)	(−38.27)
2007–2014	−5.30	0.13	−4.69	−0.77
		(−2.44)	(88.43)	(14.56)

Source: Author's calculation.

Note: Numbers in parentheses are the contribution of each factor in driving the growth of the net rate of profit.

profit fell dramatically. The stagnating RSV could not offset the effect of the value composition of capital. The rising share of unproductive sectors also repressed the net rate of profit.

UNDERMINED CONDITIONS FOR THE GROWTH OF THE RSV AND THE "NEW NORMAL"

The "new normal" of the Chinese economy witnessed the lowest net rate of profit of the reform era. The decomposition shows that the stagnation of the RSV and the rise in the value composition were the driving forces for the decline in profitability after 2008. It is worthwhile to note that the RSV and the value composition of capital are not independent of each other. One affects the other, and some common factors affect both of the RSV and the value composition of capital. However, given that the decomposition shows that the RSV was the dominant driving force from 1978 to 2007 and greatly contributed to the growth of profitability in the decade before the global crisis, we can start with the causes of the stagnation of the RSV.

First of all, the stagnation of the RSV is a result of the shrinking reserve army of labor. As discussed above, the formation and expansion of the reserve army of labor are a critical reason for the increase of the RSV in the late 1990s and early 2000s, and the two primary components of the reserve army of labor are migrant workers and laid-offs of the state-owned sector. For the laid-offs, after 2004, the employment of the state-owned sector turned to be stable, which implies that there was little increase in the number of laid-offs. Meanwhile, many of the workers being laid off in the 1990s have quit the labor force by now as they reached retirement ages. The other main component of the reserve army of labor did not continue to grow after 2008 as fast as it grew before 2008. The growth of migrant workers from 2008 to 2014 continuously declined.[19] The share of migrant workers in total urban employment was increasing in the 1990s and 2000s; by contrast, this proportion became stable after 2008, and slightly declined after 2010. Regarding wages, the economy witnessed fast real wage growth; however, fast real wage growth does not imply that workers afford decent living conditions (Li & Qi, 2014; Xu, Chen, & Li, 2015). Insufficient wages for decent living conditions imply that it might be impossible to reverse the rising trend of the real wage.

Second, the fast growth of the RSV in the decade before 2008, on the one hand, underpinned the growth of profitability; on the other, it could jeopardize profitability by repressing the domestic consumption demand. Thus, the accumulation model in the decade before 2008 had to find the sources of demand to resolve the realization problem. Export and investment played a crucial role in maintaining aggregate demand. As Zhu and Kotz (2010) observe, Chinese economic growth has increasingly relied on export and investment. After 2008, as the global capitalism entered into the great recession or secular stagnation, demand for China's export dramatically declined. As a result, the role of investment became crucial, which is one of the reasons for the substantial growth of the value composition of capital after 2008 when the state launched the four trillion yuan stimulus package in response to the economic slowdown as a result of the global crisis. The state-controlled banking system supported massive investment that concentrated in infrastructure. Infrastructure investment could expand aggregate demand for enterprises in the short run and enhance productivity in the long run; however, infrastructure investment per se was less profitable, and its positive effect on the profitability of enterprises might be limited within a few relevant industries (such as steel industry). As a result, the massive investment greatly increased the value composition of capital, which further depressed profitability.

Meanwhile, although the state-controlled banking and the relatively large state-owned non-financial sector are favorable to carry out massive investment (Lo & Li, 2011), the rising debt-income ratio along with massive investment might jeopardize the growth sustainability. The debt-value added ratio of the non-financial enterprise sector quickly rose from 195% in 2007 to 317% in 2014. The proportion of the debt of the non-financial enterprise sector to GDP was stable from 1996 to 2008 but increased from 98% in 2008 to 149% in 2014. The debt-income ratio of the non-financial sector has been the highest among major economies of the world (Li, Zhang, & Chang, 2015).

CONCLUSION

This paper has constructed homogenous series of the RSV using a Marxian approach and analyzed the relationship between the stagnation of the RSV and China's "new normal" featured by falling profitability. Dynamics of the RSV may result from changes in power relations determined by a series of economic and institutional factors such as the ownership structure of the economy, the formation of the reserve army of labor, and the reform of the state-owned enterprises. The main findings of this paper are as follows: over the reform era, the RSV decreased from 1978 to 1997, increased from 1997 to 2008, and then stagnated after 2008. The decomposition analysis has indicated that the RSV was the dominant driving force of the growth of the net rate of profit from 1985 to 2007.

The RSV might have been stagnant or slightly falling after 2008. Some important events took place along with this change. First of all, the financial and economic crisis that initiated in the United States led to a recession and stagnation for leading capitalist economies, which affected the Chinese economy through the contraction of the demand for China's exports. China's economic growth fell behind the increase of wages, leading to the decline in the

RSV. Second, as the decade-long increase of the RSV constrained workers' capacity to maintain decent living conditions, struggles of workers for a living wage surged against this background, and the reduction in the reserve army of labor also enhanced the bargaining power of workers. Given that the massive investment led to a rising value composition of capital, which repressed profitability, and a rising debt-income ratio, which jeopardized the growth sustainability, the Chinese economy might encounter serious problems to maintain profitability in the "new normal." Furthermore, the current accumulation model has also challenged the limits of environmental resources as air pollution has become a serious problem for the Chinese people. Capital accumulation has overused not only labor power but also environmental resources. Under this circumstance, maintaining the current accumulation model may prepare conditions for not only an economic crisis but also an environmental crisis. Major institutional changes favorable to pro-labor distribution, a wage-led growth model, and sustainable development might be a prerequisite to achieving prosperity in the future.

NOTES

1. Zhang and Zhao (2007) provide series of China's rate of surplus value over the period 1978–2004; however, they only cover manufacturing and do not consider the transfer of surplus value.
2. "New normal" in the west refers to the conditions of the financial market and the economy after the global crisis, which Summers (2015) interprets as "secular stagnation." In May 2014, President Xi Jinping proposed that the Chinese economy had entered into a "new normal" phase; however, what the term means for the Chinese economy is ambiguous.
3. The RSV in the United States was around 3.5 in 2008 (Paitaridis & Tsoulfidis, 2011), compared to 2.6 in China.
4. The decomposition method utilized here decomposes the growth rate of the net rate of profit into the growth rates of the RSV, value composition of capital, and the share of surplus value distributed to productive sectors. This method does not reveal the causality or interactions among variables. Nevertheless, it reveals the correlation between the growth rate of profitability and the growth rates of the other three variables.
5. This problem with GDP accounting is important especially for developing economies, where a large proportion of total employment is in agriculture (38% in 2010 for low- and middle-income economies) and a large proportion of agriculture is non-capitalist. Data sources: WDI database.
6. For example, in 1979, Deng Xiaoping cited the GDP of developed economies to illustrate the goal of Chinese economic development; in 1987, Deng illustrated the goal of Chinese economic development with GDP numbers, which pushed the shift in the statistical system (NBS, 2009b).
7. Private enterprises in this paper correspond to the statistical categories of "private enterprises," "enterprises with funds from Hong Kong, Macro and Taiwan," and "foreign funded enterprises."
8. Some self-employment units might be as large as small private enterprises in terms of employment but they are not registered as enterprises; however, there is no data to distinguish those enterprises from real self-employment units.

9. Shaikh and Tonak (1994) suggest that government enterprises in the United States are essentially capitalist enterprises but this need not be the case in other countries.

10. Royalty payments are consisted of two kinds: payments as operating surplus and payments as intermediate inputs. The first kind has been counted by the net value added of productive sectors and the total output of the commerce sector.

11. The National Bureau of Statistics conducts a national input–output survey every 5 years to compile the basic input–output table and conducts a small-scale input–output survey 3 years after each national survey to compile a simplified input–output table.

12. Data sources: China Statistical Yearbook, issues from 1981 to 1988; China Labor Statistical Yearbook, issues from 1991 to 1998.

13. Data sources: Author's collection of historical materials of the mining industry in Henan Province, Zhengzhou No. 5 Cotton Textile Factory, Guangxi No. 1 Machinery Manufacturing Factory, Changzhou Machinery Manufacturing Factory, and Luoyang Glass Group.

14. As the export declined after 2008, one may expect that the surplus value transferred to foreign economies also decreased. If that is the case, this assumption would imply that the rate of change in RSV in the recent period is also underestimated.

15. Data sources: China Statistical Yearbook 2015.

16. The RSV increased slightly from 2.55 to 2.57 from 2008 to 2011.

17. Chinese economists held five conferences on distribution from 1977 to 1979 to criticize the distribution and incentive system of the Cultural Revolution and labeled the system "egalitarianism," "big pot rice," and "doing more work is the same as doing less work" (Su & Feng, 1978).

18. It is worthwhile to note that the massive state-led infrastructure investment after 2008 was relevant to the increase of capital composition. Thus, the decline in the rate of profit might result from the massive state-led infrastructure investment rather than contradictions in capital accumulation. However, given that the state-led infrastructure investment was mostly financed by borrowing, local governments and other agencies have to repay debts with earnings from operating the infrastructure (such as income from rail transportation). Thus, the sustainability of such infrastructure investment is contingent on how profitable the newly built infrastructure is. In this sense, the rate of profit in the overall economy still reflects the health conditions of the economy.

19. Data sources: National Statistical Bureau, "Investigation Report on Migrant Workers," from 2008 to 2014.

REFERENCES

Cronin, B. (2001). Productive and unproductive capital: A mapping of the New Zealand system of national accounts to classical economic categories, 1972-95. *Review of Political Economy*, *13*(3), 309–327.

Hsueh, T., & Li, Q. (1999). *China's national income*. Boulder: Westview Press.

Kuznets, S. (1955). Economic growth and income inequality. *American Economic Review*, *45*(1), 1–28.

Li, Y., Zhang, X., & Chang, X. (2015). *China national balance sheet 2015*. Beijing: China Social Science Press.

Li, Z., & Qi, H. (2014). Labor process and the social structure of accumulation in China. *Review of Radical Political Economics*, *46*(4), 481–488.

Lo, D., & Li, G. (2011). China's economic growth, 1978-2007: Structural-institutional changes and efficiency attributes. *Journal of Post Keynesian Economics*, *34*(1), 59–84.

Luo, G. (1990). *Marx's theory of productive labor: Two contemporary systems of national accounting and issues on the reform of China's statistical system (in Chinese)*. Beijing: Economic Science Press.

Maniatis, T. (2005). Marxian macroeconomic categories in the Greek economy. *Review of Radical Political Economics, 37*(4), 494–516.

Marina, A., & Moseley, F. (2000). The rate of profit in the postwar Mexican economy, 1950-1993. In R. Baiman, H. Boushey, & D. Saunders (Eds.), *Political economy and contemporary capitalism: Radical perspectives on economic theory and policy* (pp. 184–192). Armonk, NY: M.E. Sharpe.

MOA. (2009). *New China's agriculture in 60 years*. Beijing: China Statistics Press.

Mohun, S. (2005a). Distributive shares in the U.S. economy, 1964-2001. *Cambridge Journal of Economics, 30*(3), 347–370.

Mohun, S. (2005b). On measuring the wealth of nations: The US economy, 1964-2001. *Cambridge Journal of Economics, 29*(5), 799–815.

Mohun, S. (2013). Unproductive labor in the U.S. economy 1964-2010. *Review of Radical Political Economics, 46*(3), 355–379.

Moseley, F. (1985). The rate of surplus value in the postwar U.S. economy: A critique of Weisskopf's estimates. *Cambridge Journal of Economics, 9*(1), 57–79.

NBS. (1985). *Materials of labor and wage statistics 1949-1985*. Beijing: China Statistics Press.

NBS. (1997). *The gross domestic product of china 1952-1995*. Beijing: Dongbei University of Finance and Economics Press.

NBS. (2007a). *Data of flow of funds of china 1992-2004*. Beijing: China Statistics Press.

NBS. (2007b). *Data of gross domestic product of china: 1952-2004*. X. Xu (Ed.). Beijing: China Statistics Press.

NBS. (2009a). *60 years of new China*. Beijing: China Statistics Press.

NBS. (2009b). *History of statistics in the people's republic of China*. Beijing: China Statistics Press.

Paitaridis, D., & Tsoulfidis, L. (2011). The growth of unproductive activities, the rate of profit, and the phase-change of the U.S. economy. *Review of Radical Political Economics, 44*(2), 213–233.

Piketty, T. (2014). *Capital in the 21st Century*. Cambridge, MA: The Belknap Press of Harvard University Press.

Qi, H. (2014). The labor share question in China. *Monthly Review, 65*(8), 23–34.

Qi, H. (2015). *The labor share question in China*. Dissertation. University of Massachusetts-Amherst.

SAIC. (1992). *40 Years of state administration for industry and commerce in China*. Beijing: China Statistics Press.

Shaikh, A. M., & Tonak, E. A. (1994). *Measuring the wealth of nations: The political economy of national accounts*. New York: Cambridge University Press.

Su, S., & Feng, L. (1978). Clear up the influences of the slanders of the "Gang of Four" on "Distribution According to Work". In *On the issues of "Distribution According to Work" (in Chinese)*. Shanghai: Sanlian Bookstore.

Summers, L. H. (2015). Demand side secular stagnation. *American Economic Review, 105*(5), 60–65.

Sun, Y. (1981). On productive labor and unproductive labor and the discussion on national income and gross national product. *Economic Research Journal (Jingji Yanjiu, in Chinese)*, 8, 15–24.

Tsoulfidis, L., & Tsaliki, P. (2014). Unproductive labor, capital accumulation and profitability crisis in the Greek economy. *International Review of Applied Economics, 28*(5), 562–585.

Wei, X. (1981). *On the issue of productive labor and unproductive labor. Economic theory and economic management (Jingji Lilun yu Jingji Guanli, in Chinese)*, pp. 16–22.

Weisskopf, T. E. (1979). Marxian crisis theory and the rate of profit in the postwar U.S. economy. *Cambridge Journal of Economics, 3*(4), 341–378.

Xu, Z., Chen, Y., & Li, M. (2015). Are Chinese workers paid the correct wages? Measuring wage underpayment in the Chinese industrial sector, 2005-2010. *Review of Radical Political Economics, 47*(3), 446–459.

Yu, G. (1981). Productive labor and unproductive labor in the socialist system. *Economic Issues in China (Zhongguo Jingji Wenti, in Chinese)*, 1, 1–8.

Zhang, Y., & Zhao, F. (2007). The rate of surplus value, the composition of capital, and the rate of profit in the Chinese manufacturing industry: 1978-2004. *Bulletin of Political Economy*, *1*(1), 17–42.

Zhu, a., & Kotz, D. M. (2010). The dependence of China's economic growth on exports and investment. *Review of Radical Political Economics*, *43*(1), 9–32.

APPENDIX

Capital stock K

K is the non-residential capital stock of the enterprise sector, measured by replacement costs. Use the perpetual inventory method to measure *K*. The initial year is 1952. The price index of fixed investment is from NBS (2007b) and the NBS website. The depreciation rate is assumed to be 7% for the period 1952–1978. For the period 1979–2014, the depreciation of the enterprise sector is assumed to grow at the same rate as the depreciation of the economy. The depreciation data are from Hsueh and Li (1999), NBS (2007b), and China Statistical Yearbook (hereafter, CSY) 2006–2015.

To measure *K*, we need the fixed investment of the enterprise sector. Use different methods to estimate the investment of different periods.

(1) 1952–1977

Fixed investment in the enterprise sector = non-agricultural fixed asset formation − fixed investment of non-profit institutions − urban residential investment.

Non-agricultural fixed asset formation is assumed to be 65% of total fixed asset formation (NBS, 2009a). Fixed investment of non-profit institutions is assumed to grow at the same rate as total fixed asset formation, and estimated with these growth rates and the fixed investment of non-profit institutions in 1978 (CSY 1981). Urban residential investment is from CSY 1981.

(2) 1978–1991

Fixed investment in the enterprise sector = (non-agricultural fixed asset formation − fixed investment of non-profit institutions − urban residential investment) × income-approach GDP/expenditure-approach GDP.

This equation is different from the equation for the period 1952–1977 because the income approach data for the period 1952–1977 are unavailable. Non-agricultural fixed asset formation is from NBS (1997). Fixed investment of non-profit institutions is CSY 1981–1992. Urban residential investment is from CSY 1981 and the NBS website. Income-approach GDP is from Hsueh and Li (1999). Expenditure-approach GDP is from the NBS website.

(3) 1992–2013

Fixed investment in the enterprise sector = (fixed asset formation of the non-financial enterprise sector in the flow of funds account + fixed asset formation of the financial enterprise sector in the flow of funds account) × income-approach GDP/GDP in the flow of funds account.

The flow of funds account data is from NBS (2007a) and CSY 2005–2015. Income-approach GDP is from NBS (2007b) and CSY 2005–2015.

(4) 2014

Fixed investment in the enterprise sector is assumed to grow at the same rate as total fixed asset formation in 2014 (NBS website), and estimated with this growth rate and the fixed investment of the enterprise sector in 2013.

Agriculture

NV_1: Net value added of agriculture. For the period 1956–1977, NV_1 is from CSY 1994. For the period 1978–2003, NV_1 is calculated by subtracting the agricultural depreciation of fixed assets from the agricultural value added (Hsueh & Li, 1999; NBS, 2007b). Since the definition of "net value" in CSY 1994 slightly differs from that in Hsueh and Li (1999) and NBS (2007b), all the data for the period 1956–1977 are adjusted by multiplying the ratio of "net value" in 1978 from Hsueh and Li (1999) to that from CSY 1994. For the period 2004–2012, NV_1 is calculated by subtracting an estimated depreciation from value added. The estimated depreciation share equals average depreciation share in value added over the period 1990–2003.

Industry (Mining, Manufacturing, and Utilities), Construction, Transportation, Post and Telecommunications

NV_2: Net value added of industry. The industry sector is composed of three sub-sectors: mining, manufacturing, and utilities. The data of NV_2 are from various issues of CSY and Hsueh and Li (1999) and adjusted in the same way as NV_1.

W_2: Compensation of employees in industry. For the period 1956–1977, I assume that the ratio of the compensation of employees in industry to the sum of wages, salaries, and benefits in industry is equal to that ratio in 1978. With this assumption, I estimate W_2 for the period 1956–1977. Data of wages, salaries, and benefits are from NBS (1985). I also use this method to estimate the compensation of employees in construction, transportation, post and telecommunications, food and hotel services, and social services over the period 1956–1977. For the period 1978–2003, W_2 is the compensation of employees in industry from Hsueh and Li (1999) and (NBS, 2007b). For the period 2004–2012, W_2 is derived from the predictions of the following regression with the observations over the period 1990–2003.

$$W_{2,t} = \alpha_0 + \alpha_1 \text{emp}_2 + \alpha_2 \text{mean}w_2 + \varepsilon_2$$

In this equation, $W_{2,t}$ is the compensation of employees in industry in year t, emp_2 is the urban employment of industry, and $\text{mean}w_2$ is the average wage of urban industrial units. In addition, α_0 is a constant, α_1 andα_2 are coefficients, and ε_2 is the error term. Data of employment and average wages are from various issues of CSY. I also use this method to estimate the compensation of employees in construction, transportation, post and telecommunications, food and hotel services, and social services over the period 2004–2014.

Using the same method and data sources, obtain or estimate the following variables.

NV_3: Net value added of construction.

W_3: Compensation of employees in construction.

NV_4: Net value added of transportation, post and telecommunications.

W_4: Compensation of employees in transportation, post and telecommunications.

Food and Hotel Services

NV_5: Net value added of food and hotel services. Since commerce and food and hotel services are treated as a single sector in the statistics, we need to split the sector into the commerce part and the food and hotel service part. I use the retail sale of commerce and that of food and hotel services to split the sector over the period 1956–1977 and the value added of commerce over the period 1978–2014. The retail sale data are from various issues of CSY, and the value added data are from CSY 2015. With the data of net value from CSY 1994, value added, depreciation, compensation of employees from NBS (2007b), I exclude commerce and then obtain the data for food and hotel services only. Then, I apply the same procedure used in the calculation of NV_1 to obtain NV_5.

W_5: Compensation of employees in food and hotel services. With the data for food and hotel services, I apply the same procedure used in the calculation of W_2 to obtain W_5.

Social Services

NV_6: Net value added of social services. NBS (1997) provides the value added of social services over the period 1956–1978. Hsueh and Li (1999) provide data of value added, compensation of employees, and depreciation of fixed assets of social services over the period 1978–1995. For the period 1978–1995, NV_6 is calculated with the data from Hsueh and Li (1999) by subtracting depreciation of fixed assets from value added. I assume that the ratio of the net value to the value added of social services is a constant that equals this ratio in 1978, with which I estimate NV_6 over the period 1956–1977. NBS (2007b) and CSY 2015 do not provide data of social services but provide data of "other services" which includes social services. Thus, I assume that the share of social services in "other services" is constant and that the depreciation's share in the value added of social services is the same as the share of depreciation in the value added of "other services," with which I estimate NV_6 for the period 1996–2012.

W_6: Compensation of employees in social services. I estimate W_6 for the period 1956–1977 with data of wages, salaries, and benefits from NBS (1985), using the same method for estimating W_2 over the period 1956–1977. For the period 1978–1995, W_6 is the compensation of employees of social services from Hsueh and Li (1999). I assume that compensation's share in the value added of social services is the same as compensation's share in the value added of "other services," with which I estimate W_6 for the period 1996–2003. I use the regression method for estimating W_2 to estimate W_6 over the period 2004–2012.

Commerce

TO'_c: Total output of commerce, which equals to the sum of compensation of employees, operating surplus, net taxes on production, and costs of inputs of commerce. This sum coincides with the "social total value" of commerce. CSY only provides the social total value of commerce, food, and hotel services over the period 1952–1992. In order to estimate the social total value of commerce, food, and hotel services over the period 1993–2014, I estimate the following regression.

$$\mathrm{STV} = \gamma_0 + \gamma_1 \mathrm{RS_c} + \gamma_2 \mathrm{RS_{fh}} + \varepsilon_c$$

In this equation, STV is the social total value of commerce, food, and hotel services, RS_c is the retail sale of commerce, and RS_{fh} is the retail sale of food and hotel services. In addition, γ_0 is a constant, γ_1 and γ_2 are coefficients, and ε_c is the error term. I use the estimated coefficients and the data of retail sale to estimate the social total value over the period 1993–2014. Furthermore, I use the retail sale data to split the data of social total value into the commerce part and the food and hotel service part, then obtain TO_c.

NV_c: Net value added of commerce. I use the retail sale of commerce and that of food and hotel services to split the net value added of commerce, food, and hotel services. The net value added of commerce, food, and hotel services is from CSY 1993 for the period 1952–1977 and Hsueh and Li (1999) and (NBS, 2007b) for the period 1978–2003. For the period 2004–2014, I assume the depreciation's share in value added equals the average depreciation share in value added over the period 1990–2003 and estimate the net value added with the depreciation's share and value added from the NBS website.

W_c: Compensation of employees of commerce. For 1978–2003, the compensation of employees of commerce, food, and hotel services is from Hsueh and Li (1999) and NBS (2007b), then I split it with the retail sale of commerce, food, and hotel services. For 1952–1977, I use the data for 1978 and the wages, salaries, and benefits of commerce, food, and hotel services from NBS (1985) to estimate the compensation of employees and then split it with retail sale data. For 2004–2014, I use the same procedure used in estimating W_2 to estimate the compensation of employees.

Self-employment

W_s: Compensation of employees of self-employment units. Given that wages and profits are not distinguishable for self-employment, the statistical data treat both wages and profits as compensation of employees. Estimate the compensation of employees with the following equation:

$$W_s = \frac{T_s}{T_{sv}}(W_{sv} + \Pi_{sv})$$

T_s is the taxes of self-employment units from various issues of China Tax Yearbook. T_{sv}, W_{sv}, and Π_{sv} are the taxes, wages, and profits of rural self-employment units, respectively, from MOA (2009) and various issues of China Township and Village Enterprise Yearbook.

NV_s: Net value added of self-employment units, which equals to the sum of the compensation of employees and taxes of self-employment units from various issues of China Tax Yearbook.

δ: Share of productive self-employment in total self-employment. I assume this share is the same as the employment share of private enterprises and self-employment of productive sectors. Data for estimation are from SAIC (1992) and various issues of CSY.

Finance and Real Estate

Π_{fr}: Operating surplus of finance and real estate. For the period 1978–2003, data are from Hsueh and Li (1999) and NBS (2007b). For the period 1952–1977 and 2004–2014, assuming that the operating surplus grows at the same rate as the value added of finance and real estate, estimate the operating surplus with value added data from the NBS website and NBS (1997).

T_{fr}: Net taxes on production of finance and real estate. Data are obtained or estimated with the same sources and method as used for Π_{fr}.

TO_{fr}: Total output of finance and real estate. Obtain the ratio of total output and value added of finance and real estate from input-output tables, extrapolate the missing values, and estimate the total output of finance and real estate with this ratio and value added data from the NBS website and NBS (1997).

β: The ratio of royalty payments counted as intermediate costs of productive sectors and commerce to the net value added of productive sectors and commerce. Estimate this ratio with input-output data.

Variable Capital

$$\text{VC} = \sum_{i=2}^{6} W_i - \delta W_{\text{s}}$$

Marxian Value Added

$$\text{MVA} = \text{NV}_{\text{p}} + \text{TO}_{\text{c}} + \left(\text{RY}_{\text{p}} + \text{RY}_{\text{t}}\right)$$

$$\text{NV}_{\text{p}} = \sum_{i=2}^{6} \text{NV}_i - \delta \text{NV}_{\text{s}}$$

$$\text{TO}_{\text{c}} = \text{TO}'_{\text{c}} \frac{\sum_{i=2}^{6} \text{NV}_i - \delta \text{NV}_{\text{s}}}{\sum_{i=1}^{6} \text{NV}_i}$$

$$\text{RY}_{\text{p}} + \text{RY}_{\text{t}} = \beta\left(\sum_{i=2}^{6} \text{NV}_i + \text{NV}_{\text{c}}\right)$$

Net Profit

$$\text{NP} = \sum_{i=2}^{6} (\text{NV}_i - \text{W}_i) - \delta(\text{NV}_{\text{s}} - W_{\text{s}}) + (\text{NV}_{\text{c}} - W_{\text{c}}) \frac{\sum_{i=2}^{6} \text{NV}_i - \delta \text{NV}_{\text{s}}}{\sum_{i=1}^{6} \text{NV}_i} + (\Pi_{\text{fr}} + \text{T}_{\text{fr}}) \frac{\text{RY}_{\text{p}} + \text{RY}_{\text{t}}}{\text{TO}_{\text{fr}}}$$

PART II
STATE AND HEGEMONY IN EAST ASIA IN THE CONTEXT OF TRANSNATIONAL CAPITALISM

THE TRANSNATIONAL CAPITALIST CLASS AND RELATIONS OF PRODUCTION IN ASIA AND OCEANIA

Jeb Sprague-Silgado

ABSTRACT

As components of society, social classes contain individuals who are carriers of productive relationships. In the era of global capitalism, chains of accumulation are functionally integrating across borders and regions – uniquely altering the formation of productive relationships. How can we understand class relations in the global era, and in the context of regions and countries in Oceania and Asia? How do transnational capitalist-class fractions, new middle strata, and labor undergird globalization? How have state apparatuses and other institutions in this part of the world become entwined with new transnational processes? To begin to consider these questions, this paper provides an overview and summary of studies on transnational class relations and the associated political economic changes occurring across areas of Asia and Oceania.

Keywords: Transnational capitalist class; Globalization; Asia; Oceania

Return of Marxian Macro-dynamics in East Asia
Research in Political Economy, Volume 32, 133–158

ISSN: 0161-7230/doi:10.1108/S0161-723020170000032009

Through the context of Asia and Oceania, this paper provides a synthesis of the studies that have examined and debated the growing transnationality of many social and material relations in the global era.[1] What tensions do these novel dynamics give rise to? How do transnational capitalist-class fractions, new middle strata, and labor undergird capitalist globalization in Asia and Oceania?

Social classes are relationships generated and reproduced through the productive processes and economic life of a type of society (or what Marx referred to as a "mode of production"). As components of a society, these classes contain individuals who are carriers of productive relationships. In the present global/transnational phase of world capitalism, what changes are social classes undergoing? And, importantly, how do state apparatuses and other institutions connect with new transnational processes?

For the purposes of this paper, it is important to first emphasize the difference between national, international, and transnational processes. Whereas national processes occur within the frontiers of the national state, international processes occur across borders. Transnational processes, while occurring across borders, also take place through functional integration. Functional integration refers to how amalgamations of different components (or agents) are constituted through their joint-operation. Processes that take place across frontiers in this integrated manner alter the very ways in which space and geography are implicated in material and social production.

Transnationally oriented class relations have emerged over the shift from the international to the global phases of world capitalism (Carroll, 2010; Harris, 2006; Liodakis, 2010; Robinson, 2004, 2014; Sklair, 2001). In regards to the state: earlier indicative (development) planning (with a view to foment nationally oriented economic development) continues to fragment, as markets integrated into new circuits of transnational accumulation. This has a concrete impact, for example, with massive sums of transnational capital flowing into China and other sites in different regions (with huge rises in foreign direct investment and cross-border mergers and acquisitions taking place), transforming the character and content of the capitalist-class composition.

How then can we visualize the ruling class of this emerging global system? As Gramsci (1973) explains, in different historical periods and societies, there has arisen a historic bloc, an alliance of different class forces politically organized around a set of dominant ideas that provide coherence and a planned direction. Moreover, this "historic bloc" operates under one dominant social class that has established its intellectual and moral leadership (*Ibid.*, p. 215). This historic bloc establishes its domination over society, not just through coercion (such as through the courts, police, and army), but also through consent (through culture and ideology) in the societal superstructure. In order to promote its hegemony over a crisis-prone *global* system, the transnational capitalist class (TCC) has required a new broad alliance of social forces, a *global* historic bloc. This new historic bloc (with the TCC as its hegemonic class) has been made up of the transnational corporations (TNCs) and transnational financial institutions, the elites that manage the supranational economic planning agencies, major forces in the dominant political parties, media conglomerates, and technocratic elites and state managers in both North and South (Robinson & Sprague-Silgado, 2018). Over recent decades, we can see how many national and regional contingents have undergone an insertion into this new *global* historic bloc.

Uneven and combined development has cast both the world market and world capitalism in a heterogeneous context. Different countries developed relatively independently (with their own national histories and particularities) but also through interdependent processes (such as in trade, investment, cultural diffusion, and migration). Separate national capitalist groups, for example, conflicted but also interacted with one another. Uneven and combined development also occurred through the context of the rise of imperialism, where certain powerful countries dominated weaker countries. An important factor in the uneven and combined development of different countries was the role of powerful international capitalist monopolies.

Yet, with the rise of the *globalization phase of world capitalism*, I argue, along with others (Harris, 2016b; Robinson, 2004, 2014, p. 31; Sklair, 2002) that uneven and combined development also occurs through new transnational processes. Altering forms of capitalist accumulation (and a variety of associated relations) play out conjecturally in world society, through shifting structural patterns and combinations.

A number of nuanced studies have looked at the particularities of global political economy in the context of these regions and many of the nations therein (to reference just some of these: Breslin, 2013; Chun, 2013; Jayasuriya, 2004a, 2004b; Li, 2009; Murray, 2007; Zhao, 2008). Many other scholars have written on racialized and gendered processes in Asia and Oceania, and on the way in which socialized divisions have developed in connection with diverse and interconnected histories and cultures. Yet, to date, there has been no comprehensive study focused on shifting relations of production in the context of transnationalism across these regions during the era of global capitalism (an era that we can date starting from the last quarter of the 20th century and continuing into the 21st century). By "relations of production" I refer to the sum total of social relationships that people *must* enter into, in order to survive and reproduce their existence.

Racialized and gendered class relations have formed in particular ways through world capitalism (Calinicos, 1993; Mies, 1986). The modern formation and reproduction of racialized class relations in societies in East Asia, for example, was melded through local histories and particularities alongside the spread of European and US colonial capitalism and imperialism (see e.g., Dikötter, 1997). As capitalism emerged and expanded, it also structured gendered social relations in new ways, for example, men's labor became monetized whereas women's labor often was unwaged (Federici, 2004). Into the present era, from the family unit to export processing zones, transnational capitalist accumulation benefits from un- and under-waged feminized labor, especially upon the labor of those negatively racialized women. We see this in plain view with regard to the large pools of exploited female labor across Asia and Oceania, and as reproductive labor has been devalued through capitalism. Many studies and documentaries have shown well the common struggle that women workers face in the globalizing economy. The documentary *Global Assembly Lines,* for instance, examines how women workers in the United States, Mexico, and the Philippines have faced exploitation through the rise of a new global circuit of capitalist production, which evolved through microprocessors and other new technological and organizational advancements (Gray, 1986).

When examining our present era's world society, much of the mainstream, academic, and even critical discourse takes up surface-layer views of geopolitical and national competition occurring through the interstate system: China's growing role abroad; the rise of the association of five major emerging "national" economies, the BRICS (Brazil, Russia, India, China, and South Africa); the unending political crises on the Korean peninsula; the emergent role of the developing nations of South and Southeast Asia; Australia's partnership with the North Atlantic Treaty Organization (NATO); India's competition with its neighbors; and the squabbles over islands in the East China Sea, and as Japan reasserts its power in tandem with the US foreign policy establishment's "pivot to Asia." Populations are viewed as domestically rooted and involved in national class struggles; domestic capitalist power blocs engage in international alliances and rivalries, "national" business groups and conglomerates must deal with foreign competitors; a conflict between "homelands" and between nation-state policymakers pursuing their "national" interests.

While state-centric perspectives can and do shed light on important dynamics, they ignore the emerging new social (and material) reality. The rationale for this paper is that much analysis and theorizing on contemporary events and more broadly on globalization, international relations, and the contemporary dynamics of capitalism economy remains often deeply impoverished, reflecting the stale language of Westphalian state-centrism.

The capitalist state has always functioned to institutionalize unequal power relations. Yet in the global phase of world capitalism, state elites have increasingly come to see their interests neither in national development, nor in finding strategies that meet the desires and interests of local popular classes or even of national capitalists. Instead they have seen their interests in terms of global competitiveness, transnational capitalist investment, and that of local dominant groups who are seeking to entwine with such processes. Policymakers are increasingly abandoning or are being forced to abandon polices of domestic development and "national goals," and instead are moving toward policies of elite oriented transnational engagement, where local goals emphasize constructing a climate conducive to global investors. States as political organs, with all of their repressive and ideological forces, are (to different degrees and through particular conditions and forms) being tasked for "reconfiguring sovereignty to meet challenges and demands that stem from relentless global market integration to strengthen and broaden global capital accumulation" (Watson, 2015, p. 10). This does not mean that capitalist globalization is resulting in a "borderless world." TNCs utilize borders to their advantage. While capitalist production and financial networks operate transnationally, they are at the same time able to "take advantage of labor pools and the different built environments in which they exist" (Pereira, 2017, p. 137).

Next I want to provide a brief overview of the growing body of research on transnational social and class relations that have coalesced as a collective research effort by scholars associated with the Network for Critical Studies of Global Capitalism (NCSGC). The NCSGC was founded at a conference titled "Global Capitalism and Transnational Class Formation," held in September 2011 at the Academy of Sciences in Prague in the Czech Republic. An edited book volume (Murray & Scott, 2012) and two scholarly journal issues (Haase, 2013; Struna, 2013) were published with papers from the conference. Two years after the initial conference, the network held its second conference, "Global Capitalism in Asia and Oceania," at Griffith University in Brisbane, Australia in June 2013. Together, many of these papers first presented at the conference were then published as an edited volume (Sprague, 2016). A purpose of the conference in Brisbane has been to continue the debate on the political economy of global capitalism and transnational class formation, with particular attention to Oceania and Asia.

In this paper, I want to look over how these new studies have reflected back and engaged with works of the "global capitalism school," and in particular the research of those scholars who have presented their work through the NCSGC. The work of these scholars examines changing material relations alongside the rise of transnational class relations and the subjective and objective dynamics therein. The term "global capitalism school" has been used to describe broadly a growing body of scholarly work that shares two main affinities (1) the conceptualization of a new epoch in the capitalist system and (2) an analysis of the structure of global capitalism that goes beyond traditional Marxist understandings of nation-state imperialism.

Below I will provide an overview of this new research, and in regard to Asia and Oceania. The research done as part of the recent conference at Griffith University focused primarily on Australia, China, Japan, India, Laos, Papua New Guinea, and upon global processes more broadly. Some of the major themes and questions prompting this research have been:

1) How can the political economy of Asia and Oceania be seen in light of the novel dynamics of the globalist era, with the rise of transnational social, economic, and political processes?
2) How are one-time nationally or internationally oriented state apparatuses, institutions, and corporations converging with new transnational processes?
3) How do social classes and various social groups in Asia and Oceania connect objectively and subjectively to transnational and global processes?

4) How do shifting social and material relations play out regionally or within particular frontiers or built environments?
5) What contradictions are connected to these processes? For example: (a) the crisis of legitimacy that occurs through the abandonment by state managers of national development as they seek transnational integration, (b) social polarization, and (c) the global environmental crisis.

Rather than reify the interstate system, seeing the nation-state as an end in itself, this chapter suggests we consider how a growing amount of class power is exercised transnationally, manifesting itself both across and within national borders in complex and contradictory ways. In this process, the state is utilized as a means to an end, not an end in itself. Recent studies, for example, have looked at the attempt to create the Trans-Pacific Partnership (TPP), through which many transnational capitalists from across the Pacific Rim have sought to more closely integrate their states' economic and regulatory frameworks. Through such forums, for instance, transnationally oriented dominant groups have sought to create the conditions through which TNCs can override domestic laws by appealing regulations through international tribunal. At the same time, competition between transnational conglomerates exists, and the TPP and other supranational forums can serve as a mechanism through which certain transnational capitalist fractions could gain leverage over other TCC fractions, such as the more statist-oriented Chinese fractions of transnational capital. This is reflected in the contradictory policies of US elites in seeking to secure better conditions for global capitalist accumulation, while at the same time engaging in particular hegemonic policies (Starrs, 2015) meant to most benefit certain fractions of transnational capital.

The formation of new transnationally oriented supranational frameworks occurs alongside many contradictions and different kinds of policy debates, and we can see shifting strategies undertaken. Many state managers must engage often in policies that are in apparent contradiction with transnational capital, as they must juggle their need to maintain local legitimacy and deal with local forces and particularities. With mounting crises, we see then, for instance, the rise of rightist populism where certain elites have ridden waves of discontent through nationalist rhetoric and by channeling popular discontent against marginalized groups and migrants, or against bureaucrats seen as disconnected from local particularities. Rightist currents, some within the TCC, have at times challenged the plans of "enlightened" segments of the TCC; with different parts of the ruling class engaged in varying ideological strategies to renew its legitimacy. Key among these are ideological mechanisms of splitting and disorganizing the working classes, including the old tried-and-true racism, jingoism, and xenophobia.

The activities of the TCC and the state managerial groups who promote their interests are bound up with contradictions. Take for example, the deregulation of national financial systems, allowing for the continued ease of capital mobility and flight. Key for this, as Anthony van Fossen (2016) has examined, tax havens have emerged as important nodes for transnational capitalist-class formation. Differing visions exist between state policymakers on how tax havens should function. While many state managers have become transnationally oriented, Van Fossen observes how major differences among them exist and for a variety of reasons.

Below I will provide a summary of studies on the emerging TCC and related dynamics, and in particular how this class is operating across national contexts in Asia and Oceania. Recent studies demonstrate that global capitalist integration is not motivated by the idea of contributing to national economic development or national job creation, or transforming the productive powers of labor as a national objective. The studies examined below instead illuminate shifting capital-labor relations in Asia and Oceania, considering for example how new waves of proletarianization in China and India are connected with global capitalist accumulation, as labor-power is incorporated into transnational value chains. This does not mean that class relations are not riven by conflict and impacted by historic and national differences – for instance, as workers operate in particular labor regimes and built-up environments – and fractions of capital hold closer ties with some state policymakers as compared with others.

Several studies have looked at how particular fractions of the TCC operate with regard to specific states and institutions in Asia and Oceania. As Ietto-Gillies explains, transnational-oriented capitalists with interests across various countries "use their economic position and clout to strengthen their ties and claims … [with] specific countr(ies) and exercise influence to secure special treatment" (Sprague & Ietto-Gillies, 2014, p. 44). Take, for example, the intense rivalry and competition among transnational capitalist conglomerates. While particular state policies may not benefit all transnational capitalist groups equally, many state policies facilitate transnational capital distinct from more locally or nationally oriented capitalists.

Clearly, we exist in a global system in which the United States is the major super power. The institutions of the "Washington consensus" and the US state apparatus have an oversized role in promoting global capital. This has deep historical roots. Nations around the world have undergone structural adjustment programs and faced pressures from Washington. US imperialism has left deep scars across Asia and Oceania and in regions worldwide (with tens of millions of dead in the wake of its wars and interventions).

While US state actors have played a decisive role in crafting the architecture of the interstate system (Panitch & Gindin, 2012), its policymakers increasingly act on behalf of fractions of transnational capital (Baker, 2014). Importantly, militarized accumulation is at the core of transnational capitalist accumulation (especially among those fractions that are powerful in the United States). To justify this, spending new enemies are always required. As of 2010, US expenditures accounted for 48% of the world's military spending, amounting to more than $700 billion (Golby, 2015, p. 57). The threat of war thus remains frighteningly present in our hi-tech and nuclear age. As John Pilger (2017) shows, the

United States continues its militarized policies in the Pacific. These are aimed overwhelmingly at China.

Here we see the complex, contradictory, and crisis-prone nature of our global system. Tensions continue even as transnational capitalists in China and the United States are deeply entwined and have together become ultra-wealthy (Harris, 2016). Different fractions of the TCC exist, and, as Graaff and Apeldoorn (2017) suggest, varying (transnationally oriented) elite and business networks underpin the state-capital nexus and impact interstate politics (such as between China and the United States). Different ideological and subjective factors are also present, such as nationalism, playing an important role in the political scenes of these nations.

Next, I will lay out some of the stakes of this project in regard to the broader literature that it engages with.

THE GLOBAL CAPITALISM SCHOOL

While there are differences between how global capitalism school (GCS) scholars have conceptualized the novel social and material relations of globalization, what binds them together is the argument that global capitalism represents a qualitatively new epoch in the history of world capitalism. Scholars have theorized and shown empirically many of the novel social arrangements that have come about in the era of global capitalism (Harris, 2006; McMichael, 1996; Robinson, 2004, 2014; Rodriguez, 2010; Sassen, 1991; Sklair, 2001, 2002; Van der Pijl, 1998), but have also raised questions for conceptualization (Embong, 2000). As global networks of production and finance that pushed through TNCs and other institutions redefine the scale of the world economy (Dicken, 2011), transnational relations form within and between class fractions and social groups. One of these new classes, the TCC, is tied together as a conscious class, a class in and of itself whose material basis is in TNCs and the accumulation of global capital (Robinson, 2004; Sklair, 2001). However, such a class is not monolithic. Different fractions actually exist within this class, as a segment or portion of the whole class that are grouped around different forms of economic activity.

Some scholars have begun to theorize how transnational class relations are also emerging among subaltern groups, with, for example, different static, diasporic, and dynamic global proletarian fractions coming into existence (Struna, 2009). In addition, as some class fractions are becoming transnationally oriented, others remain more nationally oriented or have not developed into a conscious class fraction, even as they have become objectively interconnected with transnational chains of accumulation. In addition to the rising vast number of human beings living in slums (Davis, 2007) and the many unemployed, in recent decades we can also see the solidification of precariaty, and as large parts of the world's population have come to be structurally underemployed and marginalized in relation to the global economy. To effectively organize transnationally, a difficult and long road ahead exists for labor unions and struggles from below (Robinson, 2014).

An important point to make here is that unlike an epistemological framework that affords primacy to the nation-state as its primary unit of analysis, the "global capitalism school" approach helps us to understand how production, labor struggles, and class and ideology formation are evolving through transnational processes over recent decades. This approach helps us to see how vital it is for working and popular classes and their organizations to interconnect their activities across borders, especially if they are to ever challenge the structural conditions brought about through global capitalism. This approach helps us to see how vital it is for humans to escape the national boxes and mindsets we often become stuck in. A "global approach," and furthermore, a global consciousness can help lead to a undermining of "nation-state" myths, where, for examples, workers who see their situation through a "national" scope then turn to blame migrants for problems that are in fact linked to upheavals and exploitative relations of global capitalism. Yet, the construction of a global consciousness and the building of coordinative relations from below are massive endeavors (Struna, 2015). Working and popular classes and their movements and organizations are far, far, far behind capital in their coordinative activities across borders, a condition that makes it difficult to mount successful alternatives. CEOs understandably often have a globally geared mindset, with contacts in different sectors, and experiences and knowledge on different international markets. By contrast, pushing for a globalization from below, this is the major challenge for subaltern forces in the coming century. They must do this all the while continuing to engage in local and national struggles.

In regard to the TCC, this is an idea that has been theorized in different ways. The TCC, as Robinson (2004), Harris (2006), and Liodakis (2010) argue, is the dominant social class in this new era, the age of global capitalism. These theorists utilize a historical-materialist understanding of the division of labor into social classes upon the basis of property ownership. They understand the individuals of the TCC as people directly involved in global capital accumulation, whereas others involved in its promotion but not accumulation are described in other ways, such as transnational elites and functionaries (but not as capitalists). By contrast, Sklair's more eclectic approach constructs a TCC model that not only includes groups directly involved in global capital accumulation, but those who promote it as well – for example, some media and state functionaries.

Sklair outlines four major propositions in regard to the TCC. First, it is a class that benefits from its connection to TNCs, emerging "more or less in control of the processes of globalization" (2001, p. 5). Second, it is acting as a "transnational dominant class in some spheres" (*Ibid.*). Third, a "profit-driven culture-ideology of consumerism" exists as a mechanism of persuasion, solidifying the participation of populations in global capitalist chains of consumption. And finally, the TCC is faced with two global crises: class polarization and ecological crisis (*Ibid.*,

p. 6). Furthermore, Sklair presents a TCC structure that includes four primary groupings. These are (1) those who own and/or control the major TNCs and their local affiliate (corporate fraction), (2) globalizing bureaucrats and politicians (state fraction), (3) globalizing professionals (technical fraction), and (4) globalizing merchants and media (consumerist fraction). In regard to the state, Sklair argues that what others term the transnationalization of state apparatuses is more accurately conceptualized in terms of ongoing individual struggles between what he describes as the state fractions of the TCC (globalizing politicians and officials) and politicians and officials who see their interests in more local terms.

Differing from Sklair, Robinson (2014) has gone into more detail in regard to the changing orientation of state policymakers and the state apparatus. Through his analytical abstraction of emergent transnational state apparatuses, Robinson (2004) argues that worldwide many state managers and policymakers are becoming transnationally oriented. The social reproduction of these state elites, he argues, is becoming increasingly linked to networks of transnational capitalist accumulation. As the state facilitates the myriad things that capital (increasingly, transnational capital) has to do in order to reproduce itself, we can appreciate more fully the "migratory propensities" of sovereign state power (Agnew, 2009).

Sklair (1996a, 1996b) was among the earliest to consider transnational class relations in regard to Oceania, through studies in which he looked at the limitations of domestic markets and growing globalist trends among leading Australian-based corporations, the rise of transnational capital in Australia, and the growing transnational orientation of leading state bureaucrats undergoing a shift from protectionism to policies of global competitiveness. In recent years, scholars have carried out expanded studies of the TCC in Australia and New Zealand (Murray & Scott, 2012; Murray, 2007). Meanwhile, the strategy of leading dominant groups over recent decades has been one of elite-oriented polyarchy, where the options in democratic elections have been limited to selecting between different groups of elites. US foreign policy in the 1970s and 1980s and an increasingly wide array of agencies (from the EU, UN, etc.) have come to promote this approach. We can see many examples of this taking root in the region, such as in the Philippines (Robinson, 1996, pp. 117, 145).

Political economists writing on modern Asia have sought in particular to understand how China's historical experience with a specific statist-developmental model has led to a unique mode of integration into the global economy. During recent decades of transition, state-owned enterprises have maintained a major role, an important factor in the lifting of 728 million out of World Bank defined poverty (Ross, 2016). Yet, simultaneously, China's integration into the global capitalist economy has spawned massive new inequalities. Harris (2006) has researched, for instance, the rise of a statist fraction of the TCC within China, its individuals becoming tremendously wealthy.

Another scholar, Zhao (2003), has examined the ways in which transnational and local social forces in China have intersected to structurally reshape China's mass media and communication industry. She first recognizes the complex constellation of interests effecting Chinese media's integration with transnational capital: from (what she describes as) integrationist, culturist, and nationalist perspectives, to the rising influence of non-Chinese capitalists on the industry and shifting alignments of social forces and power relations in the country. She points out how Chinese bureaucrats hold unique rationalizations for the neoliberal reforms that have been undertaken, which over time have helped ease China into the global system, as with its ascension into the World Trade Organization (WTO). Chinese media has been reorganized under global market logic, yet remains connected with the country's statist political model. Here her argument shares some similarity with Harris's (2009) observation of a statist TCC in China, as she describes how the country's development will continue to be heavily managed by state elite, whose interests have aligned with fractions of transnational capital. Zhao points out, for instance, how the media has come to serve dominant groups.

Whereas the rising business and urban middle classes are increasingly using the media to articulate their interests and shape state policies toward their preferred ends, the rally cries of tens of thousands of Chinese workers and farmers in their struggles for economic and social justices often fall on deaf ears in the Chinese media system (Zhao, 2003, p. 63). While occurring through local specificities, transnational media capital in China serves as a key mechanism through which information is tilted toward the interests of dominant, transnationally oriented groups, both from within and without.

In looking at Taiwan *and* China, Shen (2011) has examined how transnational capitalists in Taiwan have utilized "nationalist" state policies as favorable opportunities for their cross-strait strategies of capital accumulation and integration. A contradictory process initiated with the lifting of martial law and the opening of family and business travel from Taiwan to China in 1987, the outward orientation of Taiwanese transnational capital has greatly intensified in the years since, as Taiwanese investors have come to prefer the regimented labor system in China and have gained significant wealth through subcontracting in mainland China. By manipulating the political systems of both countries toward its own end, transnational capital has helped generate tremendous economic growth, as well as heightened social inequality in both Taiwan and China. By the late 1980s, Chinese state policymakers saw Taiwanese transnational capitalists as valuable sources of capital, and put into place special laws to encourage their investment. Scholars have also noted the role of the TCC in other parts of East Asia. For instance, in a study examining the political economy of South Korea, Moore identifies the dominant role of a TCC (2007, p. 44).

Other studies on the TCC in Asia have researched Indian and Indian diasporic transnational capitalists (Biradavolu, 2008; Upadhya & Vasavi, 2013). Writing on India in regard to transnational class relations, Upadhya (2004), for example, has shown the emergence of an early TCC fraction rooted among entrepreneurs in the software outsourcing industry. As one of the least regulated industries in India and emerging relatively autonomously from the "old economy," Upadhya traces how the software outsourcing industry expanded rapidly in the 1990s and into the 21st century, becoming globally competitive alongside underlying transformations in social and material relations. Looking at specific companies, she shows how middle-class professionals founded the initial Indian software enterprises. These companies underwent a decisive shift as foreign and cross-border capital investments grew, occurring not just through the direct investment of TNCs but also through venture capital (Upadhya, 2004). The industry's expansion was also tied to the growth of an Indian diaspora business community in the United States (most importantly in California's Silicon Valley), who use their connections with India in their business activities. She points to new contradictions and the necessity of studying how outsourced and diasporic labor – harnessed through virtual space – impacts the structure of global capital. Others have shown how these new high-technology ventures have facilitated the exploitation of segments of the Indian workforce through new 24-hour economic hubs where transnational telecommunications and sales corporations are heavily present (Sandhu, 2010).

Some studies have also begun to look at the role of state apparatuses in the region in promoting transnational labor regimes, such as Rodriguez's (2010) recent work, in which she observes how the Philippine state has become actively involved in marketing its citizens to companies and labor-receiving governments around the world for low wage and closely monitored temporary jobs. She explains how Philippine state elites have become entwined with global capitalist accumulation to such an extent that managing and promoting the exploitation of migrant workers has become an important part of their own social reproduction (Sprague, 2011). Importantly she shows how this is a gendered process, in which it is Filipino women who make up the vast majority of the exported labor. Also, many studies have looked at the growing role worldwide of policing actions targeting migrants and maintaining them as supra-exploited labor (Golash-Boza, 2015).

As such studies show capitalists rely on the state to plan and finance the infrastructure that is necessary for reproducing the productive base in political economy. In addition to facilitating the movement of low-waged labor, capitalists are forced in this regard to finance along with the state the training of highly educated and skilled cadres of scientists and other professionals. A good deal of this talent moves across territorial borders for additional training and to work in R&D and other centers to facilitate the competitiveness of industry and labor. Why do Japanese and other scientists locate their R&D operations close to research universities and centers in the United States, for example? Why and how did Singapore manage to move some distance up the investment and production food chain? They sent some of their best students to the United States for high-level training, following which they returned home to help set up and run the research and investment centers with the contacts they made overseas paying off, with some of the most advanced research groups from the US building transnational alliances with them and others in parts of Asia. This cross-fertilization and immediate cross-border relation of capital, skills, and talent is at the heart of the process for Singapore.

The static rhetoric about countries and nationally rooted power blocs competing with one another blurs our vision to reality. We could do with much less of this staid and dated rhetoric, if we are going to make sense of the globalization process in a critical and accurate way. As Jayasuriya (2012) points out: "Much of this tortured reflection is really a zombie debate where outmoded geopolitical terms such as 'power transition' are deployed to understand new patterns of international politics in a globally integrated economy." Jayasuriya points out a useful example in looking at the debate over competition and international relations between Australia, China, and the United States. He observes: "The assumption in the debate is that the strategic and economic relationships between the three countries are separate, whereas I suggest that it is the economic relationship that shapes the nature and form of the strategic relationship" (*Ibid.*). He adds:

> One of the defining features of economic changes in the region is growing regional integration within these production networks. Not only is Australia locked into these networks as supplier of resources and services, but US firms – such as J P Morgan – are as much a part of this emerging regional network. This complicates simplistic assessments of rivalry between China and the US. These production networks are complemented by the deepening capital markets. We know that China is heavily locked into US treasuries, but this is a two-way street with mutual interdependence and vulnerability. Perhaps more importantly, key government entities – not just in China, but also elsewhere such as Singapore – are now deeply embedded in capital markets through vehicles such as sovereign wealth funds. (*Ibid.*)

With similar approaches and lines of enquiry to the studies previously discussed, below I want to discuss some of the studies to appear in my recent edited book (Sprague, 2016). They help to start to form an interrelated body of work on the emergence of transnational social and class relations, and in the context of Asia and Oceania. This book in no way covered all the areas of class formation – as it was limited to the papers submitted to the Brisbane conference – and in particular, research avenues of ideological formation as well as racialized and gendered class relations are in need of more attention.

TRANSNATIONAL CAPITALIST CLASS

While the TCC is oriented toward global competiveness and profit seeking, it also includes national and regional contingents. These local and diverse factions, while not oriented toward indicative (development) planning (to foment national development), do often utilize particular national state apparatuses to advance their agendas. While oriented toward transnational chains of production and finance, this does not prevent "contingents of the TCC from drawing on particular ethnic identities and cultural practices to achieve their interests" (Robinson, 2014, pp. 27–28).

A number of recent studies have examined how there are different fractions of the TCC. Harris (2016a) has studied in detail the rise of a Chinese, statist-oriented fraction of the TCC. He explains that state enterprises have been utilized to incubate and promote this class fraction's increasing involvement in global chains of production and finance. Here he expands on his previous research on statist fractions of the TCC (Harris, 2009).

Focused on Japan, Takase (2015) argues that transnational productive capital has gained hegemonic status over other fractions of capital. To support this argument, he looks at the global orientation and activities of Toyota, showing how Japanese transnational capitalists hold a dominant influence over policymaking and push for stronger global economic integration, including the Asia-Pacific free trade accumulation strategy (the FTAAP). He points out, though, that many problems and contradictions face the implementation of Asia-Pacific economic integration, including the balance of social forces and the geopolitical conflict centered on China and the United States' role in the region.

Chesters (2015) has looked at the emergence in recent decades of leading transnational capitalists in China and India, who are integrated with chains of accumulation that span the globe. Connecting the world systems approach (Robinson, 2011; Wallerstein, 2004) with the global capitalism school approach, she argues that rapid economic growth and rising inequality within the territories of China and India has been linked to the exacerbation of wealth inequality in Australia and other parts of Oceania and Asia. The author explains how leading capitalists hailing from China, India, and Australia have become transnationally oriented and geared toward global competition, rather than localized markets or national development. Chester also looks at the number of billionaires in the region, explaining how financial speculation, rapid urbanization, and real estate development have generated much of the massive new wealth of top billionaires in India and China. Financial markets in particular have been fundamental to the functional connectivity of these capitalists with capitalists active in many others industries and based in different parts of the world. As Robinson (2014), Harris (2016a), and others show this has been a historical process through which the relationship of capitalists to each other and toward states have changed dramatically over recent decades.

In a multi-authored piece, Jones, Shrivastava, Selvarajah, and Van Gramberg (2016) examine how the rise of transnational capitalists and TNCs has occurred alongside declining well-being and job security for workers. The authors look at how processes of lean production have come to function, with case study research on the operations of Toyota in India. The standardization of lean production is enforced by a cohort of managers who are transferred between different locations around the world. Workers, meanwhile, are monitored in increasing detail by management through new technologies and organizational models. Workers who last as employees are those that remain uninjured, continually achieve cost, time, and production targets, and display themselves as compliant and loyal to management. Globally standardized labor regimes, promoted by transnational capital and operated by managerial groups, are thus used to extract more and more surplus labor from workers, with the value created incorporated into transnational chains of production.

LABOR AND THE GLOBAL ECONOMY

With vast tracts of humanity marginalized as "supernumeraries" of the global economy, many are propelled into migration as exported laborers, while others remain in relatively spatially fixed positions within nations as their labor-power. is incorporated into transnational value chains. Only in recent years have scholars begun to theorize the emergence of global proletarian fractions (Robinson, 2014, pp. 48–59; Struna, 2009), where the labor power of workers (producing their existence under various conditions) has become inserted into transnational value chains.

Lin (2016) through theories of a global proletariat and transnational capitalism has looked at the changing structural features of labor in China. With China's integration into the global economy over recent decades, Lin explains how millions of proletarianized workers have come to be embedded in new circuits of transnational accumulation. Here it is important to take into account the historical trajectory of Chinese labor through the Maoist period, up through the market reforms of Deng Xiaoping, and into the heightened capitalist globalization of recent decades. Taking under consideration Struna's (2009) theory of global proletarian fractions, Lin suggests how different fractions of the working class in China have come to exist through the era of capitalist globalization, observing how different skilled, immigrant, and statically located workers have had their labor-power transnationalized. Yet at the same time, as the author argues, many are grounded within a national context where their experiences and conditions are shaped heavily by local peculiarities. Local specificities can clash with and/or become enmeshed with transnational processes. Lin (2016) adds how these changes occur alongside open-ended labor struggles that face particular problems in building cross-border solidarity, such as being channeled through bureaucratic hierarchies and with their international ties heavily influenced by powerful state apparatuses (a problem that labor unions face in other parts of the world as well, including within the United States, as Scipes (2011) has documented).

Expanding on the work of Upadya and others who have examined the contradictory nature of India's integration into the global economy, authors Russell, Noronha, and D'Cruz (2016) have focused on business process outsourcing (BPO) as a leading up-and-coming sector of India's globally integrated economy. BPO is a type of outsourcing in which the activities of specific business functions are contracted out to a third-party service provider, often specializing in creating flexible and "more efficient" labor-intensive tasks. While

Russell, Noronha, and D'Cruz recognize the transnationalization of capital in the industry, with subcontracting forming a vital aspect of local capitalist integration into the global economy, they point to many existing problems that hold back and box in working-class organizing, subjectivity, and agency. They argue that workers within these industries have yet to exhibit tendencies that would lead to a globally oriented "class for itself," but instead remain confined to primarily local struggles, organized through national bodies and occasionally taking part in international campaigns. This points to a major problem and contradiction of capital-labor relations in the global era: whereas transnational capital intensifies its cross-border integrative practices, labor struggles are usually nationally or locally geared. Labor unions and movements from below have a long way to go in order to effectively organize against transnational capital. Yet, as Robinson (2014) and others have argued, if radical changes to this system are to occur and humanistic alternatives are to percolate, working-class organizing and consciousness too must globalize.

Another scholar, Velayutham (2016), points out how national rhetoric has become a mechanism through which policymakers of national states facilitate competitive engagement with the global economy. Foregrounded in the context of rising income inequality worldwide, Velayutham emphasizes how, through the era of global capitalism, government regulation and labor protections have been undermined through neoliberal reforms that have strengthened transnational capital. The author argues that as a part of this process, nationalism and national identity have been repackaged as a tool for competition in the global arena.

FINANCE AND PRODUCTION CAPITAL

While the globalization of capital has occurred unevenly (e.g., with divergent economic growth rates; distinctive consumer preferences; varied competitive environments; divergent regulatory standards and tax regimes; different currencies, cultures, and operating and management models), there has also been growing standardization of regulations, a wide-scale lowering of tariffs, increasing rates of cross-border mergers and acquisitions, and broad structural shifts toward global competitiveness. Financial speculation has reached unimagined heights through high-tech and organizational advancements, with stock markets and banks increasingly interconnected across borders. Areas in Asia have become nexuses for global chains of production and transnational banking and financial systems, and with highly developed "global cities" such as Singapore and Hong Kong.

Van Fossen (2016) argues that offshore tax havens have served as key nodes for transnational capitalist-class formation, observing, for example, how "[n]ew and powerful entrants to the TCC in the Asia-Pacific, such as most of China's elite, have formed symbiotic relationships with offshore tax havens." Fossen (2015) deals with how, among the TCC and their state and institutional associates, there have been different approaches toward tax havens. Van Fossen describes these factions/approaches as (1) libertarians who seek opaque tax havens that weaken the role of sovereign states to regulate capital, (2) structuralists who aim to lightly regulate havens through minimal common norms, and (3) regulationists who push for global law and regulations over tax havens. With transnational capital and power blocs not reaching a consensus over tax haven policy, there has been a relative incoherence in practical policies toward havens.

By contrast, authors Peetz and Murray (2016), through an ethnographic study, look at the TCC in connection to the global phenomenon of climate crisis, which now affects every region across the planet. Recognizing climate crisis as a by-product of capitalism, they seek to see whether fractions of transnational finance capital can be motivated to interrupt or avoid climate crisis. They seek specifically to understand how individual capitalists, as agents of the transnational capital class might be motivated to take environmentally friendly and even activist positions on matters of corporate behavior in relation to climate change. Peetz and Murray's study is particularly useful in understanding the subjective orientation of powerful transnational capitalists toward the most pressing planetary crisis: climate change. How do CEOs and major investors in the insurance industry see global climate change as impacting their global profits? Human-driven global climate change is negatively impacting species across the planet. It is a crisis that is already having a major impact on certain industries in the global economy, such as insurance corporations. The authors thus force us to consider what could happen if transnational companies, such as in the insurance industry, now integrated with global financial flows and with business activities across a range of sectors (and in different parts of the world), could push for better environmental policies and not just in one country, but globally.

Looking at transnational production capital, Cottle and Collins (2016), using the Marxian idea of ground-rent in their study of mining in Australia during the global era, make clear the role of land and nature in the creation of values of various forms of capital. Recognizing the "dominance of the transnational mining capital fraction within the ensemble of capital in Australia," they furthermore reference Bieler and Morton's argument on how the interests of transnational capital internalize within different forms of state. To articulate some contradictions they identify, their case study emphasizes "comprador" capitalists operating in "semi-peripheral" Australia. The term comprador, which is also used by Stilwell (2016), was utilized throughout much of the 20th century to describe capitalists in colonial and postcolonial societies that played a subordinate role to metropolitan capital. Future studies can debate the usefulness of the idea of comprador capitalists in understanding contemporary class relations.

TRANSNATIONAL DYNAMICS AND (UNDER) DEVELOPMENT

To understand the structures and agencies that undergird global society, scholars of the "global capitalism school" have emphasized as more determinant (of causal priority) the role of social production, and *then*, while also important, uneven geographic development. Whereas the academic field of development studies has long been wedded to nation-state centered frameworks, as Robinson suggests: "the way forward is a reconsideration of the relationship between space and development, and a new conception of development based not on territory but on social groups" (2002, p. 1048).

Examining the class nature of contemporary development and underdevelopment, Sims (2016) has looked at the social and economic transformation of Laos. Focused on the Indochinese peninsula in Southeast Asia, Sims explains how Laos has become a nexus through which people and capital move between more highly developed surrounding areas and, in the process, has become deeply incorporated into global chains of capital accumulation and rising inequality. Long considered an isolated area in the region, through secondary sources and ethnographic research the author shows the quantitative and qualitative expansion of global capital into this zone, with new city districts, transportation routes, upgraded airports, and other infrastructure developed for the purpose of facilitating the movement of transnational capital. The author connects the lived experiences of lower income communities displaced from their homes with the activities of dominant groups seeking to open space for new transnational capital investments, such as in real estate. Though looking at a much more highly developed part of the world, Harvey (2008, p. 38) has also recognized the role of transnational capitalists in reshaping cities and real estate development.

Also informed by ethnographic research, Mukherjee (2016) charts how middle-class education in India has historically been incubated in private, missionary schools. She argues that the successor models of this earlier missionary approach are now focused on their insertion into a globally competitive educational market. Seeking to adapt to shifting social and material patterns, under local and global pressures, such schools are dropping policies of social inclusion and are becoming more exclusive, increasingly immersed within structural inequalities of the global system. Mousumi provides detailed testimonials she gathered from educational workers in Kolkata to support her argument – which also help to show the ideological formation that takes place in this context.

Pacheco (2016), emphasizing the uneven nature of today's transnational chains of accumulation, looks at the local impact of transnational corporate mining on the remote island of Lihir in Papua New Guinea. He focuses specifically on how the industry seeks to measure and promote the data they have gathered. Having formerly worked in the mining industry himself, Pacheco provides an insider's view. He observes that "the worldwide deregulation of investment in mining, oil, and gas facilitated the entry of private foreign multinational companies into developing countries," with various projects starting up at that point. The growth in global capitalist industrial production in locations such as China has sent transnational capital fractions in search of new raw materials, giving impetus to new investments in oil, gas, and metal industries in the developing world. For this reason, new mining enclaves in developing countries such as Papua New Guinea have become substantial locations for global capital investment. Pacheco explains how mining companies conduct detailed studies of the impact of their operations, in part to comply with national and transnational regulatory regimes but also to show global competitiveness and secure legitimacy. He concludes that the tensions between the mining company and local communities he observed in Papua New Guinea were not diminishing, but rather were "rooted in structural, historical, and economic disparities" perpetuated by the transnational legal system that upholds international contracts while sidelining substantive debate and depoliticizing local struggles (Pacheco, 2016).

TRANSNATIONALLY ORIENTED ELITES AND THE STATE APPARATUS

In regard to the state, Robinson (2004), Harris (2006), and others have argued that a parallel political project connected to the class power of the TCC is nascent. Conceptualizing political restructuring in the global era, they have argued that transnationally oriented elites operating through various state apparatuses (often aligned with different fractions of the TCC) have become the dominant actors in most governments and major political institutions. The theory of emergent transnational state apparatuses, as coined by Robinson (2004), claims that through globalization a nascent political, juridical, and regulatory network is taking shape through numerous local, national, and supranational state institutions. The TCC, to promote and ensure its power, requires a concomitant political project. Such a political project would involve, for example: (1) promoting investor confidence in the global economy, (2) setting up mechanisms and institutions for responding to economic, political, and military crises that threaten the stability necessary for global markets, and (3) establishing a degree of macroeconomic policy uniformity across borders. Some scholars have used this approach to look at how international law has been impacted during the global era (Chimni, 2010). Cannon and Jayasuriya (2016) and Bieler and Morton (2013/2014) explain how specific state forms or subunits within states have come to incubate or be penetrated by transnational interests, emphasizing (as does Robinson) that particular mechanisms of statecraft and regulatory regimes have become sites of political contestation and transnational conflict. Cannon and Jayasuriya (2016), for instance, lay out how changes have occurred regionally and through state regulatory apparatuses, utilizing examples from Australia (such as the heightening impact of transnational Chinese mining capital on Australian institutions). Identifying the transformation of what they call subnational state institutions, the authors examine how transnational interests and processes have become embedded within governmental bodies (see also Sprague, 2010).

Robinson (2016) expanding on his earlier work argues that over recent decades, state elites operating through different national and supranational state apparatuses have worked to congeal the political project of transnational capital by way of state reforms and policies that promote the interests of transnational capitalist fractions. He examines in particular the relationship between the TCC and the BRICS association, observing how state apparatuses within the BRICS association have become transnationally oriented. While recognizing the importance of the BRICS in helping lead toward a more multipolar interstate system, Robinson (2016) argues that BRICS do not represent a liberatory alternative for the global system's class society. This is because the BRICS are deeply integrated within the highly unequal class relation of capitalist globalization. He explains that mainstream political economy perspectives, through the lens of nation-state competition, ignore the fundamental changes undergone through the transnationalization of capitalist relations, leading many to overlook how capitalists in the BRICS have become inseparable from capitalists worldwide. He observes, for instance, that the China National Petroleum Corporation (CNPC) now has "co-investments and joint ventures around the world with virtually all the major private transnational oil companies" and rather than being shut out of US-occupied Iraq, it was ushered into the Iraqi petroleum market with the assistance of US policymakers. In another example, he points out "agribusiness interests in Brazil … bring together Brazilian capitalists and land barons with the giant TNCs that drive global agribusiness, and that themselves in their ownership and cross-investment structures bring together individual and institutional investors from around the world, such as Monsanto, ADM, Cargill, and so forth". He adds, "simply put, 'Brazilian' agricultural exports are *transnational capital agricultural exports*." Brazilian state elites who promote the dropping of US agricultural subsidies in fact advance the interests of certain TCC fractions, not Brazilian national capital. The same can be said of many state elites operating through their national state institutions in Oceania and Asia, where their social reproduction has become dependent upon the investment and accumulation of global capital. Robinson (2016) has taken on some of his critics in a number of recent pieces, elaborating, for instance, upon how political economists Bieler and Morton (2013/2014) have mischaracterized his approach.

DEBATING THE GLOBAL CAPITALISM SCHOOL APPROACH

Some legitimate critiques and debates over works of the GCS approach (and with reference to inter-state politics) do exist, but too often the critiques have thrown up straw person arguments. The most recent blatant example of this is a full-length article published by Sean Kenji Starrs (2017) looking at the GCS approach through the context of Asia and Oceania. Starrs' explanation of the GCS approach is a caricature and simplification, one in which he can hold up a straw person to then take down. The number of false assertions that he makes are too many to go over here, but the most ridiculous are his claim that the GCS approach depicts the national state as a relic of the past, that it is "not taking the state seriously," that from the GCS approach "geo-political rivalry is merely a remnant from a bygone era," or that the GCS "assumes that all capitalist nation-states have a strict separation between public and private, state and capital, in which the capitalist class instrumentalizes the state" (*Ibid.*). Through these straw persons, Starrs then makes the claim that GCS scholars ignore the role of state elites and local particular interests.

GCS scholars have never argued that the nation-state is a relic of the past. State elites, as relatively autonomous, clearly carry out many particular and vital activities and through different backgrounds and local particularities. At the same time, over recent decades, many state elites have become dependent for their social reproduction on transnational capital. This is most assuredly true for the Chinese state-party elite, as Harris (2016b) has shown. Importantly, Starrs (2017) ignores the GCS analysis of fractions and fractionation, which then allows him to claim that the GCS posits a monolithic TCC. Geopolitical conflict clearly continues to exist, but the GCS approach forces us to consider how this occurs in light of the novel social and material relations of the global epoch.

Echoing Bramble (2016), who though to a lesser extent, also makes some poor caricatures of the GCS approach, Starrs (2017) conflates political analysis with the underlying structure of capital relations. At one point in his recent article, Starrs claims that Robinson utilizes the concept of base and super-structure (which, in fact, Robinson never has in any of his work). Even Marx in his use of the base and super-structure concept utilized it in a much more flexible (and less deterministic) manner than is often portrayed. Marx suggested, for example, that culture sometimes became a component of the base. Rather than sticking rigidly to a model like Starrs suggests, the method of Robinson and other GCS theorists, as Barahona (2011, p. 892) has pointed out, has been to: "study historical facts, filtering them for their significance through the lens of Marx and Gramsci, and formulate inductive theory from them. Once the theory has been universalized, he goes back and does more research to test how well the theory works, 'unpacking' the theory to see if it 'fits' new sets of facts."

Importantly, not only do we need more data, we also need to consider how data is framed and interpreted. For example, while we do have a growing amount of corporate ownership data, as Starrs (2017) rightly points out: more data on corporations is needed. However, Starrs fails to ask himself some vital questions: how do we interpret this data? How is the data framed? Starrs' interpretation of the data is to view the orientation of capital as determined simplistically by the citizenship status of a capitalist or the domicile location of a company or its investors – a gross over simplification and one that reifies nation-state centrism, ignoring so many other objective and subjective phenomena.

CONCLUSION

Much attention in recent years has turned toward understanding the so-called Asian century and the rise of China and the problems it faces, with emphasis on global finance and heated geopolitical conflicts new and old, and the governmental and business policy challenges all of this entails. Through many state-centric approaches, social scientists have often focused their attention on the development of phenomena occurring within the borders of a single nation, making comparisons between nations, or at times considering international processes that occur back and forth between countries or the role of national corporations and domestic capitalists (identified with the nation-state in which they are domiciled or a citizen). This paper, however, as I have outlined, seeks to look at how some political economic studies have broken with the Westphalian state-centric approach. I have looked at how researchers of GCS place emphasis on transnational processes, globalizing chains of accumulation, and the social reproduction therein that has come to be so entangled with local, national, and regional phenomena. The numerous studies that I have discussed in this paper illustrate the highly integrative yet intensely exploitive, dehumanizing, and crisis-prone nature of this globalization phase of world capitalism.

NOTE

1. This paper is a greatly improved upon and expanded version of a chapter titled "Global Capitalism and Transnational Class Formation in Asia and Oceania," published previously in an edited book volume (Sprague, 2016). A shorter version of this article has been translated into Mandarin Chinese and can be viewed online at: http://groundbreaking.tw/wordpress/archives/2245

REFERENCES

Agnew, J. (2009). *Globalization and sovereignty*. Rowman & Littlefield Publishers.

Barahona, D. (2011). The capitalist globalization of Latin America. *Critical Sociology*, *37*(6), 889–895.

Baker, Y. (2014). Global capitalism and Iraq: The making of a neoliberal state. *International Review of Modern Sociology*, *40*(2), 121–148.

Bieler, A., & Morton, A. D. (2013/2014). The will-o'-the-wisp of the transnational state. *Journal of Australian Political Economy*, *72*, 23–51.

Biradavolu, M. R. (2008). *Indian entrepreneurs in Silicon Valley: The making of a transnational techno-capitalist class*. Amherst, NY: Cambria Press.

Bramble, T. (2016). State, capital, and class struggle in Australia: Reflections on the global capitalism perspective. In J. Sprague (Ed.), *Globalization and transnational capitalism in Asia and Oceania*. London: Routledge.

Breslin, S. (Ed.). (2013). *East Asia and the global crisis*. London: Routledge.

Calinicos, A. (1993). *Race and Class* (Bookmarks).

Cannon, D., & Jayasuriya, K. (2016). The regionalization of capital in the patchwork economy and the transnationalization of the subnational state. In J. Sprague (Ed.), *Globalization and transnational capitalism in Asia and Oceania* (pp. 285–300). London: Routledge.

Carroll, W. (2010). *The making of a transnational capitalist class: Corporate power in the 21st century*. London: Zed Books.

Chesters, J. (2015). The rise of China and India and the formation of a transnational capitalist class in the Asia/Oceania region. In J. Sprague (Ed.), *Globalization and transnational capitalism in Asia and Oceania* (pp. 56–72). London: Routledge.

Chimni, B. S. (2010). Prolegomena to a class approach to international law. *The European Journal of International Law*, *21*(1), 57–82.

Chun, L. (2013). *China and global capitalism: Reflections on Marxism, history, and contemporary politics*. New York, NY: Palgrave Macmillan.

Cottle, D., & Collins, J. (2016). From client state to rentier state? New compradors, transnational capital, and the internationalization of globalizing dynamics in Australia, 1990-2013. In J. Sprague (Ed.), *Globalization and transnational capitalism in Asia and Oceania* (pp. 180–195). London: Routledge.

Davis, M. (2007). *Planet of slums*. London: Verso.

Dicken, P. (2011). *Global shift: Mapping the changing contours of the world economy*. New York, NY: The Guilford Press.

Dikötter, F. (Ed.). (1997). *The construction of racial identities in China and Japan*. C Hurst & Co Publishers Ltd.

Embong, A. R. (2000). Globalization and transnational class relations: Some problems of conceptualization. *Third World Quarterly*, *21*(6), 989–1000.

Federici, S. (2004). Caliban and the Witch: Women, the body and primitive accumulation. *Autonomedia*.

Feldman, D. (2016). Review of globalization and transnational capitalism in Asia and Oceania. *Journal of World-Systems Research*, *22*(2), 576–582.

Golash-Boza, T. M. (2015). *Deported: Policing immigrants, disposable labor and global capitalism*. New York, NY: NYU Press.

Golby, J. (2015). American society and its military. In H. Liebert, J. Griswold, & I. Wilson III (Eds.), *Thinking beyond boundaries: Transnational challenges to U.S. foreign policy* (pp. 55–64). Baltimore, MA: John Hopkins.

Graaff, N. D., & van Apeldoorn, B. (2017). US elite power and the rise of 'statist' Chinese elites in global markets. *International Politics*, *54*(3), 338–355.

Gramsci, A. (1973). *Letters from prison*. L. Lawner (Ed. and Trans.), New York, NY: Harper and Row.

Gray, L. (1986). *The global assembly line*. Blooming Grove, NY: New Day Films.

Haase, D. (Ed.). (2013). *Perspectives on global development and technology*, 12(1–2).

Harris, J. (2006). *The dialectics of globalization: Economics and political conflict in a transnational world*. Newcastle upon Tyne: Cambridge Scholars Publishing.

Harris, J. (2009). Statist globalization in China, Russia and the Gulf States. *Science & Society*, *73*(1), 6–33.

Harris, J. (2016a). Statism and the transnational capitalist class in China. In J. Sprague (Ed.), *Globalization and transnational capitalism in Asia and Oceania* (pp. 21–39). London: Routledge.

Harris, J. (2016b). *Global capitalism and the crisis of democracy*. Atlanta, GA: Clarity Press.

Harvey, D. (2008). The right to the city. *New Left Review*, *53*, 23–40.

Jayasuriya, K. (2004a). *Asian regional governance: Crisis and change*. New York, NY: Routledge.

Jayasuriya, K. (Ed.). (2004b). Governing the Asia Pacific: Beyond the "New Regionalism". *Third World Quarterly Series*. New York, NY: Palgrave Macmillan.

Jayasuriya, K. (2012). *Global markets are the new battlefields*. *ABC News*. Retrieved from http://www.abc.net.au/news/2012-06-26/jayasuriya-geo-economics/4091270

Jones, R., Shrivastava, S., Selvarajah, C., & Van Gramberg, B. (2016). Lean production as a tool of global capitalism in Asia: The transnational capitalist class in action. In J. Sprague (Ed.), *Globalization and transnational capitalism in Asia and Oceania* (pp. 73–88). London: Routledge.

Li, M. (2009). *The rise of china and the demise of the capitalist world economy*. New York, NY: Monthly Review Press.

Lin, K. (2016). Global capitalism and the transformation of China's working class. In J. Sprague (Ed.), *Globalization and transnational capitalism in Asia and Oceania* (pp. 91–107). London: Routledge.

Liodakis, G. (2010). *Totalitarian capitalism and beyond*. London: Ashgate.

McMichael, P. (1996). *Development and social change: A global perspective*. Thousand Oaks, CA: Pine Forge.

Mies, M. (1986). *Patriarchy and accumulation on a world scale: Women in the international division of labour*. London: Zed Books.ies.

Moore, P. (2007). *Globalisation and labour struggle in Asia: A neo-Gramscian critique of South Korea's political economy*. London: I. B. Tauris.

Mukherjee, M. (2016). From missionary to new middle-class schooling in the era of global capitalism: Dilemmas of inclusive education reform in India. In J. Sprague (Ed.), *Globalization and transnational capitalism in Asia and Oceania*. London: Routledge.

Murray, G. (2007). *Capitalist networks and social power in Australia and New Zealand*. London: Ashgate.

Murray, G., & Scott, J. (2012). *Financial elites and transnational business: Who rules the world?* Cheltenham: Edward Elgar Publishing.

Pacheco, V. (2016). From transnational trends to local practices: Monitoring social impacts in a Papua New Guinea mining community. In J. Sprague (Ed.), *Globalization and transnational capitalism in Asia and Oceania* (pp. 229–244). London: Routledge.

Panitch, L., & Gindin, S. (2012). *The making of global capitalism: The political economy of American empire*. London: Verso.

Peetz, D., & Murray, G. (2016). Conflicts within transnational finance capital and the motivations of climate-interested investors. In J. Sprague (Ed.), *Globalization and transnational capitalism in Asia and Oceania* (pp. 163–179). London: Routledge.

Pereira, A. A. (2017). Review of globalization and transnational capitalism in Asia and Oceania. *Critical Sociology*, *43*(4–5), 802–805.

Pilger, J. (2017). *The Coming War on China*. ITV. Retrieved from Film website http://thecomingwar-movie.com

Robinson, W. I. (1996). *Promoting polyarchy: Globalization, US intervention, and hegemony*. Newcastle upon Tyne: Cambridge University Press.

Robinson, W. I. (2002). Remapping in light of globalization: From a territorial to a social cartography. *Third World Quarterly*, *23*(6), 1047–1071.

Robinson, W. I. (2004). *A theory of global capitalism: Production, class and state in a transnational world*. Baltimore, MD: John Hopkins University Press.

Robinson, W. I. (2011). Globalization and the sociology of Immanuel Wallerstein: A critical appraisal. *International Sociology*, *26*(6), 1–23.

Robinson, W. I. (2014). *Global capitalism and the crisis of humanity*. Newcastle upon Tyne: Cambridge University Press.

Robinson, W. I. (2016). Global capitalism, the BRICS, and the transnational state. In J. Sprague (Ed.), *Globalization and transnational capitalism in Asia and Oceania* (pp. 247–268). London: Routledge.

Robinson, W. I., & Sprague-Silgado, J. (2018). The transnational capitalist class: Origin and evolution of a concept. In M. Juergensmeyer, M. Steger, S. Sassen, & V. Faesse (Eds.), *The Oxford handbook of global studies*. Oxford: Oxford University Press.

Rodriguez, R. M. (2010). *Migrants for export: How the Philippine state brokers labor to the world*. Minneapolis, MN: University of Minnesota Press.

Ross, J. (2016). Lessons for Latin America from China's economic success. *teleSUR*. Retrieved from http://www.telesurtv.net/english/opinion/Lessons-for-Latin-America-from-Chinas-Economic-Success-20160126-0014.html

Russel, B., Noronha, E., & D'Cruz, P. (2016). Transnational class formation: A view from below. In J. Sprague (Ed.), *Globalization and transnational capitalism in Asia and Oceania* (pp. 108–124). London: Routledge.

Sandhu, A. (2010). Servicing global capitalism: Transnational work, labor and culture in India's Silicon Valley. Santa Barbara, Dissertation for University of California.

Sassen, S. (1991). *The global city: New York, London, Tokyo*. Princeton, NJ: Princeton University Press.

Scipes, K. (2011). *AFL-CIO's secret war against developing country workers: Solidarity or sabotage?* Lanham, MD: Lexington Books.

Shen, H. (2011). Transnational or compatriotic bourgeoisie? Contesting democracy across the Taiwan Strait. In K.-S. Chang & B. Turner *Contest citizenship in East Asia: Developmental politics, national unity, and globalization* (pp. 115–132). New York, NY: Routledge.

Sims, K. (2016). Uneven geographies of transnational capitalism in Laos. In J. Sprague (Ed.), *Globalization and transnational capitalism in Asia and Oceania* (pp. 199–213). London: Routledge.

Sklair, L. (1996a). Australia in the global capitalist system. *Social Alternatives*, *15*(1), 14–17.

Sklair, L. (1996b). Conceptualising and researching the transnational capitalist class in Australia. *Journal of Sociology*, *32*(1), 1–19.

Sklair, L. (2001). *The transnational capitalist class*. Malden, MA: Wiley-Blackwell.

Sklair, L. (2002). *Globalization: Capitalism and its alternatives*. Oxford: Oxford University Press.

Sprague, J. (2010). Statecraft in the global financial crisis: An interview with Kanishka Jayasuriya. *Journal of Critical Globalisation Studies*, *3*, 127–138.

Sprague, J. (2011). Review of Robyn Magalit Rodriguez, migrants for export: How the Philippine state brokers labor to the world (2010). *Science & Society*, *75*(3), 442–444.

Sprague, J. (2016). *Globalization and transnational capitalism in Asia and Oceania*. London: Routledge, 322pp.

Sprague, J., & Ietto-Gillies, G. (2014). Transnational corporations in twenty-first century capitalism: An interview with Grazia Ietto-Gillies. *Critical Perspectives on International Business*, *10*(1/2), 35–50.

Starrs, S. (2015). Making the world safe for big business: The Trans-Pacific Partnership is about expanding US hegemony in East Asia. *Jacobin*. Retrieved from https://www.jacobinmag.com/2015/05/trans-pacific-parternship-china-united-states-asia/

Starrs, S. K. (2017). The global capitalism school tested in Asia" (a critical review of "Globalization and Transnational Capitalism in Asia and Oceania. *Journal of Contemporary Asia*, *47*(2).

Stilwell, F. (2016). Global capitalism and its discontents: Towards a political economy of the possible. In J. Sprague (Ed.), *Globalization and transnational capitalism in Asia and Oceania* (pp. 303–318). London: Routledge.

Struna, J. (2009). Toward a theory of global proletarian fractions. *Perspectives on Global Development and Technology*, *8*(2–1), 230–260.

Struna, J. (Ed.). (2013). *Globalizations*. 5(10).

Struna, J. (2015). *Handling globalization: Labor, capital, and class in the globalized distribution center*. Dissertation, University of California Riverside.

Takase, H. (2015). Japanese transnational capitalists and Asia-Pacific free trade. In J. Sprague (Ed.), *Globalization and transnational capitalism in Asia and Oceania* (pp. 40–55). London: Routledge.

Upadhya, C. (2004). A new transnational class? Capital flows, business networks and entrepreneurs in the Indian software industry. *Economic and Political Weekly*, *39*(48), 5141–5143, 5145–5151.

Upadhya, C., & Vasavi, A. R. (2013). *In an outpost of the global economy: Work and workers in India's information technology industry*. New Delhi: Routledge India.

van der Pijl, K. (1998). *Transnational class and international relations*. London: Routledge.

Van Fossen, A. (2016). Offshore tax havens: The borderlands of global capitalism. In J. Sprague (Ed.), *Globalization and transnational capitalism in Asia and Oceania* (pp. 145–162). London: Routledge.

Velayutham, S. (2016). National champions in a global arena: Rhetoric and inequality in global capitalism. In J. Sprague (Ed.), *Globalization and transnational capitalism in Asia and Oceania* (pp. 125–141). London: Routledge.

Wallerstein, I. (2004). *World-systems analysis: An introduction*. Durham, NC: Duke University Press.

Watson, H. (Eds.). (2015). *Globalization, sovereignty and citizenship in the Caribbean*. Mona, Jamaica: University of the West Indies Press.

Zhao, Y. (2003). Transnational capital, the Chinese state, and China's communication industries in a fractured society. *Javnost – The Public*, *10*(4), 54–74.

Zhao, Y. (2008). *Communication in China: Political economy, power, and conflict*. Lanham, MD: Rowman & Littlefield Publishers.

A CRITICAL REVIEW OF CHINA'S REFORM

Gyu Cheol Lee

ABSTRACT

This paper reviews the socioeconomic reform policies employed by the China's party-state between the early 1980s and mid-2000s. Unlike conventional frameworks viewing the reform as an economic development project designed for "national interests" or "ruling elites" personal interests', this paper interprets the reform as a political attempt of the state made in response to the crisis of dominance over the working class. In the face of the crisis of class dominance expressed as economic and political unrests related to low growth of labor productivity, the state managers of the post-Mao era embarked on the reform as a way of restoring the state's ability to impose work upon the workers. As is well known, the reform was "market-oriented" with the state relinquishing some of the control over economic managements, and this paper sees it as the state's strategy of reducing political risks arising from a highly politicized form of class confrontation. By making pressures upon producers look like a purely economic matter arising from private relations, that is, by depoliticizing exploitative social relations of production, the market-oriented reform helped the party-state effectively repress workers without a serious damage to political legitimacy. From this perspective, this paper examines the reform policies in management of labor, firms, and money, and how those policies contributed to the state's ability to discipline class relations of production in China. This paper, however, does not

Return of Marxian Macro-dynamics in East Asia
Research in Political Economy, Volume 32, 159–184

ISSN: 0161-7230/doi:10.1108/S0161-723020170000032010

conclude that the reform as a depoliticization strategy of class dominance was successful and nonproblematic. It is argued that beneath the success of the reform was a growing necessity of crisis; faced with re-burgeoning workers' struggles, growing problems of overproduction/overaccumulation, and the resultant looming banking system crisis, the party-state came to find it more and more necessary to bring the economic managements back into political ambit with the related political risks also growing.

Keywords: Reform in China; China's transition; class struggle; depoliticization

INTRODUCTION

It is a common conception that the market-oriented reform in China was an economic restructuring project designed either for "national prosperity" or for economic and political interests of "groups of powerful individuals." It is true that a study of the reform can explain how China's national wealth was enlarged so fast and how the cadres and their family enriched themselves at the costs of the majority of people. This paper, however, argues that "national economic growth" or "enrichment of certain groups of people" is the outcome of the reform, not the cause of it, and thus just focusing on them cannot show the fundamental nature (i.e., the class character) of the reform. This paper alternatively attempts to interpret the reform as a political attempt of the state made in response to the crisis of dominance over the working class. Faced with the crisis of class dominance manifested in the form of low growth of labor productivity and the related political unrests, the state managers devised the reform as a means of restoring the party-state's ability to pressurize defiant workers. As is well known, the reform was "market-oriented" with the state retreating from economic managements, and this paper views it as the state's strategy of reducing political risks arising from a highly politicized form of class confrontation. By making pressures upon producers look like a purely economic matter arising from private relations or so-called nature-like market discipline, that is, by depoliticizing exploitative social relations of production, the market-oriented reform helped the government effectively repress underproductive workers without a serious political damage to itself. In this framework, this paper examines the reform policies in management of labor, firms, and money, and how those policies contributed to the state's ability to discipline class relations of production in China.

This paper starts with a section dealing with a theoretical framework, including the Open Marxist concept of the state and the politics of depoliticization.

The paper then discusses a historical context of the post-Mao reform, showing how the crisis of Maoist social relations provided the basis upon which the reform process gathered momentum. Examining the first phase of reform and its limitations, this paper presents how a set of reform policies conducive to exploitation of labor came to build its own barrier in the course. Dealing with the second phase of reform, the following part of this paper analyzes how the Chinese state organized social relations as a way of lowering exploitation costs through depoliticization policies on the banking system, state-owned enterprises (SOEs), and public management of the labor force. Lastly, in lieu of conclusion, the paper briefly points out the fundamental limitations and contradictions of the second phase of reform in each economic field.

THEORETICAL FRAMEWORK: ACCUMULATION IMPERATIVE AND POLITICS OF DEPOLITICIZATION

The State and Imperatives of Accumulation

A number of commentators have sought to explain the character of the reform in China proceeded from the early 1980s. Many of them view the reform as a project of national development: the government's decision to transplant market factors into the "inefficient" state-centric planned economy. Admiring the unprecedented economic growth and national prosperity it has achieved, they tend to see the reform, albeit not without a limitation, as a successful project designed by the foreseeing party leadership. On the other hand, some critical viewers focus their attention on the struggles for material interests and political power among powerful groups of individuals (e.g., the capitalist roaders vs. the radical Maoist leaders), and then see the reform as an outcome of the struggles: abandonment of socialist principles by the ruling elite who turned themselves into self-interested "bureaucratic capitalists" (Au, 2014). It is undeniable that both points of view explain some important facts of the event, providing insights into the reform process. Despite their insights, however, those views, focusing on "nation" or "groups of people," can be criticized for failing to fully reveal the class character[1] of the reform, and it seems such a shortcoming derives from failing to see the fundamental class character of "national states."

"The state" is conventionally considered a natural thing that exists separate from society; a neutral and classless institutional structure that either acts for the sake of the "national" interest or that can be appropriated and wielded by a certain social group for their own personal benefits. Based on open Marxist perspectives (Bonefeld, 1992; see also, inter alia, Holloway, 1995; Burnham 1995, 2001, 2006), this paper views the state from a quite different perspective; in this view, the state is seen not as a "thing" naturally existing independent from society but as a political *form* of exploitative social relations of production; a formalized political way in which class relations are reproduced on the basis of extraction of surplus labor from those without control over the means of production. This conception of states explains why the core of statecraft, whatever political party is in power, always lies in political and economic policies ensuring a favorable condition for exploitation of labor and the resultant progressive accumulation growth (Burnham, 2001, p. 108). It follows, in other words, that policies for more efficient exploitation of labor and progressive accumulation (expressed in the form of a rise in labor productivity and national economic growth, respectively) are not an option but an imperative to the state as long as it is to secure its own existence. From this perspective, one can see that the reform in China was one of the political attempts of the Chinese state to regulate and reproduce class relations by imposing more "efficient and productive" work upon the working class.

This paper traces that it was political and economic unrests owing to the difficulties in extracting surplus labor on a national level (expressed as stagnating productivity growth) during the last decade of the Maoist era that made a reform in one way or another necessary. Under the so-called state capitalism, a consistent rise in labor productivity was indeed crucial for the sustainability of the system as long as the government (the sole "employer" or "capitalist") was to employ an increasing number of new workers, offering them at least the same level of social wages as that of the existent workers. Put differently, employing more workers without a rise in labor productivity meant that the government was getting less and less surplus with which it could support the existing level of social wages and investment. It follows that, one way or another, the party leadership had to figure out a way to improve labor productivity in order to reproduce the class relations including itself. One of the easiest ways for that was taking advantage of the command power of bureaucratic hierarchy; the party leadership had the administrative power to cut the real wages of workers or order the cadres on each production fields to directly put pressure upon "less-productive" workers in the name of national prosperity or "socialist victory." A critical problem of such a direct control, however, was that it could turn the Chinese Communist Party (CCP) from the "comrades" of workers into a mere dictator which would be more exposed to direct resistances of workers. It was this limit of highly politicized control over class relations that made the state managers pursue "a governing strategy of depoliticization" in the name of reforms.

Reform as Political Strategy of Depoliticization

In making socioeconomic policies, state managers, as managers of class dominance, must not only consider ensuring progressive accumulation but popular domestic support in order to retain office, strengthen personal authority, and preserve the legitimacy of the state's institutions. The problem is that the former (imperative of accumulation) often contradicts the latter (imperative of legitimacy) as it is likely to involve politically unpopular policies (involving wage cutting and work intensification, etc.). For state managers, thus, there needs to be a governing strategy through which they can reconcile the contradiction between two imperatives. Among others, this paper focuses on the strategy of depoliticization, which means "the process of placing at one remove the political character of decision-making" (Burnham, 2001, p. 128) or employing "the range of tools, mechanisms and institutions through which politicians can attempt to move to an indirect governing relationship" (Flinders & Buller, 2006, pp. 295–296).

By relinquishing direct control over particular issues or delegating it to apparently nonpolitical institutions (albeit while retaining an "arm's length" control over crucial economic and social processes), core-executives can avoid their direct political responsibility for any social consequence of unpopular policies on the issues (as they are now seen as essentially technical, apolitical, and personal matters). The concept of depoliticization as a governing strategy is a useful framework through which the market-oriented reform in China can be understood; it can be seen as the party-state's attempt to depoliticize management of class relations so that the exploitative pressures on the workers can be heightened without critically undermining the political legitimacy of the party leadership.[2] This paper explores the CCP's depoliticization strategy with special attention to the reforms in management of money, state-owned firms, and workers.

First, through a series of banking system reforms, the government transformed banks from a politically driven financial guarantor for SOEs and public agencies into seemingly independent and profit-oriented legal entities. This transformation of banks changed the nature of money from a mere means of circulation (which is simply given to producers by the state) into an independent embodiment of value (which has to be hardly earned by producers in the competitive market). With the rule of money, that is the disciplinary power of money replacing the rule of the central plan, the state was able to obtain a powerful and seemingly nonpolitical means (i.e., monetary policies instead of direct administrative directives) to impose austerities upon underproductive producers (both firms and workers).

Second, along with banks, the state also pushed SOEs outside the ambit of the political system toward the pure economic realm, making them responsible for their own losses as well as gains in competition with other firms. This privitization of state firms functioned as privitization of the politically unpopular imperative of having to impose "efficient" work on defiant state workers, thereby realizing higher productivity of labor. Put differently, the state's abandonment of ownership over firms freed the party cadres (managers in the workplace) from the politically difficult obligation to impose economically "rational" work upon their danwei "comrades"; now the obligation was moved onto the individual owners of firms whose survival in the market came to be dependent upon "competitive" productivity levels in factories.

Third, the CCP leadership transformed the political "labor system" (in which workers as "comrades" were directly regulated by the bureaucratic hierarchy) into the ostensibly nonpolitical "labor market" (in which workers and property-owners as "free and equal citizens" interact one another by legal contracts). The newly formed labor market turned out a much more effective political and economic means than the previous labor system in extracting surplus labor; first, the competition for jobs among workers now free from the forced employment of the state (e.g., millions of young migrant workers discharged from the township and village enterprises (TVEs) in the 1990s) played a critical role in lowering real wages and strengthening labor discipline in the workplace. Second, while labor disputes were soaring due to the emerging job insecurity and falling real wages, the party was able to evade the direct ire of workers by disguising itself as an "impartial arbiter" or even "workers' party" trying to impose "fair and just" rules of the game against some abusive managements.

In summary, by relinquishing the direct control (and the concomitant direct responsibility) over money, firms, and workers and by upholding the rule of money under which the exploitative class relation is seen as apolitical, technical, and personal matters between "free and equal" citizens, the party-state managed to gain (rather than lose) the power to pressurize underproductive producers, the ability to impose a stricter discipline over the class relations. Indeed, the rule of money, in the form of threat of potential bankruptcy and redundancy, triggered the endless and self-directed "race to the bottom" among the firms and workers across the industry, and this made it possible for the state to finally achieve the goal of the reform: *creating more favorable condition for accumulation without seriously undermining the legitimacy of the CCP rule*. This is the reason why the reform in China should be seen in the framework of a political strategy of depoliticization aiming at a better exploitation of labor, rather than viewing it as a technical process of employing market stimulus required for national prosperity or an outgrowth of struggles for private interests between some powerful individuals.

HISTORICAL CONTEXT OF POST-MAO REFORM

In the early years of the foundation of the People's Republic of China, the ruling CCP made it clear that its historical mission was to transform China into a fully developed industrial economy, thereby creating the "material conditions for socialism" (White, 1998, pp. 22–24). Making itself the sole owner of means of production with the monopolized power over workers and production, for the purpose, the party-state pursued economic plans focusing resources on heavy industries at the cost of the rural sector. In terms of economic achievements, such a command economy made a great success. Indeed, Mao's China had enjoyed high rates of industrial growth with agricultural production growing steadily, which successfully implemented structural change in the economy with industry's share of gross national product soaring from 25% in 1949 to nearly 60% in 1977 (Girdner, 2004, p. 125). Also, with improvements in public education and social welfare, the level of "human capital" was significantly raised, while full employment provided a certain extent of social and political stability.

Despite these figures of success, however, at the time of Mao's death (1976), the Maoist model of state capitalism was running out of steam. The most manifest sign of crisis was found in low growth of productivity throughout the national economy (i.e., the state's inability to extract surplus labor much enough to sustain progressive accumulation). While labor productivity in heavy industry was declining and output increases were sustained merely through ever-larger capital investments and a growing industrial labor force, excessive concentration on heavy industry starved other sectors of funds and retarded their growth in productivity as well (Hart-Landsberg & Burkett, 2005, p. 38). According to some estimation, by the mid-1970s about 20–25% of urban workers in state industry were employed more than was required for maximum production (Knight & Song, 2005, p. 34). In rural areas, despite the massive infrastructural projects agricultural output per worker only rose 5% in real terms over the whole period between 1952 and 1978 (Nolan, 1990, p. 11). While productivity growth was stagnating, the commitment to rapid industrialization and high levels of capital accumulation was able to be maintained only at the expense of the working population's standard of living.[3]

One of the most obvious causes of the productivity problem was technical backwardness which worsened following the break with the USSR. Another and more fundamental cause of the problem, however, was the class relations in production process that were based on the law of state-command (instead of the law of value). Although the state could force workers (who themselves had no means of production) to turn up to the factory and work for certain hours, with life-long employment guarantees and nationally set wage rates (i.e., prevalidation of the value of the labor force in the labor market), there was no effective ways for workplace managers to intensify work during working time. Also, the collective integration of large sections of the industrial workers into the party-state through the mediation of the *danwei*[4] system turned out to be a double-edged sword; while enabling the party to promote political acquiescence and often even loyalty, it also provided workers with a ready source of solidarity against managerial attempts to impose stricter working disciplines (White, 1998, p. 38).

In the case of the rural communes,[5] while the cadres could demand corvee-work on local infrastructural projects and impose policy restrictions on agricultural work, peasants were also able to exercise a considerable degree of negative control over the labor process through rural collectives. The collective organization of agricultural work and relatively egalitarian income distribution within the collectives had moreover removed competition among individual peasants as a potential disciplining mechanism that could force the peasants to deliver a higher level of labor effort (Li, 2008, p. 52). The peasantry manifested their discontent (emerging from the continuing adverse terms of trade between agricultural and industrial goods) in passivity at work and evasion of state levies (by under-reporting production), which led to slow productivity growth in agriculture. As a result, by the mid-1970s, the state was finding it increasingly difficult to appropriate surplus products from the peasantry. Indeed, the amount of grain had long stagnated and even begun to decline by that time (White, 1998, p. 40).

In the 1960s and the 1970s, the CCP leadership reacted to these problems of class dominance by emphasizing moral–ideological incentives for higher productivity, that is, self-conscious observation of labor discipline. Maoist party leaders appear to have thought that so long as workers and peasants realized the socialist state's control over work is beneficial for their long-term common interest, there would be no difficulty in raising productivity and thus accumulation could proceed at a sustainable pace (Li, 2008, p. 52). Based on these perceptions, advocates of the Cultural Revolution pointed at so-called capitalist roaders as a disturbance to inspiring "socialist consciousness." In line with this ideological strife, the party waged waves of political campaigns, reasserting hierarchical party control both in production and throughout society. Such a highly politicized form of governing strategy, however, backfired on the party; the urban population used the opportunity of the officially sanctioned campaign in venting their anger against their political and administrative masters.

After brutal crackdown on such defiant movements, popular attitudes to the party changed to cynicism, apathy, or active opposition while "ideological principles and political institutions lost much of their former meaning and authority based on revolutionary heritage" (Hart-Landsberg & Burkett, 2005, pp. 38–39). In every aspect, the governing system of exploitative class relations was clearly in crisis by the time of Mao's death. The crisis, together with the socialist legacy of social–material infrastructure, became the basis upon which the reform process gathered momentum. Although there was neither clear vision nor predetermined trajectory of reform, for the workers and peasants reform meant a promise for higher incomes, greater consumer choice and personal freedom, while for the party leaders it was considered a useful tool for restoring the battered political fortunes of the CCP without directly confronting defiant workers and peasants (White, 1993, p. 41).

FIRST PHASE OF REFORM AND ITS LIMITATIONS

In the early years of reform, the main cause of the productivity problem was considered to lie in the overly centralized decision-making system (Hart-Landsberg & Burkett, 2005). Indeed, Deng pointed to the economic management power too concentrated at the central government level and the resultant lack of incentives as a critical factor discouraging localities, enterprises, and workers to improve their productive activities (Deng, 1993, pp. 150–152). Accordingly, the main strategy of the new reformist CCP leadership was to introduce market elements into the planning system as a means of decentralization. Initially, it appeared the reform projects made a success of its purpose. However, it soon turned out the surprising growth was largely based on monetary expansion rather than improved productivity (i.e., improved class dominance). Typical fallouts of such fictitious growth soon followed: uncontrollable inflation, accumulation of trade and budget deficits, a run on the banks and ultimately serious political unrests.

Outline of Reform in Each Economic Field

Following some regional experiments, in 1984 the party embarked on radical reforms using market system; any SOEs that had exceeded their production quotas were allowed to sell their products outside the state plan at "market prices," and to use that profit in reinvesting in production or in providing workers with bonuses. Through this policy, the party-state expected to take advantage of market forces without abandoning the alleged advantages of the planning system (Lawrence, Qian, & Roland, 2000, p. 120). Together with SOE reforms, the state began to promote private firms and urban collective enterprises. This was a pragmatic response to the growing problem of youth unemployment and lack of basic consumer goods at that time; a rapid development of non-state firms was expected to provide both jobs and consumer goods (Tang & Ma, 1985, p. 614). In that consideration, many advantages such as lower tax rates and access to free labor market were given to them, and it encouraged local governments to organize them under their jurisdiction. The introduction of fiscal decentralization policy, granting autonomy to local governments in the promotion of economic growth and in the use of fiscal residuals for their own bonuses, strongly incentivized them to invest in such profitable firms.

In 1980, fundamental reforms of agricultural policy were also implemented on a national scale. First, agricultural collectives were dismantled and the government drew up contracts for the purchase of staple crops with each individual peasant household. Second, the peasant household was set free to sell in local markets anything they had produced beyond the production quotas specified in their contracts. In addition, in order to give an incentive to increase production, plan prices for compulsory grain deliveries were raised by 20% (Xu, 2012, p. 53). With the help of the pre-existing infrastructure, the effect of such reform was more than immediate; there was no more passivity at work or evasion of state levies by under-reporting production. Indeed, there was a substantial spurt in the growth of agricultural output and peasants' incomes. Meanwhile, this growing productivity combined with the limited arable land per household released the rural population from their land to work for "industries," they were absorbed by the former communes, now renamed TVEs mainly producing labor-intensive intermediate and consumer goods (Hart-Landsberg & Burkett, 2005, p. 45).

The banking system was also an important target of the reform. During the pre-reform era, the People's Bank of China (PBC), the sole monetary authority of the country, was merely an administrative agent of the state's planning system; the role of the banking system was just to provide the state with needed funds. With the reform process on track, the government passed a resolution to separate central banking from commercial banking functions. Accordingly, the PBC no longer engaged in industrial and commercial credit activities or urban and rural savings businesses, and instead concentrated its resources on performing central banking functions (CSC, 1983). Its commercial banking business was taken over by four state-owned specialized banks (SOBs) and several regional banks including non-bank financial institutions, offering day-to-day financing to firms, and dealing with saving deposits. Now the PBC came to perform standard central bank responsibilities such as issuing currency, regulating interest rates, supervising foreign exchange affairs, and setting reserve ratio for the commercial banks. SOBs also underwent "enterprization," transforming them from a type of state agency into relatively independent commercial entities.

Limitations of Reform Policies

The immediate problem faced by the reform process was that there was no breakthrough in the productivity of most SOEs, which meant the party-state failed to put effective pressures upon state workers. This undermined the whole picture of reform because the overall reform processes focusing on the provision of incentive bonuses for agricultural and consumer-oriented industries were premised on the concomitant growth of productivity in state-running heavy industries which had so far been dependent upon subsidies from the former sectors. It seems like the reformist party leadership at first envisaged state workers' pre-existing real wage could be financed by the increased productivity and profits of SOEs that would be responsive to positive incentives in the same way as the farmers' case. This meant, in other words, without sufficient SOEs' productivity growth state workers should be willing to abandon their existing level of real wages. In reality, however, neither productivity growth nor wage-benefit cuts were realized.

Despite the workers lacked formal or legal rights to form independent unions and to strike, with free housing, medical care, education and foods for families as well as "iron" job security provided by the danwei system of SOEs, managers (without effective disciplinary power over workers) found it difficult to impose new working practices conducive to improving productivity (Andreas, 2008). Further, with the paternalistic relationships within the danwei remaining pervasive, managers used their newly given discretion over company funds and wage rates just to keep workers' real wages from falling, thus buying obedience and compliance from the workers (Walder, 1994, pp. 297–323). As there was no compelling profit motives and market competition (without threat to their own careers), managers tended to accommodate workers' pressures rather than put pressure on them. In addition, the forced absorption of the unskilled youths according to the predetermined state plan greatly compounded the existing problem of excessive labor power rooted in many SOEs for a long time.[6]

While most SOEs were raising their prices to avoid an even more rapid decline in profitability, the state in an attempt to head off worker opposition to the reforms began providing additional funds to "inefficient" state enterprises so that they could raise wages. In 1988 while more than half of SOEs were running at a loss, they were recipients of subsidies amounting to nearly $11 billion – a figure representing about 50% of the total earnings of China's industrial enterprises (Southerland, 1988, p. 5), and the deficits were financed to an increasing extent by state-owned banks' credits. Despite their transformation into profit-orientated commercial corporations, SOBs passively accommodated the credit demands not only of SOEs but also of local governments that were eager to expand industrial activities. There was neither a rigorous loan screening in lending activities, nor the exertion of creditors' power to "restrict credit to loss-making enterprises and to require their restructuring," that is, any threat of bankruptcy to enterprise managers or local authorities (Bowles & White, 1993, p. 488). Not surprisingly such generous subsidies for SOEs and local firms' over-investment based on overexpansion of credit created a massive excess demand for goods and services, ultimately triggering inflation and economic instability.[7]

In summary, the party leadership expected SOEs to operate like profit-oriented corporations responsible for their own gains and losses in competition with other forms of enterprises, while at the same time it prevented them from doing so by imposing political missions (i.e., the burden of taking responsibility for defiant state workers) upon them. The contradictory dual role of SOEs was able to be assumed only through subsidies for losses in the form of easy credit. SOEs did not seriously care about "cost efficiency and profitability" (i.e., profitable exploitation of labor) because they would not be held responsible for their losses anyway. The financial shortfalls of their own operations were supposed to be subsidized (socialized) by the state or higher prices of their commodities in the market.

The reform in the banking system was not unproblematic either. Under the new banking system, credit planning was a major monetary instrument of the PBC (Ji, 2006). The PBC set credit/monetary targets for commercial banks by using instruments such as credit ceilings and quantity rationing to control money supply. This role of the central bank was supposed to be executed by local PBC branches regulating local banks according to centrally set targets. In reality, however, due to interference by local administrative authorities, local PBC branches tended to compromise macroeconomic objectives for local developmental goals. The core problem was that local PBC branches were subject to the "dual leadership" of both the PBC head-office and local governments (Ji, 2006, pp. 108–111). Whereas officially PBC branches were only accountable to the head-office, it was the provincial governments that had the authority to appoint branch managers. As local authorities were more incentivized than ever to pursue local growth following fiscal decentralization, local branches of the banking regulatory body were oriented by local governments to serve local developmental or entrepreneurial goals. This in turn resulted in loss of control over money supply and credit over-extension.

While the PBC could not assume the role of independent central bank, commercialized state-owned banks also did not act like fully profit-oriented commercial entities; rather, they had to continue to provide part of the "policy loans" to SOEs (Mehran, Quintyn, Nordmann, & Laurens, 1996). Although SOEs and SOBs were supposed to act as corporate entities with independent accounting, in practice the "soft budget constraint" still existed (Kornai, 1986, pp. 3–10). Indeed, the local government was still able to use administrative power to allocate resources among SOEs and SOBs, albeit indirectly rather than through the budget system. For Bank branches, it was rational to conform to the request of local authorities in making loans, because they were financially dependent upon the local governments whereas the risks and losses related to lending activities as a whole would be ultimately shouldered by the state. In principle, commercial banks should limit their lending volume within the "credit quota" set by the central bank. However, as the actual enforcement of this quota were being implemented by the local PBC branches where local governments already exerted their influence, "extra" credit quota was easily made available to local SOBs. It follows that the state's credit plan was actually set by such bottom-up political pressure from local production units, not the other way around.

In summary, the entrepreneurial behavior of local governments and their collaboration with state banking institutions led to over-expansions of credit. As local governments competed with each other to set up and duplicate projects, production lines, factories and shops, and as banks supplied funds to support this investment rush, the economy soon became overheated nationwide. In the second half of 1984, for example, money supply in terms of M1 increased by about 40% in the second half of the year (Ji, 2006, p. 140). The central bank, however, was not effective in taking adjustment measures to curb overheated microeconomic activities as its local branches tended to meet local governments' needs rather than follow the orders of the bank headquarters. With bank activities integrated into the state plan, the demarcation between banks and state finance remained blurred, which tended to perpetuate banks' reliance upon the state and gave rise to political lending behavior.

Meanwhile, growing problems in agriculture began creating a serious political and economic crisis. By the mid-1980s, the spurt of agricultural production began to peter out. Although the reforms gave peasants incentives to increase production, both central and local governments did little to increase the actual productive capacity of agriculture. With the drive to expand rural industries, indeed, the township and village authorities did not pay attention to maintaining the infrastructure build in the pre-reform era. Also, the breakup of collectives meant that the advantages of collectivization were lost. With decreasing productivity in agriculture, higher food prices began fueling unrest among urban workers who had already been squeezed by the rising price of necessities, whilst peasants were caught in a price squeeze with the cost of inputs such as fertilizer increasing faster than the prices of agricultural goods (Girdner, 2004, p. 130). The average annual growth of real wage for urban workers plummeted from 9.4% during the period of 1984–1986 to −1.6% between 1987 and 1989. Agricultural incomes, which had grown by 15% per year during 1978–1984, rose by 5% annually over 1985–1988, and by mere 2% in 1989–1991 (AMRC, 2007).

Ultimately, attempts at raising procurement prices to stimulate greater agricultural production only served to exacerbate the problems caused by inflation. As a result of ever mounting inflationary pressure, waves of panic buying swept across the country. Beginning in May 1988 run on banks happened in major cities. Bank savings deposit, which had been growing at an annual rate of 30% during the 1980s, fell to negative growth in August 1988, whereas average retail price nationwide rose by 18.5% (Zhao & Guo, 1998). Parallel to this economic crisis, the party-state also entered into crisis. Following the events at Tiananmen Square in 1989, Zhao Ziyang, the chief proponent of reforms was removed from office and the reform was brought to an abrupt halt. The money supply was tightened and bank loans were reduced. The old practice under the planning system was reinforced. And the economy went into a deep recession in 1989 with urban collectives and rural TVEs that relied heavily on bank loans went into bankruptcy in rows.

SECOND PHASE OF REFORM

What was absent in the first stage of reform was the means with which the state could pressurize the state workers, thereby realizing higher productivity of labor. As shown above, ironically, the lack of such means was due to the direct control power (and concomitant direct responsibility) over the economy retained by the state itself. While the state retained the direct control power, nobody actually assumed the politically unpopular responsibility of confronting defiant workers. In the second stage of the reform, thus, the state began relinquishing some of direct control over the economy and upholding the rule of money and law under which the exploitative social relation of production is seen as apolitical, technical, and personal matters between free and equal citizens. The rule of money and law, in the form of threat of potential bankruptcy and redundancy, triggered the endless and self-directed "race to the bottom" among the firms and workers across the industry, and this made it possible for the state to finally achieve the goal of the reform: creating favorable condition for exploitation of labor and accumulation of capital without seriously undermining the legitimacy of the CCP rule.

Restructuring of Enterprises Ownership

It seems reformist policy-makers began to see the failure of the first stage of reform was due to the public ownership of SOEs. Without any debtors' responsibility and threat of bankruptcy, for mangers, whose career as danwei cadres had nothing to do with the productivity levels in their factories, it was not necessary to confront workers in a more economically "rational" fashion. In other words, they were not fully pressurized to seriously attack workers (their danwei "comrades"). Of course, the party-state could have directly repressed managers and workers by means of administrative measures, but this, just as was the case in the Maoist era, would have been costly in terms of the political legitimacy. Against this backdrop, the party-state took a decisive step in pushing SOEs outside the ambit of the political system toward the economic realm where seemingly apolitical "market discipline" rules. By turning over state assets to private hands, the state was in effect privatizing the political burden of making production profitable by attacking workers. The privatization projects were supported by provincial–local party cadres "whose ability to pursue their private gains [had] been much enhanced by the material resources provided by sweeping fiscal decentralization" during the previous reform process[8] (Cheng, 1999).

In response to Deng's urge for an intensification of reform, in July 1992, the government issued regulations allowing under-performing enterprises to completely overhaul their structure and to be sold to the public or the employees. In line with privatization drives, policies that had limited the size of private firms and foreign investment were lifted and state officials were encouraged to promote both (Andreas, 2008). In 1995, ownership reform was significantly accelerated when the central government renounced the ownership of SOEs except for 500–1,000 large state firms of key strategic industries.[9] As a result, the number of SOEs fell from 64,737 in 1998 to 27,477 in 2005 (Garnaut et al., 2006, pp. 33–65). The party's push was not limited to SOEs; local governments began a rapid sell off of debt-ridden urban collectives and TVEs in the mid-1990s. The sales were expected to generate desperately needed local government revenues, and at the same time to create potentially profitable investment opportunities for cadres and foreign investors. Since then, most TVEs and collective enterprises were privatized, and TVEs owned by local states came to employ only 2% of workforce in 2003, while privatized TVEs were employing 16% (Naughton, 2007, p. 182).

As the public sector shrunk, the private sector expanded. The number of private enterprises increased from 440,000 in 1996 to 1.32 million in 2001, from 16.9% of all enterprises to 43.7% (NBS, 2003). As a result, the public sector's share of all industrial output dropped from 73.4% in 1983 to only 11.1% in 2003, while the share of the urban workers employed in the public sector plunged from nearly 82% to about 27% between 1991 and 2005 (Andreas, 2008; China Labour Bulletin, 2007). Ironically, the more private enterprises grew, the more remaining SOEs came under pressure to restructure themselves as the private firms free from obligations of social welfare and employment (thus more competitive in the market) increasingly undermined their own profitability and monopoly power. As competitive pressure on state firms from private sectors grew, deeper and more painful reforms (i.e., a series of attacks on workers) of beleaguered state firms were justified (Gallagher, 2005, p. 154). In this way, the privitization of state firms virtually functioned as privitization of the politically unpopular imperative of having to achieve higher productivity by directly confronting workers.

Restructuring of Labor Management

Freeing Workers from the Iron Rice Bowl

As part of the state's effort to remake SOEs into "modern enterprises" efficient and profitable enough to compete with private firms, a series of measures were implemented to reduce the political burden of them, and the key was transforming the "labor system" into a "labor market." First, in the early 1990s, the planning quota for recruitment by SOEs was abolished, and SOEs were allowed to recruit employees according to their own management plan (Knight & Song, 2005, p. 23). But what mattered more than freedom to hire was freedom to *fire* workers. Central to this issue was the "unproductive iron rice bowl" cherished by most existing state workers. Clearly, it was not to be possible for SOEs to be "cost-efficient and profitable" as long as they had to continue providing workers with lifetime employment and danwei-based comprehensive welfare. The new reform projects, thus, focused attention on the introduction of a universal labor contract system and the establishment of a societal-level safety net that would substitute the function of the danwei.

Unlike the previous labor contract system which covered only 6% of state workers by 1988, the Labour Law of 1994 required all employees to have such contracts, and they were thus extended to then permanent workers, re-categorizing them as fixed term contract workers (Hart-Landsberg & Burkett, 2005). According to the law, labor contracts should stipulate the legal rights and responsibilities for both parties over a specified period of time. Thus, in theory, contracts would benefit all; managers were to gain a new license to dismiss workers for productivity gains, while workers were supposed to enjoy freedom to switch jobs for higher wages. In practice, however, contracts accentuated managerial power over workers, particularly those working in less competitive and older industries. Indeed, most state workers fell vulnerable to new pressures from managers as they lacked the market capacity to change to non-state employment in competition with millions of young migrant workers flooding into cities. The more inefficient the enterprise, the more desperately dependent were its workers. To them, labor contracts meant managers' unfettered power to discipline, if not dismiss, them.

The introduction of universal labor contract system was accompanied by the establishment of a societal-level safety net as a substitute for the danwei system. The new principles of social protection were that the employer, the employee, and the state should share financial responsibility, that the funds should be pooled and administered by provincial or local social insurance departments, and that the system should be extendable to all urban workers and not just danwei members (Lee, 1999, pp. 47–48). Reforms concerning old age pensions, medical care, unemployment, maternity benefits, etc. were implemented or planned according to this principle; any employee covered by the scheme, regardless of the firms' ownership forms, was supposedly able to claim reimbursement of at least a part of the cost of public services. In the case of housing provisions, housing benefits in the form of a cash allowance would be paid out of housing funds collected from the local government, the enterprise, and the individual worker. With this allowance, workers could buy or rent low-cost accommodation to be constructed by local governments.

Reformers interpreted such changes as "severing the ties that bind workers' lives to leaders of state danwei" (Karmel, 1996, pp. 111–133). In theory, "severing the ties" meant freedom of both SOEs and state workers. SOEs would be released from the financial duty for all danwei members; they would now become liable only for the workers *employed* by them. At the same time, state workers were released from the forced dependence on any specific danwei in public services and housing; they were now given "customers' freedom." Although reformers emphasized the newly given workers' freedom from danwei, what was actually realized was SOEs' freedom from the danwei burden (Lee, 1999, p. 47). Indeed, as the coverage rates of enterprise other than large and medium SOEs remained less than 10% throughout the 1990s, the insurance programmes virtually meant that if workers move to jobs in the non-state sector, they would be much less likely to gain any insurance and welfare benefits (Lee, 1999, p. 48). It followed that the new social protection system in effect ended up pushing state workers out of the social safety net, freeing the state from the direct responsibility for them.

Allowing Rural Migrant Workers into Cities

Throughout the 1980s, most TVEs flourished, employing over 100 million rural workers, as subcontractors to urban state enterprises. Hence, when many SOEs went bankrupt in the early 1990s, thousands of TVEs were left in the lurch (Walker & Buck, 2007, p. 42). Also, credit-dependent TVEs were severely hurt by the harsh administrative measures to cut back the banks' credit quotas in 1989. The collapse of TVEs brought about a serious problem of high unemployment in rural areas.[10] As a result, the income and consumption disparity between rural and urban residents was increasingly widening. It was against this backdrop that millions of workers began migrating to the cities in search of employment and higher wages (from rapidly growing private and foreign-invested enterprises). On the other hand, many urban employers had a profit incentive to buy their labor power which was less expensive and more disciplined than urban workers'. After decades of being mobilized under the strict control of the party-state, the rural population was not merely "peasant" in the traditional sense, but rather a well-disciplined reserve army of labor ready to be exploited productively (Li, 2008, p. 36).

In line with these growing demands for rural–urban migration, regulations on residential movement, that is, the household registration system of *hukou*[11] was more or less relaxed. While permanent movement from the rural areas to the big cities was still not permitted, rural residents were largely allowed to work and live in the cities temporarily. Prior to economic reform, urban rationing made even temporary migration extremely difficult. During the first stage of reform, when the "dual track" system operated, rationed food was distributed at low prices, as before, and higher prices prevailed in the free food markets. The ration coupon system was largely abolished in 1993: it became easier for migrants to live in the city without a city *hukou*. Moreover, with free markets for food, peasants could buy grain to meet their production quotas, that is, to pay their taxes in the form of compulsory grain sales to state agencies, so that they could more easily leave their farms[12] (Knight & Song, 2005, p. 26).

Living and working in cities but still registered as "rural residents," migrant workers were welcomed by urban employers as they could hire them *without* labor contracts required by the law. According to official survey findings, only 46.3% of all migrant workers were hired with written labor contracts (China

State Council, 2006, p. 4). Employers had strong incentives to avoid signing labor contracts with workers and not reporting such employees. First, by hiring informally, enterprises could avoid having to pay required payroll taxes for pensions, unemployment insurance, medical insurance, and work injuries, which could be quite costly (e.g., in Shanghai in 2004, the regular employer contribution rate for these types of insurance totaled 36.5% of wages) (Chan, 2003, p. 137). Also, hiring workers on an informal basis would give employers greater flexibility to adjust the size of labor force in response to changes in economic conditions. Moreover, this greater managerial power of dismissal and ambiguous legal identity of migrant workers would make them more obedient than urban workers, which in turn would put disciplinary pressures on urban workers in factories.

Legalizing Labor Relations

The state's attempts to break the iron rice bowl entailed "a spectacular increase in disputes that began in the early 1990s" (Pringle, 2002). According to official statistics, collective action including strikes increased ninefold from 752 cases in 1992 to 6,767 cases in 1998 (Hart-Landsberg & Burkett, 2005, p. 83; Pringle, 2002). Many of those laid-off organized protests over their forced redundancy and insufficient compensation, demanding a new economic compensation package or new employment within the SOEs from management and local government (China Labour Bulletin, 2007). Collective organized protests by laid-off workers usually took the form of sit-ins, assembly outside government offices, petitioning to higher level government and also large-scale "mass incidents." From the mid-1990s, large-scale protests took place throughout the country and were often well planned as some older laid-off SOE workers called upon organizing skills learned during the Cultural Revolution (AMRC, 2007; for concrete instances, see Gallagher, 2005, p. 155).

To deal with growing worker resistance to structural reform without serious harm to productivity growth and political legitimacy of CCP rule, the state attempted to embed labor relations in a legislative framework. The legislative approach began in 1995 with a comprehensive Labour Law (1994) which stipulated all manner of regulations on working conditions, minimum wages, working hours, and overtime. The law also assigned to the sole official trade union the responsibility of arranging collective contracts between employers and workers, while workers right to strike and form an independent union remained denied under the law (Chan, 2008). To this it added mediation and arbitration channels to resolve industrial conflicts that had seen increasing uptake from aggrieved workers.

This legalization of labor relations had several purposes. It was a genuine attempt to rein in the most notorious abuses of worker rights, thereby preempting serious disputes and normalizing factory life. It was also an attempt to demobilize and individualize working class discontent – to drive it from collectivized strikes and demonstrations in the streets toward arbitration and mediation in government offices ("officially sanctioned resolution processes") (Gallagher, 2005, p. 103). For the CCP leadership, it was a political strategy of depoliticization to save the party-state from workers' direct ire over the restructuring process, making the party-state appear to be an "impartial arbiter" or even "workers' party" that occasionally offers workers central government directions as weapons against abusive managers and corrupt local government officials (Chan, 2003, p. 143).

Restructuring of the Banking System

Making the Central Bank "Independent"

A major step in building an independent central bank (i.e., building an apolitical rule of money) was the enforcement of the Central Bank Law enacted in 1995. The law made it clear that the central bank should be separated from the administrative authorities at various levels. Article 7 of the Law dictated that "PBC shall, under the leadership of the State Council, independently implement monetary policies, perform its functions and carry out its operations according to law free from any intervention by local governments or government departments at all levels, public organizations or individuals." Accordingly, the law stipulated that the PBC should not act as sole sales agent for state and other government bonds; it must not act as financial guarantor for any organization or individual (Ji, 2006, p. 143). In other words, the PBC was now to fully assume the role of an independent and detached regulator, whose ultimate aim is to maintain the stability of the value of money and thereby ensure a "sound" financial environment.

Dealing with the problem local governments' structural influence over PBC branches, the PBC decided to formally abolish its branches at provincial and municipal levels and instead set up a small number of regional branches (Ji, 2006, p. 146). In provinces where a PBC branch became absent, a supervisory office was established to assume the role of arms of the "cross-district" PBC branch. With this new organizational structure, the PBC would be hopefully more protected from interference by local governments. Of course, the emphasis on central bank independence did not mean that the central government was going to sit by as a spectator on banking issues. According to the Central Bank Law, the PBC would be under the direct leadership of the State Council. It follows that the central government has come to take a more active role in ensuring that the PBC is freed from the influence of undisciplined administrative authorities.

In terms of the approach to macroeconomic management, the central government dictated the PBC to use a more indirect adjustment mechanism. In the past, the focus of PBC monetary policy had been on direct control over credit volume. Under the new law, the PBC should instead focus on the control of total money supply in terms of M1. Accordingly, the PBC began to mainly rely on monetary policy instruments rather than administrative directives over credit quotas for macro financial control. Indeed, instruments such as open market operations, discount, and rediscount policy were adopted since the mid-1990s. The system of money markets was also improved by establishing a nationally unified interbank market (1996) where interest rates were formally liberalized. By using these indirect control instruments rather than resorting to administrative recentralization, indeed, the PBC successfully assisted the central government in controlling inflationary pressure, that is, imposing austerity upon the underproductive producers, between 1992 and 1993 without a serious political crisis.

Making Commercial Banks Truly "Commercial"

The clear objective of SOBs reform was to make them truly "commercial" by disentangling the banking system from SOEs and local governments. In other words, SOBs were supposed to be able to make profit an overarching goal, free from political responsibility for macroeconomic stabilizations, welfare provision, or industrial policy promotions. To this end, the central government took a series of deregulatory and liberalization measures of the banking system since the mid-1990s, and the 1995 Law on Commercial Banks was the first step. The law, bestowing legal person status on SOBs (granting legally independent status to banks), made it possible for the banks to "independently manage their businesses, shoulder their own risks, be responsible for their own profits and losses and follow the principle of self-restraint in conducting commercial activities" (Ji, 2006, p. 151).

The PBC's change to the practice of monetary management referred to above also helped commercial banks to become truly commercial. They were now allowed to determine their lending activities themselves, as long as maintaining the required level of bank reserves. This did not mean, of course, that the banks were set free from all constraints. The newly introduced asset–liability ratio system meant that they were now forced to optimize asset to liability ratios and limit their credit and loan activities accordingly. Meanwhile, one of the most difficult problems in commercial banks reform was the fact that they were carrying the burdens of the past: the huge amount of nonperforming loans (having mounted up to 25% of total loans by 1995) (China Daily, 1995). The banks' total debts had already exceeded their total assets, rendering the banking system virtually insolvent. In response to this problem, in 1998 the government executed a series of bank recapitalization, such as setting up asset management companies to take over the bad-debts, directly injecting capital into bank assets and debt write-offs (Hart-Landsberg & Burkett, 2005, p. 65). These measures were political attempts to make commercial banks "commercial" that can play a role of a pillar of the rule of money.

With a series of banking system reform, in summary, banks came to be under growing pressure to operate on a more commercial basis and to scrutinize loan applications more carefully. This pressure was directly transferred to SOEs and TVEs whose expansion until the early 1990s was largely dependent upon easy bank loans. Indeed, some 1,000 large to medium state-owned industries (let alone thousands of small collectives and TVEs) were driven into bankruptcy by the mid-1990s (AMRC, 2007). Under the invisible and seemingly nonpolitical nature-like rule of money threatening potential bankruptcy, surviving firms in turn had to undergo severe restructuring of production process (attacks on workers) or be sold to private investors who were supposed to be more "rational" in exploitation of labor. Politically unpopular goals of eliminating or pressurizing underproductive producers were attained in this apparently apolitical way of banking system reform, protecting the political legitimacy of the CCP rule to some extent.

IN LIEU OF CONCLUSION: LIMITS OF REFORM AS A GOVERNING STRATEGY OF DEPOLITICIZATION

Under the seemingly apolitical rule of money and law, firms and workers came to be working out their own salvation from natural-disaster-like bankruptcies and redundancies, and it made it possible for the state to achieve the goal of the reform: creating conditions highly conducive to exploitation and accumulation without critically undermining political stability. One of the numbers clearly showing the success would be the unit labor costs that continued to fall throughout the reform era.[13] From the early 1990s, on the back of the world's lowest costs of exploitation, China did undergo a remarkable transformation in which it turned itself literally into a "factory of the world," while the CCP's rule became more consolidated with the credit for having achieved the goal of "national prosperity." The apparent success of reform as a governing strategy of depoliticization, however, was building the barrier to itself; as a result of the reform process, there was a growing possibility of socioeconomic crisis and the resultant necessity for the state to re-politicize the management of money, production, and labor with growing political risks. As a full discussion of this issue is beyond the purpose of this paper, this section presents just a brief outline of them in lieu of conclusion.

First, the limits of reform as a strategy of class dominance was made more and more manifest in the management of labor relations. With the emergence of a "new generation of Chinese workers" (Chang, 2012, p. 11; Chen & Estreicher, 2011; Leung & Pun, 2009, p. 553) from the mid-2000s, workers, in particular migrant workers, who were supposed to be willing to work under harsh conditions with low wages and thereby weaken the position of urban workers, began refusing to be docile any longer. Through waves of strikes nationwide, challenges to injustice and inequality against migrant workers was ever-increasing in terms of numbers and "radicalizing" in terms of its form (e.g., solidarity strikes and protests)[14] (Leung & Pun, 2009). This increasing social unrest and radicalization of migrant workers forced the party-state to directly intervene into the labor market. First, the government under the banner of "harmony and stability" was forced to employ a set of pacifying labor policies including a steep rise in minimum wage. Second, the party also had to address the problem of rising unemployment partly caused by its own action: the rise in real wages (i.e., cost of exploitation of labor) through another bout of interventions possibly absorbing discharged workers. It follows that in one way or another, the workers' struggles made the state take direct political responsibility for them again.

The limits of reform were also becoming clear in the management of firms and production. In the face of rising wages and intensifying competitive pressures, individual firms did not tamely withdraw from the markets but tried to overcome the barrier by investing money (either earned profits or borrowed money) in high-tech new machinery and more advanced technologies while shedding "surplus" workers through downsizing and reengineering, in an attempt to reduce costs of exploitation further. These rational efforts of individual capitals for keeping themselves competitive were soon found contradictory and self-defeating; while maximizing productive capacity, it actually pushed the aggregate effective demand down increasingly further, thus serving to compound the problem of overproduction and overcapacity.[15] With profit rates ever-falling,[16] a growing mass of capital was to be no longer reinvested in production, which in turn would aggravate the market situation by increasing unemployment, bankruptcies, and losses to the banking system in a vicious circle. From the late-1990s, the government sought to confront this problem through debt-financed investments in huge mega-projects of building infrastructure. In the same way as the United States during the 1950s and the 1960s, thousands of highways, airports, new railroads, and huge dams were to be built in every big city. It follows that the tendency to overproduction and overaccumulation inherent in the capitalist production obliged the state to intervene further in the production process which was supposed to be an apolitical nature-like system under the rule of money.

Finally, there was a growing necessity for the state to bring money back to the political ambit. The state's (re)interventions obliged by the above-mentioned problems: intensifying workers' resistance, unemployment, and potential crisis of overproduction made it inevitable for the state to re-politicize the management of money as well. With all the potential crises looming, the state had no choice but to mobilize banks to finance a variety of local government projects, while at the same time commanding commercial banks to increase their lending and to loosen credit controls regardless of risk calculations just as was the case in the 1980s (Barnet and Brooks, 2006, p. 17). One of the immediate troubles caused by these policies was a serious bad debt problem arising again as the profitability and cash income flows of firms (the ability to pay interest) were on the steady decline. Another problem was a speculative boom or so-called bubble[17] began to form in real estate-construction sectors (Barnet and Brooks, 2006, p. 17). It seems the most serious and fundamental problem to the state, however, was the fact that such an intervention into the monetary relations, by undermining money as an independent form of value, was making it virtually impossible for the state to re-use money as a seemingly nonpolitical disciplinary means over the underproductive producers until a destructive economic crisis strikes the entire system including the state itself.

In summary, the reform as a depoliticization strategy of class dominance was not successful and nonproblematic. Beneath the success of the reform was a growing necessity of crisis; in face of re-burgeoning workers' struggles, growing problems of overproduction and overaccumulation, and the resultant looming banking system crisis, the state came to find it more and more necessary to bring the economic managements back into political system even though such policies would bring about economic and political crisis in the future.

NOTES

1. In this paper, "class" is not understood in terms of sociologically defined groups of individuals sharing common experiences or workplace relations, and nor is it seen in relation to the existence of class consciousness or political struggle, but is recognized instead as an exploitative relation arising from the process of social production. As de Ste Croix puts it, the concept of "class" refers to "the collective social expression of the fact of exploitation, the way in which exploitation is embodied in a social structure" (de Ste Croix, 1983, pp. 43–44). For an open Marxist view of class, see Bonefeld, Brown, and Burnham (1995) and Burnham (2001).

2. One can refute that the class relations of production in China is still highly "politicized," rather than "depoliticized," considering the state's widespread control over the economy. But such a view is only correct in comparison with other capitalist countries; seeing it *historically*, one can appreciate how the class relations came to be depoliticized through the reform era.

3. The per-capita grain available to rural populations barely rose over the 26 years, and urban real wages remained roughly the same, rising on average by only 0.4% per annum over the planning period (Knight & Song, 2005, p. 31).

4. A social institution based on interdependence among SOEs employees, providing members with housing, healthcare, and pensions.

5. A politico-administrative authority built with a view to improving productivity based on collectivization and a more efficient procurement system.

6. Indeed, the annual addition of more than 2.5 million new workers seriously affected the normal operation and management of factories and led to a steady reduction of their productivity and profits (Knight & Song, 2005).

7. After rising at an annual rate of approximately 8% over the years 1985–1987, prices soared by more than 18% in both 1988 and 1989. Prices jumped even more, by as much as 30%, in Beijing and other big cities (Hart-Landsberg & Burkett, 2005, p. 59).

8. Their transformation into new property-owners (so-called red capitalists) was also legitimated by Deng's newly pronounced reform direction: to develop the "socialist market economy," "a few have to get rich first," and "to get rich is glorious" (Girdner, 2004, p. 125; Meisner, 1999, pp. 516–518).

9. By 1998, a national survey showed that 50% of 87,000 SOEs had restructured or planned to do so. Among the restructured, 60–70% had been partially or fully privatized. By the end of 2001, 86% of all SOEs had been restructured and about 70% had been partially or fully privatized (Garnaut, Song, & Yao, 2006, pp. 33–65).

10. In the early 1980s, the surplus of rural workers (who were underemployed or unemployed) was an estimated 70 million, or 18% of the entire rural labor force and this surplus grew to about 130 million, or 28% in the early 1990s (Zhang, 2003).

11. Each town and city (broadly categorized as "rural" or "urban") issued its own *hukou*, which invested only its registered residents with access to public welfare services within the jurisdiction.

12. The number of rural people working in urban areas grew significantly from about 30 million in 1995 to 62 million in 2000, and further to more than 130 million in the mid-2000s (Chan, 2003, p. 135).

13. Between 1995 and 2002, unit labor costs fell by −1.2% each year (Ceglowski & Golub, 2007, pp. 605–606). As the exchange rate was almost fixed since 1995 (8.28 yuan to the dollar) unit labor costs in dollar terms were reduced at similar rates.

14. For more examples and statistical data on labor disputes, see CLB Research Report No. 5 (2007, pp. 15–24), Cai and Wang (2012, pp. 11–17), and Chan (2009, pp. 60–77).

15. The relatively low cost of production made it possible for China-based firms to enlarge the global market share that could to some extent complement inefficient domestic demands for consumer goods. But the competitive pressure intensified by the flood of commodities made in China on the world market was also forcing foreign-based firms to follow suit; they, just like firms in China, rationally reacted to the cost-cutting pressures with further mechanization, intensification of works or lower wages and thereby ending up increasing productive capacity and decreasing aggregate effective demand in the world market. This trend checked the growth of effective demands for Chinese commodities. For examples of how such trends influenced East Asian countries, see Hart-Landsberg and Burkett (2006, pp. 9–11) and Fernald and Loungani (2004, p. 2).

16. One of the symptoms clearly showing the problem was the ever-declining average capacity utilization rates (a falling capital productivity) during the period. The rate continued to fall from 82.6% in 1999 to 77.1% in 2003 and further down to 75.8% in 2006 (China Statistical Yearbook, 2008, *National accounts*: http://www.stats.gov.cn/tjsj/ndsj/2008/indexeh.htm, accessed on June 6, 2012).

17. For instance, investment in real estate soared by nearly 20% per year from 2001 to 2005 and reached 11% of GDP in 2005, boosting housing prices up by more than 50–60% in almost every major city between 2001 and 2007 (Barnet & Brooks 2006, p. 17).

REFERENCES

Andreas J. (2008). Changing colours in China. *New Left Review*, *54*, 123–142.

Asia Monitor Resource Centre (AMRC). (2007). *Labour resurgence under globalization II*, 32, October–December 2007.

Au, L. Y. (2014). What is the nature of capitalism in China? On the rise of China and its inherent contradictions. *Europe Solidaire Sans Frontières* [online]. Retrieved from http://www.europe-solidaire.org/spip.php?article35764. Accessed on 22 September 2014.

Barnett, S., & Brooks, R. (2006). *What's driving investment in China?* IMF Working Paper No. WP/06/265. Washington, DC.

Bonefeld, W. (1992). Social constitution and the form of the capitalist state. In W. Bonefeld, R. Gunn, & K. Psychopedis (Eds.), *Open Marxism: Dialectics and History* (Vol. I). London: Pluto Press.

Bonefeld, W., Brown, A., & Burnham, P. (1995). *A major crisis?: The politics of economic policy in Britain in the 1990s*. Aldershot: Dartmouth Publishing.

Bowles, P., & White, G. (1993). *The political economy of China's financial reforms*. Boulder, CO: Westview Press.

Burkett, P., & Hart-Landsberg, M. (2001). Crisis and recovery in East Asia: The limits of capitalist development. *Historical Materialism, 8*, 3–48.

Burnham, P. (2001). New Labour and the politics of depoliticisation. *British Journal of Politics & International Relations, 3*(2), 127–149.

Burnham, P. (2006). Marxism, the state and British Politics. *British Politics, 1*(1), 67–83.

Cai, F., & Wang, M. (2012). *Labour market changes, labour disputes and social cohesion in China*. Working Paper No. 307. OECD Development Centre.

Ceglowski, J., & Golub, S. (2007). Just how low are China's labor costs? *The World Economy, 30*(4), 597–617.

Chan, A. (2003). A race to the bottom-globalisations and China's labor standards. *China Perspectives, 46*, 41–49.

Chan, C. (2008). *Emerging patterns of workers' protest in South China*. Center for Comparative Labour Studies Working Papers, University of Warwick.

Chan, C. (2009). Strike and changing workplace relations in a Chinese global factory. *Industrial Relations Journal, 40*(1), 60–77.

Chang, D. O. (2012). The neoliberal rise of East Asia and social movements of labour: Four moments and a challenge. *Interface: A Journal for and about Social Movements, 4*(2), 22–51.

Chen, L., & Estreicher, S. (2011). A new labor era: Higher costs and greater pressures. *China Business Review, 38*(2), 26–29.

Cheng, E. (1999). China: Is capitalist restoration inevitable? Links 11 (January–April).

China Daily. (1995, January 9). Bold, new moves needed to make headway, p. 4.

China Labour Bulletin. (2007). *Speaking out: The workers' movement in China (2005–2006)*. CLB Research Report No. 5. www.clb.org.hk

China State Council. (1983). *Resolution on the issue of the People's Bank of China performing central bank functions*. Beijing: The State Council of China.

China State Council. (2006). *Report on rural migrant workers in China*. Beijing: The State Council of China.

de Ste. Croix, G. E. M. (1983). *The class struggle in the ancient Greek world: From the archaic age to the Arab conquests*. London: Duckworth.

Deng, X. (1993). *The selected works of Deng Xiaoping* (Vol. 3). Beijing: The People's Press.

Fernald, J., & Loungani, P. (2004). Comrades or competitors? On trade relationships between China and emerging Asia. *Chicago Fed Letter* (March 2004). Federal Reserve Bank of Chicago.

Flinders, M., & Buller, J. (2006). Depoliticisation: Principles, tactics and tools. *British Politics, 1*(3), 293–318.

Gallagher, M. E. (2005). *Contagious capitalism: Globalization and the politics of labor in China*. Princeton: Princeton University Press.

Garnaut, R. Song, L., & Yao, Y. (2006). Impact and significance of state-owned enterprise restructuring. *The China Journal, 55*, 35–65.

Girdner, E. J. (2004). China as a capitalist state: From "primitive socialist accumulation" to neoliberal capitalism. *The Turkish Yearbook of International Relations, 25*, 121–144.

Hart-Landsberg, M., & Burkett, P. (2005). *China and socialism: Market reforms and class struggle*. New York, NY: Monthly Review Press.

Hart-Landsberg, M., & Burkett, P. (2006). China and the dynamics of transnational accumulation: Causes and consequences of global restructuring. *Historical Materialism, 14*(3), 3–43.

Holloway, J. (1995). Capital moves. *Capital and Class*, *57*, 137–144.

Ji, M. (2006). *Neoliberal developmentalism: State-led economic liberalization in China*. Ph.D. thesis, Cornell University.

Karmel, S. M. (1996). Securities markets and China's international economic integration. *Journal of International Affairs*, *49*(2), 525–556.

Knight, J., & Song, L. (2005). *Towards a labour market in China*. Oxford: Oxford University Press.

Kornai, J. (1986). The soft budget constraint. *Kyklos*, *39*(1), 3–30.

Lawrence, L., Qian, Y., & Roland, G. (2000). Reform without losers: An interpretation of China's dual-track approach to transition. *Journal of Political Economy*, *108*, 120–143.

Lee, C. K. (1999). From organized dependence to disorganized despotism: Changing labor relations in Chinese factories. *The China Quarterly*, *157*, 44–71.

Leung, P. N., & Pun, N. (2009). The radicalization of the new working class: The collective actions of migrant workers in South China. *The Third World Quarterly*, *198*, 287–303.

Li, M. (2008). *The rise of China and the demise of the capitalist world-economy*. London: Pluto.

Mehran, H., Quintyn, M., Nordmann, T., & Laurens, B. (1996). *Monetary and exchange system reforms in China: An experiment in gradualism*. IMF Occasional Paper No. 141. Washington, DC.

Meisner, M. (1999). *Mao's China and after* (3rd edn.) New York, NY: Free Press.

Naughton, B. (2007). *The Chinese economy: Transitions and growth*. MA: MIT Press.

National Bureau of Statistics (NBS). (2003). *China statistical yearbook*. Beijing: China Statistical Publishing House.

Nolan, P. (1990). Assessing economic growth in the Asian NICs. *Journal of Contemporary Asia*, *20*(1), 41–63.

Pringle, T. (2002, February 1). Industrial unrest in China: A labor movement in the making?, *Foreign Policy in Focus*.

Southerland, D. (1988, September 21). China plans to sell stock in state-owned enterprises. *Washington Post*, F1–F5.

Tang, J., & Ma, L. J. C. (1985). Evolution of urban collective enterprises in China. *China Quarterly*, *104*, 614–640.

Walder, A. G. (1994). Collective behavior revisited: Ideology and politics in the Chinese cultural revolution. *Rationality and Society*, *6*(3), 400–421.

Walker, R., & Buck, C. (2007). The Chinese road. *New Left Review*, *46*, 39–69.

White, G. (1993). *Riding the tiger: The politics of economic reform in post-Mao China*. London: Macmillan.

White, G. (1998). Social security reforms in China: Towards an East Asian model? In R. Goodman, G. White, & H. Kwon (Eds.), *The East Asian welfare model: Welfare orientalism and the state*. London: Routledge.

Xu, Z. (2012). The Chinese agriculture miracle revisited. *Economic and Political Weekly*, *47*(14), 51–58.

Zhang, J. (2003). *Urban Xiagang, unemployment and social support policies: A literature review of labour market policies in transitional China*. Report to the World Bank.

Zhao, H., & Guo, T. (1998). *Twenty years of reform in Chinese financial institutions*. Henan: Zhongzhou Press.

WHY CHINA IS DIFFERENT: HEGEMONY, REVOLUTIONS AND THE RISE OF CONTENDER STATES

Lorenzo Fusaro

ABSTRACT

This paper attempts to critically question present IPE approaches and analyses that aim at assessing China's role within the international political economy. Thus, unlike common theorizations that see the country as being integrated within US hegemony (Panitch and Gindin) or those accounts that claim that we are already witnessing the "terminal crisis" of US hegemony accompanied by a hegemonic transition toward China (Arrighi), the paper will argue that China was able to gain "relative geopolitical autonomy" as a result of the revolutionary processes it went through and eventually assert itself as a contender state, now just in the process of challenging US hegemony. Dissatisfied with existent theorizations of hegemony, I will be drawing on the critical edition of Gramsci's Quaderni *and attempt to offer a new perspective regarding the conceptualization thereof. Thus applying the elaborated framework of analysis to the current situation, I argue that unlike the US's ability to counter the challenge of its traditional imperial rivals Germany and Japan as they developed under the grip of US hegemony, the country is facing difficulties in countering China's ascent. However, while maintaining that China does indeed represent a challenge to US hegemony, particularly in East Asia, I will argue that the idea of a "crisis of US*

Return of Marxian Macro-dynamics in East Asia
Research in Political Economy, Volume 32, 185–223

ISSN: 0161-7230/doi:10.1108/S0161-723020170000032011

hegemony" is premature as China remains distant from fully realizing hegemonic relations, even at the regional level.

Keywords: Gramsci; Hegemony; China; international political economy; geopolitical autonomy; contender states

INTRODUCTION: PARADOXES OF CONTEMPORARY MARXIST ACCOUNTS

In November 2011, President Obama affirmed that "the United States is a Pacific power, and we are here to stay" (*The Guardian*, 2011, November 17). This statement was made on the US president's visit to Australia, when announcing the stationing of an increasing number of US troops – a move that was part of a major economic, diplomatic and military re-orientation of the United States toward the Asian-Pacific. The context of this increasing focus on the region, the *New York Times* reported at the time, was the US's efforts to contain China as the latter "has become the largest trading partner with most of the countries in the region, undercutting American economic influence. It also is projecting military power more broadly than at any other time in modern history" (*New York Times*, 2011). The *National Intelligence Report* (NIC) "Global Trends 2025: A Transformed World" published in 2008 is perhaps the first official document that clearly and comprehensively displayed the concerns of the US administration (NIC, 2008). It envisaged a "historical transfer of relative wealth and economic power from the West to East" and considered China to be the US's biggest challenger (*Ibid.*).

Notably, this "declinist" attitude is mirrored in interventions within US academia, particularly amongst Realists. As Andrew Nathan and Andrew Scobell outlined in *Foreign Affairs*, there are fears within parts of the US establishment that China's ambitions are not only regional and that it "will soon overwhelm its neighbours and one day supplant the US as a global hegemon" (Nathan & Scobell, 2012). Unsurprisingly, it is the Liberal school of thought that has most seriously challenged these "pessimist" realist accounts. Thus, Ikenberry underlines the increasing economic importance of emerging economies and particularly China without seeing them as a challenge to the present US-led world order: "[t]he distribution of capabilities – of wealth and power – is shifting away from the North and West toward the East and South. The old Western order dominated by the United States and Europe is giving way to a world that is increasingly filled with non-Western rising states." And yet, Ikenberry maintains, "non-Western rising states" have no incentive to attempt to change the liberal international world order the US constructed: "Liberal international order offers several levels of rules, institutions, and organizational logics for collective action that serve the interests of most states – East and South as well as North and West." Eventually, this world order "is harder to overturn and easier to join" (Ikenberry, 2011a, 2011b, p. 2).

Interestingly, an important volume of Marxist accounts – "sanguine Marxists" as opposed to "anxious Marxists" according to Herman Schwartz (Schwartz, 2009, p. 32) – reaches similar conclusions to those put forward by liberal institutionalists, albeit for different reasons. Hence, building on the insights originally developed by Robert Cox (Cox, 1981, 1983, 1987) and later further elaborated, amongst others, by Gill (1993), neo-Gramscian analyses suggest that the deepening of transnational production and financial linkages has resulted in the emergence of a transnational capitalist class making geopolitical competition amongst states superseded. Therefore, following very closely and consistently the neo-Gramscian argument and underlining the integration of China's and other emerging countries' capitalist class within "international class linkages," Matthew Stephen claims that "today's rising powers are unlikely to threaten the transnationalization of the global economy or the fundamental features of global economic governance" (Stephens, 2014, p. 930). By contrast, albeit also inferring that China should not be seen as a challenge to US hegemony, Leo Panitch and Sam Gindin's (2012) award-winning *The Making of Global Capitalism* sees both the West and "the rest" (including China) as being integrated within and reproducing the "American Empire." What became to be labeled the "hegemony continuity thesis" (Schmalz, 2010) has been challenged by Arrighi who in the new edition of his renowned book *The Long 20th Century* argued that the "terminal crisis of US hegemony" occurred before the onset of the Great Recession (Arrighi, 2010). China, according to Arrighi, is indeed a strong candidate for hegemony, but its character will not only differ from US hegemony but also from all previous experiences of "historical capitalism," as it is understood as being a non-capitalist market economy therefore meant to project a different form of hegemony (Arrighi, 2010, p. 385).[1] Most recently, Radhika Desai dismissed both the idea of the "continuity" and the "crisis" of US hegemony, arguing that the United States, actually, has never been hegemonic. As she puts it, "[…] the widespread idea that the United States was (or is) hegemonic is simply false" (Desai, 2013, p. 3).

We are therefore confronted with a paradox. While there is deep concern within both influential academic circles and the US administration about the decline of US hegemony and China's potential; while the United States is strongly shifting its attention toward Asia in words and deeds, prominent Marxist authors generally tend to argue for the uninterrupted strength of US hegemony. And when the "continuity thesis" is contested as Arrighi does, we are confronted with the vision of a crisis of US hegemony accompanied by an already on-going hegemonic transition toward China, the latter conceptualized as a non-capitalist market economy. Radhika Desai, by contrast, seems to contend that the whole discussion is obsolete as the United States has never been hegemonic.

This chapter aims to contribute to these debates by arguing that neither the perspective of the continuation of US hegemony as understood by the "continuity thesis," nor Arrighi's idea of a hegemonic transition are satisfactory to understand the current developments in international political economy. For these analyses rest, I believe, on an inadequate understanding of hegemony at the international level and consequently on a not convincing interpretation of the position of China within the international political economy. Hence in the following sections I will firstly return to the critical edition of Gramsci's *Quaderni del Carcere* attempting to contribute to the conceptualization of hegemony at the international level in a way that is consistent with Gramsci's classical Marxist approach to international relations and that in substantial issues, I maintain, contrasts with neo-Gramscian analyses as well as other interpretations of Gramsci's concepts. Accordingly, in section two I will contend that China achieved what I refer to as "relative geopolitical autonomy" as a result of the revolutionary processes the country went through, arguing that the country largely developed outside US hegemonic relations. Hence in section three I will attempt to demonstrate that while the United States was able to block attempts of its imperialist rivals, Japan and Germany, to construct full-fledged hegemonic relations at the regional level, it is facing difficulties in countering China's attempt to do so. The conclusion will reiterate that China does indeed represent a challenge to US hegemony, particularly in East Asia, arguing, however, that the country remains still distant from fully realizing hegemonic relations at the regional level, not to mention the global level.

HEGEMONY AND *RELATIVE GEOPOLITICAL AUTONOMY*

Within Marxist international political economy, the concept of hegemony at the international level has been mainly developed by World-systems theory (Wallerstein, Arrighi) and the neo-Gramscian school of thought. However, the concept remains largely under-theorized from what we might refer to as "classical" Marxism, that is that school of thought within Marxist international political economy that takes Marx's *Capital* as point of departure, counting, amongst others, the works of Lenin, Bukharin, Luxembourg, and most recently, works associated with the *New Imperialism* (Callinicos, 2009; Harvey, 2003). What characterizes existing conceptualizations of hegemony at the international level is a *talis qualis* transposition of particular interpretations of Gramsci's concept of hegemony (as well as other Gramscian concepts) to the field of international relations. The most notorious analyses are those put forward by Robert Cox and Giovanni Arrighi. Common to the two conceptualizations of hegemony is their emphasis on the *consensual* aspect of power: hegemony thus understood, refers to an "addendum" to domination for Arrighi (Arrighi, 1994, p. 28) and a condition, according to Cox, in which "the consensual aspect of power is in the forefront" (Cox, 1983, p. 164). Yet where the two approaches strongly differ from each other, when applied to the international field, is on question of national states. Arrighi retains the centrality of national states in his analysis, maintaining that at the international level a state is hegemonic over the State system when it can credibly claim, thanks to its material and later financial supremacy, to be a motor force of a general expansion, thereby presenting its interests as being also those of subordinated states (Arrighi, 1994, p. 28). By contrast, according to Robert Cox, hegemony refers to a particular condition of the "world order" that can be hegemonic when there is a fit between the way in which production takes place, institutions and ideologies. Hence social forces, transnationally interrelated, may bring about a "hegemonic world order" by diffusing similar production practices as well as cultural and ideological values across the world.

It is on the above theoretical assumptions that neo-Gramscian scholarship reaches conclusions that strongly resemble those reached by the liberal school of thought, while World-systems theory appears to flirt with *economism*: for here the redistribution of economic power at the international level seems to *immediately* bring about crises of hegemony. Hence, for example, Arrighi's "signal crisis" of US hegemony in the 1970s as the US's economic supremacy faced serious setbacks and, eventually, its "terminal crisis" as a result of the expiration of the US's "financial expansion" (Arrighi, 1994, 2010). But what moreover characterizes both schools of thought, eventually, is a departure from Marx's enquiry into the capitalist mode of production and its laws of motion as described in *Capital*. Additionally, and paradoxically one might think at first sight, what also characterizes their theoretical framework is a *departure* from crucial features of Gramsci's body of thought as developed in the *Prison Notebooks*. By contrast, what might be referred to as classical Marxism, as for example the theory of the *New Imperialism*, takes Marx's *Capital* as point of departure for assessing developments within the world economy, while not offering a substantial theorization of hegemony at the international level.

A return to the critical edition of Gramsci's *Quaderni* suggests that Gramsci not only developed the concept of hegemony at the international level, but also that the way in which he did so, is consistent with the overall framework developed by classical Marxists thereby building a concept that, in my opinion, strongly contrasts with neo-Gramscian analyses. Hence Gramsci's *Notebooks* make a *talis quails* transposition of the concept of hegemony at the national level in order to characterize hegemony at the *international level* problematic. To be sure, the two concepts remain interrelated and Gramsci's conception of hegemony at the national level offers important methodological insights that can inform the further elaboration of hegemony at the international level. An exhaustive account of Gramsci's body of thought cannot be offered here, yet

I wish to briefly point to three aspects in Gramsci's work that I consider to be crucial for understanding his conceptualization of hegemony at the international level. Firstly, relying on Gramsci's approach and method as detailed in *Notebooks* 10 and 11 in particular, it can be argued that Gramsci's concepts should be understood as "organic unities" composed of different contradictory parts, whereby it is possible to distinguish methodologically (but not organically) between the two parts that constitute the organic unity. Secondly, Gramsci's Marxism is further clarified when dwelling on *Notebook 13*, which contains a note of central importance: the "Analysis of Situations." Here we cannot but take notice that Gramsci's starting point is the economic structure as indicated in Marx's *Preface to the Critique of Political Economy* (Marx & Engels, 1956–1990, MEW, Bd. 13, p. 7) representing "the most important authentic source for the reconstruction of the Philosophy of Praxis" (Gramsci, 2001, Q.11 §29, p. 1441) and that Gramsci follows *ad litteram* providing a non-determinist reading. Thirdly, Gramsci's famous "Revolution against Capital" (Gramsci, 2007, p. 22) should not be read too literarily as his critique to the "stagist" and economistic interpretation of Marxism should not be understood as a departure from Marx's main work and approach that would legitimate the deployment of Gramsci's thought outside *Capital*. The *Prison Notebooks* still remain permeated by the law of value and the crisis tendencies as analyzed by Marx. With this in mind, we aim at presenting relevant aspects of Gramsci's conception of hegemony at the national level that might be useful to further elaborate on the author's conceptualization of hegemony at the *international* level.

Elements of Gramsci's Conception of Hegemony at the National Level

In light of the above-enounced elements, a good starting point to address Gramsci's concept of hegemony is, I believe, beginning from Marx's *Preface*. In particular, on the author's statement that when analyzing epochal transformations,

> it is always necessary to distinguish between the material transformation of the economic conditions of production, which can be determined with the precision of natural science, and the legal, political, religious, artistic or philosophic – in short, ideological forms *in which men become conscious* of this conflict and fight it out. (Marx & Engels, 1956–1990, MEW, Bd. 13, p. 9, own emphasis)

For as Gramsci's "Analysis of Situations" clarifies, his enquiry, as Marx's, also starts from *objective changes* in the economic structure. What Gramsci seems to elaborate on throughout the *Prison Notebooks* is Marx's idea that *only* in cases in which "men become conscious of this conflict" within the structure, epochal change has the *potential* to occur. By implication a lack in the acquisition of consciousness that occurs at the level of ideologies (hence Gramsci's interest ideology, intellectuals etc.) changes, to put it crudely, absolutely nothing. Hence, Gramsci portrays how a social group related to the economic structure, going through different phases – "different moments of the collective political consciousness" (Gramsci, 2001, Q.13 §17 p. 1583) – *might* become hegemonic. This can occur when the fundamental social group can supersede its narrow corporate interests, understanding that its interests "in their actual and future development" go beyond their corporate milieu and as such *can and must* become the interests of other subordinate groups (Gramsci, 2001, Q.13 §17, p. 1585). Crucially, the realization of hegemony involves, eventually, the seizing of the state, whereby the state "is conceptualised as the organism of a group destined to create favourable conditions for the maximal expansion of the same group," underlining at the same time that "this development and this expansion are conceptualised and presented as motor force of a universal expansion, of the development of all national energies" (Gramsci, 2001, Q.13 §17, p. 1585). Hence, this reading of Gramsci's *Quaderni* suggests that the *full realization of hegemony* occurs only when the fundamental social group is able to grasp power and take over the state. Conversely, hegemony "at this side of possession of the state" (Gramsci, 2001, Q.16 §9, p. 1861), that is before taking political power during the "Sturm und Drang" or "Romantic" phase of political struggle as Gramsci calls it (Gramsci, 2001, Q.11 §70, p. 1508), can "only" be "political hegemony" or "hegemonic activity." "Hegemonic activity" is then a fundamental precondition for the full realization of hegemony: "There must be *hegemonic activity* even before the rise to power" as Gramsci puts it (Gramsci, 2001, Q.19 §24, pp. 2010–2011, own emphasis).

In opposition to Arrighi who identifies "domination" as being a precondition for hegemony, the contrary seems to be the case: a certain degree of hegemony ("political hegemony" or "hegemonic activity") is a precondition for taking political power and hence for domination. In addition, once political power has been grasped and hence domination attained, the exercise of leadership continues to be a condition for its maintenance. As a consequence, domination and hegemony are interrelated: the attainment of domination requires a *certain form* of hegemony ("political hegemony" or "hegemonic activity" or "leadership") and the realization of hegemony requires political power and domination. Hence, hegemony should be understood as the dialectical unity between "leadership" (also referred as "hegemonic activity" or "political hegemony") and "domination."

The importance of both domination *and* leadership, coercion *and* consensus is further appreciated when considering Gramsci's concept of "integral State" that should be understood as a further dialectical or organic unity: the one between civil society and political society. Significantly, the exercise of hegemony involves both spheres and cannot be reduced to civil society alone. Thomas and Burgio go as far as to argue that this form of rule can be compared to the Foucauldian concept of "biopolitcs" emphasizing, however, that in Gramsci it is based on class power (Burgio, 2007; Thomas, 2009, p. 225). Importantly, it is the relative stability of this form of class rule that eventuate in the fact that, according to Gramsci, changes within the economy, as, for example crises, *do not* immediately result in "fundamental historical events" or crises of hegemony. As Gramsci writes, "It may be ruled out that immediate economic crises of themselves produce fundamental historical events" (Gramsci, 2001, Q.13 §17, p. 1587). As I shall argue below when elaborating on the concept of hegemony at the international level this holds true also for the latter.

Hegemony at the International Level and Relative Geopolitical Autonomy

As has been mentioned above a transposition of Gramsci's concept seems not pertinent, for as also Adam Morton (who took a distance from other neo-Gramscians on this issue) has in our opinion correctly emphasized, international relations are not only *present* within the *Prison Notebooks*, they also retain crucial explanatory significance (Morton, 2007a). Moreover, as I wish to argue below, Gramsci's *Notebooks* provide clear elements of what hegemony at international level entails. When addressing the latter, it should be emphasized that Gramsci provides a "dialectical" understanding of the international. Hence, figuratively Gramsci compares the "national personality" with the "individual personality" arguing that,

> [...] the national personality (as the individual personality) is a mere abstraction if considered outside the international (or social) nexus. The national personality expresses a 'distinct' of an international complex, for this reason it is bound to international relations (Gramsci, 2001, Q.19 §2, p. 1962)

And yet, as his theoretical reflections and historical examples suggest (e.g. his analysis of Italy) the influence that states are able to exercise over others varies. It is here that Gramsci explicitly introduces the concept of *hegemonic states*. What characterizes a hegemonic state then is "its ability to impress upon state activity an autonomous direction, of which other states need to support the influence and repercussion." Thus, elsewhere Gramsci writes: "The line of a hegemonic state (hence of a great power) does not oscillate because it does determine the will of others and it is not determined by them" (Gramsci, 2001, Q.13 §32, p. 1629).

Following the above definition of hegemony, a nation state can be a world hegemonic power if it has "the possibility to imprint upon its activities an absolutely autonomous direction, of which all other powers, great and minor, have to feel the influence" (Gramsci, 2001, Q.2 §16, p. 166). According to Gramsci, the status of a hegemonic power can be "calculated" looking at "the extension of territory," "economic power" understood as "productive capacity" and "financial capacity" and finally, and very importantly, considering "military power" (Gramsci, 2001, Q.13 §19, p. 1598). Thus, according to this view, hegemony does not only rest on economic power as the latter needs to be realized as politico and military power.

Hence in contrast to neo-Gramscian accounts, according to Gramsci, hegemony at the international level is exercised by *national states*. While in his early writing Gramsci reflects about liberalism's "nice dream" that consists in the "attempt to adapt international politics to the requirements of international trade" (Gramsci, 2007, p. 27) and that might be seen an invitation to conceive the possibility of the supersession of national divisions and the formation of transnational classes exercising hegemony, throughout the *Prison Notebooks* he asserts that the liberal dream remained just that: a dream. Therefore, it seems, Gramsci is critical of any conception of transnational classes and transnational states *under capitalist relations of production*. Worth noting is the fact that this is historically specific, as in the case of the Roman Empire Gramsci identified a cosmopolitan transnational class and state. Certainly Gramsci recognizes the cosmopolitan character of capitalism; however, he nonetheless recognizes the limits to that posed by "national life" upon which capitalism is also based. This, according to Gramsci, constitutes a fundamental contradiction of capitalist modernity:

> One of the fundamental contradictions is this: that whereas economic life has internationalism, or better still cosmopolitanism, as a necessary premise, state life has always developed in the direction of 'nationalism', of 'self-sufficiency' and so on. (Gramsci, 2001, Q.15 §5, p. 1757)

At the same time, also in the case of hegemony at the international level, the latter cannot be reduced to the consensual aspect of power only, for a state exercises hegemony using both leadership and domination, consensus and coercion. Generally, according to Gramsci, "the peripheral nation's economic life is subordinated to international relations" (Gramsci, 2001, Q.13 §2, p. 1562), arguing, eventually, that "war remains the ultimate arbiter for hegemony." Moreover, as his analysis on Italy reveals hegemony is maintained through "implacable repression" by the "police system" as well as "political measures" (Gramsci, 2001, Q.1 §43, p. 36). One element amongst the latter, Gramsci demonstrates later, is the so-called "party of the foreigner." This party does not represent the "vital forces of the country" but rather represents "the subordination and subservience to hegemonic nations or groups of hegemonic nations" (Gramsci, 2001, Q.13 §2, p. 1563).

While not diminishing the consensual aspect of power as well as ideological and symbolic features, one should not confuse, I believe, hegemony at the international level with the *diktat* of the *law of value*. This is strongly manifest in Gramsci's discussion of *Americanism and Fordism*: In fact, Gramsci generally points out that Americanism – with its "café life" and "ideology of the Rotary Club" (Gramsci, 2001, Q.22 §15, p. 2180) – does not represent something particularly new, pointing to the fact that in the United States the relation between classes has not changed. At the same time, according to Gramsci, Ford's method of production will spread. This occurs because of the "implacable weight" of US production and, immediately, because of "American super-power" rather than through ideology and culture. Forced by US competition, European states will have to develop new forms of states and life adequate to the new production methods, although by finding original combinations to do so:

> The problem is not whether in America a new civilisation and a new culture exists [...] and if these are invading Europe: if the problematic is posed in this way, the answer would be easy: no it does not exist. The problem is rather this; whether America, through the implacable weight of its economic production (and therefore indirectly), will compel or is already compelling Europe to overturn its excessively antiquated economic and social basis. This would have happened anyway, though only slowly. In the immediate perspective it is presented as a repercussion of American super-power. (Gramsci, 2001, Q.22 §15, p. 2178)

Therefore, Gramsci's argument strongly recalls Marx's analysis of relative surplus value production. In *Capital*, Volume one, Marx abstractly defines what Gramsci would later apply in analyzing the United States and Europe: while innovative capitals acting as "first movers" within the market (read: the US) might obtain extraordinary profits, "the law of the determination of value by labour-time [...] acting as a *coercive law* of competition," Marx argues, forces competitors (read: Europe) to adopt the new methods of production. Thus he emphasizes that the advantages that accrued to the "first mover" disappear "so soon as the new method of production has become general" (Marx & Engels, 1956–1990, MEW, Bd. 23, pp. 337–338). To be sure, and as evident from the above evocation of "US super-power," Gramsci also considers how the *law of value* is *mediated* by introducing national states in the analysis. Moreover, it considers the superstructural transformations that the adaptation to the new production process would result in.

In addition, the *Prison Notebooks* also emphasize that hegemonic powers should be simultaneously understood as imperialist states, whereby Gramsci adopts a "classical" understanding of imperialism that strongly recalls Lenin's (Gramsci, 2001, Q.19, §24 p. 2018). What my analysis suggests is that imperialist states *must* become hegemonic in order to secure the accumulation of capital. This is based on a further implication of the law of value that compels capitals to grow and expand:

> the development of capitalist production makes it constantly necessary to keep increasing the amount of the capital laid out in a given industrial undertaking, and competition makes the immanent laws of capitalist production to be felt by each individual capitalist, as external coercive laws. It compels him to keep constantly extending his capital, in order to preserve it, but extend it he cannot, except by means of progressive accumulation. (Marx & Engels, 1956–1990, MEW, Bd. 23, p. 618)

The reproduction of capital and the related endless accumulation of capital cannot be confined between the borders of a national state. Being an international tale, the accumulation of capital requires that states secure the necessary conditions for the accumulation of "their" capitals.[2] Subaltern states might be differently integrated in the hegemonic nation's circuit of (and hence as providers of raw materials, labor power, production sites, market for realization etc.) and/ or for geopolitical reasons necessary for the containment of rival states. It is therefore necessary to qualify Arrighi's claim that states become hegemonic by virtue of their ability to lead other states through a period of economic expansion. Following the above understanding of hegemony, states *must* become hegemonic and enforce the latter by means of both consensus and coercion if the accumulation of capital is to take place. This is reminiscent of Gramsci's theorization, where, as we have seen, a fundamental social group *must* become hegemonic if it wants to expand and develop.

Restricting the concept to hegemonic relations amongst "core" or "imperialist states," it refers to the hegemonic position of an imperialist state over other imperialist states. A regional hegemon is hegemonic at least in its respective region. A world hegemonic (imperialist) state prevents the construction of hegemonic relations by rival imperialist states. In fact, a crisis of world hegemony refers to the ability of rival (imperialist) states to become hegemonic at least in its respective region thereby challenging the position of the former world hegemon.

But there is, finally, a further important refinement of the concept of hegemony at the international level I wish to propose. Drawing on Gramsci's discussion of hegemony at the national level and its distinction between "hegemonic activity" (before the seizure of the state) and the effective realization of hegemony that only occurs through the seizure of the state, I distinguish between two "levels" of hegemony at the international level: "Sturm und Drang hegemony" and "fully realised hegemony." Also at the international level the construction of hegemony should therefore be understood as a process. In the first case – Sturm und Drang hegemony – the concept refers to a weak form of hegemony as the latter includes mainly the economic moment. "Fully realised hegemony," by contrast, represents a far more robust form of hegemony as it involves the economic, political and military moments. Thus unlike World-systems Theory or cases of "Sturm und Drang hegemony" where the redistribution of economic power (usually associated with economic crises) might immediately lead to a crisis of hegemony, in cases of fully realised hegemony, hegemonic states can resort to battery of means in order to avoid crises of hegemony. These include the influence over currency exchange rates, but also political and military measures.

As we shall see later, this differentiation might be helpful for understanding the process of construction of hegemonic relations as well as for understanding why the redistribution of economic power did not result in a crisis of United States *fully realised* hegemony. But before entering into the analysis of the current situation, it is important to clarify a further point: how can the emergence of "contender states," to use Kees Van der Pijl's term (Van der Pijl, 1984), be conceptualized?

The Rise of Contender States

As is well known, Gramsci argues that changes in the fundamental social relations have the potential to result in economic development and thereby creating the potential for reaching the status of a great power. As Gramsci puts it:

> Do international relations precede or follow (logically) fundamental social relations? There can be no doubt that they follow. Any organic innovation in the social structure, through its technical- military expressions, modifies organically absolute and relative relations in the international field too. (Gramsci, 2001, Q.13§2, p. 1562)

In his work, the above-mentioned experience of the United States represents a clear example. The dramatic process of uneven development and amelioration of the US position within the world economy from the late 19th century onwards represents a successful the dramatic process of uneven development and amelioration of the US position within the world economy from the late 19th century onwards represents a successful attempt to counteract declining profitability, thanks to "the accelerated rhythm in the progress of production and labour methods and the modification of the traditional worker" (Gramsci, 2001, Q.10 §41, p. 1313). Americanism and Fordism are hence associated with productivity increases, including the introduction of new technology and the scientific managing of production accompanied by adequate or corresponding institutional and ideological arrangements within the United States. At the same time, it is worth noting that "organic innovation in the social structure" refers to deep, long-lasting structural societal changes (Gramsci, 2001, Q.13§17, p. 1579). As again Gramsci's *Analysis of Situations* show, these are brought about by *revolutions*.[3] Within this context it should be emphasized that Gramsci also dwells on the *pre-condition* that enabled the United States to detach itself from hitherto hegemonic relations and subsequently to *relatively autonomously shape* its development. Thus, the primary conditions for "the formation of the power of United States" were, Gramsci outlines, first and foremost the revolutionary processes, from "Independence" to the Civil War, the result of which posed the conditions for the US's subsequent development (Gramsci, 2001, Q.2, pp. 166–168). Hence what are now referred to as the first and second American Revolution, by *breaking dependent relations* vis-à-vis the British Empire (independence) and establishing the modern liberal capitalist state under the leadership of the industrial north as a result of the Civil War, can be seen as having posed the *precondition* for both the astonishing results the US economy achieved and the creation of the potential to establish itself as a hegemonic state. Building on Gramsci's insights I shall attempt to argue further below that it was the Chinese Revolution that resulted in what I refer to as the country's "relative geopolitical autonomy" thereby also making China, I believe, a category of its own amongst other "emerging economies" or the so-called BRICS states.[4] As we shall see, it was the Chinese Revolution that posed the seeds for China's relative autonomous development that eventually resulted in its ability to establishing itself as a great power now in the process of challenging US hegemony, remaining, however, far from replacing it.

US HEGEMONY AND CHINA'S RELATIVE GEOPOLITICAL AUTONOMY

Following the analysis outlined in the previous paragraphs, I contend that the construction of US hegemony should be understood as a process going through different phases. Here we can only very briefly sketch out elements thereof in order to highlight the different position that China achieved compared to some of the US's imperialist rivals.[5] Differently from Arrighi (1994) and in stark contrast to the analysis provided by Desai (2013), I wish to argue that the United States became hegemonic already during the interwar period, with the qualification that the latter form of hegemony was deficient: while backed by the state *strictu sensu*, hegemony was exercised via private channels rather than public ones and took mainly an economic dimension. Political and military involvement, while occurring, would be relatively restricted compared to the post World War Two order the United States would establish. This is why, relying on Gramsci's characterization of a still incomplete form of hegemony, I refer to it as "Sturm und Drang hegemony." As a result of the "endless accumulation of capital" and capital's drive to expand beyond its borders, nation-states are compelled to become hegemonic in order to secure the accumulation and reproduction of "their" capitals. Thus given the standing the US attained within the world economy already by the 1920s as confirmed by any important indicator (production, trade, finance), it was "imperative" as Gilbert Ziebura has aptly underscored that the United States took control not only of the European but also the world economy as a whole (Ziebura, 1990). The United States would do so by launching the Dawes Plan (1924) in Europe, forcing most countries (including Britain) into the Gold Standard, the rules of which benefited the United States and blocked Britain's attempt to revitalize its declining position. Moreover, through a series of agreements signed during the 1921/1922 Washington Conference the United States was able to shape the balance of power in Asia as well as limit the military ambitions of its competitors. Hegemony was mainly exercised by private forces (analytically different from the state "*strictu sensu*," but still part of the state integrally understood) and was prevalently economic as direct political and military involvement, while existent, was limited. But it was exactly the relative weakness of this form of hegemony that resulted in the fact that the Great Depression of the 1930s caused a crisis of US hegemony. Thus, rival imperialist states were able to start constructing hegemonic relations at the regional level (Germany and Japan) or attempting to reinvigorate their declining empire (Great Britain). Here, it can be argued that symbolically September 1931 was the point at which the foundation upon which US hegemony was constructed started to unravel. On the 18th of September Japan invaded Manchuria thus breaking the status quo imposed in occasion of the Washington Conference; on the 21st of September Britain abandoned the Gold Standard. In figurative and descriptive terms, we may characterize the Great Depression as bringing about the negation of a first, weak version of US hegemony, the further negation of which resulted in the post-World War II hegemonic order.

It is therefore only after World War two that the United States became *fully hegemonic*, now involving the economic *cum* the political and military moment. US economic recovery was eventually brought about by rearmament worth around 50 times government expenditures under the New Deal and, eventually, through participation in World War II in which the United States was able to create the conditions for re-launching its world hegemonic project by militarily defeating Germany and Japan and by forcing the opening up of the biggest remaining closed trading block, that is Britain's Empire, through various mean, including Lend Lease (starting 1941). The full realization of US hegemony occurred only by circa 1950, and, reflecting the changes that occurred during the Great Depression and during the war, it became increasingly *state-led, institutionalized and eventually was cemented politically and militarily*. Through the Marshall plan in Europe and similar policies in Japan, the US set the conditions for Germany and Japan to regain partially their former role as economic powerhouses in order to revive the respective economic areas under strict US control, while Great Britain would retain a different role given the importance of the Empire she still controlled. Yet in all cases, and differently from the 1920s, the US's grip was secured militarily, through NATO, for example.

It was on this background that the US thought of and gave an impulse to the process of European Integration which was spelled out by Hoffman in 1949 and which foresaw "the formation of a single large market within which quantitative restrictions on the movements of goods, monetary barriers to the flow of payments, and eventually, all tariffs are permanently swept away" (Hoffman quoted in Block, 1977, p. 99). In Japan, similarly, as both Pollard and Wells have pointed out the US saw Japan's recovery as pivotal for the development of the whole area:

> The United States restored Japanese industry for roughly the same reason it restored German manufacturing capacity. American officials saw Japan as the key to general Asian reconstruction. American planners had originally hoped to disperse Japanese industry or trade throughout other Asian and Pacific countries (especially China, the Philippines and Australia) partly through Japanese reparations and American aid. But by 1947 they realised that that these largely underdeveloped courtiers could not fill the economic void left by the Japanese collapse. (Pollard & Wells, 1984, p. 348)

As we shall see in greater detail later, Germany's and Japan's economic development from the 1970s onwards must be comprehended as having been influenced by both the profitability crisis and the constraints imposed by the

United States. By contrast, I wish to argue that China developed largely outside US hegemonic relations.

China's Relative Geopolitical Autonomy

China's extraordinary economic growth over the past decades has enabled the country to achieve, at least in quantitative terms, a central position within the world economy. Yet, as mentioned previously, the nature of its position is highly contested. Panitch and Gindin claim that China is far from posing a challenge to US hegemony: "China may perhaps emerge eventually as a pole of interimperial power, it will obviously be very far from reaching such a status for a good many decades" (Panitch & Gindin, 2004, p. 22). This thesis, reiterated in the two authors' book *The Making of Global Capitalism* (Panitch & Gindin, 2012, pp. 292–301), is substantiated by the work of Hung Ho-Fung (Hung, 2009) and, from a different perspective, by Martin Hart-Landsberg and Paul Burkett (2006): they claim that China is subordinated either to the United States (Hung, 2009) or to the operations of "transnational capital" (Landsberg and Burkett). Arrighi, in stark contrast to the former authors, and as has been mentioned, contends that "China has emerged as an increasingly credible alternative to US leadership in the East Asia region and beyond" (Arrighi, 2009, p. 385). Yet conceiving China as non-capitalist market economy he argued that the sort of hegemony China might construe would strongly differ from previous and current experiences within "historical capitalism" (*Ibid.*).

Contra the above interpretations, we wish to argue that China's development has been far more *autonomous* (in relative terms) than the above-mentioned authors concede and that the Chinese State plays a significant role in orchestrating the economy and its direction. By implication we wish to claim that China represents a potential challenger to US hegemony, particularly so in East Asia, but economically also in other parts of the globe. Yet we want to emphasize that this does not amount to imply that China's development is spared from deep contradictions: after all, and differently from Arrighi's assessment, we want to argue that China is a capitalist economy.

The relative geopolitical autonomy and the central role the Chinese State plays emerges when reflecting on the modalities of the "Rise of China." Hart-Landsberg and Burkett's analysis seems to share the claim that China's rise occurred as a consequence of ("transnational") capital's path to incorporating nations where labor was cheaper and China "became the most likely ultimate destination of this labour-seeking snowballing process" (Arrighi, 2009, p. 37). Given the large reservoir of cheap labor available elsewhere, this alone, however, can hardly explain why China got targeted. Helmut Peters and Hyekyung Cho have proposed a different interpretation. According to the German sinologist Helmut Peters the "Rise of China" should be understood within a specific geopolitical context recognizing two central factors: the 1949 revolution and later the break with the Soviet Union, which by the end of the 1960s was perceived as "chief enemy of and chief threat" (Peters, 2012). Maurice Meisner recognizes the realization of "national unity" and "national independence," the latter understood as "the elimination of the foreign imperialist impingement that had humbled and humiliated China for almost a century" as the two great achievements of the Chinese revolution (Meisner, 1999, 2008). As Wei underscores, it was "the humiliating memory and consequences of the foreign imperialist invasions of China, as well as their perceptions of existential threats, provided the cultural atmosphere within which their individual actions, preferences, and calculations were framed" (Wei, 2011, p. 5). Theda Skocpol's famous *States and Social Revolutions* also underlines the critical significance of the revolution while pointing to the fundamental importance of a states' *autonomy* a social revolution might help to achieve: for here social revolutions are said to "break the chains" of dependency. Moreover, she underlines that social revolutions "have given birth to nations whose *power and autonomy* markedly surpassed their own pre-revolutionary past and outstripped other countries in similar circumstances." Thus referring China (and Russia) she maintains that the revolutions were conductive to very rapid and successful development: "within the space of two generations" the revolution "transformed a backward agrarian country into the second-ranked industrial and military power in the world. What the Russian Revolution was for the first half of the twentieth century, the Chinese has been for the second half" (Skocpol, 1979, pp. 3–4, own emphasis).[6] Following Peters, according to the concept of the "three worlds," China should emerge as a third independent and sovereign power alongside the Soviet Union and the United States. Under Mao, China made initial steps toward this goal. Starting with Deng Xiaoping's reforms and opening in 1978, both China's ambitions and means to achieve them changed. Nonetheless, unlike the majority of analyses that take 1978–1979 as the starting point for China's successful development, Meisner (1999), Lippit (1987), and Wei (2011) underline the legacy of Mao's period (notwithstanding the human suffering during the period) in posing the seeds that enabled China to develop at the well-known pace thereafter. In the words of Wei "China's successful reform is in fact the legacy of the Mao era and the Cultural Revolution" (Wei, 2011, p. 2). The concept of the "three worlds" was eventually abandoned and later substituted by the concept of the "one world," *the capitalist world*, developed under Hu Jintao (Peters, 2012). The means, from the 1978 reforms onwards, involved China's opening up, in order to gain access to modern technology and, structural changes, that is the establishment of capitalist relations of production. It was the Chinese State and the Chinese Communist Party that promoted this.

Zhao has thus well described the very important role the Chinese State plays in the economy:

> China has [...] engaged with global markets to attract foreign capital, technology and management skills, and participated in the global economic division of labour by taking advantage of its cheap labour and huge domestic market. The Chinese economy, however, is only selectively free. The state still keeps ultimate control over strategic sectors of the economy and a large range of core industries, including utilities, transportation, telecommunications, finance, and the media. (Zhao, 2010, p. 422)

By implication, Hart-Landsberg and Burkett, in my opinion, underrate the significance of the Chinese state. Hence throughout the 1980s, the 1990s and the 2000s economic growth in China, has not only been export-led (certainly not during the 1980s and the early 1990s), but also investment led: state investments represented by far the greatest quota of investment, despite the continuous decline in the state's quantitative share within the economy. China's subsequent increasing reliance on exports over the years has been a conscious strategy pursued by the Communist Party. As Hyekyung Cho has shown, this largely occurred as reaction to the slowdown of domestic economic activity. Hence the sharp deceleration of China's growth rates at the end of the 1980s was followed by a surge in exports starting from the early 1990s. Similarly, the slowdown that occurred at the end of the 1990s resulted in China's accession to the WTO which again led to a steep upraise in exports (Cho, 2005a, Chapters 4 and 5, 2005b). In this light, Hung's claim that China's holding of US treasury bonds is indicative of the former country's dependence on the latter, can also be read the other way round: As Hung himself writes "the drastic expansion of China's export industries not only accounts for its stellar growth, but also, through its enlarged trade surplus, *its global financial power*" (Hung, 2009, p. 10, own emphasis). Even considering low returns on US treasury bonds, this disadvantage can be seen as being offset by the advantages the country got by keeping the yuan low compared to the dollar thereby enabling to increase the volume of exports to the United States.

Importantly, the state also set the legal framework (and ad hoc rules) under which so-called FIE (Foreign Invested Enterprises) or FOE (Foreign-Owned Enterprises) operate in China and which Hart-Landsberg and Burkett underestimate. FIEs are in many cases bound to Chinese firms (usually directly controlled by the Chinese Communist Party) via joint ventures, which allow the latter to obtain technology from the former. Frank Sieren refers to the relationship between foreign firms and the domestic economy as "*Konkubinenwirtschaft*" (Concubine economy): As concubines at the emperor's court, foreign companies are required to make serious concessions, particularly relating to the transfer of technology, in order to gain access to the Chinese market and profit from highly favorable conditions (Sieren, 2008, p. 208). Last but not least, Hart-Landsberg and Burkett as well as Hung, while emphasizing China's emergence as a colossal export platform and its weight within the world economy, are silent on China's major shifts in foreign (economic) policy, which paralleled the country's ascent. Yet in order to understand the latter, it is necessary to engage with Arrighi's claim that China is not capitalist.

Arrighi's claim that China developed along a non-capitalist Smithian path centers on the agrarian reforms which represent "*the critical factor*" (Arrighi, 2008, p. 361) for his assessment. The reforms included the institution of the Household Responsibility System and the development of Town and Village Enterprises (TVE). Given the redistribution of land amongst peasants, Arrighi refers to the process as one of "accumulation without dispossession" arguing that China does not present the main preconditions of capitalist relations of production and development envisaged by Marx and elaborated later, amongst others, by Brenner (1977). Yet a look at the longer term repercussions of the agricultural reforms suggest that also in China the agrarian population eventually felt compelled to sell its labor power in order to survive: peasants, now relating to each other as individual producers, eventually were bankrupted and proletarianized. As both Cho and Hung have argued, despite its early successes, the agrarian reform led to the often mentioned "unlimited supply of labor" exemplified by the rise of rural labor force engaged in non-agricultural activities from 28 million in 1978 to 176 million in 2003 (Arrighi, 2009, p. 39). As Hung has argued, eventually the government's rural-agricultural policies served to "bankrupt the countryside and generate a continuous rural exodus" (Hung, 2009, p. 12). While the means changed slightly the end result was the same: primitive accumulation.

Again, relying on the work of Hyekyung Cho, China is best understood as "State-capitalism." The author considers the transformation that started in 1978 as a "revolution from above" that got completed with the opening of the Chinese Communist Party to private entrepreneurs in 2001 (Cho, 2005a, p. 217). On the occasion of the 80th anniversary of the formation of the Communist Party, Jiang Zemin reiterated the solution to the dilemmas between "capitalism" and "socialism" as well as "private" and "public." It found the solution the "socialist market economy" and "mixed property relations." Here the Communist Party's open commitment to capitalism is justified on the basis that the forces of production still have space for development. This possibility should be exploited before socialism can be implemented, whereby the Party remains committed to do so at some point in the future (Peters, 2012).

THE US AND ITS IMPERIALIST RIVALS: JAPAN'S AND GERMANY'S SUBORDINATION, CHINA'S RELATIVE AUTONOMY

The difference between Germany's and Japan's subordination as opposed to China's relative geopolitical autonomy can be exemplified by the countries' development from the 1970s onwards. Hence Germany's and Japan's economic development from the 1970s onwards must be comprehended as having been influenced by both the profitability crisis (I cannot deal with here) and the constraints imposed by the United States. Significantly, and in contrast to the view presented by Panitch and Gindin, given the economic position these economies achieved, this involved, according to my analysis, the attempt to become hegemonic in their respective regions rather than contributing to the reproduction of the "American Empire" – processes that were successfully prevented by the United States. Also, Japan's and Germany's turn to neoliberalism, should be understood not as a mere emulation of the US model, but rather as having been influenced by the law of value and hence the very same downward pressure on profitability the United States was confronted with. It is worth noting in this context that Germany's turn to monetarism, for example, happened before the famous 1979 Volcker shock usually taken as neoliberalism's starting-point; Japan's loose monetary policy and the ensuing real estate bubble also *anticipated* similar processes that characterized the US response to the crisis.

Panitch and Gindin acknowledge that the United States could not maintain the economic position attained after World War Two as its share in world output, which stood at roughly 50 per cent in the immediate post-war period, declined to 25 per cent by the end of the 1970s. Yet they argue that the US remained *unchallenged,* then and in subsequent decades. The US economic performance, they observe, surpassed that of major advanced economies: between 1984 and 2004 the rate of economic growth in the United States, averaging 3.4 per cent exceeded the one achieved by Germany and Japan; R&D expenditures by far outpaced those of other advanced economies; between 1987 and 2004 exports were rising at a pace of 6.8 per cent per annum in the US compared to 4.5–5.8 per cent in other G7 economies (Panitch & Gindin, 2005, pp. 113–114) (Figs. 1–3).

Yet the 20 years' averages (1984–2004) Panitch and Gindin take in order to sustain their argument, obfuscate the developments that occurred during these years. While it is true that on *average* during the period the US's economic performance was superior compared to other advanced economies, breaking down the period tells a different story which can be summarized as follows: firstly, the data indicate the *rise and retreat* of the US's potential challengers Germany (and with it the EU) and Japan between 1980 and the year 2000. Secondly, from the year 2000 onwards the hitherto prevailing mechanisms are greatly unsettled by the emergence of China. Therefore, *contra* the analysis presented by Panitch and Gindin, while the US economy grew more rapidly immediately after the 1982 recession, between 1985 and 1991 Japan's and later Germany's rates of economic growth exceed that of the United States, averaging 4.1, 3 and 1.8 per cent, respectively. During those years the US's per capita income was surpassed by both Japan (1985), and by Germany (around 1990) as the above chart indicates. Japan's and Germany's superior growth rates are also reflected in increased shares in world output: after a substantial but brief recovery between 1980 and 1985 (from 25 to 35 per cent of world output), the US share falls back to one-quarter, while Japan dramatically increases its own to nearly

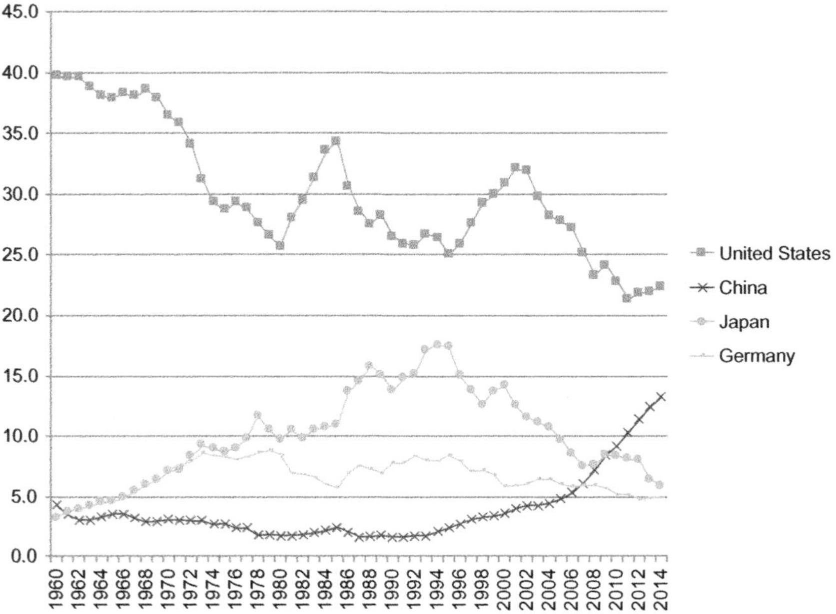

Fig. 1. World Share of GDP 1960–2014 (Current USD). *Source:* World Bank.

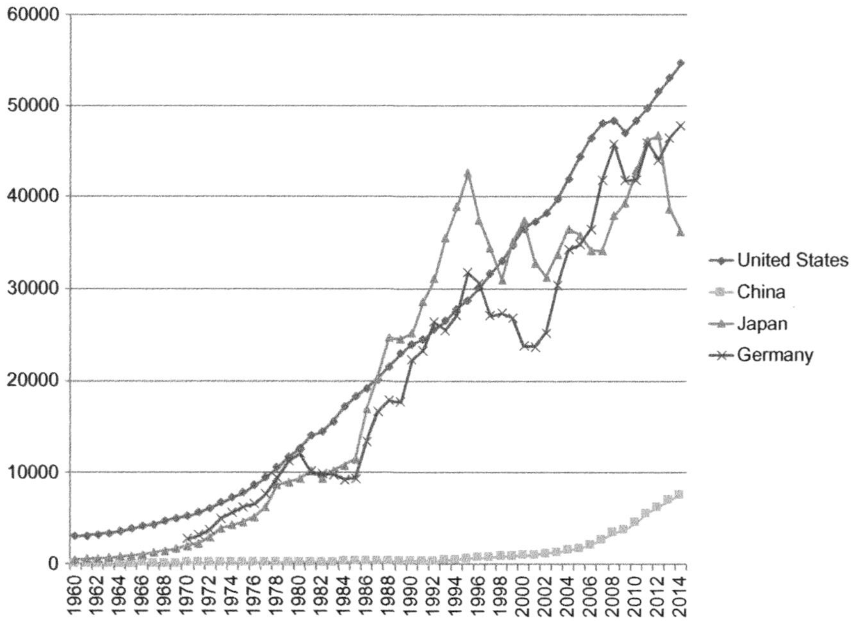

Fig. 2. GDP per Capita 1960–2014 (Current USD). *Source:* World Bank.

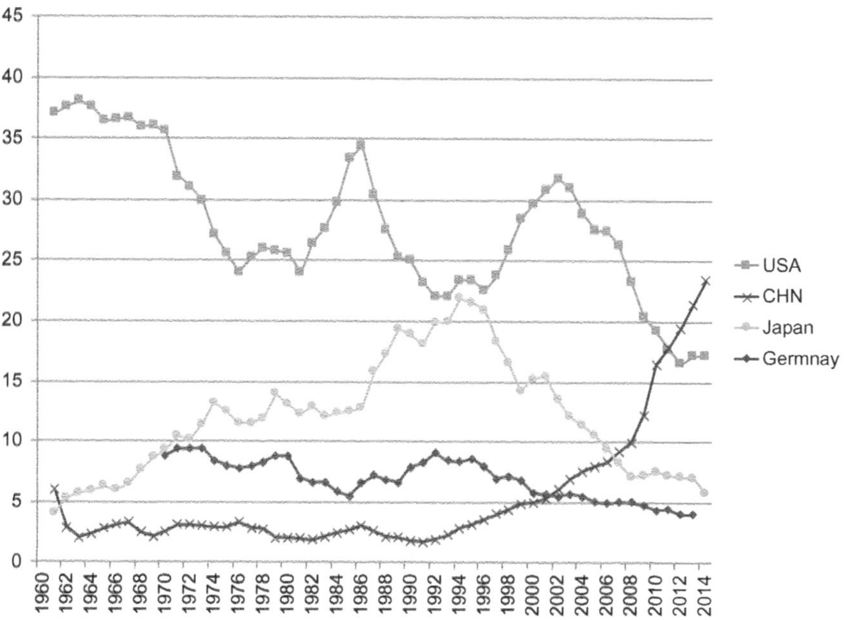

Fig. 3. World Share – Fixed Capital Formation 1970–2014 (Current USD). *Source:* World Bank.

20 per cent, accompanied by a modest increase in Germany's share (from five to eight per cent). But the trend in all mentioned indicators is reversed by the mid-1990s. Indeed, between 1995 and 2000 the US grew again more rapidly, its GDP per capita tops again Japan's and Germany's. In addition, the United States was able to increase its share of world output again to roughly one-third, while Japan's share strongly and Germany's modestly declined.

The year 2000 represents a significant turning point: between the year 2000 and 2007 (but the trend is already clearly visible already in 2004) the US share in world output declines from 33 to 25 per cent, its world share in exports drops to 7 per cent from 14 per cent and its share in fixed capital formation, passing from 28 to 20 per cent, also experiences a dramatic downward turn. Yet, importantly, this time round the decline is not, as previously, accompanied by a rise in Japan's and Germany's shares, but only by the rise of one other country: China. Its share in world output, which, at the beginning of the 1990s stood at around 2 per cent, shows a very strong acceleration surpassing Germany's and Japan's by 2007. China's growing share in world output expresses the country's extraordinary rise in GDP. China's share in world exports surpasses Japan's in 2003 and outpaces Germany's and the US's by 2013. The rise in China's share of world fixed capital formation is even more pronounced.

Offsetting Germany's and Japan's Challenges

As Joseph Halevi has argued, already at the onset of the profitability crisis Germany significantly shifted its accumulation strategy, in which export-led growth was now to be based on a strong currency, industrial restructuring and Foreign Direct Investment (Halevi, 1995, p. 268). Within this strategy, both Riccardo Parboni and Joseph Halevi argue, the accumulation of surpluses from trade with the rest of Europe was necessary to finance Germany's exports as well as foreign direct investments. In contrast, major changes in Japan's accumulation strategies occurred during the mid-1980s, in particular as a reaction to the revaluation of the yen imposed through the Plaza Agreement. In particular, Japanese capital engaged in the process of construing regional production networks. "In the second half of the 1980s Japanese elites," Gowan notes, "[...] did start to develop a new accumulation strategy: the development of a strong regional network in East and South East Asia and one not based on West European-style neo-mercantilist regional trade policy, but rather on the export of productive capital" (Gowan, 1999, p. 47). As Katzenstein has detailed, "Japanese multinationals tripled their foreign output between 1985 and 1994 to 9 percent of total output, and by 1994 had captured over 25 percent of the Japanese import market" (Katzenstein & Shiraishi, 1997, p. 346). At the same time, the Bank of Japan engaged in very loose monetary policy with the main aim of boosting domestic consumption (Schmidt, 2010, p. 516).

As a result, both strategies enabled the two countries to deepen their economic weight within Europe and Asia, respectively. Regarding Germany, we notice a strong increase in exports toward, and surpluses from, the rest of the continent, making Europe Germany's major source of effective demand. As Halevi writes: "In 1970 the FRG's trade with the rest of the EEC was nearly balanced. Twenty years later, in spite of steadily declining growth rates, the EEC provided the vast majority of the FRG surpluses, the main source of which are net exports of investment and capital goods" (Halevi, 1995, p. 286).

While Pempel's assessment of Japan's economic might within the region is drawn by comparing the country to a colossus, the widely accepted description of Japan's relation to other East Asian economies is the one of the "flying geese" originally developed by Akamatsu in the 1930s (Pempel, 1997, p. 52):

> Under the domination of Japanese capital either through Japanese foreign direct investment or the multilayered subcontracting system centred on Japanese corporations, Japan maintained a stable division of labour along the value chain with other East and Southeast Asian economies. Japan always specialised in higher value-added products, and the four original Tigers, together with other late-coming new tigers such as Thailand and Malaysia, concentrated on lower-value-added ones. (Hung, 2009, p. 10)

With the economic weight the two countries achieved within their respective regions came also the necessary attempt to translate economic leadership into political leadership. Thus, Germany's effort to institutionalize its economic position can be traced to the foundation of the European Monetary System (EMS) established in 1979. As Halevi has argued, "[...] with the EMS, Germany acquired the freedom to fight the fluctuations of the dollar through internally coordinated restructuring. At the same time, Bonn prevented the other European countries from using the exchange rate instrument to undercut its policies" (Halevi, 1995, p. 280).

There are different interpretations as to why the European Monetary System eventually led to the creation of the euro. According to Carchedi, Germany had a strong interest in the development of a world currency and "to become a truly international currency, it had to become the currency used in the whole Community (even though under different clothing), in a market comparable to that of the US and served by an efficient and technologically advanced production system" (Carchedi, 2001, p. 141). Unlike Carchedi, Gowan maintains that it was in the interest of Germany to keep the mark: "the spontaneous rationality for German capitalism would have required a smaller mark union, without the Mediterranean countries, and with an eastward orientation" (Gowan, 1999, p. 58). Here, the introduction of the euro is understood as having occurred as a result of a political compromise as "Germany was pushed politically into the big EU monetary union" (*Ibid.*). This line of argument is also preferred by Michael Baum who argues that both the Maastricht Treaty and the euro resulted from an arrangement between Germany and other members of the European Community, particularly France (Baum, 1995/96, p. 623).

Looking at Japan we notice that its ability to engage autonomously in the construction of hegemonic relations that would institutionalize its economic leadership politically, not to mention militarily, was even more seriously limited by its geopolitical subordination to the United States. As Katzenstein and Shiraishi detail:

> Dependence on U.S. protection [...] meant that Japan remained a semi-sovereign state. Its defence forces are fully integrated into the U.S. military. Loosely speaking, the United states became part of Japan's ruling conservative coalition in the form of the politics of gaiatsu (external pressure). In the 1970s and 1980s, the United States compelled Japan to link economics and politics with security. When Japan redefined its strategic posture in 1976, the military component of defence became important for the first time. U.S. pressure and Japanese interest in continued access to U.S. markets made this concession to the United States a foregone conclusion; however, Japan's idea of 'comprehensive security' underscored the point that a substantial military build-up was not on the cards. There was no real inclination to make Japan into a 'normal' state. This continues to be the case two decades later in the mid-1990s. (Katzenstein & Shiraishi, 1997, p. 361)

But both Japan and Germany started to represent serious challenges to US hegemony. According to Ho–Fung Hung, and as the literature on the "Japanese threat" that flourished in the United States during the 1980s suggests, by the early 1990s some believed that Japan could challenge the economic leadership of the United States. Hence Hung writes:

> this model of capitalist development through regionalisation was so successful that many saw in the early 1990s the emergence of a Japan-centred 'Greater Asian Co-Prosperity Sphere', a prospect for which Japan had longed since the early twentieth century but militarism in the 1930s and 1940s failed to achieve. With the whole East Asian Region behind it, Japan posed an increasing threat to the global economic leadership of the United States. (Hung, 2009, p. 10)

"European integration" under German leadership, despite its limitations, posed a potential threat to US hegemony over Europe. Gibbs has identified three important reasons for this: The European Union was developing into one of the largest single economic units in the world; secondly, the consolidation of the EU was pursued independently from the United States; thirdly, at the military level the EU was embarking on the development of its own European Security and Defence Identity. In particular, Gibbs writes, "the possibility of an independent European foreign and military policy was immediately viewed as a potential threat to Nato and U.S. dominance," whereby, as Gibbs correctly states and as we have argued, NATO was a vital element of US hegemony over Europe (Gibbs, 2001, p. 23).

Nevertheless, both Germany's and Japan's efforts to translate their economic leadership into political and military supremacy within their respective region were seriously limited by action undertaken by the United States. As the above analysis has already made clear the fluctuations of the dollar and US monetary policy strongly influenced Germany's economic strategy and consequently the *mode* of European integration. As attentive observers of the process, both Carchedi and Gowan have showed its limitations. Thus, Gowan points to the flawed architecture of the euro given the lack of "a solid political base that could be counted upon to act as single political unit in a crisis" and "a major military-political capability autonomous from the US" (Gowan, 1999, p. 75). Carchedi makes a very similar point and writes: "a world currency must be supported both by a sovereign political entity and by an overpowering military force" (Carchedi, 2001, p. 142) nothing though "the military dependence of the EU, and of its military arm, the West European Union, upon the USA and NATO" (*Ibid.*). Significantly, the EU eastward enlargement occurred under the auspices of the US controlled IMF and new member countries were integrated into NATO. Concerning Japan, the political institutionalization of Japan's economic leadership in the region, autonomously from the United States, did not occur: most of the countries' currencies were tied to the dollar and the United States were heavily involved in regional economic organizations, such as APEC (Asia-Pacific Economic Cooperation), founded in 1989. Yet a further example of Japan's failure to create a cohesive regional pole can be discerned from the East Asian crisis. In Gowan's account of the deep crisis that affected East Asian economies at the end of the 1990s (with GDP declining between 6 and 13 per cent) the US efficaciously achieved that Japan would not take the lead in the "rescue" of the troubled economies:

> Japan, at the onset of the crisis, was the first country to offer remedial action with its proposal to create an Asian Monetary Fund (AMF). The proposal was for the region's richer countries to provide $100 billion in needed liquidity to the crisis-affected countries. Japan's proposal was quickly shot down by the United States and the International Monetary Fund (IMF) as well as by China. (Pempel, 2011, p. 265)

As a result, the effects of both the operation of the countertendencies to defy declining profitability and US actions resulted in deep economic contradictions within Europe and Japan. Thus, the European Monetary Union was not backed by a political and fiscal union and took the form of a fixed exchange rate system of the most rigid form. Its central bank was modelled according to the Bundesbank. Perry Anderson has well summarized the resulting economic developments since the introduction of the euro:

> German capital enforced an unprecedented wage repression [...]. As manufacturing productivity rose and relative labour costs declined, German export industries became more competitive than ever, taking an increasing share of Eurozone markets. In the periphery of the Eurozone, on the other hand, the corresponding loss of competitivity of the local economies was anaesthetized by a flow of cheap capital borrowed at interest rates held virtually uniform across the space of the monetary union, according to German prescriptions. (Anderson, 2012, p. 56; see also Lapavitsas et al., 2011)

While in the 1990s the contradictory developments in Europe did not *yet* lead to a full-fledged crisis, Japan, as is well known faced a deep and long lasting economic crisis. In fact, Japan's apparently successful economic performance described above must be drastically revised when considering other developments within Japan's economy, particularly as a result of loose monetary policy which fueled an economic bubble characterized by over-indebtedness, real estate and stock market speculation (Turner, 2008, p. 137). The bursting of the bubble in the early 1990s had devastating effects on Japan's economy reversing many of the relative gains made earlier. Hence Pempel gives the following assessment:

> For the subsequent 20 years [after the bursting of the bubble], Japan's economy was locked in a spiral of debt, deflation and declining productivity. In the process per capita gross domestic product declined from third highest in the world in 1991 to eighteenth in 2008. Household income fell from its peak in 1994 to a 19-year low of 5.56 million yen, or about $58,000, in 2007. By 2009, nominal GDP was barely above its 1991 levels while Japan's share of world GDP – that had risen so parabolically from roughly seven percent in 1970 to ten percent in 1980 and nearly 18 percent in the early 1990s (an increase of roughly 250 percent) – had fallen back to eight percent in 2010. In other words, in the 20 years from 1990 to 2010 Japan surrendered virtually all of the relative global economic gains it had so spectacularly achieved in the two prior decades. (Pempel, 2011, p. 261)

Therefore, while the strategies initially adopted by both Germany and particularly Japan brought more success than the one adopted by the United States, with the effect of increasing their weight within the world economy, this did not translate into the creation of hegemonic blocks sufficient to induce a crisis of US hegemony. The latter country was able to block these advances and contributed, together with the already contradictory character of capitalist development, to the growth of deep incongruities within Europe's and Japan's economies.

China's Expansion and Its Initial Bid for Hegemony...

Following the understanding of hegemony developed above, China's increasing weight within the world economy has compelled the country to attempt to construct hegemonic relations in order to guarantee the accumulation of its capitals. This can be appreciated when considering the changes in Chinese foreign policy and economic diplomacy, which coincide with the economic turning point described by Hung and Hart-Landsberg/Burkett. As Rosemary Foot has put it the "passive and unspecific approach" China pursued earlier "was replaced with something more active and with real policy content" (Foot, 2006, pp. 84–85). This refers to China's "new foreign policy" made official in the early years of Hu Jintao's leadership (2002–2012): according to Hu Jintao, Peters writes,

> [...] economic diplomacy amounts to an opening of the country towards the outside which combines the 'coming-in' (import of raw materials, technology, capital etc.) with 'going-out'. 'Going out' means to fight for positions on the world market by developing competitive products, to invest in the raw material sector abroad, to gain technology and markets through the acquisition of foreign companies, and to participate in the economic improvement of developing countries with China's own capital and labour. (Peters, 2012)

During this initial phase of China's outward expansion, the country pursued efforts to secure the provision of raw materials and energy resources. The official guidelines for China's offensive have been "mutual respect for sovereignty and territorial integrity, mutual non-aggression, non-interference in each other's internal affairs, equality and mutual benefit, and peaceful coexistence" (Mills, 2012). This has given rise to the idea of the "China Model" or "Beijing Consensus" as opposed to the "Washington Consensus." But as Paul Ciccantell argues,

> China's raw materials access strategies combine reliance on existent systems built by earlier ascendant economies with efforts to steal these earlier ascendant's raw material peripheries by offering what appear to be better deals to raw materials exporting states and firms. (Ciccantell, 2009, p. 109)

In doing so, the author argues, China is actually pursuing strategies "similar to those the US used against Great Britain" a century ago (Ayers, 2013; Ciccantell, 2009, p. 109).

China's thirst for raw materials resulted in the country becoming a major trading partner for raw material exporting nations, which China supplied and continues to supply largely with manufacturing products and machinery. As a result, already before the Great Recession both in Latin America and Sub-Saharan Africa, China started to challenge the economic position held by the

United States and European countries – hitherto the two regions' greatest trading partners.

Importantly, deepening trade relations between China and the two continents have been accompanied by an increase in Chinese Outward FDI, which, however, only took considerable size during the Great Recession (see below). In fact, before the Great Recession total Chinese Outward FDI passed from ca. $3 billion in the year 2000 to $17 billion in 2006, and even if increasing nearly six fold, were still very low by international comparison (about 2.3 per cent of the world's total and less than half of Italy's or less than a fifth of the UK's FDI, e.g.) (Morck, Yeung, & Zhao, 2008, p. 338). Data from the Chinese Ministry of Commerce collected by Morck suggest that by 2006 "Asia, Latin America, and Africa account for 63.9, 26.3, and 3.4% of the FDI stock, respectively, and the shares for North America and Europe are each below 3%" (*Ibid.*).

These trade relations have been somewhat politically substantiated by the establishment of "strategic partnership agreements" with Latin American countries (Jenkins, 2010) and the Forum on China-Africa Cooperation (FOCAC) set up in the year 2000. Yet where economic leadership started to translate into political leadership is East Asia. As Meideros and Fravel have underscored,

> [...] starting in the second half of the 1990s, China began to engage with the Association of Southeast Asian Nations (ASEAN). In 1995, Beijing began holding annual meetings with senior ASEAN officials. Two years later, China helped initiate the "ASEAN +3" mechanism, a series of yearly meetings among the ten ASEAN countries plus China, Japan, and South Korea. Next came the "ASEAN +1" mechanism, annual meetings between ASEAN and China, usually headed by China's premier. (Medeiros & Fravel, 2003, p. 25)

As Foot highlights a major turning point occurred in the East Asian crisis of 1997 as "Beijing moved swiftly to offer economic assistance to countries affected and announced that it would not be devaluing its own currency as a response to the crisis" (Foot, 2006, p. 85). Ming Wan argues in *Asian Survey* that China has strong preferences for the ASEAN +1 which excludes Japan. A first important step to consolidate China's influence in the region can be recognized in the 2001 proposal for a free trade agreement (implemented in 2010) and a further proposal made in 2003 for a "strategic partnership of political and economic cooperation with the association" (Wan, 2010, p. 527).

But China did not only increase its political weight in the region. Unlike Germany and Japan earlier, China also increased its military capability outside the control of the United States and in opposition to it. Thereby China made some considerable changes in its defense strategy accompanied by a surge in military spending, which in absolute terms still remain much lower to US military expenditures. Yet according to Friedberg China's "anti-access/area-denial" can be relatively effective:

> Since the mid-1990s, China has been piecing together what Pentagon planners describe as asymmetric 'anti-access/area-denial' (A2/AD) capabilities. At their heart is the development

> of an arsenal of accurate, relatively inexpensive, conventionally armed ballistic and cruise missiles. With these weapons, China can target virtually every air base and port in the western Pacific, as well as threaten to sink enemy surface vessels (including U.S. aircraft carriers) operating hundreds of miles off its coasts. The People's Liberation Army has also been experimenting with cyberwarfare and antisatellite weapons, and it has begun to expand its small force of intercontinental nuclear missiles (Friedberg, 2012, pp. 4–5)

The period of the still on-going Great Recession marked by Xi Jinping's more assertive presidency since 2013 presents an acceleration of the above trends. Between 2007 and 2014, China's GDP (measured in current US$) *nearly tripled*, passing from $3.5 trillion to $10 trillion (World Bank), while it should be noted that the country's economy grew at a pace between 9 and 10 per cent until 2012, whereas its growth rate decreased to circa 7 per cent thereafter. Of course, the stimulus program adopted by China rather than alleviating, intensified the contradictions of its economic model, particularly considering an enormous increase in overall indebtedness between 2007 and 2014 (passing from $7.4 trillion to $28 trillion that corresponds to 282 per cent of GDP), whereby "nearly half of the debt of Chinese households, corporations, and governments is directly or indirectly related to real estate, collectively worth as much as $9 trillion" (McKinsey Global Institute, 2015, p. 10). Yet despite the problems related to its attempt to counter the effects of the crisis, China expanded its economic position in Asia and beyond, and products "made by China" started to enter the world market more assertively. During the crisis China's total trade with ASEAN reached $232 billion and the country thus became ASEAN's major trading partner surpassing both the EU and the United States as it also became Australia's, and, between 2009 and 2012 even Japan's major export destination (*Financial Times*, 2013). Significantly, in East Asia the Yuan became an important reference currency. As the Financial Times reported "East Asia is now a renminbi bloc because the currencies of seven out of 10 countries in the region – including South Korea, Indonesia, Taiwan, Malaysia, Singapore and Thailand – track the renminbi more closely than the US dollar" noting that "even during the heady days of the Japanese miracle, the yen never came close to rivalling the dollar as a reference currency" (*Financial Times*, 2012).

China also deepened its trade relations with Latin America, which grew at a pace of 5 and 6 per cent annually, making China the third largest trading partner for the region as a whole (*China Daily*, 2012). But particularly relevant has been China's overtaking of the United States as Brazil's largest trading partner, a position the latter country held since the 1930s (*The Telegraph*, 2009). Similar developments occurred in Sub-Saharan Africa. Also here already in 2009 China overtook the United States as largest trading partner: while in 2011 US imports from the region ($70 billion) were still slightly higher compared to China's ($65 billion), China's exports to the region reached $60 billion while US exports stood at $20 billion (GAO, 2013, p. 20).

Importantly, trade with Brazil has been accompanied by a 20-fold increase in outward FDI. As *The Economist* reported at the time, "Chinese investment in Brazil is taking off. Until 2009 this amounted to only about $500m. But in 2010 investment of $19 billion was announced, and $12.7 billion finalised" (*The Economist*, 2012). Outward FDI to Brazil is indicative of a general trend: during the crisis there was a major surge in Chinese outward FDI, which reached $84 billion in 2012 making China the third biggest investor worldwide (UNACTAD, 2013, p. XV). Crucially, thereafter, as Chinese economic growth rates decelerated, Outward FDI did not decrease, on the contrary. Hence according to Chinese Outward FDI reached $120 billion at the end of 2014, up $40 billion compared to 2012 making China also a net creditor for the first time (Herrero & Casanova, 2015). What the same authors remark is a qualitative shift in overseas investments. As a result of excessive capacity reached in sectors such as steel, cement, construction and as a result of rising wages, the country increasingly invested in locations where wages are lower, while also increasing its investments at the higher end of the technology ladder. As the two authors put it:

> Boosting ODI to overseas markets where demand is still on the rise, as is the case with most ASEAN countries, will enable China to outsource this excessive capacity [in steel, cement and construction sectors]. Labor-intensive sectors will also seek to expand overseas in order to benefit from relatively lower labour costs and maximize profit margins, favouring ODI flows to manufacturing activities in ASEAN and to a lesser extent Africa. On the other end of the spectrum, TNC's on the high value-added segment will look to expand overseas to purchase technology that will facilitate China's shift up global value chains (GVCs). This quest for technology has already driven many TNCs to purchase assets in the EU and the US. (Herrero & Casanova, 2015, p. 9)

In addition, Chinese firms, fully backed by the state, started aggressively to enter the world market thereby representing a formidable form of competition. So far this has not occurred in traditional sectors as the car industry, but in so-called "markets of the future." A paradigmatic example is the market for solar panels. As the Guardian has detailed, "[i]n four years, the solar manufacturing sector shifted from being led by a geographically dispersed number of companies to one dominated by Chinese companies" (*The Guardian*, 2011) as China now controls 62 per cent of manufacturing in the sector. It is worth stressing the strategy according to which Chinese companies operate:

> The Chinese strategy is very clear. They are engaging in predatory financing and they're trying to drive everybody else out of the market. When you've got free money you can out-dump everybody below cost. (*Ibid.*)

Significantly, China's economic deepening has been accompanied by substantial progress also in consolidating its political position, particularly in East Asia. It also started to openly voice its territorial claims while continuing to develop its military forces. Hence, trade relations with ASEAN have been backed through a free trade agreement that came in place in 2010. In addition, China pressed for stronger financial integration. While the United State was able to avoid Japan's Asian Monetary Fund in the aftermath of the East Asian crisis, this crisis led to the so-called post-Chiang Mai Initiative in 2009. Even if funded with only $120 billion it has been considered by some as a "milestone achievement" (Pilhyun, 2012). Incidentally, the acceleration of these trends occurred as China's economic growth slowed. Hence in 2014 China launched the Silk Road Fund, the Asian Infrastructure Investment Bank (AIIB) as well as the BRICS New Development Bank. According to Casanova and Herrero, as well as Charles Clover and Lucy Hornby from the *Financial Times* these projects' main aim is to "exporting overcapacity." As Casanova and Herrero write:

> The need to offshore excess capacity and expand overseas markets for Chinese TNCs coincides with an increase in the assertiveness of Chinese economic diplomacy, a shift which is embodied by China's 21st Century Silk Road. The initiative, announced in 2014, comprises the creation of a USD 40 billion Silk Road Fund to boost infrastructure investments and foster economic integration with countries along the historic Silk Road (Highlighted in green on Figure 4). The Silk Road Economic Belt (the land bound leg of the initiative), will target countries in Central Asia (many of which are important suppliers of oil and natural gas to China) and will finish in Turkey. The 21st Century Maritime Silk Road (the sea bound leg) will target ASEAN countries and will reach East Africa via the Malacca Strait as well as India and Sri Lanka. (Herrero & Casanova, 2015, p. 10)

At the military level, China continued to increase military spending already rising "at a double-digit rate for all but one of the past 23 years," reaching $120 billion in 2012 and set to raise to $215 billion by 2015 (the United States: ca. $700 billion in 2012 and prospected $600 billion in 2015) (*Financial Times*, 2012, February 13). Also, it continued to improve its military capabilities, focusing in particular on the development of its naval power. As the new Chinese passport issued in 2012, whose map includes the South China Sea, indicates, China sees it as mare nostrum. There are at least two reasons for this. On the one hand, the South China sea is rich in natural resources: "The South China Sea" Su Hao, from the Center for Strategic and International Studies writes "is rich in natural resources, such as phosphoric acid and lime mines on islands, the world's largest tropical fishery in the sea, large quantities of metallic ores on the sea floor, and oil and gas on the continental shelf" (Hao, 2012, p. 9). On the other hand, it is vital for Chinese trade. In the words of Su Hao, "China's foreign trade, energy transportation, transfer of personnel and tourism are mainly implemented through the South China Sea. Among the big powers in the world, China has the highest needs for the freedom of navigation in the South China Sea." From the Chinese perspective, the author hence concludes: "therefore, China needs the most to maintain and protect such freedom" (Hao, 2012, p. 10).

... And the United States Difficulties in Countering It

China's relative geopolitical autonomy resulted in greater difficulties for the United States to counter its rise as well as the construction of hegemonic relations. This compared to the US's ability to deploy its power able to block

Japan's and Germany's bid for hegemony. Hence unlike the US's ability to determine the exchange rate of Japan and Germany, China determined the Yuan – dollar exchange rate largely autonomously. China strongly devalued the Yuan to the US dollar between 1980 and 1995, and thereafter pegged its currency to the dollar. Later, as a result of the strengthening dollar that made Chinese exports more expensive, in 2015 China unpegged its currency by devaluing the renminbi by roughly 5 per cent. Equally unsuccessful has been the US attempt to ameliorate its bilateral trade balance by pressing China into the WTO hoping that this would ease the US balance of payments by augmenting US exports to China. US exports to China did indeed increase considerably passing from an average yearly growth of 6 per cent (1995–1999) to 20 per cent after China's WTO accession. However, imports from China increased even more strongly thereby increasing the US trade deficit with China (Cho, 2006, p. 45).

Symptomatic of the essential role China played for the US economy, during the George W. Bush presidency (2001–2009) economic pressures on the Asian country were largely abandoned. Yet military pressures started to increase, not least with the US's attempt to control the "oil spigot" and the "war on terror." Arrighi has well described the different strategies the US evaluated in order to deal with China. The first of them, advocated by Kaplan, consists in containing or encircling the country militarily by strengthening PACOM, the US Pacific Command, and military alliances in the Asian Pacific region with the aim to neutralize China as NATO did with the USSR (Arrighi, 2008, pp. 284–289). The second strategy Arrighi recognizes is the one advocated by Henry Kissinger. As Arrighi remarks the latter comes very close to China's official doctrine of the "peaceful rise" and maintains that China has no hegemonic ambitions. Correspondingly, "US interests therefore lie in cooperating with China in the pursuit of a stable international system" rather than confronting it (Arrighi, 2008, p. 291). Pinkerton, according to Arrighi proposed yet another plan he labels "*tertium gaudens*" (the happy third). According to this view, "instead of confronting directly the rising Asian powers, the United States should play them off each other" (Pinkerton quoted in Arrighi, 2008, p. 296).

Claudio Katz, referring to the same three strategies, has recently argued that none of them prevailed (Katz, 2012, p. 96). However, looking at events, it is not biased to argue that the "encirclement" strategy is the one the United States is pursuing. This involves an increased political, economic and military focus in the region. Already before the Great Recession, under the George W. Bush administration, we notice some diplomatic efforts, as, for example the US's renewed interest toward India. According to Robert D. Blackwill, former US envoy to India, "President George W. Bush based his transformation of US-India Relations on the core strategic principle of democratic India as a key factor in balancing the rise of Chinese power" (Blackwill, quoted in China US Focus, 2013). But very important has been the "War on Terror," which enabled the United States to increase its military presence at China's borders. Nathan and Scobell thus write:

> before September 11, 2001, CENTCOM had no forces stationed directly on China's borders except for its training and supply missions in Pakistan. But with the beginning of the 'war on terror', CENTCOM placed tens of thousands of troops in Afghanistan and gained extended access to an air base in Kyrgyzstan. (Nathan & Scobell, 2012)

The US reaction to China's increasing influence, as we have mentioned, has been political, economic and military – a process captured by the notion of the so-called "Pivot to Asia" or "Rebalancing." Significantly Obama's first trip after re-election in November 2012 was to East Asia: to Burma, Thailand and Cambodia, preceded by then US secretary of State Hillary Clinton. As the Guardian reported, the United States is, on the one hand, determined to win "south-east Asian states to present a united front to the Chinese in dealing with territorial disputes in the South China Sea" (*The Guardian*, 2012). On the other hand, the United States is interested in challenging the ASEAN + 3 from which they are excluded. Thus major economic and political maneuvers have been the Obama administration's attempt to reenergize the APEC forum, and the proposition of the Trans-Pacific Partnership (TPP) already in 2010. The eventual signature of the TPP agreement in February 2016 represents a significant success for the Obama administration, yet the treaty has not been ratified so far and the outcomes of its implementation, remain to be seen. As the *New York Times* reported, China and its trading partners, might need to find ways to circumvent it, given their strong and now established economic ties:

> there's not a major business anywhere in the region, including in Japan, that doesn't have to factor China in [...]. With China out of TPP for the foreseeable future, the incentive for China and its East Asian partners to ramp up their economic ties will be more powerful. (*New York Times*, 2015)

The signing of the TPP by some Latin American countries is indicative of a further very important effort the United States is pursuing: challenging the economic and political ties that China constructed over the past decade in Latin America. Significant in this respect is the setback experienced by the so-called "pink tide" and hence the fall (as in Argentina and more recently Brazil) of left leaning governments that came to power over the last decades and that incidentally had close relations with China.

At the military level, as the latest Strategic Defence Review outlined, the United States is rebalancing its forces toward Asia. According to the New York Times, this concerns particularly the navy: "The Navy [...] would reconfigure its forces from a 50-50 split between the Atlantic Ocean and the Pacific to 60 percent of the Navy's assets assigned to the Pacific Ocean" (*The New York Times*, 2012). Indicative as it is for the US containment strategy, also what Arrighi referred to as "tertium gaudens" seems to play a role. Hence with reference to China – Japanese tension over the Senkaku/Diaoyu islands that erupted in autumn 2012, a New York Times report suggested it could be considered as a "time bomb planted by the U.S between China and Japan" (*The New York Times*, 2012). Despite these efforts, the preoccupation expressed by Friedberg in *Foreign Affairs* is that the relation of military forces in East Asia, given the US's "current fiscal climate," could favor China in the future. As Friedberg puts it,

> The problem with the pivot is that to date it has lacked serious substance [...]. Apart from vague references to a new "air-sea battle concept" [...] the administration has not made clear how it actually intends to respond to China's increasing military capabilities. (Friedberg, 2012)

Yet the weakening of the United States in East Asia is not accompanied by a crisis of US hegemony: despite the economic, political and even military advances in East Asia which do make China a strong challenger to US hegemony in the region, the former country's grip over the region remains, for the moment, far from completed. As Evelyn Goh puts it, "China's economic power outstrips that of the United States in Southeast Asia in terms of rates of growth, intensity of interdependence, policy activism, and regional integration," whilst at the same time maintaining that even though "the power gap between China and the United States has narrowed in this region, the United States is far from being a 'declining' power. It maintains military superiority, strategic and economic leadership, and political engagement in Southeast Asia" (Goh, 2015, p. 216). Thus China's ability to determine other states' conduct, despite its economic standing, remains limited as the United States retains influence over its key allies as, for example, South Korea and, very importantly, Japan (Kim, 2013).

CONCLUSION

This chapter started by considering a paradox when juxtaposing US foreign policy toward China and East Asia, backed by influential academic circles within the US administration that voiced their concerns about the possible or already perceived decline of US hegemony and China's potential, and the ideas put forward by Marxist authors. For they generally tend to argue for the uninterrupted strength of US hegemony, or, as in the case of Giovanni Arrighi, that we are already in the process of a hegemonic transition toward China, whereby the "future" hegemon is understood as a non-capitalist market economy.

Pointing to some shortcomings in existing conceptualizations of hegemony, I have argued for the need to attempt to re-conceptualize hegemony at the international, and have returned to the critical edition of Gramsci's *Prison Notebooks* in order to do so. Thereby I have emphasized that hegemony also includes the coercive moment and that unlike the proposition of neo-Gramscian analyses it is exercised by national states. My analysis suggests that (imperialist) states *must* become hegemonic in order to secure the accumulation of capital. Gramsci understands the construction of hegemony at the national level as a process that goes through the economic, the political and culminates, or is *fully realised*, by the seizure of the state. Likewise, we argued that the construction of hegemony at the international level be understood as *processes* going through different levels or phases: the economic, political and military. Hegemony is *fully realised* when it involves the economic, political and military moments. Instead, when it entails only the economic and partially the political moment, we refer to it as "Sturm und Drang Hegemony." Thus we maintained that the United States became fully hegemonic over Germany and Japan, enabling the country to withstand attempts by its imperialist rivals to construe hegemonic relations in their respective regions. By contrast, we maintained that China, thanks to its successful revolution, was able to retain what we referred as "relative geopolitical autonomy" making US efforts to counter its rise less effective.

It is then on this background that we sketched out elements of China's rise also emphasizing that the country should be understood as being state capitalist, drawing attention to the very important role the state plays within China's economy. At the same time, we maintain that given the position that China reached within the world economy, it also *had* to start embarking in the construction of hegemonic relations. However, our general assessment has been that while US hegemony weakened in East Asia, this was not sufficient to induce a crisis of US hegemony. Hence we underlined that China expanded its economic position in East Asia and beyond, maintaining that the country's economic deepening has been accompanied by substantial progresses in consolidating its political and military position, whilst not being able to oust the United States from the region as the latter still retains significant allies and military presence.

NOTES

1. Van der Pijl (2012, p. 503), arguing that China 'may well veer back to a State-socialist line of development', comes close to the position developed by Arrighi.

2. To be sure, and as Gramsci observes, the law of value undergoes mediations and does not immediately result in corresponding state action. An exhaustive investigation would therefore require an analysis at a concrete level of analysis taking into account the struggles within the ruling class and amongst classes as well as international factors in determining state action, starting from the constraints posed by the operation of the law of value. Unable to cover these important aspects in this chapter, in the following analysis I will have to abstract from those.

3. Gramsci (2001, Q.13). Gramsci, of course, distinguishes between thorough revolutions and 'passive revolutions', a concept we cannot present here. See Kanoussi and Mena (1985), Voza (2004), Callinicos (2010), Morton (2007b, 2010), and Thomas (2009).

4. Russia, given the revolutionary processes it went through, might also represent an exception, albeit having other characteristics. For further critical analyses of 'emerging economies' and their position within the world economy see Kiely (2016) as well as Bond and Garcia ed. (2015).

5. For a more comprehensive analysis, see Fusaro (forthcoming).

6. While a comparative analysis with other BRICS states cannot be offered here, consider, for example the case of Brazil and its revolution for Independence. In contrast to China, Brazil's revolution has been far weaker (a dependent 'passive revolution' according to Ansaldi & Giordano, 2012) and did not result in the country's relative geopolitical autonomy. On the contrary, as Keen and Hayes (2009, p. 176) state, for example, 'Brazil's new status substituted one form of dependence for another. Freed from Portuguese control, Brazil came under the economic domination of England'. This has led Halperin Donghi (2013, p. 211) to refer to the new order as 'neo-colonial' dooming the country to 'dependent development' notwithstanding periods (even longer ones) of economic growth.

ACKNOWLEDGMENT

I wish to thank Alex Callinicos for his very useful comments on earlier versions of this chapter as well as Alejandro González for his assistance with the data.

REFERENCES

Anderson, P. (2012). After the event. *New Left Review*, *73*, 49–61.

Ansaldi, W., & Giordano, V. (2012). *América Latina. La construcción del orden.* Ariel: Buenos Aires.

Arrighi, G. (1994). *The long twentieth century: Money, power, and the origins of our times.* London: Verso.

Arrighi, G. (2008). *Adam Smith in Beijing: Lineages of the twenty-first century.* London: Verso.

Arrighi, G. (2009). China's market economy in the long run. In H.-F. Hung (Ed.), *China and the transformation of global capitalism.* Baltimore, MD: Johns Hopkins University Press.

Arrighi, G. (2010). *The long twentieth century: Money, power and the origins of our times* (2nd ed., p. 258). London: Verso.

Ayers, A. (2013). Beyond myths, lies and stereotypes: The political economy of a 'New Scramble for Africa'. *New Political Economy*, *18*(2), 227–257.

Baum, M. J. (1995/96). The Maastricht Treaty as high politics: Germany, France, and European Integration. *Political Science Quarterly*, *110*, 605–624.

Bond, P., & Garcia, A. (Eds.). (2015). *BRICS.* An anticapitalist critique. Chicago, IL: Haymarket.

Brenner, R. (1977). The origins of capitalist development: A critique of Neo-Smithian Marxism. *New Left Review*, *104*, 25–94.

Burgio, A. (2003). *Gramsci storico: una lettura dei Quaderni del carcere.* Roma: Editori Laterza.

Burgio, A. (2007). *Per Gramsci: crisi e potenza del moderno.* Roma: Derive Approdi.

Callinicos, A. (2009). *Imperialism and global political economy.* Cambridge: Polity Press.

Callinicos, A. (2010). The limits of passive revolution. *Capital and Class*, (34), 491–506.

Carchedi, G. (2001). *For another Europe: A class analysis of European economic integration.* New York, NY: Verso.

China Daily. (2012, October 18). Deeper Sino-Latin American trade cooperation urged, by Jiabao, Li and Jianming, Zhang. Retrieved from http://www.chinadaily.com.cn/cndy/2012-10/18/content_15826118.htm. Accessed on October 2016.

Cho, H. (2005a). *Chinas langer Marsch in den Kapitalismus*. Münster: Westphälisher Dampfboot.

Cho, H. (2005b). Chinas langer Marsch in die neoliberale Weltwirtschaft. *Prokla*, *141*(4), 601–618.

Cho, H. (2006). Die USA: Ein unbequemer Patron für Chinas Wirtschaftswunder. *Das Argument*, *268*(5,6), 40–52.

Ciccantell, P. S. (2009). China's economic ascent and Japan's raw material periphery. In H.-F. Hung (Ed.), *China and the transformation of global capitalism*. Baltimore, MD: Johns Hopkins University Press.

Cox, R. (1981). Social forces, states and world orders: Beyond international relations theory. *Millennium – Journal of International Studies*, *10*(2), 126–155.

Cox, R. (1983). Gramsci, hegemony and international relations: An essay in method. *Millennium – Journal of International Studies*, *12*(2), 162–175.

Cox, R. (1987). Production, power, and world order: Social forces in the making *of history*. New York, NY: Columbia University Press.

Desai, R. (2013). *Geopolitical economy: After US hegemony, globalization and empire (the future of world capitalism)*. London: Pluto.

Financial Times. (2012, February 13). Chinese defence budget set to double by 2015 by Hoyos, Carola. Retrieved from http://www.ft.com/intl/cms/s/0/7b58ac0a-5592-11e1-9d95-00144feabdc0.html#axzz2PEigLy77. Accessed on July 09, 2016.

Financial Times. (2013, April 18). US becomes Japan's top export market By McLannahan Ben. Retrieved from http://www.ft.com/cms/s/0/c1440782-a7c1-11e2-9fbe-00144feabdc0.html. Accessed on July 10, 2016.

Financial Times. (2012, October 21). China's currency rises in the US backyard by Subramanian. Arvind and Kessler, Martin. Retrieved from http://www.ft.com/cms/s/0/5a34c410-19d6-11e2-a379-00144feabdc0.html#axzz2OV0iR6om. Accessed on June 10, 2016.

Foot, R. (2006). Chinese strategies in a US-hegemonic global order: Accommodating and hedging. *International Affairs*, *82*(1), 77–94.

Friedberg, A. L. (2012). Bucking Beijing: An alternative U.S. China policy. *Foreign Affairs*, *91*(5). Retrieved from http://www.foreignaffairs.com/articles/138032/aaron-lfriedberg/bucking-beijing. Accessed on July 08, 2016.

Fusaro, L. (forthcoming). *Crises and hegemonic transitions. From Gramsci's Quaderni to the contemporary world economy*. Leiden: Brill.

Gibbs, D. N. (2001). Washington's new interventionism: U.S. hegemony and inter-imperialist rivalries. *Monthly Review*, *53*(4), 15–37.

Gill, S. (1993). *Gramsci, historical materialism and international relations*. Cambridge: Cambridge University Press.

Goh, E. (2015). China's power in the regional context (II): Southeast Asia. In J. H. Chung (Ed.), *Assessing China's Power*. New York: Palgrave Macmillan.

Gowan, P. (1999). *The global gamble: Washington's Faustian Bid for world dominance*. London: Verso.

Gramsci, A. (2001). *Quaderni del Carcere (edizione critica dell'Istituto Gramsci a cura di Valentino Gerratana)*. Torino: Einaudi.

Gramsci, A. (2007). *Nel mondo grande e terribile. Antologia degli scritti 1914-1935*. Roma: Einaudi.

Halevi, J. (1995). EMS and the Bundesbank in Europe. In P. Arestis & V. Chick (Eds.), Finance, development, and structural change: Post-Keynesian *perspectives*. Aldershot: Edward Elgar.

Halperin Donghi, T. (2013). *Historia contemporánea de América Latina*. Madrid: Alianza Editorial.

Hao, S. (2012). *China's positions and interests in the South China Sea: A rational choices in its cooperative policies*. Center for strategic and international studies Working Paper. Retrieved from http://csis.org/files/publication/110912_Hao_South_China_Sea.pdf. Accessed on July 10, 2016.

Hart-Landsberg, M., & Burkett, P. (2006). China and the dynamics of transnational capital accumulation. *Historical Materialism*, *14*(3), 3–43.

Harvey, D. (2003). *The new imperialism*. Oxford: Oxford University Press.

Herrero, A., & Casanova, C. (2015). *Chinese outbound foreign direct investment: How much goes where after round- tripping and offshoring? BBVA Research*. Working Paper, 15/17. Retrieved on https://www.bbvaresearch.com/wp-content/uploads/2015/06/15_17_Working-Paper_ODI.pdf

Hung, H.-F. (2009). America's head servant? The Prc's dilemma in the global crisis. *New Left Review*, *60*, 5–25.

Ikenberry, J. (2011a). *Liberal leviathan: The origins, crisis, and transformation of the American world order*. Princeton, NJ: Princeton University Press.

Ikenberry, J. (2011b). America's challenge: The rise of China and the future of liberal international order. *New America Foundation*, 12 July.

Jenkins, R. (2010). China's global expansion and Latin America. *Journal of Latin American Studies*, *42*(4), 809–837.

Kanoussi, D., & Mena, J. (1985). *La revolución pasiva: una lectura de los Cuadernos de la cárcel*. Puebla: Universidad Autónoma de Puebla.

Katz, C. (2012). *Bajo El Imperio del Capital*. Bogotà: Espacio Crítico.

Katzenstein, P. J., & Shiraishi, T. (1997). *Network power*. Ithaca, NY: Cornell University Press.

Keen, B., & Haynes, K. (2009). *A history of Latin America*. New York, NY: Houghton Mifflin Harcourt Publishing Company.

Kiely, R. (2016). *The rise and fall of emerging powers. Globalisation, US power and the global north-south divide*. Cham: Palgrave Macmillan.

Kim, H.-Y. (2013). Imperialism and instability in East Asia today. *International Socialism*, 138. Retrieved from http://www.isj.org.uk/index.php4?id=882&issue=138. Accessed on July 10, 2016.

Lapavitsas, C., Kaltenbrunner, A., Labrinidis, G., Lindo, D., Meadway, J., Michell, J. ... Vatikiotis, L. (2012). *Crisis in the urozone*. London: Verso.

Lippit, V. (1987). *The economic development of China*. New York, NY: M.E. Sharpe.

Marx, K., & Engels, F. (1956-1990). *Marx-Engels-Werke (MEW)* (43 Bände). Berlin: Dietz Verlag.

McKinsey Global Institute. (2015). *Debt and (not much) deleveraging*. Retrieved from www.mckinsey.com/mgi

Medeiros, E., & Fravel, T. (2003). China's new diplomacy. *Foreign Affairs*, *82*(6). Retrieved from http://www.foreignaffairs.org/20031101faessay82604/evan-s-medeiros-m-taylor-fravel/china-s-new-diplomacy. Accessed on September 20, 2012.

Meisner, M. (1999). *Mao's China and after. A history of the People's Republic* (3d ed.). New York, NY: The Free Press.

Meisner, M. (2008). *The significance of the Chinese Revolution in world history?* In Working Papers. Asia Research Centre, LSE, London.

Mills, I. (2012). Should China abandon its non-interference policy? *World Politics Review*. Briefing 8.2. Retrieved from http://www.worldpoliticsreview.com/articles/11416/should-china-abandon-its-noninterference-policy. Accessed on July 10, 2016.

Morton, A. (2007a). *Unravelling Gramsci: Hegemony and passive revolution in the global political economy*. London: Pluto.

Morton, A. D. (2007b). Waiting for Gramsci: State formation, passive revolution and the international. *Millennium – Journal of International Studies*, *35*(3), 597–621.

Morton, A. D. (2010). The continuum of passive revolution. *Capital & Class*, *34*(3), 315–342.

Nathan, A. J. & Scobell, A. (2012). How China sees America. *Foreign Affairs*, *91*, 5. Retrieved from http://www.foreignaffairs.com/articles/138009/andrew-j-nathan-and-andrew-scobell/how-china-sees-america. Accessed on July 05, 2016.

New York Times. (2011, November 16). As U.S. looks to Asia, it sees China everywhere, by Johnson, Ian and Calmes, Jackie. Retrieved from http://www.nytimes.com/2011/11/16/world/asia/united-states-sees-china-everywhere-as-it-shifts-attention-to-asia.html?pagewanted=all&_r=0. Accessed on October 2016.

New York Times. (2015, October 6). U.S. allies see trans-Pacific partnership as a check on China. *New York Times*, by Perlez, Jane. Retrieved from http://www.nytimes.com/2015/10/07/world/asia/trans-pacific-partnership-china-australia.html

Panitch, L., & Gindin, S. (2004). Global capitalism and American empire. In *Socialist register 2004: The new imperial challenge* (Vol. 40). Retrieved from http://www.nodo50.org/cubasigloXXI/congreso04/panitch_060404.pdf. Accessed on July 08, 2016.

Panitch, L., & Gindin, S. (2005). Superintending global capital. *New Left Review*, *35*, 101–123.

Panitch, L., & Gindin, S. (2012). *The making of global capitalism*. London: Verso.

Pempel, T. J. (1997). Transpacific Torii: Japan and the emerging Asian regionalism. In P. J. Katzenstein & T. Shiraishi (Eds.), *Network power*. Ithaca, NY: Cornell University Press.

Pempel, T. J. (2011). Japan's search for the 'sweet spot': International cooperation and regional security in Northeast Asia. *Orbis*, *55*(2), 255–273.

Peters, H. (2012). Chinas Weg zur eigenständigen Weltmacht Teil 1: Vom Weltrevolutionär zur unabhängigen und selbständigen politischen Großmacht. *Z. Zeitschrift Marxistische Erneuerung*, *89* (März). Retrieved from http://www.schattenblick.de/infopool/medien/altern/z-156.html. Accessed on July 05, 2016.

Pilhyun, K. (2012). The global financial crisis and its implications for East Asian financial integration. In J. Park, T. J. Pempel, & G. Xiao (Eds.), *Asian responses to the global financial crisis*. Northampton: Edward Elgar.

Pollard, R., & Wells, S. (1984). 1945-1950: The era of American hegemony. In W. Becker & S. Wells (Eds.), *Economics and world power: An Assessment of American diplomacy since 1789*. New York, NY: Columbia University Press.

Schmalz, S. (2010). China's Neue Rolle im globalen Kapitalismus. *Prokla*, *161*(4), 483–505.

Schmidt, I. (2010). Exportortientiertes Wachstum in China, Deutschland und Japan – Herausforderung oder Bestandteil der US Hegemonie? *Prokla*, *161*(4), 505–525.

Schwartz, H. M. (2009). *Subprime nation: American power, global capital, and the housing bubble*. Ithaca, NY: Cornell University Press.

Scokpol, T. (1979). *States and social revolutions: A comparative analysis of France, Russia, and China*. New York, NY: Cambridge University Press.

Sieren, F. (2008). *Die Konkubinenwirtschaft: Warum westliche Unternehmen in China scheitern und die Chinesen an die Weltspitze stürmen*. Muenchen: Carl Hanser Verlag.

Stephen, M. D. (2014). Rising powers, global capitalism and liberal global governance. A historical materialist account of the BRICs challenge. *European Journal of International Relations*, *20*(4), 912–938.

The Economist. (2012, January 14). Brazil's trade policy. Seeking protection. Retrieved from http://www.economist.com/node/21542780. Accessed on July 06, 2016.

The Guardian. (2011, September 12). How China dominates solar power by Lacey, Stephen. Retrieved from http://www.guardian.co.uk/environment/2011/sep/12/how-china-dominates-solar-power. Accessed on July 06, 2016.

The Guardian. (2012, September 3). Hillary Clinton wades into south-east Asian disputes. By Associated Press. Retrieved from http://www.guardian.co.uk/world/2012/sep/03/clinton-wades-in-south-east-asian-disputes. Accessed on July 05, 2016.

The New York Times. (2012, June 01). Panetta outlines new weaponry for Pacific by Perlez, Jane. Retrieved from http://www.nytimes.com/2012/06/02/world/asia/leon-panetta-outlines-new-weaponry-for-pacific.html. Accessed on July 08, 2016.

The Telegraph. (2009, May 09). China overtakes the US as Brazil's largest trading partner by Moore, Malcolm. Retrieved from http://www.telegraph.co.uk/finance/economics/5296515/China-overtakes-the-US-as-Brazils-largest-trading-partner.html. Accessed on July 07, 2016.

Thomas, P. (2009). *The Gramscian moment. Philosophy, hegemony and Marxism*. Leiden: Brill.

Turner, G. (2008). *The credit crunch: Housing bubbles, globalisation and the worldwide economic crisis*. London: Pluto.

UNACTAD (2013). *World investment report 2013*. Retrieved from http://unctad.org/en/pages/PublicationWebflyer.aspx?publicationid=588. Accessed on October 2016.

US Government Accountability Office, GAO. (2013). Sub-Saharan Africa: Trends in U.S. and Chinese Economic Engagement. *Report to Congressional Requesters*. Retrieved from http://www.gao.gov/products/GAO-13-199. Accessed on October 2016.

Van der Pijl, K. (1984). *The making of the Atlantic ruling class*. London: Verso.

Van der Pijl, K. (2012). Is the east still red? The contender state and class struggles in China. *Globalizations*, *9*(4), 503–516.

Voza, P. (2004). Rivoluzione Passiva. In F. Frosini & G. Liguori (Eds.), *Le parole di Gramsci. Per un lessico dei Quaderni dal carcere*. Roma: Carocci.

Wan, M. (2010). The Great Recession and China's Policy toward Asian Regionalism. *Asian Survey*, *50*(3), 520–538.

Wei, G. (2011). Mao's legacy revisited: Its lasting impact on China and post-Mao era reform. *Asian Politics & Policy*, *3*(1), 2–27.

World Bank. http://data.worldbank.org/. Accessed in October 2016.

Zhao, S. (2010). The China model: Can it replace the Western model of modernization? *Journal of Contemporary China*, *19*(65), 419–436.

Ziebura, G. (1990). *World economy and world politics, 1924 – 1931. From reconstruction to Collapse*. Oxford: Berg Publishers.

PART III
CONSIDERATION OF ASPECTS FOR A MARXIAN ALTERNATIVE FOR EAST ASIA

THE CHONGQING MODEL – SOCIALIST ALTERNATIVE OR PROPAGANDA CLICHÉ?

Anna Zakharzhevskaya

ABSTRACT

This paper examines diverging views on the Chongqing model, the policy experiment led by Bo Xilai from 2007 to 2012 that was famous for its "red songs" and the campaign against organized crime. It has impressed both the supporters of socialist identity of China and the supporters of liberal identity and led to an intense debate concerning China's path of development. This paper attempts to discuss and clarify to what extent the Chongqing model represented a genuine socialist experiment and the implications of the model for China's future.

Keywords: The Chongqing model; economic reforms; socialism; Bo Xilai

From 2007 to 2012, China's Chongqing Municipality undertook a number of bold policy experiments, including a successful campaign against organized crimes, promotion of "red songs" and red culture, and a more egalitarian-oriented economic development model under the leadership of Bo Xilai, the Municipality's Party Secretary. In 2012, Bo Xilai was suddenly dismissed

Return of Marxian Macro-dynamics in East Asia
Research in Political Economy, Volume 32, 227–252

ISSN: 0161-7230/doi:10.1108/S0161-723020170000032013

because of corruption charges and an incident that involved the murder of a British businessman by his wife. The Chongqing incident attracted widespread attention throughout the world. After the dust settled, the time has come to consider whether the Chongqing model was a socialist way of development.

This paper examines diverging views on the Chongqing model. The model has impressed both the supporters of socialist identity of China and the supporters of liberal identity – but of course, their attitude to it was different. Some leftists perceived the Chongqing model as a turning point, a return to the genuinely socialist way of development. In their opinion, the Chongqing model was a sign of the shift to the left in the policies of the Communist Party of China (CPC), which would avoid a decline in the standards of living of people and, moreover, avoid political turmoil, which could be caused by such a decline. At the same time, other leftists criticized the Chongqing model. According to them, there was nothing socialist in it and the Chongqing model was just another liberal variant. By contrast, the liberals tried to present the Chongqing model, first and foremost, as a return to Mao's Cultural Revolution, although it is doubtful that all of them really believed it. They criticized violations of the law in the anti-corruption campaign and the "Red Songs" campaign. Liberal opponents of the Chongqing model denied Chongqing's economic success as a debt dependent investment bubble. Finally, there is the view that the Chongqing model has never actually been a model at all. Against the background of such different views, there is a need to clearly define what was the essence of the Chongqing model, whether it was socialistic, whether there was the real threat of a return to the Cultural Revolution. It is also necessary to understand whether the Chongqing model was utterly smashed, as some publicists have written, and whether the model has good prospects in the future development of China.

WAS THERE EVER A CHONGQING MODEL?

First of all, it should be noted that not all scholars acknowledge the existence of the Chongqing model. Some of them believe that Chongqing Municipality was never that different from other regions of China for people to talk about a special model. Furthermore, after Bo Xilai's dismissal in 2012, Zhang Dejiang, who replaced Bo as the party secretary of Chongqing at the 18th Party Congress in 2012, stated that "there is no such thing as the Chongqing model" (*IFeng News*, 2012).

But what, in fact, caused this claim? Politicians and scholars in China are careful to choose their terminology, and such caution is founded on a solid basis. For example, Zhao Qizheng (the former Director of the State Council Information Office) objected to the use of the term "Chinese Model," although it had already been well known throughout the world. The use of the term "model" implies that China can export it, and that kind of talk can become an occasion for promotion of the theory about the Chinese expansion (Fewsmith, 2011). Zhao Qizheng's concerns were not groundless. For instance, it is exactly the Chinese expansion what the famous American political scientist Fukuyama (2016) tells about in his article *Exporting the Chinese Model*. In his view, competition between the Chinese and the American (and other Western) models of development is gaining momentum. He believes that the question which model will win has become a key issue for global politics. Chinese initiative "One Belt, One Road" proves to Fukuyama that China is seeking to export its developmental model. If the initiative meets the expectations, Eurasia will change in a positive direction, and the Chinese authoritarian form of government will achieve immense prestige – what, according to Fukuyama, would undermine democracy around the globe. As a result, the United States is risking to lose an argument with China over the future of Eurasia and other key regions of the world. This case clearly shows that denying of the existence of one or another model can be related to political considerations.

The term "Chongqing model" deserves to exist and is based, for the most part, on the economic foundation. You and Lei (2013, p. 51) from Xiamen University uphold the following view: the momentum of the reforms in Chongqing was much stronger than in other cities and provinces, so it could not be claimed that the term "Chongqing model" is a misnomer. They believe that Zhang Dejiang denied the existence of the Chongqing model for political reasons.

You and Lei (2013, p. 54) also point out that in September 2010, the official central media first used the expression "Chongqing model" in the title of the article: *Explaining and analyzing the "Chongqing model" in constructing public rental housing*. The article was published by *People's Daily* (Wang & Cui, 2010).

The notion of "Chongqing model" was introduced into common parlance by journalists of the Hong Kong magazine *Yazhou Zhoukan* in February 2009. They wrote about the Chongqing government's policy as an interesting experiment to counteract the impact of the world crisis on the Chinese economy. They described the Chongqing model solely in economic terms and compared it with other regional models – the Guangdong model, the South Jiangsu model, the Wenzhou model, etc. (Karneev, 2014, p. 130).

The famous economist Cui Zhiyuan, who participated in work of the Chongqing government, considers that in this particular case we can talk exactly about a new model. First, it differs from the experience of economic reforms in other regions; secondly, it is not a return to the pre-reform period, when the state also had many national assets (one of the features of the Chongqing model) (Frenkiel, 2010).

As for Zhang Dejiang's statement about non-existence of the Chongqing model, it may be not as adamant as it might seem at first. During the press conference at which he said that phrase (Available at: https://www.youtube.com/watch?v=itY1ahGOI18, 11 January 2016), Zhang was asked whether or not the Chongqing model would be eliminated after the Bo Xilai's takedown. In fact, he did not give a straight answer to that question.

EARLY HISTORY OF THE CHONGQING EXPERIMENTAL ZONE

In mass media, the majority of articles and disputes about the Chongqing model paid attention to Bo Xilai's personality. But Chongqing has become an experimental zone for reforms long before Bo's arrival in the city.

It is well known that reforms in rural areas of China started in 1978 after the death of Mao Zedong. But what was effective in the countryside often were not suitable for urban areas, so the Central Committee of the CPC launched the work on the establishment of urban "test fields."

At first, experiments were carried in small- and middle-sized towns: Shashi (Hubei province) and Suzhou (Jiangsu province). On February 8, 1983, the Central Committee of the CPC and the State Council decided to establish Chongqing as the first big city among "test fields" for reforms (Gou, 2008).

Chongqing was chosen as a typical Chinese inland city. Bo Xilai's father Bo Yibo, who was the member of the State Council at that time, said: "In implementing the reforms of economic system in Chongqing, it is necessary not to pay attention only to Chongqing but to look at the entire southwest, at the whole country."

In 1983, the leadership of Chongqing gave the rights of autonomy to the city's enterprises, allowing them to establish their own prices of goods. In the same year, the Chongqing government launched the first set of administrative reforms: the size of executive personnel was decreased and subordinate authorities were granted more rights.

In 1984, in Chongqing was established the country's first mall of industrial goods, as well as the financial market, a labor exchange, etc.

After 1991, Chongqing emerged at the forefront of trade liberalization in China: management of trade organizations, prices, and recruitment were liberalized. At the same time, reforms under the theme "Industry – five autonomies" were tested: regulations on pricing of manufactured goods, on recruitment, on technology upgrading were eliminated or reduced.

The changes at the "reforms test field" promoted development of Chongqing's economy: Chongqing's GDP grew from 13.1 billion yuan in 1984 to 117.9 billion yuan in 1996.

In March 1997, Chongqing became the only directly administered municipality in western and central China (with a provincial status) (Gou, 2008).

In 2007, Hu Jintao (the Chinese President) defined the new role of Chongqing in the national development strategy. This time Chongqing was chosen as an experimental zone for integration of rural and urban development. Such integration was seen as a key to the stimulation of Chinese domestic demand (Cui, 2012, pp. 27–28).

As part of this integration, Chongqing offered concessions for housing purchases for migrant workers; children of migrant workers from countryside were entitled to free education at occupational schools (Gou, 2008).

Lu (2012) argued that Bo Xilai turned Chongqing into a place for experiments of alternative development strategies, aimed at resolving centuries-old problems between urban and rural areas. However, as noted above, economic experiments were launched in Chongqing before Bo's arrival and were initiated by the central government.

When Bo arrived, the city in many ways had already been in the frontline of market-oriented reforms, which undoubtedly were not aimed at a returning to the days of Mao.

In the Chongqing model, it was not politics or "confrontation" with Beijing but the economy that had played a leading role. In fact, the Chongqing model could not seriously entertain a conflict with the central government because of its dependence on government investment.

COMPONENTS OF THE CHONGQING MODEL

The Land Certificates Market

To understand the Chinese land policy, we need to keep in mind that the country's government seeks to promote urbanization, but does not want to be dependent on food imports. On the one hand, the local authorities did not have the right to reduce the amount of agricultural land below the level set by the central government. On the other hand, they wanted to urbanize their peripheral areas (Lafarguette, 2011). How could they reconcile these contradictory goals?

In December 2008, the country's first "market of land" was organized in Chongqing. Objects to be sold at this market were "land certificates" (*dipiao*), not land itself (Frenkiel, 2010). These certificates allowed villagers to sell the right to use land. If a developer wanted to build an industrial zone, he could buy at the land exchange market the certificates for appropriate amount of land (Lafarguette, 2011). To have more land certificates available for sale, rural residents made their living pattern more compact and turned old, demolished and abandoned plants, factories and roads into arable land. In so doing, the total amount of arable land in the municipality was not decreasing (Frenkiel, 2010). For example, in some villages, residents restructured their houses to convert part of the land back to arable land (Cui, 2012, p. 28).

With this system, on the one hand, the urban area was expanded not at the expense of agricultural land and on the other hand, rural residents could benefit from the growth of cities, because they would get 80% of the value of land certificates (the remaining 20% went to the village authorities) (Lafarguette, 2011). The average price of land certificate per *mu* was 150,000–200,000 yuan (*mu* is the Chinese land unit; one *mu* equals 600 square meters of one-sixth of an acre), which made life of the villagers who moved into the city more comfortable. In many parts of China, industrialization has not been beneficial even for the peasants who live close to cities. But in Chongqing, even peasants who lived far away from the city benefited from the urban growth during the Bo Xilai years (Cui, 2012, p. 29).

Household Registration Reform

The *dipiao* system contributed to the influx of migrants to the city. The land certificates market encouraged rural residents to give up their land in the countryside. It required a fundamental reconsideration of the Chinese household registration system (*hukou*). In Chongqing, the change in registration rules allowed anyone who had been a worker in the city for longer than five years to change their household registration from rural residence to urban one (Cui, 2012).

Huang Qifan (he was the Mayor of Chongqing for seven years since January, 2010, to December, 2016; then he became Vice-Chair of the National People's Congress Financial and Economic Affairs Committee) believed that migrant workers and young graduate, who moved to Chongqing for work, had benefited most from public housing in the city and from the 3.38 million new *hukou* distributed in 2010–2011. Residents of other regions who came to Chongqing also had the right to participate in the program.

The Chongqing administration intended to distribute 10 million *hukou* from 2010 to 2020. This would be the largest such distribution in the history of the People's Republic. Through this measure, the administration planned to increase the Chongqing's rate of urbanization from 29% in 2011 to 60% in 2020. In the local authorities' view, the policy would lead to agricultural growth, the development of the peripheral areas, housing boom, and the growth of public infrastructure (Lafarguette, 2011).

According to *The Economist* (2016), 4 million *hukou* had been distributed by the Chongqing Municipality during 2010–2015, lagging behind the official objective. Some rural migrants chose to keep their attachment to land rather than giving it up completely. The local authorities, however, took new measures to attract peasants to the urban areas. For example, now rural migrants could change their decision about *hukou* within three years of change of residence. In addition, the Chongqing administration took steps to further reduce the differences between the urban residents and the rural residents. In September 2015, the administration extended the access to most of the urban public services to residents registered under the rural *hukou*.

The Public Housing Program

Migrants from the countryside are in need of urban housing. In 2010, Huang Qifan and Bo Xilai announced an ambitious program of public housing construction. The local government declared that tenants of public housing could become owners of their units after five years of renting, although they would not have the right to sell these units in the commercial housing market (but they could sell back these units to the local government). Huang Qifan compared this system with similar systems in Hong Kong and Singapore. Huang argued for government intervention to ensure supply of affordable housing. By contrast, in many Chinese cities, less than 10% of the sold public land had been used for public housing construction (Lafarguette, 2011).

Huang (2011, pp. 592–593) argued that the Chinese government had been influenced by neoliberal ideology and relied excessively on private commercial housing market. As a result, only 3–5% of the urban population had access to affordable public housing. In Chongqing, the public housing program was designed to benefit the low income population that accounted for about 30% of the urban residents.

The first stage of the program envisaged the construction of more than 40 million square meters of public housing in the period 2010–2020. Eventually, public housing would cover 30–40% of the local real estate market. The renting cost was expected to be 40% lower than the market cost. This housing was intended for unmarried individuals whose income was less than 2,000 yuan per month or married couples whose income was less than 3,000 yuan per month. In order to implement the project, the municipality provided more than 2,000 hectares of land (Lafarguette, 2011).

According to *The Economist* (2016), the plans for the construction of public housing had not been fully implemented. About 15 million square meters of housing had been constructed by early 2016. The investment cost is considerable. The municipality has already spent 50 billion yuan on the project and 50 billion yuan of additional investment is needed in order to achieve the established targets.

Because the program would not make profit, commercial housing developers were not interested. Chongqing's investment in public housing had been financed by profits of local state-owned enterprises (Frenkiel, 2010). According to *The Economist* (2016), local governments in other parts of China would not spend their money on housing for migrant workers.

In most parts of China, local governments chose to sell undeveloped public land to private developers who would later make huge profits on land value appreciation. In Chongqing, the government-owned enterprises had developed most of the land and participated in housing construction. In effect, the government captured much of the land price increase and used it for public good rather than giving it away for private enrichment (Huang, 2011, p. 592).

The Public-Land Leasing System and Government-Owned Enterprises

When Huang Qifan came to Chongqing, he was surprised that the Municipality government's revenue from leasing public land was not more than 200 million yuan per year. In 2002, he launched a campaign to increase the revenue from public-land leasing and Chongqing's revenue from this source rose to 98 billion yuan by 2010. As the government received high revenue from land leasing, it was able to lower the business income tax rate for private businesses to 15%.

In other regions, the local governments also tried to reduce taxes for businessmen. In January 2000, the State Council created the Leadership Group for Western China Development, which covered six provinces (Gansu, Guizhou, Qinghai, Shaanxi, Sichuan, and Yunnan), five autonomous regions (Guangxi, Inner Mongolia, Ningxia, Tibet, and Xinjiang) and one municipality (Chongqing). Its objectives included promotion of economic growth, reduction of socioeconomic inequalities and ensuring social and political stability. The central government gave special privileges to all 12 regions: they could lower the business income tax rate to 15%, while the national average rate was 33% (until 2008, now it is 25%). However, most of the local governments gave up their privileges and returned to the 33% tax rate, because they had implemented too much privatization and if they did not levy 33% of enterprise income tax, they would not be able to carry out their functions. Only Chongqing retained the 15% tax rate, due to which it attracted enormous foreign investments and stimulated the development of local business (Frenkiel, 2010).

Huang Qifan also initiated the establishment of eight public investment firms in 2002, when Huang was Chongqing's deputy mayor. The eight public investment firms were government-owned enterprises that helped to implement the public infrastructure policy (Lafarguette, 2011).

The Municipality government took over unprofitable banks and enterprises, and then reorganized them into completely new and dynamically developing state corporations. The first step was the establishment of a government-owned assets management company ("Chongqing Wealth," or Yufu Assets Management Company, 渝富资产管理公司) (Huang, 2011, p. 579).

An important moment was the establishment of Chongqing's Municipal government commission for state-owned assets (*guoziwei*) in 2003. This reinforced Chongqing government's capacity to intervene in the economy (You & Lei, 2013, p. 52).

In Chongqing, there was no zero-sum game between public ownership and private business, that is, there was no redistribution of assets from the State to private owners or vice versa. Instead, they mutually reinforced each other (Cui, 2012, pp. 29–30). While many regions in China undertook privatization in the early 2000s, the state-owned assets in Chongqing had increased by six-fold from 2003 to 2009. In this way, the Chongqing experiment demonstrated that state ownership and private business were not necessarily in conflict with each other (Frenkiel, 2010).

Economists who criticized the Chongqing model argued that the Municipal government had privatized too little of state-owned property. In the view of Cui Zhiyuan, they drew attention only to the growth of the state sector in Chongqing, but did not understand that the private sector had actually grown more rapidly than the state sector (Frenkiel, 2010).

"Striking the Black" – A Campaign against Organized Crime

The Bo Xilai's campaign against mafia was the cause of considerable discussion, because it was conducted without due respect for the law. In June 2011, at the Faculty of Law at Peking University (FLPU) there was debate among lawyers, where they denounced abuses that had taken place in Chongqing. He Weifang, professor at FLPU, stated that more than 5,000 suspects had been arrested only on the basis of letters of accusation, which reminded him of prosecutions during the Cultural Revolution. Zhong Zhiwei, another discussant, said that the Chongqing government used that political campaign to control society, intimidate citizens and businessmen. The police was granted with special powers. Anything that threatened public order had been attributed to mafia. It had placed restraints on freedom of association, freedom of speech and publication was reduced (Cabestan, 2011).

On the other hand, Lu (2012) believed that even if Bo Xilai was a con man, he did his job well: in Chongqing public security was improved, infrastructure was built, there was innovation in the urbanization process, and Chongqing attracted foreign direct investment.

According to Zhao (2012), regardless of whether or not Bo Xolai used the campaign against organized crime for illegal expropriations and submission of political enemies, it eradicated powerful officials and mob businessmen protected by those officials. Huang (2011, p. 603) emphasized the difference of the Chongqing campaign from other similar campaigns. In other regions, only "black organizations" were brought down but not their protective "umbrellas."

The famous Chinese leftist activist Yang Fan was of the view that Chongqing's politics should not be discredited simply as the return of the Cultural Revolution, which allowed masses to take the law into their own hand, although certain acts of the Chongqing government did not comply with the principles of legality, especially measures against mafia (Yang, 2011).

Karneev (2013a, p. 37) considered that the negative reflections on the activity of law enforcement authorities were made by Bo Xilai's opponents. Neutral observers noted that as far as respect for the law was concerned, the practice in Chongqing had not been very different from what was typical in the rest of China, and the campaign *dahei* ("striking the black") was little different from periodic Chinese campaigns against crimes known as *yanda* ("striking hard"). Allegations that Bo Xilai established "a reign of terror" in Chongqing involve a significant element of exaggeration.

The "Red" Ideological Campaign

One of the elements of the Chongqing model that was particularly stressed by the model's enemies was its propaganda campaign, which they called the Maoist one.

The best known element of this campaign was the so-called "Red Songs." For instance, there were bulk mails of lyrics of revolutionary songs in Chongqing. On May 19, 2009, about 200 descendants of famous revolutionaries, including the major CPC leaders, participated in the singing performance in the Concert Hall of Chongqing. They sang old songs such as *The East Is Red*. Among them there were both common people and individuals from the upper class such as bankers, heads of large corporations, and politicians (Gabuev, 2012).

Zhao (2012) observed that among liberal intellectuals and mass media this campaign caused a knee-jerk reaction against the "revival of the Cultural revolution." On the basis of this reaction, Wen Jiabao unleashed the critique of Chongqing.

But, as sarcastically noted by Bo's opponents, the "Red Songs" are not *The Internationale* or *Tremble! Tyrant!* There were two types of songs, which had been promoted in Chongqing: traditional peasant songs and songs praising the CPC and Chairman Mao. Under specific conditions of the early 2000s, these songs were more bourgeois than revolutionary. In the view of some enemies of the Chongqing model, all these songs were nothing but a smokescreen, but meanwhile the "Red Songs" campaign costed Chongqing 2.7 billion yuan (Cabestan, 2011).

There were positive views on the "Singing Red" campaign, too.

Yang Fan said that this initiative brought back the bad memory of the Cultural Revolution, and for that reason could give rise to resentment among the elite. But it also raised the morale of the common people.

Zhang Musheng saw the campaign of "Singing Red" as completely positive: it recalled the Yan'an period, when the CPC was the most democratic, and helped to restore the people's faith in the CPC's honest and legitimate governance.

Yang Ping argued that the "Red Songs" campaign was an ideological support to other activities of the government (Yang, 2011).

According to Cui Zhiyuan, Bo's "Red Songs" might be seen as a way of reconstruction of relations between the CPC and the masses (Cui, 2012, p. 31).

Finally, it is possible to conclude that the "Red Songs" campaign could not be considered as an anti-government one, and claims that it intended to bring back the Cultural Revolution has not been based on facts.

MASS COVERAGE OF THE EVENTS IN CHONGQING

For mass media, the main interest of the events in Chongqing was in scandalous details. Most assessments of the events were highly emotional, for example: "The dramatic fall of Chinese Politburo member Bo Xilai is a truly Shakespearean saga of an overambitious prince, corruption, treason, murder and revenge – with even a distressed Lady Macbeth dispensing poison" (Keatley, 2012) or "revealing the skeletons in Bo's closet also meant revealing the secret world of the 'red aristocracy'" (Ma, 2012).

Internet search engines often take readers interested in information about the Chongqing model to sources provided by the opposition sect Falun Gong. Zhao (2012) considered that such sources could not be trusted. According to her, Falun Gong's sites and the Western media spread rumors and unconfirmed information to the detriment of Bo Xilai and the Chongqing model.

Sisci's article (2012) could give an example. The author looked forward to the upcoming political reforms in China and expected that new political experiments would differ from the Chongqing experiment, which was characterized by slogans and songs of the Cultural Revolution. Sisci focused on the Maoist past when considering the Chongqing model and the Chongqing incident. He expressed hope that "this experiment has ended," "China cannot turn back," and "the future of the country has nothing to do with red squads." In his view, the Chongqing incident should be a warning for the future leaders, who were coming to power in 2012: "They could be participants of red squads in the past, but they are expected to understand that such historical period should never happen again." In fact, even Bo Xilai himself, as shown below, cannot be unconditionally defined as a leftist.

The authors of the editorial article in the Japanese newspaper *Nikkei* (2012) stated that Bo Xilai pushed forward ideas, which ran counter to the CPC's dictatorship, by using the public dissatisfaction at the worsening of social inequalities. Japanese journalists rightly pointed out that in China there is a serious problem of social inequalities, but they significantly overestated Bo Xilai's opposition to the central government policies.

More than a year after the Chongqing incident, Garnaut (2013) came to the conclusion that the fall of Bo Xilai was supposed to free the country from the Maoist past. But, in assessing the political platform of Xi Jinping, Garnaut noted with dismay that seasoned with the Maoist ideas, Bo's program seemed to be very attractive for many people – even for princelings whose families suffered during the Cultural Revolution. Writing about Bo Xilai's activities, this author in the first place mentioned the popularization of the red culture, undertaken by Bo. Garnaut considered that the red culture was a sign of the revival of Maoism. Trying to explain the phenomenon, the author wrote that Bo, just like Xi, was raised in the family, where the communist ideals of equality, asceticism and emancipation of all humanity prevailed. The revival of the image of Mao, on the one hand, symbolized the recovery of old ideals, and on the other hand, it reminded people about the contribution which their own families made for the construction of the People's Republic. In terms of governance, the revival of the Maoist iconography and methods, according to the article's author, was necessary to keep power in the hands of the ruling families in the post-communist country that had become more and more cynical and fragmented every day.

In this respect, it would be interesting to consider the orthodox leftist reactions to the events in Chongqing. Devrim (2013), an activist of Turkish Revolutionary Workers' Party, wrote in the Russian magazine *Alternatives*. He stressed that the Chongqing model was not anti-capitalist (Devrim did not consider that the Chinese model was socialist, either). He drew attention to the fact that Bo Xilai, during his leadership of the Chongqing Municipality, did not change the capitalist system. Furthermore, such large foreign corporations as Hewlett Packard, Foxconn, and BASF moved parts of their production and management to Chongqing, and Chongqing was included among 15 new cities, which offered the best potential for business, in the July 2011 edition of the magazine *Fortune*. This would not have happened if corporations had seen anti-capitalist experiments in Chongqing.

Devrim mentioned about the information publicized by *Bloomberg* on April 23, 2012, according to which Bo's family owned at least 136 million US dollars. And on this basis, the author came to the conclusion that Bo Xilai was a "bureaucrat-bourgeois," like many other representatives of the CPC (the anti-corruption campaign in the PRC confirms that in fact there are a lot of such officials). What about Bo's "leftism," Devrim considered that this opinion, shared by some left-wing commentators both inside and outside China, was evidence of their ideological and political "poverty."

WAS THE CHONGQING MODEL "LEFT"?

Is the Chongqing model a model of "leftism"? The problem is that the belief that the Chongqing model was "left" is generally disseminated by detractors of this model – supporters of neoliberalism. On the other hand, the orthodox Marxist Li Minqi (an economics professor at the University of Utah) expresses the opposite view: he is sure that the Chonqging model is definitely not a socialist model but it carries progressive economic and political implications.

The Chongqing reforms could be largely considered as implementation of ideas of New Leftists, or Liberal Leftists – of course, given that they have diverse views among themselves.

Cui Zhiyuan, the political economy and political philosophy scholar from the School of Public Policy and Management of Tsinghua University, participated in the work on the Chongqing model. He prefers to be called not a New Leftist but a liberal socialist (Frenkiel, 2010) and even wrote *A Petty Bourgeoisie Manifesto* (Cui, 2005) which claims that socialism does not perpetuate the proletarian status of the working class but promises this class a future of petite bourgeoisie. He was closely acquainted with Huang Qifan and Bo Xilai and was even seconded to the Chongqing government (Leonard, 2012, p. 26) as a special assistant to the director of Chongqing's municipal government commission for state-owned assets. One might say that this scholar found an opportunity to put into practice his theoretical propositions (Frenkiel, 2010), which were not leftist at all.

But most commentators (as can be seen from the previous part of the paper) associate the Chongqing model with the extreme left part of the politico-ideological spectrum and attribute the desire to start a new Cultural Revolution to its supporters, although in fact the representatives of New Leftists who approve the Chongqing model do not want to apply the policies of the Cultural Revolution in current conditions.

Karneev (2013b, p. 51) considered that polarization of political and social forces in China significantly affected perception of the events in Chongqing. He wrote that during the term of the Bo Xilai's administration in Chongqing the authorities of the region had done a great deal to promote the Chongqing model by organizing seminars, conferences, invitations of distinguished guests to study the Chongqing experience, and so on. But gradually the term "Chongqing model" came to be associated with the idea about a sort of "restoration" of socialism of the Mao Zedong era by the efforts of left-wing scholars and publicists and their opponents (Karneev, 2014, p. 130).

Left-wing radicals saw in Bo Xilai a long-waited charismatic leader. In addition, he had significant administrative and financial resources. Radical left publicists in their statements often insinuated that major changes would have occurred at the upcoming 18th National Congress of the CPC, a new era would have begun in China, etc. (Karneev, 2013b, pp. 45–52). On the left-wing website *Utopia* some authors posted appeals (often allegoric ones) to appoint Bo Xilai as a new Prime Minister of China and thereby radically change the direction of economic reforms. For example, on March 9, 2012 (i.e., on days when the events of the Chongqing incident have been unfolding) on *Utopia* appeared the article *The Chongqing Model revisited* (Sun, 2012), which claimed that fighting crime and integration of rural and urban areas had been carried out in other places, too, but it was Chongqing that had turned into a "model," thanks to Bo Xilai: "Of course, the notion of a 'Chongqing Model' is very much related to Bo Xilai and the patrons who stand behind him."

Obviously, such publications did not improve the atmosphere around Bo and even gave his opponents an excuse to accuse him of a desire to take power in China, bring the days of the Cultural Revolution back, and so on. Su Wei, one of the authors of the book *The Chongqing Model*, concluded that the Chongqing model was exploited by radical leftists and that *Utopia* did more harm than good to Bo Xilai and the Chongqing authorities (Karneev, 2013b, p. 51).

Unfortunately, the Chongqing model was strongly associated with the personality of Bo Xilai both among the supporters and the opponents of the Chongqing model. Consequently, some people think of this model as one of Bo Xilai's own creation. Naturally, from this perspective, personal shortcomings and mistakes of the ruler become shortcomings of the whole system. But even if we consider the concrete identity of Bo Xilai, there is a question of whether he really was as "leftist" as the critics of him claim.

Although Bo was a Red Guard in his youth and even had a conflict with his father because of it, his lifestyle during the period when he was an official does not reveal a strong belief in socialist ideals. On the other hand, due consideration should be made of the fact that his mother was killed or was forced to commit a suicide in times of the Cultural Revolution (Garnaut, 2013). Some commentators think that the promotion of Maoism by people whose parents suffered during the Mao era seems to be very cynical. They are sure that these people do not truly believe in Maoist ideals and just imitate its style in order to exploit nostalgia of a part of the population. Such politicians bring back the attributes of Maoism but not its policies, they are interested in ideology solely from the perspective of enhancing their own popularity (Hille & Anderlini, 2011). For instance, Hu Deping (a Chinese politician, the eldest son of Hu Yaobang) stated, referring to Bo, that "some do not believe in the Cultural Revolution but nevertheless exploit it and play it up" (Garnaut, 2013).

Karneev (2013a, p. 39) noted that Bo Xilai at his previous tenures (he was the Mayor of Dalian, the Governor of Liaoning, the Minister of Commerce of the PRC) never showed leftist tendencies. Aside from propaganda of leftists and their opponents (it was in their mutual interest to emphasize Bo's "leftism"), Bo Xilai was not an embodiment of the Chongqing model, he even could not be seriously considered as a leftist. Jiang Weiping simply described Bo as a marginalized and lonely figure, who kept moving from one political project to another. His fall, according to Jiang Weiping, could be explained by the fact that he had reassessed his "red" policies to please Hu Jintao (Doyon, 2011).

A clear example of relationship between Bo Xilai and radical leftists is the so-called "15 October incident." In 2009 on that day the representatives of Mao Zedong ideological followers from more than 20 provinces gathered in

Chongqing. They were planning to form a new party, adopt its Charter, etc. The authorities of Chongqing not only did not support them, but even dispersed the event, and four of the planners were sentenced to prison terms ranging from 5 to 10 years. This incident clearly demonstrated that the relations between the Chongqing authorities and representatives of radical left organizations were far from friendly (Karneev, 2013b, pp. 50–51).

On the other hand, another leftist Yang Fan argued that since 2011 Maoists and other radical leftists from Beijing had begun to be financed by the Chongqing authorities. However, he did not give any evidence of that (Karneev, 2013b).

Some people believe that the true architect of the Chongqing model is Huang Qifan – he had served six "emperors," that is, he has served as a Mayor under six Chongqing Party Secretaries. Huang (2011, p. 572) claimed that he was Chongqing's key business strategist.

Huang Qifan became a famous figure in Shanghai, where he was the Deputy Director of Shanghai Pudong New Area Administration Commission in the 1990s. There he participated in designing successful strategies of financial sector development. In 2001, Huang was transferred to work in Chongqing. He remained at the Mayor post even after the Chongqing incident. It is important that there is no way to call Huang Qufan a supporter of returning to the time of Mao Zedong (Karneev, 2013a, p. 39).

On the basis of public statements of Bo Xilai and other leaders who were close to him, it cannot be concluded that they sought to oppose the central government instructions with their own socioeconomic and socio-political activities. Furthermore, the leaders of Chongqing periodically exonerated themselves from any claims to any independent policy-making. For example, in April 2011 Huang Qifan stated in an interview to journalists of Hong Kong television that he and Bo Xilai did not implement any new policy in their work, did not create any model, they had only one goal – in accordance with the requirements of the concept of scientific development to change mode of development, to find out solutions to arising questions (Karneev, 2013a, p. 35).

Many of Bo Xilai's initiatives did not suggest a returning to the time of the Cultural Revolution. For example, he launched the "Five Chongqing" program: he planned the building of Chongqing into a green Chongqing, transport Chongqing, safe Chongqing, healthy Chongqing, and livable Chongqing. None of these goals was Maoist or radical left, instead, they reminded people of European social democratic policy.

When Bo ruled the city, policies where shaped to highlight people's welfare, such as equitable wealth distribution, use of state-owned enterprises to promote public welfare, construction of low-cost housing, development of social support programs, etc. (Karneev, 2013a, p. 40). All these endeavors were nor contrary to the central government's policies: in March 2011 it was officially announced that improving the livelihoods of the people would be a main direction of economic and social policies of China's 12th Five-Year Plan (Cui, 2012, p. 27).

In 2008 Hu Jintao excluded the phrase of "efficiency first, equity second" from his report in the 17th Party Congress in favor of "greater emphasis on equity in redistribution" (再分配更加注重公平). It was a sign of a leftward correction. In fact, Chongqing was the main "test-point" for that reorientation (Huang, 2011, p. 608).

The slogan "equitable wealth distribution" was even included in Hu Jintao's report at the 18th National Congress of the CPC (Karneev, 2013a, p. 40).

The foregoing information leads to the conclusion that the Chongqing model was not in conflict with the central government policies in the field of economic policy and solving social problems, on the whole it was consistent with the basic principles and approaches that existed in the PRC (Karneev, 2013a, p. 39). According to New Leftists that do not reject the advantages of the market economy, this model could be considered progressive. The "Maoist" label, which is being put on it, is related not to its real features, but to propaganda battles between radical leftists and radical rightists.

THE DEVELOPMENT OF CHONGQING AFTER THE FALL OF BO XILAI

According to Cui Zhiyuan, Chinese mainstream economists are under the strong influence of neo-liberal thinking, and that is why the Chongqing government's politics often became targets of criticism (Frenkiel, 2010). Naturally, since the Chongqing incident such criticism has increased.

Especially strong criticism was directed at the nostalgic "Red Songs" campaign and the campaign against organized crime. Many elements of the Chongqing model, however, are still popular among the local population. It is important to understand the causes of this situation. Zhao (2012) stressed that Chongqing reforms had the integrated nature, and without the programs that improved people's livelihood, the "Singing Red" campaign would not have any foundation for popularity between the population.

As an example, the Chinese mass media criticized the campaign of tree planting, which cost 1.5 billion dollars, as profligacy. But it actually had a positive impact on the air quality of the industrial city (Lu, 2012). But now, this "profligacy" looks different against the background of the urgent need to improve environment in China.

Of course, if Bo Xilai is considered a creator of the Chongqing model, then his dismissal seems to be the model's complete collapse. Obviously, much has changed in the municipality, especially in its ideological policies. But in terms of the economy, it is incorrect to talk about total defeat of the Chongqing model.

During the five years from 2007 to 2012, Chongqing's GDP grew at an average of 15.8% annually, when the national average rate was 10.5% – undoubtedly a very respectable result (Lu, 2012). The pace of Chongqing's development has been ahead of the national average: according to the data for the first three quarters of 2015, among 27 provincial-level regions the highest growth rates of GDP were shown by the Western and Central provinces, and Chongqing was at the top of the ratings with its 11% GDP growth. By October 2015 Chongqing had been ranked first in the GDP growth among all Chinese provinces for seven months in a row.

One of the main factors for Chongqing's economic success is consumption growth: for the first three quarters of 2015 in Chongqing retail sales increased by 12.3% (the national average growth rate was by 10.5%). Zhang Fumin, vice director of the Chongqing Statistics Bureau, considered that Chongqing's outstanding economic growth was due to the rapid development of manufacturing and high-tech industries. The city's high-tech sector has become a new growth engine. The city's auto and IT industries maintain relatively rapid growth, they are two backbone industries of the Chongqing's economy, which grew by 13.4% and 24.8%, respectively, for the first three quarters of 2015 (*China Daily*, 2015).

The stagnation in the United States, Western Europe, and Japan has strongly affected China's coastal provinces. In contrast, Chongqing's economic growth continues to improve (Steinbock, 2012).

The critics of the Chongqing model state that after Bo's dismissal the local government has had to pay high debts. But it needs to be recognized that Chongqing received a difficult economic inheritance from the past: a need to resettle Three Gorges migrants; problems of the care of the elderly and children, who were left behind in depressed rural villages by the migrant working-age population. Since 2009, under a program known as "Ten Points on People's Livelihood," Chongqing spent more than a half of all government expenditure to improve the well-being of the population. A state investment firm, rather than private capital, took over "poor assets" from more than 1,160 state-owned enterprises of the Mao era, and then turned them into viable businesses (Zhao, 2012).

Chongqing is still one of the most economically successful regions of China, despite the fact that the Chongqing incident has had a negative impact on the inflow of foreign investments. In 2012, there was no growth of direct foreign investments. In spite of that, in 2012 Chongqing's economic growth rate stood at 13.6%. At the same time, the average per capita income in Chongqing is still lower than the national average. The policies of reforms, implemented in Chongqing, also have a positive impact on the development of the city's economy (*Gbtimes*, 2013).

Speaking about the consequences of Bo's rule, Huang Qifan said that the city's government "worked hard to banish the serious impact of the Bo Xilai and Wang Lijun cases." Also he declared that the experience of the last five years (that is from 2008 to 2012) had shown that only under the direction of the CPC it had become possible to enjoy real economic and social success in Chongqing. This phrase shows that economic and social successes of

Chongqing are beyond doubt and they should not be associated only with the identity of the former Communist Party Secretary of Chongqing (Blanchard, 2013).

It now appears that the concerns that existed before the Chongqing incident that strong leadership of Bo Xilai could, in the long term, hamper the region's normal development were fully justified, because Chongqing's economic success seemed to be related to the personal abilities of Huang Qifan and Bo Xilai and to financial and political support from the central government (Yang, 2011). After the dismissal of Bo Xiali, in August 2012, Lu (2012) predicted that, in the short term, the Chongqing model reputation would be damaged both inside and outside China because of the reaction to Bo's political ambitions and missteps. But when the dust settles and the mist clears, the Chongqing model may be remembered as a useful economic and social experiment that effectively dissipated tensions between state and people at a time when China needed to rebalance its economy and policies.

Indeed, the editorial of *Global Times* (2016) published in March 2016 reported that a new round of discussion over the Chongqing model was launched recently. In spite of debates about it, some analysts believe that the city's growth model could make recommendations for resolving economic problems facing some local authorities.

China's leadership still remains mindful of this region. During his first inspection trip of 2016 (4–6 January) Xi Jinping visited Chongqing and emphasized particular importance of the integrated development of rural and urban areas (*Xinhua*, 2016). That visit was widely interpreted as a sign of his approval of the efforts of the Chongqing government. Now the system of land certificates continues to operate in Chongqing, although some officials initially hoped that, ultimately, the free land market would appear on the basis of this system (*The Economist*, 2016).

Therefore, Bo Xilai's dismissal has not led to the complete elimination of the economic part of the Chongqing model. As described above, economic experiments were started in Chongqing long before Bo's arrival, the results of the introduction of them are still obvious and reforms still continue.

SIGNIFICANCE OF THE CHONGQING MODEL FOR THE WHOLE COUNTRY

Huang (2011, p. 607) wondered whether Chongqing's experiment was "an isolated incident in China, an island in capitalist or state capitalist sea"? What are the odds that this experiment might turn into something of greater influence for the whole country?

The experience of the Chongqing experimental zone was initially intended to be extended to other regions, especially to Central and Western regions of China which could not follow the example of developed coastal regions. The local governments of other regions showed an interest in the work of Chongqing's municipal government commission for state-owned assets. Initially, they expected that after privatization they would receive support of private owners. But privatization provoked social unrest, and the local authorities lost revenue from public assets. They had to levy high tax on enterprises, which resulted in displeasure among private owners. Therefore, officials form other provinces, for example form Shandong province, had come to Chongqing to learn how state-owned assets and tax system was organized in the city. There was also interest in the Chongqing experiments at the level of the central government (Frenkiel, 2010).

For example, Chongqing's public rental housing has drawn the public's attention and was perceived as a model, which has got central-level approval to be used more widely throughout the country. On November 16, 2010, the Ministry of Finance, the Commission for Development and Reform, and the Ministry for the Development of Urban and Rural Housing, with the approval of the State Council, issued a joint communiqué, in which they called for construction of such housing throughout the country (Huang, 2011, p. 593).

In January 2016, Chinese Minister of Finance Lou Jiwei said that now other places could try out *dipiao* trading (*The Economist*, 2016), that is, this innovation, initially tested in Chongqing, could be extended to other parts of the country.

According to Karneev (2013a, p. 38), Bo Xilai probably was hoping to influence the national policy development by conducting the Chongqing experiment. Frenkiel (2010) also considered that the Chongqing experiment gave an opportunity to get an insight into what could happen at the national level. However, economic experiments are conducted not only in Chongqing. Local officials in different regions implement institutional innovations to pacify social tensions and increase their own legitimacy. The most successful of these innovations have been implemented at provincial or national scale (Frenkiel, 2010). One of the most famous regional models is Guangdong model, that is often considered as the antithesis of the Chongqing model: neoliberal intellectuals favor its economic and political features. In 1992, Deng Xiaoping visited Guangdong and praised it as a model for the rest of China (Li & Yang, 2003, p. 210). But the regional models of development are not limited to the Chongqing and the Guangdong ones, there are also Xiamen, Wenzhou, and other options (Scrimenti, 2011).

Wang (2012, pp. 60–66) is of the view that one-size-fits-all model of socialism does not exist: the socialist ideal must be applied in different ways in different countries and at different stages of development. According to him, the Chinese people will "upgrade" socialism with Chinese characteristics by experimenting with a wide range of new policies after they reach a new stage of development.

In the opinion of Steinbock (2012), Western observers wrongly consider the Chongqing model and the Guangdong model as antagonistic. In fact, these models represent different sides of the same coin: different types of reforms for a country that features huge regional differences. Growth models that are appropriate in developed coastal regions do not work in relatively poor and less industrialized central and western areas. As an example, Steinbock compared the United States, where GDP per capita exceeded 48,000 dollars in 2012, and Thailand, where the figure was 4,900 dollars. It is obvious that an identical model of development could not be used in these countries – and in different regions of China, too, where the difference of GDP per capita between the richest and the poorest province is almost 10-fold. The Guangdong experience is unique because of the geographical features that helped the province to come to the forefront of the national development. The coast has natural advantages; therefore, the Guangdong model could not be applied wholesale to central and western provinces (Scrimenti, 2011). In addition, most investments in Guangdong have been related to its geographical, economic and cultural closeness to Hong Kong and Macao. Other provinces do not have such relations, and after all, Hong Kong and Macao could not invest so heavily in all provinces of China.

On the other hand, as noted above, in 2015 central and western regions had obvious advantages in economic growth. The fact that during the global economic crisis, western provinces stayed ahead of eastern ones in economic growth confirms that the establishment of different regional models was a right decision: in conditions of global economic slowdown it turned out to be good for the country.

Steinbock (2012) considered that the true challenge was not between Chongqing and Guangdong, but between more and less advanced regions of China, and successful reforming of China required a strong and united leadership that would be supported by the majority of the CPC and people.

Except searching for the best ways of development, establishment of reforms experimental zones is intended to discover errors in work. Special Economic Zones became experimental grounds where new methods of administration and governance were tested, where the government monitored the disruptive effects that could cause significant damage in the case of rapid wholesale introduction of free trade (Li & Yang, 2003, p. 211). Deng Xiaoping said in an interview with the American journalist Mike Wallace that all measures that had been implemented at that time were experiments and innovations for the Chinese people, that is why they had to find their own way. Chinese rulers understood that the implementation of innovations would be coupled with making some mistakes, and the Chinese way to correct them was to integrate best practices, not let a little mistake turn into a big one (Gou, 2008).

Pivovarova (2011, p. 64) drew attention to the fact that the leaders of China had been looking for administrative model that in the case of error would let avoid China a national crisis. The organization of "testing grounds" of reforms in different regions has become such a model: the government protected the country's economy against huge mistakes by conducting experiments with different models in different provinces.

This system of testing of economic models in different regions allows, while preserving political unity, decentralized decisions in as many areas as possible, and in this way creates conditions for seeking different methods of problem-solving through decentralized practices and experiments. Local authorities have no objection to these experiments, as their performance is no longer assessed only in terms of economic growth (Frenkiel, 2010).

In spite of advantages of the Chongqing model, it would be risky to use it as a template for the whole country (Lafarguette, 2011). The same could be said of the Guangdong model. Most likely, certain elements of each model will be chosen to use in other regions, and for different regions these elements are useful at different rates. For example, Scrimenti (2011), answering the question of which model will rule China, said that "it'll be a little bit of Chongqing and Guangdong, mixed in with whatever that province has cooked up on its own." And he suggested that in 20 or 30 years the world would be dealing with the United Provinces of China, not the People's Republic. Cui Zhiyuan also saw the European Union as a role model: all countries of EU have common goals but each member country can have large freedom in experimenting different ways of achieving these goals. He considered that it was a good formal mechanism that China could learn from (Frenkiel, 2010). Such statements might seem to be too bold, and such suggestions be fairly unlikely, taking into account the negative attitude of the central government to any manifestations of separatism. However, if we believe Wang Shaoguang, these suggestions are already behind the times: in China now there is a huge degree of decentralization of power and the country in many ways is more decentralized than France or even federal systems like the United States or India (Frenkiel, 2009).

What elements of the Chongqing model could be used in other regions of China in the future?

(A) The land certificates (*dipiao*) market. It was already mentioned that recently the government announced that other provinces now would have the right to apply this system, too.

(B) Household registration reform (distribution of *hukou*). For example, the National New-type Urbanization Plan (2014–2020) which is being implemented in China now provides for distribution of 100 million urban *hukou* among migrant workers within 6 years, and is aimed at urbanization of central and western regions of China (*Xinhua*, 2014). In is obvious that the ways of urbanization were tested in Chongqing.

(C) The public-land leasing system. Cui Zhiyuan (2012, pp. 28, 31) believed that the innovations undertaken by Huang Qifan had been watched closely throughout China and could indicate the way forward for the whole country.

IMPLICATIONS OF THE CHONGQING INCIDENT FOR THE LEFT WING

The Chongqing incident certainly was a monstrous assault on the left camp in China (Karneev, 2013b, pp. 45–52).

Wang (2012a, p. 94) drew parallels between the events in Chongqing and the Tiananmen Square incident: in 1989 the crackdown on the protests was also used to push through "price reforms," and the Chongqing incident could be a subterfuge of the right camp that is aimed at putting China back on the path of neoliberal reforms.

Li Minqi considered that Bo's dismissal pointed to consensus among the Chinese leadership, the purpose of which was to push ahead with economic liberalization, in spite of the increasing social problems (Spegele, 2012). According to Wang (2012a, p. 95), in this way, a climate of political repression was created in China to continue further neoliberal reforms, that the Chinese people would not like. He noted that some of the consequences of the privatization of state-owned enterprises were large-scale layoffs of workers and systemic corruption. The marketization of social security systems, including medical coverage, has widened the gap between rich and poor and between urban and rural areas.

On March 18, 2012, only a few days after the Bo's takedown, the National Development and Reform Commission published a report on the perspectives of extending economic reforms. It contained plans for the privatization of large sections of the railways, education, healthcare, communications, energy resources, etc.

Vinogradov (2014, p. 93) drew attention to the calls of Wen Jiabao for urgent reforms on the eve of the 18th National Congress of the CPC. In his opinion, the reforms offered by Wen did not question a leading role of the party. They would legitimize long-standing relations between authority and business and guarantee the safe mutual conversion of power and property. The result of these reforms, in the view of Vinogradov, would be political legitimization of family ties between businessmen and officials, opening up opportunity to become a member of the party and government leadership to business people. However, the society would be in danger of being excluded from this alliance.

According to Wang (2012a, p. 98), another adverse implication of the Chongqing incident is the fact that many young people throughout China, for whom the concept of common prosperity – a distinctive feature of the

Chongqing experiment – has become a source of inspiration and enthusiasm, could now become political nihilists.

CONCLUSION

The Chongqing model was formed under the influence of two main circumstances: the global financial and economic crisis which, according to Wang (2012b), made a new generation feel less confident of the advantages of free-market ideology and the central government strategy of rapid urbanization in rural areas.

During the global crisis, China lost a significant part of export markets, and because of this the government accelerated a shift toward the domestic market. Chongqing appeared to be at the forefront of this policy. In that period, views were widely disseminated through the world that the Western liberal model of economic policy is in deep crisis, whereas China and several other rapidly developing countries are finding some kind of "third way" in their development (Karneev, 2013a, p. 38).

The widely held view about the Maoist focus of the Chongqing reforms, as shown above, is unfounded. The widespread attention paid to Bo Xilai and the Chongqing model was used by his opponents as evidence that Bo wanted to return to the times of the Cultural Revolution. Such charges were not officially pressed in court, which is an indication of their falseness.

Some critics of the Chongqing model stated that Chongqing's rapid economic growth was achieved, as elsewhere in China, through cheap labor and foreign investments. But foreign investors were attracted by favorable tax system, which was made possible because of the Municipality's large revenue from the public sector. State-owned enterprises were important to this model (Wang, 2012a, p. 96).

Chongqing had its own specific features in social policies. For example, during the leadership of Bo Xilai, the IT manufacturer Foxconn which is known for its super-exploitative treatment of staff was lured to the city. It relocated part of its jobs to Chongqing from Shenzhen. But in Shenzhen company employees had to live in military-barrack-style dorms, while in Chongqing they were provided cheap public rental housing (Zhao, 2012). *China Labour Bulletin*, a non-governmental organization based in Hong Kong, says that there were 42 known labor-related protests in Chongqing in 2015, whereas in Shenzhen there were 121 such protests, although its population was less than one-half of Chongqing's (*The Economist*, 2016). Thus, despite Bo's negative personal traits and the mistakes he made, Chongqing's progress in raising people's living standards and improving relationship between the people and the authorities cannot be denied. In fact, the Chongqing model has been popular among the local people even after the fall of Bo Xilai.

Lu (2012) was correct in saying that the Chongqing model was an experiment, conducted in the interest of the common people while preserving the leading role of the CPC and the State. Also Lu rightly pointed out that it was because of the significant economic measures, not populist campaigns, that made Bo popular in Chongqing even after his fall.

Wang (2012a, p. 96) considered that the Chongqing model was much more attractive than other regional models. During the period, when the national authorities struggled to promote further neoliberal reforms, Chongqing demonstrated a move away from neoliberalism. In this city, unlike other regions, more attention was paid to redistribution, justice and equality. Whether or not Bo himself was corrupt, he emphasized the importance of equality and common prosperity.

Huang (2011, p. 600) stressed the role of government-owned enterprises in Chongqing. He considered that the experience of this municipality questioned the dogma of a clear division of the private and the public sector. Huang (2011, pp. 570–571) argued that Chongqing's experiment showed the possibilities that could not be provided by either free market capitalism or planned socialism.

Thereby, despite of the fact that the Chongqing model was not anti-market, it was more socialist than other provincial models. To answer the question raised in the title of this paper, "The Chongqing Model – Socialist Alternative or Propaganda Cliché?," it can be said that this model was not just a propaganda cliché, it really was one of the possible ways to build a socialist country.

Can Chongqing preserve its socialist features and advantages against the background of growing marketization and privatization in China? This will be the subject for a separate study.

REFERENCES

Blanchard, B. (2013). China's Chongqing mayor says has banished Bo Xilai's influence. Reuters, January 26. Retrieved from http://www.reuters.com/article/us-china-politics-bo-idUSBRE90P06E20130126. Accessed on January 21, 2016.

Cabestan, J. (2011). The implications of the Chongqing Model for the reform of China's legal system. In *One or two Chinese models?* London: European Council on Foreign Relations.

China Daily. (2015). *China's regional growth indicates economy bottoming out*. October 29. Retrieved from http://www.chinadaily.com.cn/business/2015-10/29/content_22311911.htm 2015-10-29. Accessed on December 21, 2015.

Cui, Z. (2005). Liberal socialism and the future of China: A Petty Bourgeoisie Manifesto. In Y. Tian (Ed.), *The Chinese model of modern development* (pp. 157–174). New York, NY: Routledge.

Cui, Z. (2012). The Chongqing experiment: The way forward for China? In M. Leonard (Ed.), *China 3.0* (pp. 26–31). London: European Council on Foreign Relations.

Devrim, A. (2013). Podzemnyie tolchki v kompartii Kitaya [Underground tremors in the Communist Party of China]. *Alternativy [Alternatives]*, *2*, 73–88.

Doyon, J. (2011). The view from Hong Kong: Bo Xilai's opportunism is not paying off. In *One or two Chinese models?* London: European Council on Foreign Relations.

Fewsmith, J. (2011). Debating "the China Model". *China Leadership Monitor, 35*. Retrieved from www.chinaleadershipmonitor.org. Accessed on October 4, 2015.

Frenkiel, E. (2009). Political change and democracy in China. Books & Ideas, July 15. Retrieved from http://www.booksandideas.net/Political-change-and-democracy-in.html. Accessed on November 20, 2015.

Frenkiel, E. (2010). From scholar to official. Books & Ideas, December 6. Retrieved from http://www.booksandideas.net/From-Scholar-to-Official.html. Accessed on November 20, 2015.

Fukuyama, F. (2016). Exporting the Chinese model. Project Syndicate, January 12. Retrieved from https://www.project-syndicate.org/onpoint/china-one-belt-one-road-strategy-by-francis-fukuyama-2016-01?barrier=true. Accessed on January 12, 2016.

Gabuev, A. T. (2012). Zolotaya molodej [The Gilded Youth]. Commersant, October 22. Retrieved from http://www.kommersant.ru/doc/2046240. Accessed on February 11, 2016.

Garnaut, J. (2013). The east is still red. Foreign Policy, August 22. Retrieved from http://foreignpolicy.com/2013/08/22/the-east-is-still-red/. Accessed on December 12, 2015.

Gbtimes. (2013). Probl'emy chuncina v pobestle dnya "dvuh sessiy" [Problems of Chongqing on the agenda of The "Two Meetings"]. March 7. Retrieved from http://ru.gbtimes.com/kitay/problemy-chuncina-v-povestke-dnya-dvuh-sessiy. Accessed on January 29, 2016.

Global Times. (2016). Chongqing's industrial clusters, forward thinking offer useful example amid tricky environment, March 8. Retrieved from http://www.globaltimes.cn/content/972442.shtml. Accessed on March 14, 2016.

Gou, X. (2008). Xian xing xian shi: gaige kaifang 30 nian Chongqing shijian ji lishi zuoyong [To go first, to test first: practical and historical role of Chongqing in 30 years of reform and opening up]. *Journal of Chongqing University (Social Science Edition)*, *14*(6), 1–7.

Hille, K., & Anderlini, J. (2011). China: Mao and the next generation. *The Financial Times*, June 2. Retrieved from https://next.ft.com/content/eb239472-8d48-11e0-bf23-00144feab49a. Accessed on January 15, 2016.

Huang, P. C. (2011). Chongqing: Equitable development driven by a "third hand"? *Modern China*, *37*(6), 569–622.

IFeng News. (2012). Zhang Dejiang: wo renwei genben jiu bu cunzai chongqing moshi [Zhang Dejiang: I think there is no such thing as the Chongqing model]. November 8. Retrieved from http://finance.ifeng.com/news/special/zhonggong18da/20121108/7272343.shtml. Accessed on January 17, 2016.

Karneev, A. N. (2013a). "Chuncinskaya model'": chto eto bilo? Ch. 1. [The Chongqing model: what was it? Part 1]. *Probl'emi Dal'nego Vostoka [Problems of the Far East]*, *3*, 33–41.

Karneev, A. N. (2013b). "Chuncinskaya model'": chto eto bilo? Ch. 2. [The Chongqing model: what was it? Part 2]. *Probl'emi Dal'nego Vostoka [Problems of the Far East]*, *4*, 45–52.

Karneev, A. N. (2014). Chuncinskaya model'. Posleslovie. [The Chongqing model. Afterword]. In *Kitay na puti k vozrizhdeniyu [China on the road to recovery]* (pp. 121–138). Moscow: Publishing House "Forum".

Keatley, R. (2012). The fall of Bo Xilai. The National Interest, April 24. Retrieved from http://nationalinterest.org/commentary/the-fall-bo-xilai-6838?page=1. Accessed on November 25, 2015.

Lafarguette, R. (2011). Chongqing: A model for a new economic and social policy? In *One or two Chinese models?* London: European Council on Foreign Relations.

Leonard, M. (Ed.). (2012). *China 3.0*. London: European Council on Foreign Relations.

Li, J. Z., & Yang, D. C. (2003). Guangdong: China's economic powerhouse – The past, the present and the future. In T. Bui, D. Yang, W. Jones, & J. Li (Eds.), *China's economic powerhouse: Reform in Guangdong province* (pp. 208–230). Basingstoke: Palgrave Macmillan.

Lu, K. (2012). The Chongqing model worked. Foreign Policy, August 8. Retrieved from http://foreignpolicy.com/2012/08/08/the-chongqing-model-worked/. Accessed on February 11, 2016.

Ma, J. (2012). China's show trial of the century. Project Syndicate, August 20. Retrieved from https://www.project-syndicate.org/commentary/china-s-show-trial-of-the-century-by-ma-jian. Accessed on January 13, 2016.

Nihon Keizai Shinbun [The Nikkei]. (2012). Chugoku no taisei no mondai o shimeshita "hakukirai juken" [The "Bo Xilai incident" showed the problems of the Chinese system]. October 3. Retrieved from http://www.nikkei.com/article/DGXDZO46838130T01C12A0EA1000/. Accessed on December 22, 2015.

Pivovarova, P. E. (2011). *Socialism s kitajskoj specifikoj [Socialism with Chinese characteristics]*. Moscow: Publishing House "Forum".

Scrimenti, M. (2011). Chongqing vs Guangdong: Which model will rule China? ChinAnalyst, December 1. Retrieved from http://chinanalyst.com/archives/629. Accessed on December 4, 2015.

Sisci, F. (2012). Wen, Bo Xilai e la Cina che verrà. Limes, March 15. Retrieved from http://www.limesonline.com/rubrica/wen-bo-xilai-e-la-cina-che-verra. Accessed on December 13, 2015.

Spegele, B. (2012). China's 'New Left' Grows Louder. The Wall Street Journal, October 5. Retrieved from http://www.wsj.com/ARTICLES/SB10000872396390443493304578038121620762516. Accessed on November 26, 2015.

Steinbock, D. (2012). Guangdong and Chongqing: Two sides of the same coin. China-US Focus, December 11. Retrieved from http://www.chinausfocus.com/political-social-development/guangdong-and-chongqing-two-sides-of-the-same-coin/. Accessed on November 19, 2015.

Sun, W. (2012). The Chongqing Model revisited. *Yumpu*, February 9. Retrieved from https://www.yumpu.com/en/document/view/11577714/the-chongqing-model-revisited-china-policy-brief. Accessed on November 11, 2015.

The Economist. (2016). Reform's big taboo. March 26. Retrieved from http://www.economist.com/news/china/21695556-ambitious-plan-social-change-has-run-trouble-reformu2019s-big-taboo. Accessed on April 7, 2016.

Vinogradov, A. V. (2014). Vlas't', bisnes I korrupcia v Kitae [Power, business and corruption in China]. *Probl'emi Dal'nego Vostoka [Problems of the Far East]*, *1*, 89–96.

Wang, H. (2012a). Political repression and the resurgence of neoliberalism in China. In M. Leonard (Ed.), *China 3.0* (pp. 94–99). London: European Council on Foreign Relations.

Wang, H. (2012b). The rumour machine. *London Review of Books*, *34*(9), 13–14. Retrieved from http://www.lrb.co.uk/v34/n09/-wanghui/the-rumour-machine. Accessed on November 23, 2015.

Wang, J., & Cui, J. (2010). Jiexi gongzufang jiangshe de "chongqing moshi" [The analysis on the "Chongqing model" of construction of public housing]. Renmin ribao [People's Daily]. Retrieved from http://paper.people.com.cn/rmrb/html/2010-09/13/nw.D110000renmrb_20100913_1-01.htm. Accessed on January 15, 2016.

Wang, S. (2012). Chinese socialism 3.0. In M. Leonard (Ed.), *China 3.0* (pp. 60–67). London: European Council on Foreign Relations.

Xinhua. (2014). China Focus: China's new plan targets quality urbanization. March 19. Retrieved from http://news.xinhuanet.com/english/indepth/2014-03/17/c_133192840.htm. Accessed on January 15, 2016.

Xinhua. (2016). Xi stresses coordinated development of southwestern Chongqing. January 6. Retrieved from http://www.kitaichina.com/se/txt/2016-01/07/content_710862.htm. Accessed on February 20, 2016.

Yang, C. (2011). Chongqing and Guangdong: Two conflicting models. In *One or two Chinese models?* London: European Council on Foreign Relations.

You, Y., & Lei, Y. (2013). "Chongqing moshi" de jingji weidu [Economic quantities of the "Chongqing model"]. *Ershi'yi shiji [The Twenty First Century]*, *135*, 50–56.

Zhao, Y. (2012). The struggle for socialism in China. The Bo Xilai Saga and beyond. *Monthly Review: An Independent Socialist Magazine*, *64*(5), 1–12. Retrieved from http://monthlyreview.org/2012/10/01/the-struggle-for-socialism-in-china/. Accessed on November 2, 2015.

SUBVERSIVE MIGRATION, CITIZENSHIP FROM BELOW AND DEMOCRACY AGAINST BORDERED CAPITALISM

Dae-oup Chang

ABSTRACT

Neoliberal globalization is not a process in which capital freely moves around the globe and exploits labor tied to families, communities and nation states. Labor often moves, wants to move and has to move in this process. Labor required by the expanding circuit of capital exists as mobile labor. However, the movement of labor is allowed in a highly selective manner, depending upon the changing needs in the spaces of capital accumulation. Nation states continue to utilize borders to control labor mobility. These borders are boundaries built upon segregation between and discrimination against people of different races, genders, nationalities and residential statuses. Whereas this "bordered global capitalism" certainly made migration more costly, uncomfortable and risky process, it could not stop the increasing flow of migration. In fact, the mobility of labor has always been central to the reproduction of capitalism while the excessive mobility of labor or "escape" of labor often threatens capitalism maintained by borders as an external expression of exclusive citizenship that gives coherence to the otherwise class-divided population. This chapter looks into the ways in which migrant labor, despite all the constraints imposed upon them by borders, struggles to form "citizenship from below" by exercising social movement citizenship and

Return of Marxian Macro-dynamics in East Asia
Research in Political Economy, Volume 32, 253–283

ISSN: 0161-7230/doi:10.1108/S0161-723020170000032014

thereby ruptures the fixed notion and institution of citizenship and migrant control regimes. The chapter does so by critically engaging with existing theories of labor migration and citizenship and presenting cases of the struggle of mobile labor in Hong Kong and South Korea.

Keywords: Neoliberal globalization; migrant labor; social movement citizenship; labor migration; Hong Kong; South Korea

INTRODUCTION

Neoliberal globalization is not a process in which capital freely moves around the globe and exploits labor tied to families, communities and nation states and sharing same national or communal identities. Contrary, labor constantly moves, wants to move and often has to move in this process. Labor required by and necessary for the expanding circuit of capital is not tied to a locality but exists as mobile labor in motion between jobs and occupations, rural communities and cities as well as one and another nation state. Indeed, the movement of labor is allowed in a highly selective manner, depending upon the changing needs for capital accumulation of given national economies. Nation states continue to utilize borders in different kinds to control labor mobility. These borders are geographical boundaries built upon segregation between and discrimination against people of different races, genders, nationalities and residential statuses. However, while this "bordered global capitalism" certainly made migration more costly, uncomfortable and risky process, it could not stop the increasing flow of migration. In fact, the mobility of labor has always been central to the reproduction of capitalism while the excessive mobility of labor or "escape" of labor often threatens the smooth reproduction of capitalism. This chapter looks into the ways in which migrant labor, despite all the constraints imposed upon them by borders, struggles to form "citizenship from below" by exercising social movement citizenship and thereby ruptures the fixed notion and institution of citizenship and migrant control regimes which form the core of the interstate management of bordered capitalism. I do so by critically engaging with existing theories of labor migration and citizenship and presenting cases of the struggle of mobile labor in Hong Kong and South Korea. These struggles of migrant workers to pursue social movement citizenship offer us an important ground for universal citizenship as an alternative to bordered capitalism.

MOBILE LABOR

A major consequence of neoliberal globalization is that the global population has become capitalist subjects who for survival have to rely directly or indirectly on the different moments of the expanding circuit of capital. It is not unusual for us to regard these new laboring populations as someone fixed and immobile whereas capital is depicted as inherently mobile. Analyses of neoliberal globalization, including that of Marxists, tend to begin with citizen-workers who hardly move beyond territories within which they reside. They therefore largely fail to integrate mobility as an inherent nature of capitalist labor. Neoliberal globalization is however *not* a process in which capital freely moves around the globe and uses labor tightly tied to families, communities and nation states and sharing same and unchanging national or communal identities. Contrary, labor also constantly moves, wants to move and often has to move in this process. Labor required by and necessary for the expanding circuit of capital is not fixed within local and national boundaries but exists as "mobile labor." That is, labor in motion between jobs and occupations, rural communities and global cities as well poorer and richer nation states.

The contemporary capitalist development provides us with ample evidence obvious enough for us to believe mobility as a central characteristic of capitalist labor. The most dramatic case of late capitalist development, that is the rise of China as a global manufacturing center demonstrates this quite clearly. The influx of young internal migrant workers from rural villages to China's coastal cities has eroded to a significant extent perhaps the most strict institutional barrier against mobile labor – the *hukou* system which was originally introduced to control rural to urban migration during the socialist era. This gradual loosening of the hukou system began with the desperate attempts of the population to escape from rural poverty and the need for global capital to take advantage of mobile labor. The number of workers employed more than six months outside their home township has reached 153 million by 2010. They account for more than half of the urban workforce and have become a "major component of the new Chinese working class" (Leung & Pun, 2009, p. 552).

Mobile labor has become an essential component of the national workforce in more advanced economies in East Asia such as South Korea and Hong Kong. The so-called "guest workers" have become a central figure in Korea's small and medium size enterprises and farms whose competitiveness relies entirely on cheap labor offered by the guest workers. South Korea's international migrant population has been growing since the government introduced the "Foreign Industrial Trainee Program" (FITP) in 1994. As a revised version of the Industrial Technical Training Program introduced in 1991 to allow companies investing overseas to bring workers to their Korean subsidies as trainees, the FITP was a desperate attempt of South Korean capitalism to overcome increasing competitive pressure in the globalizing market and the increasing labor cost in South Korea after democratization in the late 1980s (Chang, 2009, pp. 118–121). In response to the new challenges, South Korean capitalism introduced mainly two methods. On the one hand, capital began to move to countries where labor cost was cheaper. On the other hand, small and medium size firms whose capacity to move abroad was limited begun to import cheap mobile labor to South Korea. Targeting nothing but cheap and replaceable short-term labor, the FTIP naturally produced a numerous cases of verbal and physical abuse, unpaid and delayed wage, forced overtime and a wide range of discriminatory practices (Kim, 2009, p. 76; Lee, 2009, p. 370; Seol & Han, 2004, pp. 47–49). In face of the emerging criticism of the program as a modern form of slavery, the industrial trainee program has been partially replaced by the Employment Permit System (EPS) in 2004. By 2007, a renewed version of the permit program was introduced, discarding the infamous industrial trainee program. The new program allowed migrant workers to change employers but only with a consent from the previous employers and extended maximum contract period from 36 months to 58 months (Kong, Yoon, & Yu, 2010, p. 681). In 2012, the government also introduced a new scheme which allows employers to renew once more the 58-month contracts with "exemplary" workers. The South Korean government signed MOU for this program with most developing countries in Asia.[1] Since the introduction of the FTIP, the number of migrant workers had more than 10-folded, reaching approximately 720,000 by 2010 (about 24 percent of them being undocumented). These migrant workers form a significant part if not majority of the workforce in small-scale manufacturing, construction, agriculture and fishery and in doing so actually allow these industries to survive.

Mobile labor has also been a constitutive part of Hong Kong's rise to Asia's international city. Hong Kong maintained its initial industrialization by utilizing cheap refugee labor from the mainland for the emerging international division of labor since the 1960s. "Feminized off-shore proletariat" became the backbone of Hong Kong's transformation into a manufacturing city producing garment and textiles products for the markets in advanced capitalist economies during the post-war period (Sassen, 2000). Later, mobile labor has become an integral part of the reproductive sphere too as female foreign domestic workers replaced unpaid middle-class housewives for domestic labor. The increasing number of female migrant domestic workers in Hong Kong pertains to the increasing feminization of labor in Hong Kong and the persistent gender division of labor. Hong Kong shifted from manufacturing to more service and finance-driven development in the 1980s which attracted many middle-class "housewives" to jobs in the service and financial sector (Constable, 2007). By 1986, women's labor force participation exceeded 50 percent. However, pay gap between men and women persisted in these sectors and women workers could barely earn a "family wage." A solution to the absence of carers at homes and incapacity of middle-class families to afford well-paid domestic workers led to increasing demand for cheap foreign domestic workers. Consequently established was a "global care chain" (Perrons, 2004, p. 106) between domestic workers from the Philippines, Indonesia and Thailand and middle-class families in Hong Kong. As of 2015, Hong Kong has about 336,000 migrant domestic workers (Justice Centre, 2016, p. 20). They accounted for about 4.4 percent of the total Hong Kong population and 10 percent of the total workforce in Hong Kong (Justice Centre, 2016, p. 20). They are mostly women and maintain the reproduction of Hong Kong's economy by taking care of children and other domestic "duties" in middle and upper class households.

In fact, in every phase of East Asian development, from the industrialization of so-called tiger economies to the emergence of China as a global factory, mobile labor played a crucial role. Colonial development of the late 19th and early 20th in Southeast Asia involved the large-scale international migration of millions of Chinese and Indian "coolies" to work in private plantations (Breman, 1989; Kaur, 2004). It was them who maintained the "old" division of labor between the West producing manufacturing goods and the East producing primary commodities. The miraculous industrialization of Japan, Korea as well as China involved massive population flow from rural to urban cities who then participated in the newly emerging international division of labor that connects producers in the East and consumers and retailers in the West (Faison, 2007; Koo, 1990, 2001; Leung & Pun, 2009; Tsurumi, 1990). Without these mobile workforces, the current form of capitalist development would have not emerged.

Despite mobile labor persistently being an integral part of national development, the movement of mobile labor is not always viewed positively. Contrary, the movement is one of the major concerns of nation states and allowed in a highly selective manner. More often than not, the mobility of labor is regarded as a threat to national economy and security. Labor's "excessive" mobility could cause a serious problem in maintaining the space of capital accumulation. From the perspective of sending countries where often cheap labor is the only "competitive advantage," excessive mobility interrupts a smooth provision of workforce the exploitation of which is essential for capital accumulation and therefore capitalist development within the territories. From the perspective of the states of receiving countries, it undermines, as we see in what follows, the fetishized nation-state form of the space of accumulation which is maintained by borders as an external expression of exclusive citizenship that gives coherence to the otherwise class-divided population. Therefore, labor's mobility over the borders is easily criminalized and people in this "excessive" movement more often than not get excluded from access to resources, services and rights (Anderson, Sharma, & Wright, 2009, p. 10). However, labor keeps moving.

The persistent movement of labor across the world is not really new but clear manifestation of the dilemma inherent in capitalism regarding labor mobility, a dilemma between the much needed utilization of labor mobility for capital accumulation and desperate need to contain "excessive" labor mobility that possibly undermines the management of the spaces of capital accumulation (Mezzadra, 2010, p. 4). This fundamental dilemma imposes on labor a peculiar mode of mobility. On the one hand, it is necessary for labor to be mobile because otherwise, capitalist labor markets cannot function properly. None of local, regional and global labor market can be maintained without labor being mobile. On the other hand, any excessive mobility of labor or labor's attempt to escape from the spaces of exploitation is a fundamental threat to the reproduction of capitalism (Papadopolous, Stephenson, & Tsianos, 2008). The birth of capitalism began with primitive accumulation through which the ties between people and land were no longer in place. However, capitalism not only set the working people in motion but also required them to be mobile in a particular way that was conducive to capital accumulation. Once set in motion, labor during primitive accumulation has to be captured and territorialized within certain spaces of capital accumulation to provide capital with labor power. Throughout the period of primitive accumulation in Europe, the poor unsettled masses were therefore regarded a threat (Anderson, 2011) and subjected to brutal control over vagabondage (Federici, 2004; Linebaugh & Rediker, 2012; Marx, 1976). The introduction of the Poor Law made sure that the floating population was recaptured by the emerging industrial capitalists. In advanced European capitalist economies, challenges posed by mobile labor escaping from both slavery and wage labor played an important role in the way in which capitalist labor gradually took its historically specific form of "free wage labor" as "a historical compromise designed to integrate the newly released, disorganised and wandering workforce into a new regime of productivity" (Papadopolous et al., 2008, p. 204).

In *Capital*, Marx describes in his detailed chapter on primitive accumulation in England that the formation of wage labor and capitalism "proper" went through a long period of chase between escaping labor and discipline of this mobile workforce (Marx, 1976, pp. 873–940). Even after primitive accumulation and the establishment of capital relations as a natural reproductive mechanism of human societies, the possibility of "escaping the position of the seller of labour power" for another mode of subsistence continued to be an essential threat to capitalism in general (Papadopolous et al., 2008, p. 204). Since then, the history of capitalism is marked by the constantly changing balance between the utilization and containment of mobile labor. As both take turns to emerge as a more decisive element shaping particular capitalist developmental pathways throughout the history of primitive accumulation, national industrialization, colonization, empire and nation-state building and neoliberal globalization, we also witness continuing struggles between the movement of labor beyond the given space of capital accumulation and the reterritorialization of labor within the newly formulated spaces of accumulation. This fundamental dynamics of capitalist development continues to play an important role well into the 21st century as primitive accumulation and/or neoliberal accumulation by dispossession involve the release of labor from land and non-capitalist social relations, followed by the massive escape of people from extreme dispossession and subsequent attempts of capital and the state, often with fear from the excessive movement of the "mob," to recapture labor by containing labor mobility to the extent it does not undermine but serves valorization of capital (Ferguson & McNally, 2015).

VALORIZATION BORDERS, CITIZENSHIP AND BORDERED CAPITALISM

This fundamental dilemma of capitalism necessitates capitalism to establish and maintain what can be called "*valorization borders*" – the borders that regulate labor's mobility in a way it can be utilizable for the valorization of capital without moving beyond the requirement of valorization. Valorization borders are essentially a filtering device that decides (1) who are allowed to move, (2) when they are allowed to move and (3) how they are allowed to move. Valorization borders take many different spatial and institutional forms as they unfold. When hundreds of thousands of Chinese and Indian Collies were brought into Java and Sumatra in the Indonesian archipelagos for booming private plantations in the late 19th and the early 20th centuries, valorization borders did not exist in the form of national borders. It is true that Southeast Asia was experiencing for the first time clearly defined borders that could be drawn on the maps of the new colonial states.[2] However, borders were at best flexible while the colonial authorities were busy sourcing plantation labor from all over Asia. The actual borders were therefore drawn not between national territories but in the middle of thick tropical forests within the Dutch colonial territory, separating those workers from the local population and subjecting them to the private rule of planters. Those workers were allowed to sell their labor power by migrating all the way from China and India to the Dutch colonial territory. However, they were contained within the boundary of private plantations they worked (Breman, 1989). For many, the jobs they found after a long journey shared more features with slaves than with free wage workers. Although there was no border agency in the Dutch territory, "the use of the indenture contract in reality restricted mobility and prevented the free operation of market force" (Kaur, 2004, p. 53), functioning as a *de facto* valorization border within which the workers had to serve for the valorization of capital.

In contemporary capitalism, it is the territorial borders of nation states that are the central valorization borders managing this peculiar mobility of capitalist labor. The nation-state system that governs global capitalism relies upon national borders, first of all, to contain the national workforce within the national space of accumulation. In this sense, national borders resemble the boundaries of colonial plantations which restricted the movement of slaves. Contained within the boundaries of the plantation, workers became slaves. Contained within national borders, workers become the national workforce. Although containing the national workforce within the national space of accumulation is an important function of contemporary national borders, this function has not been focused much because this can be achieved only by another function of borders that is to protect national space of accumulation from the excessive inward movement of foreign workforce.[3] Nation states introduce various new border controls to curve the excessive inward mobility of labor. They do so collectively to one another and thereby effectively build borders between spaces of accumulation. Bold racist discrimination, incarceration, torture and forced deportation are commonly used methods to control the inward movement of labor. On the other hand, nation states also recognize the necessity to utilize mobile labor. Borders often allow labor to flow into the national space of accumulation according to the varying need of the valorization of capital.

The borders of the nation-state system are far from being perfect in managing the threat of excessive mobility. As we observe in the current attempts of European countries and the United States to reduce the number of migrant workers from poorer neighboring countries, these national borders certainly made the movement of labor more uncomfortable, expensive and dangerous process for many. However, their effort to do so has not been effective enough to stop the increasing flow of mobile labor beyond the territorial borders of nation states. Labor constantly moves no matter what, escaping from misery and insecurity caused either by capitalism itself or dispossession caused by capitalist development. Hence, what the increasing securitization of borders, the "proliferation of borders" (Mezzadra & Neilson, 2013) and the emergence of a global Apartheid (Balibar, 2004) manifest is not the strength of borders but the increasing tension between the containment and movement of labor. In face of increasing tension, borders are almost always defensive rather than offensive. As De Genova (2016, p. 50) puts it:

> Much as the subjective (creative, productive) force of labour necessarily always precedes its objectification as capital, the primacy of the autonomy and subjectivity of human freedom of movement is a recalcitrant and obstreperous force that precedes and exceeds any border authority's capacities for comprehensive regimentation and control.

The constant movement of labor and "irregularity" of labor mobility forces nation states to regularize the flow by constantly reterritorializing mobile labor. In this way, the national space of accumulation is constantly challenged and maintained (Papadopolous et al., 2008). All the institutional arrangements making the borders into what we know now, including clearly defined frontiers, passport control, visas, immigration laws and residency permits, have emerged from the constant attempts to maintain national space of accumulation. These institutions have not been around for a long time, though. Individual travelers were barely carrying passports before the modernization of national borders (Morris-Suzuki, 2006, p. 11) although the origin of passports can be dated back to the reign of William the Conqueror, who feared that others would emulate his successful invasion (Cohen, 2006, p. 4). Despite frequent warfare between appearing and disappearing kingdoms, few territorial borders were heavily fortressed or guarded constantly. It was only the first two decades of the 20th century when European nation states began to introduce modern border control. Even then, modern borders were not about preventing human mobility in general. As a form of valorization borders, national borders evolved essentially as a filtering device for "undesirable" people. Just as the early control of the movement of people within the national territories targeted the poorest segment of the population, modern national borders had specific targets to control. First of all, newly introduced restrictive border control was a matter of national security against the "subversive migration" of foreign radicals spreading potentially dangerous ideas. For example, the first Aliens Bill in England was introduced in 1793. The target of this legislation was revolutionaries from France whose possible infiltration would spread the spirit of the French Revolution (Torpey, 2000, p. 94). The First World War also encouraged Britain to strengthen border control to prevent both subversives and enemy agents from entering its territory (Morris-Suzuki, 2006, p. 13). The fear of being infiltrated by clandestine revolutionary organizations and enemies increased even more in the face of the Russian Revolution (Morris-Suzuki, 2006, p. 13). Japan also introduced modern border control in the 20th century in an attempt to reduce the number of subversive foreigners who were likely to undermine Japan's interest. Communist expansion in the Korean Peninsula and Chinese mainland in the early 1950s encouraged Japan to tighten its border control by introducing the Migration Control Ordinance in 1951 (Morris-Suzuki, 2006, p. 17).

Border control designed to curve subversive migration cannot be separated from a broader institutional arrangement to control the movement of labor. It is quite apparent that national borders as a filtering device are designed most of all as a class institution. In fact, up until now, poor workers from poorer countries form the majority of "unwanted people" subjected to a strict filtering process. For instance, Japan's earlier border regime was largely a product of constant efforts of the Imperial government to put under control the flow of the poor segment of colonial subjects, mainly Korean peasants and workers. While national borders were increasingly becoming the supreme institution to regulate the flow of the laboring population, a complicated system of classification of the Imperial population also developed to give different status to different people with different ethnic and class backgrounds (Kim, 2014). The post-War Japanese government used this border regime to contain "illegal" migration of laborers from Korea in the 1950s and 1960s (Morris-Suzuki, 2006, p. 17). It was the case in the United Kingdom too. The British Alien Act of 1905 stipulated that non-British subjects who were poor would be categorized as "undesirable immigrants" and denied their entry to Britain (Anderson, 2013, p. 37). When the cross-border mobility of the working class population is tolerated, they are taken not as full humans but as a container of labor power. The once-popular Gastarbeiter system, introduced to address acute labor shortage in advanced European economies during the post-War boom, strictly controlled the in-and-out flow of the working class population by bilateral agreements denying their rights to abode in the countries where they worked and resided for several years. Perhaps, the best example of the border being a class institution is the so-called investment migration schemes that the states of advanced capitalist economies such as the United Kingdom and Australia have been introducing competitively. This is a means of attracting foreigners carrying a significant amount of capital and reveals the nature of the apparently class-based decisions about migration cases. Current border control clearly manifests that "the anxiety about immigration is an anxiety about the mobility of the global poor" (Anderson, 2014, p. 9).

National borders are also *racial institutions*. It has been so from the very beginning. In all advanced capitalist economies, restrictive border regulations were particularly designed to prevent the movement of not just poor people but specifically poor people of particular colors and ethnicities, creating a racial hierarchy cutting across the flow of the working class population of different origins. Race-based categories and hierarchy were by and large products of European colonialism, with which colonizers could naturalize and thereby justify their rule over colored colonial subjects. These categories and hierarchy not only helped colonial masters keep colonial subjects where they were but also created a persistent hunger for whiteness as a symbol of ideal humans. As white supremacy became an important justification for their colonial rule abroad, constituting and maintaining internal white homogeneity vis-à-vis external heterogeneity became increasingly important concerns of the colonial projects of European states (Anderson, 2013). As a result, maintaining whiteness had become a constitutive part of the establishment of modern border control. It was particularly so for settler colonies where white supremacy needed to be maintained not only in relation to the newly immigrating population but also in relation to the colored indigenous population.

As Morris-Suzuki (2006, pp. 11–12) pointed out, Australia's Immigration Restriction Act of 1901 was introduced specifically to curve the immigration of colored people, particularly Chinese immigrants. This legislation later became a founding stone for White Australia' policy (Anderson, 2013, p. 34). Nothing could be more apparently racist than America's early immigration control which aimed to satisfy both the desperate need for labor and whiteness of the United States by allowing only European and non-European white migrants to cross US border. The US government introduced the Immigration Act of 1882 which prevented a certain group of people, such as "convicts, lunatics, idiots and person likely to become public charges" (Torpey, 2000, p. 97). Along with these unwanted people, all Chinese laborers were banned from entering the United States by the Chinese Exclusion Act of 1882, which was introduced together with the general immigration law. The Immigration Act of 1924 revealed this discrimination is not about certain nationality but about skin color. The Act comprised the National Origins Act and Asian Exclusion Act, which banned the immigration of people from *all* Asian countries. Britain also invented a complicated system of categorizing foreigners to filter the human flow from former colonies. Initially, British border control was not about aliens or immigrants but about the movement of British subjects within the British dominions. It was the 1962 Common Wealth Immigrants Act that began to deal with the movement of subjects as an immigration issue. The Act "recognized different classes of British Subjects by differentiating passports" (Anderson, 2013, p. 39). Citizens of the United Kingdom and Colonies (CUKC), although they were all British subjects, were now differentiated according to the passport-issuing authorities. The CUKC whose passports were given by the British government, mostly white British subjects, were not subjected to immigration control whereas the holders of CUKC passports issued by colonial governments, mostly non-White British subjects, could have been denied to enter Britain (Anderson, 2013, p. 40).

The fact that modern borders function as a class and racial institution shows that borders are not only territorial relations but also, more importantly, social relations. Borders represent unequal social relations between the rich and poor, white and colored. Furthermore, borders do not only represent these social relations but also reproduce them in a fetishistic way. In other words, as the guardians of the state, national borders are not only a form of valorization borders but also a fetishistic form of valorization borders. First of all, borders effectively translate gendered and racialized class relations of global capitalism into a binary relation between "us and them" (Anderson, 2013). While it is quite obvious that borders are racial and class institutions to "THEM" waiting for entry permission or deportation in detention camps, they are not so apparently discriminatory institutions to "US" residing within the heavily protected borders. To "US," borders appear to have nothing to do with social relations of inequality. Rather they appear to be a mere territorial demarcation which distinguishes "our" communities with locally grown values, lifestyles and often "artificially constructed" ethnic homogeneity from THEM. The functions that national borders as valorization borders essentially play to reproduce capitalist social relations in the national spaces of accumulation appear to be "natural" functions that protect national interests and interests of citizens. In doing so, national borders increase the fetishistic nature of the reproduction of unequal class and gender relations through the state form by diluting the inherent tensions between "US."[4]

Here "we" are basically holders of citizenship. Citizenship in its most simplistic definition is membership of a nation state that allows those members' to enjoy rights and entitlements. However, citizenship is not merely a legal entitlement and status. According to Anderson (2014, p. 3), nation states "do not simply portray themselves as arbitrary collections of people held together by a common legal status but as *communities of value,* comprised of people who share common ideals and patterns of behaviours." Citizenship is, therefore, the *membership of the particular community of value* while the role of the border is to "protect" the community of value by filtering unacceptable outsiders possibly undermining the particular set of local values and thereby deciding who is in and who is out. Indeed, values that make a particular community unique are imagined and fabricated rather than real. Nevertheless, borders present these values as a set of necessary virtues of all citizens. In so doing, borders effectively present citizens within the national borders as if they are all hardworking and law-abiding. Although hardworking is an essential requirement for migrant workers to be accepted, it is not the only requirement. "Good characters" required for them also include being "'good wives' who do not challenge patriarchal families, 'straight guys and gals' who adhere to correct sexual scripts, and 'good parents' whose parenting accords with the requirements to produce 'good children'" (Anderson et al., 2009, p. 7). Borders impose these values upon migrants.

Those who are allowed to cross territorial borders therefore still have to deal with borders (of the community of value) that not only require them to serve the economic needs of hosting countries, cities and communities but also request them to follow the "ideal types" of the locals that are "imagined" against unwanted people. In this sense, borders do not exist in the frontiers but follow migrants into the society. As a result, accepted migrants often become the guardians of the community of value, striving to be good citizens (Anderson, 2014, p. 6). In so doing, mobile labor is *constantly disciplined* in a way that it cannot be a threat to the imagined local ideal types. Also importantly, borders also constantly remind citizens of the "values" of the community, their entitlement and "privileges" by imposing these values upon migrants. Furthermore, it sets up standards for citizen's proper social and political behavior so that they can only pursue their rights within the existing system of justice. Subversive acts of citizens pursuing their rights beyond the existing system of justice are deemed undesirable and punishable. In this way, citizenship, which was achieved through centuries of struggles for radical social transformation, turns into an *anti-democratic machine* that reproduces status quo within borders, constantly disciplines non-citizen others and thereby becomes a border itself. This is the reason why borders are central to the reproduction of global capitalism. This central role played by borders to the central and distinctive feature of capitalist labor allows us to define contemporary capitalism as "*bordered capitalism*." They divide and rule the global working class by turning them into "US" and "THEM." Consequently, they strengthen the fetishistic state function to dilute tensions and conflicts among "US." They constantly force migrants to fit into communities of value and remove the subversive nature of citizenship once created through struggles for democracy.

SUBVERSIVE AGENCY OF MIGRANT LABOR

The vast majority of migrant workers have no citizenship or opportunity to gain one. But they do manifest agency, the nature of which can often be more antagonistic than that of citizen-workers. The subversive agency of migrant labor is almost completely neglected in mainstream migration literature. Neo-classical migration theories describe migration as a trans-historically "natural" process through which the supply and demand in the labor market move towards equilibrium. It is a natural phenomenon that labor migrates from places where labor is abundant and cheap to places where labor is expensive and short of supply. Cheap labor cost is the most important "push" factor while real or "expected" higher income in the destination is the single most important "pull" factor (Borjas, 1989; Todaro, 1969; Harris & Todaro, 1970). Although labor migration is a consequence of labor market conditions given to the individuals, the act of migration is deemed as a consequence of the rational cost–benefit calculation of the individuals. Therefore, migration is a consequence of an individual's rational choice in maximizing economic interests within the given structural position. At a glance, it seems that the neo-classical theory of migration recognizes agency of human individuals. However, it is not that difficult to notice that the theory has nothing to do with the agency of migrant labor. Here, individuals, who make decisions to move, are not "living individuals" but an embodiment of economic rationality whose function is constantly calculating cost effectiveness in market conditions *on behalf of* the market. This neo-classical "agency" is utterly one-dimensional in the sense that it is at best half a human agency whose capacity is constrained as a factor of production. The neo-classical theory of migration is therefore essentially a dead labor theory of migration, a theory that sees labor as a commodity, an object, and a means of production.

This fundamental shortcoming is at least partially shared by both the new economics of migration and Marxist political economy of migration. The new economics of migration emphasizes the mediation of other social institutions, such as families and kinship networks in making decisions to migrate. The theory presents the market as a social institution in an attempt to overcome the methodological individualism of the neo-classical theory and offer a better explanation of the reasons why some people migrate and some do not despite the same push and pull factors conditioning them. Although this approach to migration can reveal much more subtle social dynamics underneath the complexity of migration by paying proper attention to more diverse subjective dimensions, this does not, or perhaps does not intend to, provide "a way out of conceiving mobility in terms of coercion, or simply as an economically or socially induced trigger to migration" (Andrijasevic & Anderson, 2009, p. 364), nor does it provide politics of migration that "structurally exceeds the (re)bordering practices of politics of control" (Mezzadra, 2010, p. 1). Migration is still regarded as a flight for better economy. What the act of migrating ultimately aims appears to be "commercial citizenship" (Mezzadra, 2010, p. 7), the image of which is migrants running corner shops and Kebab restaurants without being threatened daily by life and death matters. Therefore, the neo-classical dead labor theory of migration remains intact – migration is essentially a flight of laborers in search for a better opportunity to sell commodity labor. In this theory, the migrant agency remains to be incomplete as migrants appear to have only economic subjectivity without political subjectivity. The Marxist political economy of migration brings a political dimension to the understanding of mobile labor by emphasizing the political origin and consequence of migration. Marxists focus on unequal relations and centuries-long exploitative infrastructure between economies at cores and peripheries (Baran, 1957; Frank, 1966, 1967; Wallerstein, 1974, 1979). These relations promote constant flow of migration from poverty-stricken developing countries to wealthier countries and also subject workers from developing countries to the extreme forms of exploitation and discrimination in developed countries (Castle & Kosack, 1973; Cohen, 1987; Potts, 1990). The Marxist political economy of migration has also addressed the need of developed economies to utilize cheap migrant workforce for services essential to their ever growing and internationalizing urban economies (Piore, 1979; Sassen, 1988, 1991). Harvey's theory of accumulation by dispossession (Harvey, 2005, 2006) and flexible accumulation (Harvey, 1990) offers a firm analysis of both the reason why despite risks involved in migration journeys an increasing number of workers decide to migrate and the necessity for developed economies to host cheap and flexible migrant workforce. However, Marxist studies tend to view migrant workers simply as victims and migration as something to be treated with proper national capitalist development or socialist restructuring of the global order. Whereas the Marxist political economy of migration rightly presents a political theory of migration, the politics of migration is politics without agency. In doing so, the traditional Marxist theory often fails to recognize the agency of migrant labor fully.

In all these theories, migration is presented something abnormal or negative. It is associated with inequality in contrast to equality or imbalance in contrast to the perfectly functioning market. For these theories, "migration is always-already a problem: an aberrant form of behaviours in need of fixing" vis-à-vis "an ideal view of the world that is one in which people seldom, if ever, move and societies more or less 'closed'" (Anderson et al., 2009, p. 9). Solutions for this social "problem" are always out of the hand of migrants themselves. A solution either lies in the development of the underdeveloped or political mobilization of someone else – mostly the citizen-workers of hosting countries. The agency of migrants as political subjects is therefore implicitly transferred to someone else who could do politics properly. In other words, migrants are "constructed as objects of control, rescue, and redemption rather than as full human beings" through either humanitarian actions of "others" or freer market flow of labor power commodity (Anderson et al., 2009, p. 8). These theories peripheralize migrants vis-à-vis citizen-workers. In these theories, migrants can show the incomplete agency of themselves only through the mirror of the complete agency of citizen-workers. Migrants are presented as congealed desires to become like "US." In fact, this resembles the relations between the proper self of colonial masters and the permanently incomplete self of colonial subjects in which the colonial subjects are constantly reminded of the inferior self vis-à-vis the modern and superior white masters. This is the educational impact of many programs and campaigns "for" migrants, which are run by pro-migrant organizations of citizen-workers.

In an attempt to address the incapacity of migration theories to recognize the agency of migrant labor, more contemporary Marxian critiques, loosely associated with the discussions of the autonomy of migration, provide rather very insightful points for a better theory of migration. Their starting point is to consider "migrant agency as a constituent force of social change and the primacy of mobility for investigating the present political conjuncture" (Andrijasevic & Anderson, 2009, p. 366). It is an effort to shed light on the role of the migrant agency as living labor in social transformation (Anderson, 2009; Andrijasevic & Anderson, 2009; Andrajasevic, 2009; De Genova, 2002, 2005, 2009; Mezzadra, 2010; Mezzadra & Neilson, 2013; Papadopolous et al., 2008). Emphasizing the agency of migrants is not to argue that migrants are "inherently" *more subversive* than citizens. It is rather to recognize the fact that migrant labor is not less a contradictory combination of living and dead labor than that of citizens. It is important to notice that "the subversive potential is characteristic of the social force of all labor, ever indeterminate in its centrality – as subject – within while yet against capital" (De Genova, 2009, p. 461). It is however equally important to realize that "the question of the subjectivity of labour is especially acute in the socio-political predicaments of migrant workers, particularly at the apparently opposite extremes of (guest workers) 'legality' and undocumented 'illegality'" (De Genova, 2009, p. 461). It is this particularly harsh conditions within which migrant workers survive and possibly become a dangerous class with transformative power. Migrants are understood as transformative social actors not simply because of their mode of existence of being mobile but because of their acts as real political subjects in their migrant journeys, the acts taken "at the edges of the space of citizenship" (Mezzadra & Neilson, 2013, p. 256).

This new trend of radical migration studies focuses not only spatial mobility but also on "real political dynamics and the ruptures" migration "produces within the existing order, in particular in relation to what is supposed to be its opposite, namely citizenship" (Andrijasevic & Anderson, 2009, p. 364). In doing so, they avoid "seeing migrants as either the thoroughly commodified victims of a singular logic of global capitalism, or pioneers who through their agency, border-crossings and forms of hybridity are in the vanguard of progressive post-colonial and post-national possibilities" (Chalcraft, 2007, p. 46). It is only in concrete *acts of subversion* through which migrants "might also provide a way for counter-hegemonic practice, rather than demeaning or fetishising its commodified subjects, to make linkages to existing elements within subaltern practice and ambition" (Chalcraft, 2007, p. 47). De Genova (2009, p. 453), witnessing the collective actions taken by migrants in the United States, describes the way in which the defetishizing acts of migrant agency transformed themselves from objects to subjects:

> Thus, undocumented labour, which the legislative debate had sought to render its *object*, audaciously stepped forward again, now on a genuinely massive scale, to effectively reaffirm that migrant workers were truly *subjects* in this struggle. Indeed, they were the subjects in a double and inextricably contradictory sense. They were subjects as labour *for* capital, and thus, the veritable source of value, upon which capital is constitutively dependent. They were also subjects as labour *against* capital, engaged in a mass act of insubordination and an expression of the irreconcilable antagonism that conjoins labour and capital in a mutually constitutive social relation.

Migrant labor reveals its subversive agency through repeated challenges to borders constantly (re) created by the attempts of capital and the state to balance the utilization and containment of labor mobility. In doing so, they show us that migrants have agency for transformative social changes (Anderson, 2009, p. 11). These challenges posed by migrant agency bring a new tension to citizenship, which lies at the center of the liberal democratic form of capitalism, as a dynamic institution of domination and empowerment (Isin, 2009, p. 371). As we saw above, exclusive citizenship itself is a border drawing a line between rights-holding insiders and rights-lacking outsiders. By challenging the border of citizenship, migrants can become "a key actor in reshaping, contesting, and redefining the borders of citizenship" (Mezzadra & Neilson, 2013, p. 257). They rely upon self-claimed citizenship that is different from citizens' citizenship protected and expressed by borders. It is rather "social movement citizenship" that is *a social movement towards universal citizenship that goes beyond borders*. This is an unknown territory and has never been achieved by citizen-workers living in bordered capitalism who have been "enjoying" exclusive citizenship. The social movement citizenship builds citizenship from below just as the early democratization movement has done once, challenging the existing mode of citizenship as a border institution based on immobility, fixed territoriality and identity distinction between us and them.

SOCIAL MOVEMENT CITIZENSHIP TOWARDS DEMOCRACY AGAINST BORDERED CAPITALISM

The struggles of migrant workers in Hong Kong and South Korea are quite illustrative to prove that migrants with its potentially subversive agency are becoming a key actor in challenging the borders of citizenship. In Hong Kong, foreign domestic workers from the Philippines, Indonesia and Thailand form the bottom layer of the labor market. The monthly minimum wage for migrant domestic workers increased only 3.9 percent between 1998 and 2012 whereas Hong Kong's median monthly income rose about 15 percent during the same period (Justice Centre, 2016, p. 21). Hong Kong's new minimum wage of HKD32.5 per hour, introduced in 2015, does not cover migrant domestic workers. In addition to low wages, they are often subjected to extreme forms of exploitation, including a slave-like contract with employment agencies, non-payment of wages, verbal abuses, physical punishment, controlled food provision and sexual harassment, by more powerful actors along the care chain. They are more vulnerable to such forms of exploitation largely because their labor process and relations are "domestically ruled" due to the live-in arrangement commonly imposed on migrant domestic workers. This allows direct control over their bodies rather than their "labor power." Consequently, workers' hair-style, dress-code, bathing time, habits and cultural and religious values all became a matter of control and discipline. Also, this allows extremely vague separation between working and non-working hours, which make them literally 24-hour on-call workers. While the government's standard labor contract cannot prevent abuses in confined and isolated workplaces, employers consider domestic labor personal rather than public and therefore constantly attempt to modify state-regulations written in the contract (Constable, 2002, 2007). Regarding domestic work as personal also encourages these employers to think that it is an easy job to be done without any skills – therefore "natural" to be cheap. It is through these harsh working conditions that migrant workers who were normally "humble" and "afraid of employers" in their home become increasingly defiant and begin to take action for change (A Thai domestic worker-activist, personal interview, March 20, 2016).

However, increasing discontent among migrant domestic workers does not easily turn into collective subversive action. Migrant domestic workers in Hong Kong have great difficulties in mobilizing protests against the extreme forms of exploitation mainly because of two reasons: firstly they are essentially two-year contracted workers and the renewal of their labor contracts entirely depends on the unilateral evaluation of the employers. They have to leave the city after termination of a contract unless they manage to find another employer in two-week; secondly, as mentioned above, they are to reside in the employers' homes and therefore live and work in isolation from workers in the same working environment. These are the reasons why, in the face of long working hours and ingenious disciplinary measures devised by employers and employment agencies, the majority of migrant workers rely on more passive and individual forms of resistance at work, such as foot-dragging. However, migrant domestic workers are also increasingly demonstrating their subversive agency, and their protest takes more and more collective forms, often challenging their non-citizen status and moving beyond "limited" citizenship Hong Kong residents enjoy.

Migrant workers' activism has at least a three-decade-long history in Hong Kong. As early as the 1980s, migrant workers started forming grass-root help groups and associations as well as opening shelters for migrant workers who had been victimized by their employers. At this initial stage, helps from concerned locals and religious organizations played a vital role in publicizing cases of abuses mostly against Filipino migrant workers and establishing migrant organizations aiming to enhance living and working conditions of migrants workers. The Mission for Filipino Migrant Workers (MFMW), pursuing a liberation-theology type of social justice popular in democratization movement in the Philippines at the time, was established as the first of such kind organizations in 1981. By engaging with several campaigns addressing anti-migrants policies of the Hong Kong and Filipino authority and the government of the Philippines, this initiative later developed into multiple directions, making alliances with other small migrant campaign groups as wells as domestic labor movement organizations in Hong Kong. The struggle against Filipino government's attempt to introduce a stricter remittance requirement in 1982, for instance, made Filipino organizations work together and gave birth to United Filipinos in Hong Kong (UNIFIL) in 1985 (Constable, 2007, pp. 160–161). While UNIFIL continued to be an effective vehicle for campaigns for rights of Filipino workers, Filipino migrant workers' movements in the early days also influenced Indonesian and Thai migrant workers whose number was steadily increasing in the 1990s (Hsia, 2009).

The increasing visibility and strength of the migrant movement encouraged Indonesian, Thai and South Asian domestic workers to form their own grassroot organizations such as Association of Indonesian Domestic Workers (ATKI, established in 2000), Far East Overseas Nepalese Association (FEONA, established in 1993) and Thai Regional Alliance in Hong Kong (2001). These new organizations have been built upon the earlier experience of Filipino organizations. Both MFMW and UNIFIL have been instrumental for the attempts of diverse migrant communities to build such organizations (Hsia, 2009). Bethune House, a shelter established in 1987 for distressed women migrants of any nationality played an important role in the passing experience of organizing and protesting from the earlier to newer generation migrant activists from different countries. Many migrant workers who had once relied upon services provided by Bethune House played important roles Hong Kong's migrant movement later. Individual workers' struggles against injustice also often led to more collective initiatives of migrant workers. Indonesian workers' legal battle against employers' abuses in 1993 led to the formation of the Indonesian Group of Hong Kong. Also important was that migrant groups from different countries began to build solidarity between different nationalities. This effort led to the establishment of Asian Migration Coordination Body (AMCB) in 1996

Since the late 1990s, migrant workers movements made several important developments. First of all, there has been quantitative and qualitative development regarding the number, capacity and scope of migrant organizations. The migrant workers movement became vocal and visible by launching several city-wide campaigns, including the campaign against 20 percent cut in minimum allowable wage during the Asian economic crisis of 1998, the campaign against HK$ 400 levy in 2001 and the campaign against government-proposed wage cut in 2002 all of which involved intensive mobilization of mass-rallies participated by thousands of migrant workers. At the same time, migrant organizations and Asian Migrant Centre (AMC), a Hong Kong-based regional NGO, enthusiastically assisted workers from different countries to set up trade unions of workers with same nationalities (Filipino domestic worker-activists, personal interview, April 10, 2016), leading to the establishment of a numerous trade unions, including Filipino Migrant Workers Union (established in 1998), the Indonesian Migrant Workers Union (established in 2000), the Filipino Domestic Helpers General Union (established in 2003), Filipino Domestic Workers General Union Hong Kong (established in 2005), the Union of Nepalese Domestic Workers (established in 2005), Thai Migrant Workers Union (established in 2009), Overseas Domestic Workers Union (established in 2012) and Progressive Labor Union of Domestic Workers (established in 2012).

These migrant organizations are most of all service providing organizations. They provide migrant workers with legal education programs about their rights in Hong Kong, communities of belonging and shelters. They also offer their members troubled with employers various personal advice on how to take suitable action to handle individual cases. Their methods include T-shirts campaign,[5] legal disputes, changing employers, negotiation etc. Their constant organizing campaign is often done at the massive gathering of migrant workers who become the majority "occupying" the Central on every Sunday (Constable, 2007, pp. 166–167). By taking advantage of this occasion, migrant organizations turned the subtle individual resistance of migrant workers into a more active form of collective resistance against their lack of rights at work. By joining the subtle form of resistance, migrant workers turn their individual problems into a collective issue. Again by joining activities of migrant associations and unions, they turn these collective actions into political actions and in so doing claim universal citizenship for all. The basis of their claim for universal citizenship is quite simple and straight forward. Migrants are "humans" and therefore "same" as locals. Hong Kong is a "society" which has a duty to "protect labor" (A Thai domestic worker-activist, personal interview, March 20, 2016).

By 2000s, migrants' struggles not only dealt with migrant issues but also began to address local political issues as a part of their claim for universal citizenship. Their effort to build citizenship from below met local attempts to attain half-achieved citizens' rights in increasingly authoritarianizing Hong Kong. Migrant workers have also become one of the most supportive groups in Hong Kong's democratization movement, often forming a majority group in anti-government rallies. It is an interesting dimension of migrants' subversive action in Hong Kong – migrant workers who live without citizenship in Hong Kong participate in democratization rallies with local Hong Kong citizens who have every right but the right to elect their government. Non-citizens' aspiration for democracy goes beyond that of the local majority population, reminding locals of the missing elements in their citizenship that look otherwise just fine to many local citizens. In other words, migrants act as more citizens than local citizens.

Through this mutual support between local and migrant social movements, another important step forward has been made by an on-going effort to build solidarity between migrant and local domestic workers. This effort has been finally materialized with the establishment of a Hong Kong Confederation of Trade Unions (HKCTU) affiliated federation, the Federation of Asian Domestic Workers Unions in Hong Kong (FADWU) in November 2010, which comprise of Thai, Indonesian, Hong Kong, Filipino and Nepalese domestic workers (Choi, 2011). The solidarity building between the Hong Kong labor movement and migrant movements has been a mutual process. In other words, migrants' claim of their political subjectivity would not have been possible without support from local social movements. While the HKCTU has been supportive of migrant workers movement from the very early days despite heavy criticism of local population against the HKCTU (Tang, 2010), the migrant workers movement has become an integral and important part of the social movement of Hong Kong in general and the labor movement in particular.

Perhaps, the culmination of the attempt of migrant workers to pursue social movement citizenship was migrant workers' involvement in an anti-WTO protest in 2005. It was the migrant movement that was at the frontline of publicizing the issues of injustice caused by neoliberal globalization in Hong Kong during a week-long protest. At the beginning of the People's Action Week (11–18 December 2005), it was migrant workers organizations which played an important if not a leading role in mobilizing the struggle. More than 1,500 migrant workers participated, for example in the first mass demonstration in protest to the 6th WTO ministerial conference. The Hong Kong SAR government raided an office of an Indonesian migrant workers organization on 13th, in an attempt to stop migrant workers from being involved in upcoming protests. Nevertheless, migrant workers mostly from the Philippines, Indonesia and Thailand participated in the protest until the end of People's Action Week as a third biggest group next to delegates from South Korea and volunteers and activists of the Hong Kong People's Alliance. In doing so, they risked arrest and deportation and exercised social movement citizenship.

Despite all predicaments, migrant domestic workers in Hong Kong have been struggling not to accept their migrant status as given, by acting as what Isin calls "activist citizens" who are "not priori actors recognised by law" – but "by enacting themselves through acts they affect the law that misrecognizes them" (Isin, 2009, p. 382). "By contrast to active citizens who act out already written scripts such as voting, taxpaying and enlisting, activist citizens engage in writing scripts and creating scene" (Isin, 2009, p. 381). "Acts of citizenship produce subjects as citizens" and activist citizens "constitute themselves as those with the right to claim right" (Isin, 2009, p. 371). In the search for universal citizenship, they claim more than they are granted by policies balancing the utilization and containment of labor mobility. In doing so, they are resisting the attempt to fix their identity according to the needs of the expanding circuit of capital and questioning the local mode of citizenship itself. In 2010, migrant workers in Hong Kong with support from various migrant advocacy groups finally initiated a legal challenge to the fundamental basis of the full-scale discrimination against women migrant workers – the fact that they are the only ones not entitled to the right to abode among many "types" of migrants. Although the campaign was unsuccessful, this campaign has put the issues of migrant workers' rights at the center of political debates in Hong Kong.

Social movement citizenship is also pursued by migrant workers in South Korea. The long history of the hyper-exploitation of migrant workers through the exploitative FITP, the flawed EPS, and the border agency's infamous manhunt-style seasonal deportation campaigns have created a fairly militant migrant movement in South Korea.[6] Like in Hong Kong, migrant workers' movement has emerged in close cooperation with local social movement organizations and Korean trade unions. The movement was initiated in a desperate attempt of the industrial trainees to secure basic human rights for migrant workers. Under the Industrial Trainee System, migrant workers had "no basic rights, no human rights, no labour rights and discrimination was rampant" (The President of Migrant Workers Trade Union, personal interview, April 18, 2016). In 1994, victims of industrial accidents and employers' abuse organized a protest action accusing the industrial trainee program of being modern slavery and calling for respect for the human rights of those recruited (Jung, 2012, p. 67). In 1995, the migrant workers' movement began to earn more public attention with a sit-in strike of 13 Nepalese industrial trainees in the Myungdong Cathedral in downtown Seoul that is well-known as the birthplace of the 1987 democratization movement (Kim, 2012, p. 682). Many demands of the striking migrant workers, such as "We are not slaves" "Don't hit us please" (Kim, 2012, p. 683), were echoing the slogans of the great workers struggle of 1987, reminded the Korean labor movement that these problems were still not things of the past, and attracted the solidarity of social movements in Korea. As a consequence, a nation-wide support network called the Joint Committee for Migrants in Korea (JCMK) was formed by as many as 38 Korean civil, religious and labor organizations in the aftermath of the first sit-in strike of migrant workers (Kim, 2012, p. 682).[7]

In following years, the migrant workers movement in South Korea gained confidence through well-organized struggles against the industrial trainee program, such as 69 days of sit-in strike in 2002. This period was a turning point for the migrant workers movement in South Korea in many senses. First of all, a group of activists in the JCMK and first-generation migrant worker-activists became increasingly critical of the organization's strategy. Although the JCMK played a major role in supporting the migrant workers movement, some major participants of the JCMK have also been criticized regarding their view of migrant workers as passive victims to be protected by Korean citizens rather than proper political subjects capable of building their own movement. These activists proposed to see migrant issues from a perspective of the working class rather than from the philanthropic or religious point of view (The Coordinator of Migrant Workers Support Network, personal interview, April 20, 2016). This critique of the citizen-oriented approach to migrant issues led to the establishment of the first migrants-only branch in the Seoul-Gyeongi Equal Trade Union in 2001. The migrant branch argued that (1) migrant workers needed to represent themselves rather than being represented by citizens, (2) class-based approach should replace human right–based approach, and (3) comprehensive labor rights rather than policy reform had to be the ultimate aim of the migrant workers movement (Jung, 2014, p. 13).

The migrant workers movement was no longer a movement of a small group of migrant activists who could not sustain their movement without support from Korean activists. Rather, the migrant branch of the Equal Trade Union got successfully embedded in migrant communities (The Coordinator of Migrant Workers Support Network, personal interview, April 20, 2016) so that the union could mobilize a rally with more than a thousand strong migrant workers against the government's crackdown on undocumented workers by 2002 (Jung, 2014, p. 13). As a consequence, a large number of migrant communities in remote provinces could be mobilized for major protests against the crackdown in Seoul in 2002 (Lee, 2014, pp. 50–51). In October 2002, another trade union, the Seongseo Industrial Park Trade Union, has been established with an aim to organize particularly migrant workers, becoming the first trade union with migrant members outside the Seoul metropolitan area. These struggles contributed to the eventual abolition of the notorious FITP.

The transformation from a philanthropic campaign to a migrant workers' movement with a class perspective has been consolidated through the 380 days sit-in strike between 2003 and 2004 at the Myungdong Cathedral. In 2003, the South Korean government tightened up its crackdown on undocumented workers before the implementation of the newly passed law that was about to replace the industrial trainee program with the Employment Permit System (EPS) by 2004. Some undocumented workers committed suicide in desperation while others got injured in their attempts to escape sudden arrest operation of the border agency. In protest to the manhunt-style crackdown, the migrant branch of the Equal Trade Union initiated an indefinite sit-in strike in the Myungdong Cathedral on 15th November 2003, calling for the regularization of all irregular migrants before the introduction of the new system (The President of Migrant Workers Trade Union, personal interview, April 18, 2016). They protested not only the crackdown of irregular migrants by the government but also some of the JCMK member organizations which rather surprisingly supported the government scheme for the voluntary deportation of undocumented workers for the smooth operation of EPS (Interview with the

Coordinator of Migrant Workers Support Network, April 20, 2016). This was conceived of as a shortcoming of the existing migrant movement as "a movement for migrant workers not a movement of migrant workers" (The Coordinator of Migrant Workers Support Network, personal interview, April 20, 2016). Migrant activists began to have a belief that "they have to be an independent agent of their own movement. They wanted to be treated equally as workers in Korea, no matter where they were from" (Interview with the Coordinator of Migrant Workers Support Network, April 20, 2016).

Increasingly confident actions taken by migrant workers themselves have made it clear that migrant workers were no longer poor foreigners in desperate need of protection from Korean citizens but an integral part of *the working class in Korea* if not part of *the Korean working class*. Soon, the migrant workers movement diversified into two main strands, one emphasizing class-based struggles, and the other focusing on service provision and humanitarian approaches. Migrant workers, as well as Korean activists aligned with the class-based approach, succeeded in establishing the Migrant Trade Union (MTU) in 2005. In doing so, they attracted attention from major trade unions such as the Korean Confederation of Korean Trade Unions. Korean unions' view on migrant labor has changed over the years since the early 1990s. During the earlier period, the Korean Confederation of Trade Unions (KCTU), focused on protection and support rather than organizing or integrating migrant workers as active participants of the Korean labor movement despite the rhetoric of international working class unity (Jung, 2012, pp. 69–71). In the face of the explosion of migrant workers protest in 2003, the KCTU "did not really know what to do" (A KCTU Staff for Migrant Workers, personal interview, April 21, 2016). However, the confederation began to join the protest in a way it would for any other protests of marginalized workers in South Korea. It was the sit-in strikes of migrant workers between 2002 and 2004 that made the KCTU more engage with the migrant workers movement. The KCTU dispatched an officer to take care of the administrative body of the sit-in strike and fundraising while the official title of the group of protesters in Myuongdong Cathedral became "a struggle collective of the KCTU" (Jung, 2014, p. 14). The KCTU also appointed a staff taking care of migrant-related issues in its headquarter (Jung, 2014, p. 14). Since then, the KCTU has shown more genuine interest in working with and representing migrant workers.

From its establishment in 2005, the MTU has been affiliated with the Seoul Branch of the KCTU. As the suppression of migrant workers' movement by the South Korean authority got heavier,[8] the KCTU's support as an umbrella organization has become stronger than before. The KCTU mobilized protests against the arrest and deportation of the MTU leaders and set up a monthly meeting for union officers dealing with migrant issues in its city, provincial and industrial branches in 2005 (Jung, 2014, p. 16). Although the KCTU seemed to be much more dedicated to building solidarity with migrant workers in the first half of the 2000s, these actions taken by the KCTU were largely reactive than proactive (A KCTU Staff for Migrant Workers, personal interview, April 21, 2016). In an attempt to move from a reactive to a proactive mode of engagement with the migrant movement, the KCTU has recently introduced many different policies. From 2010, migrant workers began to be represented in the general congress of the KCTU. Also, the MTU participates in the Special Committee for Irregular and Unorganized on a regular basis (A KCTU Staff for Migrant Workers, personal interview, April 21, 2016). The KCTU also now employs a full-time migrant worker-activist in its headquarter. The confederation now runs educational programs on migrant issues to raise awareness among its rank and file members (A KCTU Staff for Migrant Workers, personal interview, April 21, 2016). Now the KCTU's major national demands include the removal of the EPS, the introduction of Labor Permit System, and the immediate legalization of all undocumented workers. More importantly, the KCTU endorses the on-going campaign of the newly recognized MTU to attain right to collective bargaining and action as well as right to strike.

Local branches and KCTU-affiliated industrial and enterprise unions have also initiated some proactive policies to integrate the migrant workers movement. The Metal Workers Federation has allowed migrant workers to be members since 2005 and now has a quota for migrant delegates for its congress. The KCTU Daegu Special Metropolitan Branch has a quota for migrants too. Since its establishment, the Seongseo Industrial Park Trade Union has allocated its vice-president to migrant members and runs the Committee for Migrant Workplaces to address particular concerns of migrant members (A KCTU Staff for Migrant Workers, personal interview, April 21, 2016). In recent years, despite anti-migrant nationalist sentiment among citizen-workers, more enterprise, regional and industrial unions began to invite migrant worker to join. Enterprises unions under the Metal Workers Union such as Samwoo Precision Industry Union, Korea BorgWarner Changwon Union, and Youngjin Industry Union organized migrant workers and represented them in their collective bargaining (*Kyunghyang Shinmun*, 2010). The case of MS Autotech in 2013 is particularly important as the migrant workers from Indonesia, the Philippines, Cambodia and China took a part in local workers' struggle to build a democratic union despite the desperate attempts of the management and embassies to discourage their nationals to be involved (Kim, Oh, & Yim, 2014, pp. 159–171). The collective bargaining agreement between the company and newly established union covers many demands of migrant workers including longest possible employment contract allowed in law (4 years and 10 month), 300 percent bonus for workers employed more than 6-month, welfare benefit same as benefit for local workers, same vacation allowance, humane treatment and improvement of dormitory facilities (Kim et al., 2014, p. 165).

Much progress has been made but not without problems. Apart from the institutionalized discrimination the EPS imposes upon migrant workers, the Korean state continues to criminalize undocumented migrant workers and the migrant workers movement. The MTU has been outlawed from its establishment in 2005. Most of MTU leaders have been arrested and deported by the border agency without regard to their legal status. The consequence is the absence of a large pool of dedicated migrant activists which once existed in the aftermath of the explosion of migrant protests between 2003 and 2004. The majority of migrant workers is no longer undocumented workers whose apparently desperate situation led to the strong militancy of early migrant workers' movement. The attitude of the majority of local workers towards migrant workers also remains to be changed. Although the leadership of the KCTU shows a commitment to migrant workers' movement, Korean rank and file workers more often than not see migrant as competitors. It is particularly so in industries such as construction where migrants are becoming a majority. The language barrier between migrant workers and Korean unionists requires a much longer term plan to overcome. Nevertheless, the migrant workers movement in Korea and its strive for social movement citizenship continues to advance. Their struggle with strong determination for equal rights finally forced the supreme court of South Korea to rule in favor of the rights for migrants to join trade unions without regard to their legal status in 2015. In so doing, migrants are not only becoming an integral part of the South Korean economy as cheap labor but also turning increasingly into political subjects embedded in Korean society.

As Isin points out, "the actors of citizenship are not necessarily those who hold the status of citizenship" (Isin, 2009, p. 370). Migrant workers' struggles extend citizenship beyond legal entitlement given by the state and thereby challenge the exclusive nature of citizenship. It is in this sense that "emerging migrant collective subjectivities through political mobilisations have a direct bearing on our understanding and conceptualisation of citizenship" (Andrijasevic & Anderson, 2009, p. 366). Migrants in Hong Kong and South Korea, in their pursuit of social movement citizenship, build citizenship from below and extend the notion of citizenship by claiming universal citizenship. They not only demonstrate their desire to gain existing citizenship but also transform the existing concept of citizenship, turning it again into a contested arena of domination and resistance not only within but also beyond borders. In so doing, they undermine the glory of citizenship given and granted by borders that hide the fundamental injustice done to "THEM" by "US" inside borders, reinvigorate the concept of citizens as a radical agent for real democracy against bordered capitalism, and shake theories and practices of justice and social movements that often refuse to go beyond a singular and homogeneous identity of citizen-workers. They show that an alternative to bordered capitalism cannot be built upon social movements relying on the mundane notion of citizenship based on borders.

What emerging migrant workers' movement and their pursuit of universal citizenship shows us is that any attempt to overcome contradictions and injustice of capitalism need to deal with borders as a central institution of capitalism and an important social form of capitalist social relations. Understanding global capitalism as "Bordered Capitalism" requires us a different approach to transformative social changes. Overcoming capitalism is often regarded, implicitly if not explicitly, as a national project in which (the mythical notion of) the homogeneous national class of citizen-workers plays a revolutionary role for transformative social changes. From this perspective, international solidarity is solidarity among these separate national projects while internationalist perspective means prioritizing unity between separate national projects. This perspective indeed contradicts what Marx and Engels stated when urging "working men of all countries" to be united in 1948. They said:

> Working men have no country. We cannot take from them what they have not got. Since the proletariat must first of all acquire political supremacy, must rise to be the leading class of the nation, must constitute itself the nation, it is so far, itself national, though not in the bourgeois sense of the word. (Marx & Engels, 1948, p. 25)

This statement was written before the establishment of formal citizenship and "Bordered Capitalism" that divides the global working class into "US" and "THEM." But still, their kind of internationalism is much richer than what we consider as "Internationalism" now. This statement clearly indicates the lack of citizenship for the working class population in the mid-19th century when it says the working class "has no country," indicating the working class is inherently a global being which cannot be contained by borders. They urged the working class to be the leading class of the nation, but not in the sense that the working class should establish the nation vis-à-vis other nations and become national working classes in nation states of bordered capitalism. Rather unfortunately, history did not unfold the way Marx and Engels wanted. The working class became "a" leading class in many nations but in a very bourgeois sense of the word. Together with that, internationalism evolved in the bourgeois sense of the word too. This is the reality that Bordered Capitalism reproduces. Now, we tend to think the statement "working men of all countries' to be united!" as a call for a unity of different national working classes. Understanding contemporary capitalism as Bordered Capitalism let us reconsider the prevalent form of "internationalism" as cooperation between parallel attempts of national working classes to change their own worlds within borders. Challenging capitalism requires us to challenge borders as a central class and racial institution to the reproduction of global capitalism *while, rather than after*, we try to overcome the injustice of capitalist social relations. It is important to notice that the citizen working class is as much product of bordering as that of struggles for democracy. Cotemporary citizenship is both a set of rights and entitlements and a bordering device. This transformation of the working class from "workers without nations" to citizen-workers through the making of bordered capitalism requires us to rethink the starting point of labor's challenge to global capitalism. Members of communities of value divided by borders, in other words, the agency of citizens juxtaposed to THEM should not be taken for granted as a supreme transformative agency. In their search for universal rights refused by borders, migrant workers demonstrate its subversive agency and become a potentially "dangerous class."

CONCLUSION

As much as mobile labor is central to the reproduction of global capitalism, borders are necessary for the maintenance of global capitalism. Despite the repeated attempt of nation states to come up with new borders to utilize and contain mobile labor, the potentially subversive nature of migration has manifested throughout the history of capitalist development. Migrants' subversive agency exists not only in theory but also in practice. Migrant workers in Hong Kong and Korea went beyond the boundary between us and them to claim what they are not entitled to, acting as activist citizens. Migrants are revealing their subversive agency and build citizenship from below through their social movements for universal citizenship in and beyond both spaces of accumulation. The current waves of subversive migration across the world show that, as long as capitalism requires mobile labor, it cannot avoid facing the subversiveness of migration. Subversive migration can effectively revitalize the radical elements once contained in the concept of citizenship by bringing citizenship out of its comfort zones protected by borders. This chapter contended that we need to recognize the subversive agency of mobile labor and thereby bring the agency of migrant labor back into the center of our discussion about capitalist development and possible social transformation towards better alternatives. This is not a purely theoretical claim but based on the recognition of the importance of the various struggles of migrant labor against nation states, their regimes of migration control and exploitation at the different moments of the expanding circuit of capital.

NOTES

1. They include Bangladesh, Cambodia, China, East Timor, Indonesia, Kyrgyzstan, Mongolia, Myanmar, Nepal, Pakistan, the Philippines, Sri Lanka, Thailand, Uzbekistan and Vietnam.

2. Prior to European expansion, Southeast Asia was governed by the Mandala system in which borders were actually defined by areas and extent of "influence" of rulers rather than based on clearly geographical territories.

3. Therefore, border protecting national spaces of accumulation from the excessive inward mobility of labor is a mode of existence of the borders containing national workforce within national spaces of accumulation.

4. Perhaps, it is easier to understand the fetishistic reproduction of capitalist social relations through borders by looking at the ways in which the capitalist state and market reproduce the unequal social relations of capitalism. The state is a form through which capitalist social relations appear and exist as political relations between individual

citizens. In other words, the state translates class relation into relations between individual citizens or different interest groups. It is the state in liberal understanding, the pluralist theory of the state. Meanwhile, the market presents class relations as technical or functional relations between owners of different sources of revenue as in the trinity formula of mainstream economics. In this sense, the market is a form through which capitalist social relations appear and exist as "economic" relations between different sources of revenue or different economic classes. The state and market are indeed rooted in unequal class relations. However, they appeared to be distinctive from class relations and present themselves as class neutral institutions. It is particularly so in the case of the democratic capitalist state because the relations between citizens it represents have little trace of class relations and material inequality whereas market relations still carry them (Chang, 2009; Clarke, 1991). Because of its distinctive mode of existence, the state appears to have autonomy from class relations.

5. It is an interesting form of protest in household. Migrant domestic workers wear t-shirts that have written slogans like "respect labor rights" or "we are not slaves" in protest to labor right abuses by employers (Interview with Filipino domestic worker-activists, April 10, 2016).

6. The EPS, introduced in 2004, is known a better program than the previous FITP. However, it also does not grant migrant workers the freedom to change employers and allows only employers to terminate the contract. Migrant workers cannot change the employer without employers' consent and therefore often have to endure abusive employers. It also limits the maximum period of stay for a workers to 4 years and 10 months, effectively denying an opportunity for workers to apply of permanent residents which requires applicants to stay at least five years in South Korea.

7. The first office of the JCMK was hosted by the KCTU. However, the KCTU did not participate in the JCMK actively in the 1990s. Rather, the KCTU's engagement with migrant workers was rather formal than real.

8. Most of leaders of the MTU from 2005 to 2010 have been trained through the vehement struggles between 2002 and 2004. Later many of these leaders were targeted, followed, arrested and deported by the government's special operations, without regard to their legal status. The government also denied their application for re-entry.

ACKNOWLEDGMENT

Research for this chapter received support from the National Research Foundation of Korea Grant NRF2013S1A5B8A01055117 as well as Sogang University Research Grant. Some interviews included in this chapter have been done together with Dr. Raees Baig, the Chinese University of Hong Kong as a part of a research project titled "Capacity and agency of migrant worker activism: A Hong Kong and South Korea comparison" (funded by Chinese University of Hong Kong Research Grant).

REFERENCES

Anderson, B. (2009). What's in a name? Immigration controls and subjectivities: The case of Au pair and domestic worker Visa holders in the UK. *Subjectivity*, *29*, 407–424.

Anderson, B. (2011). Migration: Controlling the unsettled poor. *Open Democracy*. Retrieved from https://www.opendemocracy.net/5050/bridget-anderson/migration-controlling-unsettled-poor. Accessed on March 15, 2013.

Anderson, B. (2013). *Us and them? The dangerous politics of immigration control*. Oxford: Oxford University Press.

Anderson, B. (2014). *Exclusion, failure, and the politics of citizenship*. RCIS Working Paper No. 2014/1. Retrieved from http://www.ryerson.ca/content/dam/rcis/documents/RCIS_WP_Anderson_No_2014_1.pdf

Anderson, B., Sharma, N., & Wright, C. (2009). Editorial: Why no border? *Refugee*, *26*(2), 5–18.

Andrijasevic, R. (2009). Sex on the move: Gender, subjectivity and differential inclusion. *Subjectivity*, *29*(1), 389–406.

Andrijasevic, R., & Anderson, B. (2009). Conflicts of mobility: Migration, labour and political subjectivities. *Subjectivity*, *29*, 363–366.

Balibar, E. (2004). *We, the people of Europe?* Princeton, NJ: Princeton University Press.

Baran, P. (1957). *The political economy of growth*. New York, NY: Monthly Review Press.

Borjas, G. J. (1989). Economic theory and international migration. *International Migration Review*, *23*, 457–485.

Breman, J. (1989). *Taming the collie beast: Plantation society and the colonial order in South East Asia*. Oxford: Oxford University Press.

Castle, S., & Kosack, G. (1973). *Immigrant workers and class structure in Western Europe*. Oxford: Oxford University Press.

Chalcraft, J. (2007). Labour in the Levant. *New Left Review*, *45*, 26–47.

Chang, D. (2009). *Capitalist development in Korea: Labour, capital and the myth of the developmental state*. London: Routledge.

Choi, S. (2011). *Domestic Workers in Asia-campaign and organising updates*. Retrieved from http://www.amrc.org.hk/system/files/Domestic%20Workers%20in%20Asia%202011.pdf. Accessed on April 11, 2012.

Clarke, S. (1991). *Marx, marginalism and modern sociology: From Adam Smith to Max Weber*. London: Macmillan.

Cohen, R. (1987). *The new helots: Migrants in the new international division of labour*. Aldershot: Avebury.

Cohen, R. (2006). *Migration and its enemies: Global capital, migrant labour and the nation-states*. Aldershot: Ashgate.

Constable, N. (2002). Filipina workers in Hong Kong homes: Household rules and relations. In B. Ehrenreich & A. R. Hochschild (Eds.), *Global woman: Nannies, maids, and sex workers in the new economy*. New York, NY: Owl Books.

Constable, N. (2007). *Maid to order in Hong Kong, stories of migrant workers*. Ithaca, NY: Cornell University Press.

De Genova, N. (2009). Conflicts of mobility, and the mobility of conflict: Rightlessness, presence subjectivity, freedom. Subjectivity, *29*, 445–466.

De Genova, N. (2016). The "crisis" of the European border regime: Towards a Marxist theory of borders. *International Socialism*, *150*, 33–56.

Faison, E. (2007). *Managing women: Disciplining labor in modern Japan*. Berkeley, CA: University of California Press.

Federici, S. (2004). *Caliban and the Witch: Women, the body and primitive accumulation*. Brooklyn, NY: Autonomedia.

Ferguson, S., & McNally, D. (2015). Precarious migrants: Gender, race and the social reproduction of a global working class. *Socialist Register*, *51*, 1–23.

Frank, A. G. (1966). The development of underdevelopment. *Monthly Review*, *18*(4), 17–31.

Frank, A. G. (1967). *Capitalism and underdevelopment in Latin America*. New York, NY: Monthly Review Press.

Harris, J., & Todaro, M. (1970). Migration, unemployment & development: A two-sector analysis. *American Economic Review*, *60*(1), 126–142.

Harvey, D. (1990). *The conditions of postmodernity: An enquiry into the origins of cultural change.* Oxford: Blackwell.

Harvey, D. (2005). *A brief history of neoliberalism.* Oxford: Oxford University Press.

Harvey, D. (2006). *Spaces of global capitalism: Toward a theory of uneven geographical development.* London: Verso.

Hsia, H.-C. (2009). The making of a transnational grassroots migrant movement: A case study of Hong Kong's Asian Migrants' Coordinating Body. *Critical Asian Studies, 41*(1), 113–141.

Isin, E. F. (2009). Citizenship in flux: The figure of the activist citizen. *Subjectivity, 29*, 367–388.

Jung, Y.-S. (2012). Hangukui nodongundonggwa ijunodongjaui areumdaunyeondaeneun ganeunghanga? [Is solidarity between the Korean labour movement and migrant workers possible?]. *e-Journal Homo Migrants, 5*(6), 65–84.

Jung, Y.-S. (2014). Ijunodongjaundongae Daehan Minjunochongui Jeongchek Byunhwa Huireum [evolution of KCTU policy for migrant workers]. In KCTU (Ed.), *Ijunodongja Nojojojikhwa Saryeyeongu* [a case study of organising migrant workers]. Seoul: KCTU.

Justice Centre. (2016). *Coming clean: The prevalence of forced labour and human trafficking for the purpose of forced labour amongst migrant domestic workers in Hong Kong.* Retrieved from http://www.justicecentre.org.hk/framework/uploads/2016/03/Coming-Clean-The-prevalence-of-forced-labour-and-human-trafficking-for-the-purpose-of-forced-labour-amongst-migrant-domestic-workers-in-Hong-Kong.pdf. Accessed on August 1, 2016.

Kaur, A. (2004). Labour dynamics in the plantation and mining sector. In R. Elmhirst & R. Sapptari (Eds.), *Labour in Southeast Asia: Labour processes in a globalised world.* London: RoutledgeCurzon.

Kim, A. E. (2009). Global migration and South Korea: Foreign workers, foreign brides and the making of a multicultural society. *Ethnic and Racial Studies, 32*(1), 70–92.

Kim, G. R., Oh, S. Y., & Yim, B. N. (2014). Saryemouem [a collection of cases]. In KCTU (Ed.), *Ijunodongja Nojojojikhwa Saryeyeongu [a case study of organising migrant workers]*. Seoul: KCTU.

Kim, N. (2012). The migrant workers' movement in the democratic consolidation of Korea. *Journal of Contemporary Asia, 42*(4), 676–696.

Kim, J. (2014). The colonial state, migration, and diasporic nationhood in Korea. *Comparative Studies in Society and History, 56*(1), 34–66.

Kong, D., Yoon, K., & Yu, S. (2010). The social dimension of immigration in Korea. *Journal of Contemporary Asia, 40*(2), 252–274.

Koo, H. (1990). From farm to factory: Proletarianization in Korea. *American Sociological Review, 55*, 669–681.

Koo, H. (2001). *Korean workers: The cultural and politics of class formation.* Ithaca, NY: Cornell University Press.

Kyunghyang Shinmun. (2010, February 2). Retrieved from http://news.khan.co.kr/kh_news/khan_art_view.html?artid=201002020132275&code=940702. Accessed on March 11, 2012.

Lee, Y. (2009). Migration, migrants, and contested ethno-nationalism in Korea. *Critical Asian Studies, 41*(3), 363–380.

Lee, Y.-J. (2014). Inotubon, Pyeongdeungnojo Ijunodongjajibu Sarye (~2003nyeon 5wol): Nodongundongeuroseo Ijunodongjaundongui Daedu [the case of migrant workers struggle committee and migrant branch of equal trade union (up to May 2003): The rise of migrant movement as a labour movement]. In KCTU (Ed.), *Ijunodongja Nojojojikhwa Saryeyeongu [case study of organising migrant workers]*. Seoul: KCTU.

Leung, P. N., & Pun, N. (2009). The radicalisation of the New Chinese working class: A case study of collective action in the gemstone industry. *Third World Quarterly, 30*(3), 551–565.

Linebaugh, P., & Rediker, M. (2012). *The many-headed hydra: The hidden history of the revolutionary Atlantic.* London: Verso.

Marx, K. (1976). *Capital* (Vol. 1). London: Penguin Press.

Marx, K., & Engels, F. (1848). *Manifesto of the communist party.* Retrieved from https://www.marxists.org/archive/marx/works/download/pdf/Manifesto.pdf

Massey, D. S., Arango, J., Hugo, G., Kouaouci, A., Pellegrino, A., & Taylor, J. E. (1998). *Worlds in motion, understanding international migration at the end of the millennium*. Oxford: Clarendon Press.

Mezzadra, S. (2010). *The gaze of autonomy. Capitalism, migration and social struggles*. Retrieved from http://www.mara-stream.org/wp-content/uploads/2011/10/Sandro-Mezzadra_The-Gaze-of-Autonomy.-Capitalism-Migration-and-Social-Struggles.pdf. Accessed on April 11, 2012.

Mezzadra, S., & Neilson, B. (2013). *Border as method, or, the multiplication of labor*. Durham: Duke University Press.

Morris-Suzuki, T. (2006). Changing border control regimes and their impact on migration in Asia. In A. Kaur & I. Metcalfe (Eds.), *Mobility, labour migration and border control in Asia*. Basingstoke: Palgrave Macmillan.

Papadopolous, D., Stephenson, N., & Tsianos, V. (2008). *Escape routes. Control and subversion in the 21st century*. London: Pluto.

Perrons, D. (2004). *Globalization and social change: People and places in a divided world*. London: Routledge.

Piore, M. J. (1979). *Birds of passage: Migrant labour and industrial societies*. Cambridge: Cambridge University Press.

Potts, L. (1990). *The world labour market: A history of migration*. London: Zed Books.

Sassen, S. (1988). *The mobility of labor and capital*. New York, NY: Cambridge University Press.

Sassen, S. (1991). *The global city*. Princeton, NJ: Princeton University Press.

Sassen, S. (2000). Counter-geography of globalization and the feminization of survival. *Journal of International Affairs*, *53*(2), 504–524.

Seol, D.-H., & Han, G.-S. (2004). Foreign migrant workers and social discrimination in Korea. *Harvard Asia Quarterly*, *8*(1), 45–50.

Tang, E. (2010). *Spotlight interview with Elizabeth Tang*. Retrieved from http://www.theglobalnetwork.net/news/92/. Accessed on March 4, 2012.

Todaro, M. P. (1969). A model of labor migration and urban unemployment in less-developed countries. *American Economic Review*, *59*, 138–148.

Torpey, J. (2000). *The invention of the passport: Surveillance, citizenship and the state*. Cambridge: Cambridge University Press.

Tsurumi, E. P. (1990). *Factory girls: Women in the thread mills of Meiji Japan*. Princeton, NJ: Princeton University Press.

Wallerstein, I. (1974). *The Modern World-System, volume I: Capitalist agriculture and the origins of the european world-economy in the sixteenth century*. London: Academic Press.

Wallerstein, I. (1979). *The capitalist world economy*. Cambridge: Cambridge University Press.

PART IV
COMMUNICATIONS ON CHAPTERS ON SRAFFA IN *RPE*

ADDENDUM TO CARTER'S "RESPONSE TO PROFESSOR SOLOW"

Yoann Verger

INTRODUCTION

In the debate between Scott Carter (2014a, 2014b) and Solow (2014), I was a bit disappointed about Scott's Response to Solow's comments. He did not try to challenge Solow's reading of Sraffa (he just said that he "fundamentally disagrees" about the fact that Value or exploitation play a role into the definition of prices, but without referring to what Sraffa would have answered, Carter, 2014b, p. 72), whereas I think at least three misreadings must be highlighted. This chapter tries to challenge Solow's vision on these three points. Carter also underline in his Response that he may have tried to "equate Sraffa with Marx" (Carter, 2014b, p. 70). I argue that Professor Solow's misreadings originate from the same kind of approach, in his case trying to equate Sraffa with neoclassical theory.

ON THE ASSUMPTION OF CONSTANT RETURNS TO SCALE

The first misreading is the following: Solow claims that Sraffa makes an assumption of constant returns to scale (Solow, 2014, p. 64). On the contrary, Sraffa explicitly says in the first sentences of his introduction of his book *Production of Commodities by Means of Commodities* that:

Return of Marxian Macro-dynamics in East Asia
Research in Political Economy, Volume 32, 287–294

ISSN: 0161-7230/doi:10.1108/S0161-723020170000032016

> Anyone accustomed to think in terms of the equilibrium of demand and supply may be inclined, on reading these pages, to suppose that the argument rests on a tacit assumption of constant returns in all industries. If such a supposition is found helpful, there is no harm in the reader's adopting it as a temporary working hypothesis. In fact, however, no such assumption is made. No changes in output and (at any rate in Parts I and II) no changes in the proportions in which different means of production are used by an industry are considered, so that no question arises as to the variation of constancy of returns. The investigation is concerned exclusively with such properties of an economic system as do not depend on changes in the scale of production or in the proportions of "factors" ...
>
> when in 1928 Lord Keynes read a draft of the opening propositions of this paper, he recommended that, if constant returns were *not* to be assumed, an emphatic warning to that effect should be given. (Sraffa, 1960, Preface, v–vi)

So Sraffa explicitly argues that "he is only concerned with a snapshot of interindustry commodity in an economy, with no technological assumptions of any kind" (Solow, 2014, p. 64), and he does so right in the beginning of his book.

Now the "hundred thousand dollar question," to rephrase Carter (Carter, 2014b, p. 72), is: why does Solow overlook the emphatic warning?

Apparently, Solow is misled by the fact that Sraffa assumes a uniform rate of profits, and by the fact that he constructs the standard system using constant returns to scale: "without the standard technological assumptions there is no point to the various balance conditions [Sraffa] introduces" (Solow, 2014, p. 64).

On the first point, the uniform rate of profits assumed by Sraffa may be an incitation to think that he considers an economy in a long-term equilibrium, the result of a process of gravitation of prices and investment, which is a process where constant returns to scale are always assumed. But this view is in contradiction with Sraffa's claim that he looks at a system in a given instant of time:

> As regards your own interpretation, I must say frankly that you have gone astray the moment you speak of "equilibrium" or of "elasticity of factor supply": all the quantities considered are what can be observed by taking a photograph, there are no rates of change, etc. This point of view was that of the classical economists (e.g. Ricardo) whereas supply and demand curves were introduced in the middle of the 19th century. Economists are now obsessed with them and cannot think without them. (1 March 1968, letter from Sraffa to Rüdiger Soltwedel, preparing a PhD thesis on "Sraffa's *Production of Commodities by Means of Commodities*" and writing to Sraffa on 28th February 1968 to get advice; Sraffa Papers – C294/1-2)

Actually, Sraffa needs the uniformity of the rates of profits so that the lesson learnt from the standard system (the linear relation between the rate of profits and the wages, when the standard commodity is the numeraire) also applies to the real system: there is no linear relationship between the wage and the average rate of profits when the standard commodity is the numeraire and the rates of profits are not uniform, as soon as we are not anymore in the standard proportions.[1] Therefore, Sraffa applies an average rate of profits to all industries. This does not preclude that, in the real market, different rates of profits prevail.[2]

On the second point, Sraffa constructs the standard system by applying constant returns to scale. But this is an "imaginary experiment" (Sraffa, 1960, § 37), whose meaning is only to clarify the relationships between the rate of profits and the wages. This imaginary construction has no relation with the real technical possibilities about constant, increasing or decreasing returns to scale.

"There is no harm" to adopt the hypothesis that there are constant returns to scale, as Sraffa recalls. But no such hypothesis is made by Sraffa himself. And actually, as we will see, such hypothesis can be harmful, if it is combined with other mistaken assumptions.

ON THE PROBLEMS RESULTING FROM APPLYING A GENERAL EQUILIBRIUM FRAMEWORK TO SRAFFA

The second misreading is the following: Solow claims that Sraffa makes an "assumption of zero pure profit" (Solow, 2014, p. 64). Nowhere in Sraffa have we found the expression "pure profit": Sraffa only talks about profits and the rate of profits. Solow calls Sraffa's rate of profits, the rate of interest, whereas Sraffa only once talks about a rate of interest on money:

> The rate of profits, as a ratio, has a significance which is independent of any prices, and can well be "given" before the prices are fixed. It is accordingly susceptible of being determined from outside the system of production, in particular by the level of the money rates of interest. (Sraffa, 1960, § 44)

As Pasinetti (1988) argues, this incidental remark does not seem to justify that, in Sraffa's mind, the rate of profits is equal to the rate of interest. A more logical view is that Sraffa follows the distinction drawn by Adam Smith and Karl Marx between profit, which is the part of the surplus which does not goes to the wages and the rents, and interest, which is the part of the profit which goes into the hand of capitalists who had advanced a capital to the entrepreneur, be it in money form or not.

Again, why does Solow call Sraffa's rate of profits, the rate of interest, and why does he think that no pure profit should appear?

It seems that he tries to use concepts he learned from neoclassical theory in order to explain Sraffa's theory. In the neoclassical framework (general equilibrium models), pure profits are the difference that exists in each industry between the price of outputs and the cost of inputs, the latter being multiplied by a rate of interest. This rate of interest is equivalent to the inter-temporal discount rate of the commodity produced, and it is also called the commodity's own rate of profits.[3] Pure profits can exist if decreasing returns to scale are assumed, but they disappear as soon as there are only constant returns to scale, because otherwise "there can be no equilibrium" (Solow, 2014, p. 64) between offer and demand (the suppliers, seeking to optimize their profits, would offer an infinite supply).

Hence, Solow thinks that Sraffa's prices are equilibrium prices, and because he thinks that Sraffa assumes constant returns to scale, Solow concludes that pure profits cannot appear in Sraffa's system.[4] The logic of Sraffa's model, concerned with the relation between prices and distribution variables, is transformed into a neoclassical logic, concerned about finding the equilibrium prices.[5] Here, we see that the assumption of constant returns to scale, far from being ancillary, becomes necessary: if prices are equilibrium prices and are independent from demand, then it means that there should be constant returns to scale. But Sraffa, in letter to Arun Bose written in 1964, recalls that the fact that demand functions are not considered to calculate prices does not mean that demand does not influence the choice of the techniques of production, the quantity produced and the distribution of the surplus, and thus that prices should be considered to be influenced by demand:

> The fact is that your opening sentence is for me an obstacle which I am unable to get over. You write: "It is a basic proposition of the Sraffa theory that prices are determined exclusively by the physical requirements of production and the social wage–profit division with consumers demand playing a purely passive role."
>
> Never have I said this: certainly not in the two places to which you refer in your note 2. Nothing, in my view, could be more suicidal than to make such a statement. You are asking me to put my head on the block so that the first fool who comes along can cut it off neatly.
>
> Whatever you do, please do not represent me as saying such a thing. (Sraffa Papers, C32: 3)

In fact, Sraffa is not concerned about the possibility to satisfy both the suppliers and the consumers, in present and future exchange periods. He is only concerned about the relation that we can find between the rate of profits, the wage and the prices, when we observe a snapshot of a system of production, that is, after decisions about the choice of technique and the quantity to produce have been taken. Solow and Sraffa do not develop their theories inside the same paradigms, and this is also reflected in their different views about the relations between metaphysics and economics.

ON EXPLOITATION AND METAPHYSICS

The last misreading made by Solow is about metaphysics: he argues that it is possible to justify the rate of profits without using any metaphysical concept, and especially without referring to the exploitation of the labor class. Moreover, he seems to argue that Sraffa had a bad opinion on the labor theory of value and the notion of exploitation, because he described them as part of "metaphysics" in one of his notes (Solow, 2014, p. 65).

For Solow, the reason for a positive rate of profits lies in the scarcity of capital and in the fact that capitalists should receive a reward for their "abstinence" for consuming their capital (Solow, 2014, p. 67). For him, this justification makes "some sense" at the level of "the economy as a whole," and furthermore, this justification does not require any metaphysics: "the important thing is to distinguish carefully between economics and the metaphysics, or what Duncan Foley calls the theology" (Solow, 2014, p. 67).

On the contrary, "exploitation" is presented as a metaphysical concept. We do not need it to find the prices, and even Sraffa in his papers "labels these issues as part of the "metaphysics" of Ricardo, or Marx, or Marshall, or Sraffa" and "this was certainly not to pay it a compliment" (Solow, 2014, p. 64). Solow argues that exploitation does not explain the rate of profits, because even if the rate of profits is set to zero, we could find differences in wages between workers which could also be related to a kind of exploitation by the "high wages" on the "low wages" (Solow, 2014, p. 67).

To start with exploitation, Marx states that there is exploitation as soon as the rate of profits is different from zero, but this does not preclude that there cannot be any exploitation in the case the rate of profits equals zero. The position of Sraffa is that the level of the rate of profits may be "susceptible of being determined from outside the system of production" (Sraffa, 1960, § 44), instead of the wage being the exogenous variable (he then investigates what would be the wage and the prices depending on the rate of profits), meaning that the level of exploitation of the working class by the capitalist class is not decided by the system.[6] But as soon as the rate of profits is different from zero, Solow's argument that exploitation does not play any role in Sraffa's prices is wrong, if we agree with Marx's point of view.

About metaphysics, Sraffa never says that he is against the use of metaphysics to describe a system. Solow probably refers to the following note:

> The difference between the "Physical real costs" and the Ricardo-Marxian theory of "labour costs" is that the first does, and the latter does not, include in them the natural resources that are used up in the course of production (such as coal, iron, exaustion {*sic*} of land) – [Air, water, etc. are not used up: as there is an unlimited supply, no subtraction can be made from ∞]. This is fundamental because it does away with "human energy" and such metaphysical things. (Sraffa's Papers, D3/12/42: 33)

However, in another note from November 1927, Sraffa also says that he will develop its own metaphysics:

> I foresee that the ultimate result will be a restatement of Marx, by substituting to his Hegelian metaphysics and terminology our own modern metaphysics and terminology {...} This would be simply a translation of Marx into English, from the forms of Hegelian metaphysics to the forms of Hume's metaphysics (Keynes to-day, 26 XI. 27 has clearly outlined the divorce between English and Continental thought: the first descending from Descartes {and} Hobbes, the two original geniuses, to Locke, Hutcheson and ultimately Hume, the second from Spinoza (did he say that of S.?) from Kant to Hegel: they always remained foreign to one another). (Sraffa's Papers, D3/12/4: 15)

In the same note, Sraffa explains his definition of metaphysics:

> By metaphysics here I mean, I suppose, the emotions that are associated with our terminology and frames (schemi mentali) – that is, what is absolutely necessary to make the theory living {...}, capable of assimilation and at all intelligible. (Sraffa's Papers, D3/12/4: 15)

Then metaphysics means explanations that are necessary to make a connection between the results of the theory and what we experience in the real world. In this view, no scientific discourse can escape from one or another metaphysics, otherwise it would be non-sense.[7] In this perspective, the discourse about abstinence as the source of profits is a metaphysical one, as it relates the logical existence of profits to a justification that makes "some sense" to some people.

Sraffa warns about the possibility to forget the fact that each scientific technique hides a metaphysical discourse:

> Our metaphysics is in fact embodied in our technique; the danger lies in this, that when we have succeeded in thoroughly mastering a technique, we are very liable to be mastered <u>by</u> her. (Sraffa's Papers, D3/12/4: 15)

There is no doubt that Solow mastered the neoclassical technique, but unfortunately to the point that it seems that he cannot anymore escape from the neoclassical metaphysics.

NOTES

1. For a given average rate of profits, when the numeraire is the standard commodity, we can observe that wage is different when the rates of profits are uniform and when they are not. The only obvious exceptions are when the average rate of profits is at its maximum (wage equals zero in both cases), when the average rate of profits equals zero (the rate of profits must be zero in all industries, and thus the wage is equal in both cases), and when the real system is already in the standard proportions, that is, when the standard system is identical to the real system.

2. This explanation of the need for one uniform rate of profits has been challenged by one reviewer. Sraffa does not explain why rates of profits must be uniform: "accordingly we add the rate of profits (which must be uniform for all industries) ..." (Sraffa, 1960, § 4), hence different interpretations may be submitted (e.g., see Garegnani, 1984 or Kurz, 2012, where the uniform rate of profits is supposed to be the long-term result of competition between capital owners). However, the reviewer's proposal that this uniformity is mainly needed for the reproduction of the system ("the assumption of a uniform rate of profits in Sraffa is primarily due for satisfying the reproducibility of system, although, under well specified conditions, vectors of rates of profits might be compatible with the reproduction of the system – but in general they are not," anonymous reviewer) cannot be true, as Sraffa explicitly says that there is no connection between prices and a possible reproduction of the system: "the exchange ratios are, of course, determined by the equations of production and not by the ratios between the excess productions of the commodities. Sir Roy has been misled by the fact that the two ratios happen to be equal in the first example given (a no-surplus two-commodity system which is in a self-replacing state). Even in this simplest case, however, if, with the same equations, the two commodities were produced in different proportions (so that the system ceased to be in a self-replacing state) the exchange ratio

would remain the same but the ratio between the excess productions of the two commodities would be changed, so that the two would no longer be equal" (Sraffa, 1962). Furthermore, I may add that any vector of rates of profits can ensure positive prices and wage, provided that the average rate of profits does not exceed the maximum average rate of profits.

3. The inter-temporal discount rate is then different from Sraffa's rate of profits, as Sraffa does not consider successive periods of production in his book; see also Sinha and Dupertuis (2009).

4. Actually, if we apply the neoclassical theory to a system of production with no technical change during successive periods (an attempt can be found in Hahn, 1982), a uniform rate of interest will emerge and it would also be equal to zero.

5. This kind of misreading is also made by Samuelson and Etula, see Sinha (2007).

6. We can relate this view about the exogenous determination of the rate of profits with the neo-realist stand-point that the average rate of profits may be an institution, that is, a rule expressing a compromise between the different demands and interests of the different social groups composing the society (see Amable & Palombarini, 2009, for a description of the neo-realist approach; see also Gramsci, 1975/1977; Castoriadis, 1975).

The same point of view is described by one reviewer: "as far as the exploitation is concerned, in my view Solow's and Marx's notions refer to different objects. Solow aims to a general and abstract definition of exploitation, independent of the social context, while Marx's and possibly Sraffa's definition of exploitation is linked to particular institutional contexts. It is the exploitation of a social class by another class, caused by the possession of the means of production. It is true that this kind of exploitation is present in different modes of production (in a slave economy as well in the feudal economy and in capitalism), but it is linked by definition to the separation between the ones that own the means (as well as the conditions) of the productive process and the workers. In this sense, one could say that in Sraffa's framework exploitation, rather than depending on prices, determines the prices, as it determines the social rules concerning the distribution of surplus both between and within social classes (which are different in the different modes of production)" (anonymous reviewer).

7. This relates with the fact that each scientific discourse needs to rely on some ontological assumptions about the real world, in order to explain how the theory can have an impact on the real world. For instance, on the ontological assumptions of Sraffa, and their difference with Marshall's assumptions, see Martins (2013).

REFERENCES

Amable, B., & Palombarini, S. (2009). A neorealist approach to institutional change and the diversity of capitalism. *Socio-Economic Review*, *7*, 123–143.

Carter, S. (2014a). From 'Pool of Profits' to surplus and deficit industries: Archival evidence on the evolution of Piero Sraffa's thought. In P. Zarembka (Ed.), *Sraffa and Althusser reconsidered; neoliberalism advancing in South Africa, England, and Greece* (Vol. 29). Research in Political Economy. Bingley: Emerald Group Publishing Limited.

Carter, S. (2014b). Response to Comments of Robert M. Solow. In P. Zarembka (Ed.), *Sraffa and Althusser reconsidered; neoliberalism advancing in South Africa, England, and Greece* (Vol. 29). Research in Political Economy. Bingley: Emerald Group Publishing Limited.

Castoriadis, C. (1975). *L'institution Imaginaire de la Société*. Paris: Points Seuil.

Garegnani, P. (1984). Value and distribution in the classical economists and Marx. *Oxford Economic Papers*, *36*(2), 291–325.

Gramsci, A. (1975/1977). *Quaderni del Carcere*. Torino: Einaudi.

Hahn, F. (1982). The neo-Ricardians. *Cambridge Journal of Economics*, *6*, 353–374.

Kurz, H. D. (2012). Don't treat too ill my Piero! Interpreting Sraffa's papers. *Cambridge Journal of Economics*, *36*, 1535–1569.

Martins, N. O. (2013). Sraffa, Marshall and the principle of continuity. *Cambridge Journal of Economics*, *37*(2), 443–462.

Pasinetti, L. L. (1988). Sraffa on income distribution. *Cambridge Journal of Economics*, *12*, 135–138.

Sinha, A. (2007). Sraffa and the assumption of constant returns to scale: A critique of Samuelson and Etula. *Contributions to Political Economy*, *26*, 61–70.

Sinha, A., & Dupertuis, M.-S. (2009). Sraffa and the question of equilibrium. *Cahiers d'économie Politique*, *56*(1), 91–100.

Solow, R. M. (2014). Comment on Scott Carter. In P. Zarembka (Ed.), *Sraffa and Althusser reconsidered; neoliberalism advancing in South Africa, England, and Greece* (Vol. 29). Research in Political Economy. Bingley: Emerald Group Publishing Limited.

Sraffa, P. (1960). *Production of commodities by means of commodities*. Bombay: K. K. Vora, Vora & Co.

Sraffa, P. (1962). Production of commodities: A comment. *The Economic Journal*, *72*(286), 477–479.

COMMENTS ON VERGER'S "ADDENDUM"

Scott Carter

INTRODUCTORY

I would like to thank Yoann Verger for his insightful and well-argued *Addendum* on the 2014 exchange between Professor Solow and myself. I am especially grateful since Verger is correct that I did not challenge Solow on his (Solow's) reading of Sraffa in my original "Response to Comments of Robert M. Solow," some reasons for which are provided at the end of this short Comment. Verger attempts what I did not try, and in so doing identifies three areas of contention that highlight Solow's misreading of Sraffa. I would like to briefly address each of these three points of contention raised by Verger.

THREE POINTS OF CONTENTION THAT DEMONSTRATE SOLOW'S MISREADING OF SRAFFA

Verger identifies the following three contentious points that illustrate Solow's misreading of Sraffa:

1. The assumption of constant returns to scale in all production, the construction of the Standard commodity, and the notion of the uniform rate of profit and the attendant notions of equilibrium this entails
2. The conflation of the "economic profit" of neoclassical theory with Sraffa's notion of profit

Return of Marxian Macro-dynamics in East Asia
Research in Political Economy, Volume 32, 295–299

ISSN: 0161-7230/doi:10.1108/S0161-723020170000032017

3. The role of metaphysics in the Marxian notion of exploitation and the erasure of any such metaphysical concepts attributed to neoclassical theory

On the role of constant returns to scale, there has been an ocean of ink spilled over this and it has led to many-a-debate (some acrimonious) between scholars sympathetic to Sraffa's approach but differing on this assumption. The same can be said for the assumption of a uniform rate of profit in that there are differences of opinion regarding the reasons why Sraffa makes this assumption as well. On each of these points I remain relatively agnostic, an approach I increasingly take with respect to Sraffa's theory as more of the archive is made available for all scholars to study (more on this latter point below). Being agnostic means that I do not claim to know unequivocally what Sraffa "really meant" on these matters, nor do I think discerning such is a very interesting exercise all-in-all. Indeed, Sraffa tells us in the subtitle that *Production of Commodities by Means of Commodities* (PCMC) is a Prelude, which in my reading means that all of the discoveries made must be qualified as being part of a larger endeavor the ultimate results of which have yet to be determined.

On the first point Verger notes with disapproval that Solow views Sraffa's argument as a "snapshot of interindustry commodity flows in an economy" but then cites with approval Sraffa's own caution in 1968 in a letter to Rudiger Soltwedel that "all the quantities considered are what can be observed by taking a photograph." Clearly there seems to be a confusion here: is it a snapshot or not? Verger relates this seeming confusion (perhaps I am the only one confused) in a disquisition of the efficacy of the uniformity assumption of the profit rate. But the fact remains that the reasons why Sraffa made the assumption of uniformity in the profit rate are unknown, and any attribution to Sraffa's reasons are nothing more than that – mere attributions – since so far we have yet to uncover in the archival material a "smoking gun" that unequivocally states Sraffa's rationale.

The latter two points of contention Verger has with Solow's reading are cogently argued in my opinion. In the first instance the notion that Solow had in mind the economic profits of a (perfectly) competitive firm is well-taken. Yes, that is precisely what Solow does, and in so doing he is unable to remove himself from the neoclassical baggage that conditions his views. But Solow is quite clear about such intentions and says as much with the salvo that he would consider the matter as "how a run-of-the-mill late 20th century economist would approach the particular propositions" (Solow, 2014, p. 64). Here, Verger is correct that for Solow, "[t]he logic of Sraffa's model, concerned with relation between prices and distribution variables, is transformed into neoclassical logic, concerned about finding equilibrium prices" (Verger, 2016, p. 4).

Which brings us to the last misreading Verger attributes to Solow, namely the role of exploitation, as well as that of metaphysics in economic theories of all types. Regarding the latter point, I am in agreement with Verger that

Sraffa's use of the term "metaphysics" in his archival notes (evidence cited by Verger) is not meant in the same vein as Solow's notion of the term. Solow clearly derides the use of the term "metaphysics" as something that Sraffa would not have considered to be scientifically cogent. But Verger correctly in my view points out that Sraffa's referent is to consider "metaphysics" as "explanations that are necessary to make a connection between the results of the theory and what we experience in the real world. In this view, no scientific discourse can escape from one or another metaphysics, otherwise it would be nonsense" (Verger, 2016, p. 7).

Regarding the former point of exploitation, clearly Solow and Sraffa have different notions in mind, and the idea of Solow's that even when there is zero profit, exploitation can still exist as low wage workers are "exploited" by high wage workers amounts to nothing more than an application of the neoclassical notion of opportunity cost as "exploitation," itself not a new argument. But this is not the notion of exploitation used by Marx and Sraffa, where exploitation is not possible in the no-profit situation. For Marx and Sraffa "exploitation" in my reading is synonymous with unpaid labor time. No such unpaid labor time exists when there is zero profit and remunerated wages are equal to labor productivity. At the other extreme complete unpaid labor time exists when the rate of profit is at its maximum value and workers are remunerated nothing. Moving between these scenarios of "complete wage remuneration" where capitalists "live on air" and "complete profit remuneration" where it is now workers who "live on air" is in my reading the entire point of Sraffa's analytical framework of surplus and deficit industries in the face of distributional changes. Exploitation emerges here as a "pool" of unpaid labor time performed by workers during the working-day which is subsequently doled-out to the capitalist-owners through the distributional relation of a uniform profit rate of industry, and it is this above all else that in my opinion connects Sraffa's theoretical project to that of Marx's. Of course Solow does not agree with this, nor would I expect him to no matter how blue-in-the-face I got from arguing such.

CONCLUDING REMARKS

In conclusion, I would like to explain why my original Response to Solow did not take issue directly with his misreading of Sraffa. We are at the cusp of a tremendous change in Sraffa scholarship. For the first time since Sraffa's death in 1983 interested scholars everywhere will in short order finally have unfettered access to Sraffa's archival material as it is made available online at the Wren Library's web portal.[1] In my opinion several of the standard "Sraffian" interpretations must be revisited, as will many of the commonly thought aspects of Sraffa's theory. Simply put, the jury is out with respect to Sraffa's theory, and no scholar has unequivocal authority to exclaim what Sraffa "really meant."

I take this charge very seriously, and my 2014 Response nine years after I originally drafted the Pool of Profits paper and seven years after Solow first wrote his "Comment on Carter" reflected this change in my thinking. Of course Solow's reading of Sraffa is different than mine, and having him read my original paper was more of an effort to bring the limelight on the groundbreaking archival work of my original "Pool of Profits" paper, not lure him into a debate over matters the two of us would never agree on.

And my own interests are more concerned with exploring the positive aspects of Sraffa's theory that have yet to be developed – after all it is only a Prelude – and not debating and thereby criticizing the efficacy of different individuals' interpretations, no matter how valid or flawed they may be. This "open" approach to interpretational matters is articulated by Sraffa himself and can be found in archival notes of early drafts of the Preface written around 1956–1957 where Sraffa admits that the purpose to which he wrote the book may not be the one that is actually applied by other scholars:

> What is presented in the following pages is a hulk rather than a finished piece of work. Although it contains no discussion of marg{inal} theory It was intended to serve as the basis for a critique of that theory. *It is now submitted by itself, that it may be judged on its own merits, independently of the use for which is was intended.* The critique may, or may not, be attempted later. (D3/12/46/21; emphasis added)[2]

Especially important is the italicized passage where Sraffa openly admits that the use to which his ideas may lead scholars could possibly be something completely different than that which he intended it to be. And it is this aspect of Sraffa's theory as somewhat of a "wild card" that I find most appealing and which makes the theory most alive, since by Sraffa's own admission the direction to which the theory can be developed is more of an open canvass than those scholars who have made a cottage industry from the alchemy of discerning what Sraffa "really meant" can readily admit; and this remains true no matter Professor Solow's own take on these matters.

NOTES

1. Wren Library, Trinity College, University of Cambridge. The online effort is directed by Giancarlo de Vivo and Murray Milgate with the collaboration of the Wren archivist Jonathan Smith. It is expected to be completed in 2017 and can be found at the following URL: https://janus.lib.cam.ac.uk/db/node.xsp?id=EAD%2FGBR%2F0016%2FSRAFFA. I too am engaged in digitally arranging the archival material specially on the section of the archive devoted to Sraffa's Notes on PCMC archived as D3/12, the fruits of which can be found here: www.sraffaarchive.org

2. The file folder D3/12/46 is one of the key transition files with respect to the Wren Trinity meta-arrangement of the files in D3/12, where ideas from different time periods are brought together; other such key transition files are D3/12/2 and D3/12/16. In total D3/12/46 consists of 98 original archival pages (including backs of documents), 28 of which are dated in Sraffa's hand. Of these 28 the dates range from 1940 to 1941

(8 documents) and then skips to 1955–1958 (20 documents). These 98 individual archived pages break down into 18 independent documents of various page length (this result is taken from the Trinity 2.0 conceptual arrangement of the material in D3/12; see Carter, forthcoming). The file includes several drafts of the Preface as well as inserts for specific sections made in the late 1950s, and also very important documents from the 1940s that Sraffa obviously drew from within the context of the file.

REFERENCES

Solow, R. M. (2014). Comment on Scott Carter. In P. Zarembka (Ed.), *Sraffa and Althusser reconsidered; neoliberalism advancing in South Africa, England, and Greece*. (Vol. 29, pp. 63–67). Research in Political Economy. Bingley, UK: Emerald Group Publishing Limited.

Verger, Y. (2016). *Addendum to Carter's 'Response to Professor Solow'*.

REPLY TO YOANN VERGER☆

Robert M. Solow

Constant returns to *scale:* Mr. Verger writes that I ignored Sraffa's warning that he was making no technological assumptions. This is simply false. I remarked quite explicitly that Sraffa makes that claim. My point was that the claim makes no sense. Without constant returns to scale or some close equivalent, there is no good reason why the price system should eliminate all "pure profit." Mr. Verger suggests that Sraffa would simply include pure profits in his "rate of profit." But this device would create new problems and confusions. First of all, there is no good reason why pure profit (i.e., monopoly profit, scarcity rents, and so on) should be taken as proportional to the amount of (circulating) capital tied up in production. Besides, if that were done anyway, the otherwise natural assumption of a uniform rate of profit becomes wholly artificial. This is especially clear if one takes seriously Sraffa's assertion, quoted by Verger, that "The (sic) rate of profits ... is susceptible of being determined from outside the system of production." In that case, how can it absorb pure profit, which may depend on input prices?

Exploitation: Of course one can define exploitation as occurring if total revenue exceeds the wage bill. In that case there is exploitation everywhere and every day, and it is easily measured. Whether that is a good or useful definition can

☆I thank Mr. Verger for his comments and will try to respond briefly to those that make sense to me.

Return of Marxian Macro-dynamics in East Asia
Research in Political Economy, Volume 32, 301–302

ISSN: 0161-7230/doi:10.1108/S0161-723020170000032018

be argued, but not here. Mr. Verger attributes to me the belief that "capitalists should receive a reward for their 'abstinence'." Once again this is simply false. What I actually wrote is that capital is scarce to the economy, and should therefore attract a return under almost any institutional circumstances. I then went on to say: "I have sympathy with the cynical view that talk about abstinence and waiting performed by individual capitalists seems excessively solicitous."

Metaphysics: I said in my original note that I could not remember where I had noticed that Sraffa referred to some aspects of concepts like exploitation as metaphysical. I certainly can't remember now. I am pretty sure, however, that the passage quoted by Mr. Verger is not the one I had in mind. That paragraph would never have attracted my attention. I then went on to say that Sraffa had flourished for a time in an intellectual atmosphere where "metaphysical" was not an adjective of praise. That may have suggested an incorrect inference. It is possible that Sraffa believed that the metaphysics of such disputed concepts contributes to our understanding of the way an actual capitalist economy works. If so, I do not share that opinion. But there lies a discussion in which I have neither the wish nor the capacity to participate.

INDEX

Printed and bound by CPI Group (UK) Ltd, Croydon, CR0 4YY

13/09/2026

14961058-0004